STUDIES IN NAVAL HISTORY

General Editor
N. A. M. RODGER

THE TUDOR NAVY

An administrative, political and military history

THE TUDOR NAVY
An administrative, political and military history

David Loades

Scolar Press

Published by
SCOLAR PRESS
Gower House
Croft Road
Aldershot
Hants. GU11 3HR
England

Ashgate Publishing Company
Old Post Road
Brookfield
Vermont 05036
USA

British Library Cataloguing in Publication Data

Loades, D. M.

The Tudor Navy – an administrative, political, and military history / by David Loades.

p. cm. — (Studies in naval history)

Includes bibliographical references.

ISBN 0–85967–922–5

1. Great Britain — History, Naval — Tudors, 1485–1603. 2. Great Britain. Royal Navy — History. I. Title. II. Series.

DA86.L63 1992

359′.00941—dc20 91–43374

CIP

ISBN 0–85967–922 5

Typeset in 10 point Times by
Poole Typesetting (Wessex) Ltd., Bournemouth
Printed in Great Britain at the University Press, Cambridge

CONTENTS

PREFACE

It seems a long time ago that Nicholas Rodger invited me to write this book, and my first gratitude is to him for his patience. As will soon become apparent to the reader, I have come to the Tudor navy via other aspects of Tudor history, and not via other periods of naval history. I make no apology for this, because the navy was an integral part of royal government, as well as being closely related to the developments of the commercial and maritime communities. The tradition of naval history has tended to be isolationist, and that makes for unnecessary difficulties of understanding. This is also a general work. Although based partly on my own researches, it makes no claim to technical originality, aiming instead to present a profile of the sixteenth-century navy which may be different from that customarily received. Above all it aims to place the navy in its proper political and administrative context.

In the course of the last four years, I have accumulated many obligations and debts of gratitude, apart from that to my long suffering General Editor. First to the Warden and Fellows of All Souls College, Oxford, for electing me to a visiting Fellowship in the academic year 1988–9; secondly to the staff of the Bodleian Library, the Pepys Library at Magdalene College, Cambridge, and the Public Record Office, where the bulk of the research was undertaken; and thirdly to the British Academy for a grant to cover travel and other expenses. My colleagues and students have also had to bear with me during the period of gestation, when my thoughts were on victualling rather than the Pilgrimage of Grace or the rebellion of the northern earls. But above all my gratitude is due to my wife, for her constant encouragement and support among the innumerable preoccupations of running her own business. Her example in diligence and self-discipline has been an inspiration.

DL

ABBREVIATIONS

APC	*Acts of the Privy Council*
BL	British Library
AGS	Archivo General de Simancas (Spain)
CPR	*Calendar of the Patent Rolls*
Cal. Scot.	*Calendar of State Papers relating to Scotland*
Cal. Span.	*Calendar of State Papers, Spanish*
Cal. Ven.	*Calendar of State Papers, Venetian*
EHR	*English Historical Review*
Hall, Chronicle	*The Union of the two noble and illustre families of York and Lancaster*, by Edward Hall
L and P	*Letters and Papers, Foreign and Domestic, of the reign of Henry VIII*, ed. J. Gairdner *et al.*
MM	*Mariner's Mirror*
TRHS	*Transactions of the Royal Historical Society*
PRO	Public Record Office

(*for details see Bibliography*)

Places

1. Broughty Crag
2. Leith
3. Newcastle upon Tyne
4. Hull
5. Kings Lyn
6. Great Yarmouth
7. Deptford
8. Gillingham
9. Colne
10. The Downs
11. Cinq Ports
12. Portsmouth
13. Southampton
14. Plymouth
15. Bristol
16. Beaumaris
17. Calais
18. Brest
19. Coruña
20. Lisbon
21. Cadiz
22. Rouen
23. Kinsale

✂ Battles

– – – – – route of the Armada

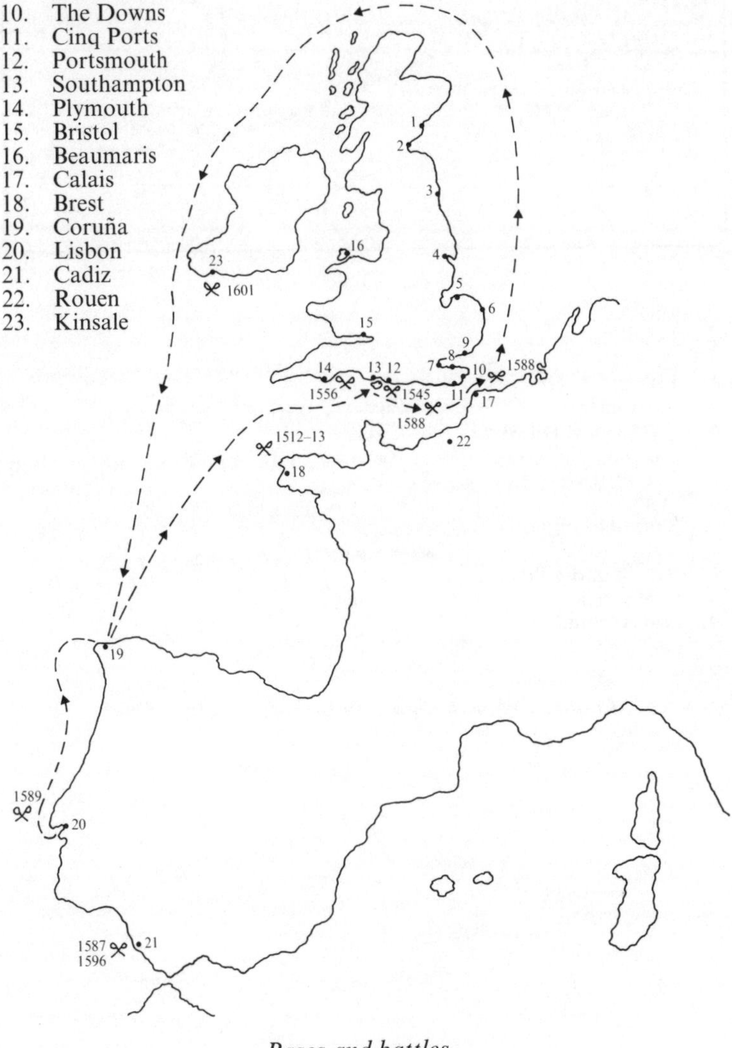

Bases and battles

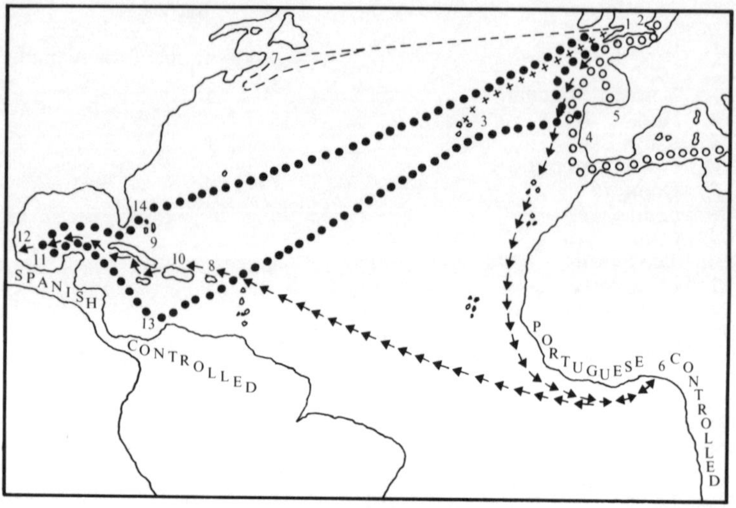

1. Bristol
2. London
3. Azores
4. Lisbon
5. Santander
6. Gold Coast (El Mina)
7. Nova Scotia
8. Puerto Rico
9. Hispaniola
10. Santo Domingo
11. Vera Cruz
12. San Juan d'Ulloa
13. Cartagena
14. San Antonio

voyages

– – – – –	Cabot, 1497
+ + + + +	Azores voyages (1450→)
○○○○○○○	Trade routes to Spain and Italy
→ → → → →	Hawkins, 1562–8
● ● ● ● ● ● ●	Drake, 1585–7

English expansion into the Atlantic, 1450–1600

1
INTRODUCTION

The sovereignty of the seas, wrote Sir John Borough in 1633, was 'the most precious jewel in his Majesties crown . . . and the principal means of our wealth and safety.'[1] Borough was arguing in favour of a *mare clausum*, and like many antiquarian lawyers of his generation, felt compelled to trace his sources back to Julius Caesar. The Saxon King Edgar, he declared, had maintained a navy of 400 ships to assert his authority at all four corners of his realm, and he went on to describe how John, Edward I and Edward III had defended this same ascendancy. In the absence of any agreed definition of territorial water, it is not quite clear how far Borough's concept of sovereignty extended. He wrote of Edward IV granting licences to foreigners to fish off the Yorkshire coast, and of Queen Mary selling fishing rights in Ireland to her husband's subjects. But his main concern was with the Narrow Seas where, he claimed, all other ships 'vaile Bonnet' in acknowledgement of English superiority 'to this day'. The main political thrust of Borough's treatise was against the Dutch, who were getting rich and immensely strong at sea by taking £300 000 worth of fish a year out of English waters without either fee or licence – an argument which echoes that of John Dee over sixty years before.[2] Queen Elizabeth had not been as remiss as Charles I:

> I remember that those of Hamburg and other Easterlings (though in amitie with us) in the late reign of Queen Elizabeth of famous memory were notwithstanding stayed from passing through our

[1] Sir John Borough, *The Sovereignty of the British Seas . . . written in the year 1633.*
[2] John Dee, *The Perfect Arte of Navigation* had suggested financing the navy by levying a toll on all foreign fishermen in English waters.

> seas towards Spain, and good prize made of all other nations that attempted to do the like.

What he did not remember, or did not choose to remember, was that the actions of the English navy at that time had very little to do with the assertion of abstract concepts of sovereignty and everything to do with waging war on Spain. Nevertheless his point was valid. Authority over the sea, like authority over colonial territories, could only be claimed if it could be exercised, and what concerned him was less Hugo Grotius's doctrine of *mare liberum* than the power of the Dutch navy. Whatever may have happened in the time of King Edgar or Edward III, the Elizabethan navy had controlled the Channel, and effectively extended the authority of the English Crown beyond the shores of the realm.

Sea power had always been expressed in royal or imperial fleets, but such fleets had been the personal creations of the monarchs who had led or operated them. The Tudor navy, on the other hand, was an aspect of the state, and its history has to be seen in that connection. Its establishment and early development was an act of political will which had very little to do with the maritime history normally associated with it. Only after the middle of the century did the two begin to converge, as naval strategy assumed an oceanic aspect, and mercantile entrepreneurs acted as an auxiliary navy. It is consequently a serious mistake to study the Tudor navy in isolation from other facets of government, with which it had much in common. The king's ships, like his artillery, were an expression of his power. Dependence upon noble support was second nature to any medieval king, and the fact that the Earl of Warwick had more ships than Edward IV does not seem to have taught that highly conservative monarch any urgent lessons. Most of Edward's ships, when he needed them, came from the port towns, like the cash which he borrowed from the citizens of London when his land revenues were slow to arrive. Edward, relying upon his personal ascendancy, did not object to this kind of dependence, but Henry VII set out systematically to reduce it. By increasing his revenues he reduced his reliance on short-term loans, and on grants from parliament. By taking more gentlemen directly into his service he made himself less dependent upon the nobility. By building two large warships and constructing an embryonic naval base at Portsmouth he lessened his need to call upon the ships of his subjects. In spite of the contrast in their personalities, Henry VIII followed his father's policies in many respects. Less suspicious in his relations with his nobility, he nevertheless continued to build up his affinity at a lower level, a strategy urged upon him, and largely executed, by Cardinal Wolsey and Thomas Cromwell, his successive chief ministers. The result was a steady growth in the importance of royal commissions of all kinds, which were largely served by knights and gentlemen. Unwilling to rely upon personal or *ad hoc* arrangements in the remoter parts of the kingdom, he reformed the royal councils in the north and in the marches of Wales, and brought the remaining franchises under his direct control by a statute of 1536. His privy council was reorganized to make it more efficient and accountable, and new revenue courts were established to handle the income resulting from the Royal Supremacy over the church. It is in this context that the creation of the Council for Marine Causes in 1545 must be viewed.

At the same time Henry VIII was a warlike King, much given to military bravado of a kind which his resources could not really support. His contemporary and arch-rival Francis I of France established a small standing army of mercenary soldiers, and Henry needed an effective riposte. Armed ships were his chosen status symbol, a symbol appropriate to the nature of his realm, and also to his personal tastes. There was nothing very original about that, but by creating an infrastructure of dockyards and storehouses, and drawing the whole establishment into the institutional framework of government, he detached it from his own preferences and priorities. A standing navy changed the nature of the King's relationship with his seafaring subjects, just as the Royal Supremacy changed the nature of his relations with the clergy. To what extent either Wolsey or Cromwell appreciated the significance of this development is unclear, but both were dedicated to the augmentation of the King's power, and Cromwell certainly had the necessary strategic grasp. He was deeply involved in questions of naval administration during the formative years 1535–40, and the Council for Marine Causes seems to bear traces of his influence. The testing time for the navy as an institution of state came with Henry VIII's death, when his creative drive was removed. He had, however, reigned long enough for it to have been no shallow growth by 1547. Also, its advantages had become sufficiently obvious for his successors to need no further education in the merits of preserving it. In that respect also it was very much like the Royal Supremacy, which had begun as a personal ascendancy and during this period was recognized as an aspect of the Crown's authority. Both Edward Seymour and John Dudley, the two regents for Edward VI, were knowledgeable in maritime affairs, and maintained both the structure and function of the navy; in the latter case far better than he is normally given credit for doing. By 1553 there was really no question of the navy being an optional or expendable item, and during Mary's short reign its integration into the machinery of state was carried a stage further. The Queen's suspicion of the officers whom she had inherited brought about a thorough stock taking, and the elimination of the last traces of *ad hoc* improvisation, with the introduction of the Ordinary, or regular budget. Placed under the supervision of the Lord Treasurer, the Admiralty survived when both the Royal Supremacy and the Court of Augmentations[1] went down. By the time that Elizabeth's council carried out another survey in 1559, and sketched out a policy for the future, the issue was about ways and means, not about the nature or the scale of the enterprise.

However, just as the early Tudor navy had reflected the growing power and self-confidence of the state, so the Elizabethan navy reflected its problems and ambiguities. Thanks to the independent commercial developments which had taken place, particularly since 1553, and the growth of a new breed of maritime adventurer, Elizabeth was quickly faced with a challenge and an opportunity. If the navy was to 'cover' the worldwide operations of the new companies in the way it had covered the Merchant Adventurers, who traded cloth to northern Europe, then it needed either a major injection of capital or some fresh strategic thinking. What happened was in many respects a retreat from the position which had been reached by 1557. The 'ordinary' was steadily reduced in significance as more and more work was contracted out, often to the officers themselves; and the navy began to cover long distance operations by taking part on a joint stock basis. Elizabeth, having inherited a situation where political dependence upon the nobility was largely a thing of the past, found the cure in some respects as bad as the disease. The gentry, who had been increasingly introduced into government earlier in the century, and who had provided her father with much of the solid support which he had needed for his controversial policies and expensive wars, were now indispensable and in some respects intractable allies. Willing to serve but unwilling to pay, they imposed limitations upon the Queen's freedom of action which could not be transcended. The Queen was forced to purchase their co-operation because she could not afford to bypass them. Much of Elizabeth's celebrated parsimony was not her fault, and on the whole in naval

[1] A financial court to administer former monastic lands. Absorbed into the Exchequer in 1554.

matters the arrangement worked well enough for most of the reign. Gentry, and even nobles, invested heavily alongside the merchants, and enabled the small royal navy to appear much more omnipresent than it really was. But the price was high. Private warships, and even private fleets, reappeared in a manner which had not been seen since the reign of Edward IV. The Queen's monopoly of force at sea was not challenged, but it was undermined. Whereas her father and grandfather had hired private ships on their own terms, Elizabeth was often constrained to co-operate as a more or less equal partner. This erosion of control was partly concealed by the Queen's success in maintaining a consensus support for the war with Spain, but it began to have a deleterious effect upon the Admiralty, where private interest began to undermine professional integrity, as it did in so many other aspects of the late Elizabethan administration.

This history, in consequence, is a history of the navy as an aspect of the Tudor state. It is not a technical history of ships and guns. These objects are constantly present, and discussed as appropriate, but the conflicting nature of much of the detailed evidence, and the confusions of contemporary terminology, make them intractable subjects except at a very general level.[1] Nor is it a history of English seafaring. Before 1550 the English were, with occasional exceptions, mere apprentices in the navigational sciences, and it was not until the reign of Elizabeth that they caught up, and began to teach their neighbours. Maritime enterprise has never lacked for scholarly exposition, and in recent years the works of E. G. R. Taylor, D. W. Waters, D. B. Quinn, K. R. Andrews and G. V. Scammell have provided learned and comprehensive coverage.[2] The English have, since the days of Hakluyt and Purchas, been profoundly interested in their seafaring past, and that interest has shown no sign of slackening in the second half of the twentieth century. But the navy, or at least the Tudor navy, has fared less well. After the great works of Laird Clowes, Michael Oppenheim, J. S. Corbett, Alfred Spont and others between 1890 and 1920, the subject seems to have lost its

[1] There are innumerable technical discussions of Tudor ordnance. The most up-to-date summary is that contributed by David Lyons to *Armada*, the catalogue of the official exhibition at the National Maritime Museum. For the difficulties of classifying oared ships, see particularly T. Glasgow jnr, 'Oared vessels in the Elizabethan navy' *MM*, 56, 1970. The best and most recent discussion of carracks and galleons is P. Kirsch, *The Galleon*.

[2] E. G. R. Taylor, *Tudor Geography, 1485–1583*, and *Later Tudor and Early Stuart Geography, 1583–1650*; D. W. Waters, *The Art of Navigation in England in Elizabethan and Early Stuart Times*; D. B. Quinn, *England and the Discovery of America, 1481–1620* and many other works; G. V. Scammell 'Manning the English merchant service in the sixteenth century' *MM*, 56, 1970, and many other works.

appeal.[1] There has been no general work, and more specialized studies have been patchy. In 1965 C. S. L. Davies published an excellent article on the origins of the Council for Marine Causes, in the *English Historical Review*,[2] and since then the American scholar Tom Glasgow jnr has written a number of highly informative articles on the Marian and early Elizabethan period, which have appeared in the *Mariners Mirror*.[3] The *Mirror* has also published, and continues to publish, many specialized and technical articles of relevance. More recently there has been a spate of publication, mostly of no academic significance, in celebration of the fourth centenary of the Armada. Exceptions to the general rule are the works of Geoffrey Parker, Colin Martin, I. A. A. Thompson, Felipe Fernandez Armesto and Mia Rodriguez Salgado, the last in the catalogue of the superb exhibition which was mounted at the National Maritime Museum.[4] Finally, this is not a history of the Admiralty jurisdiction. The Admiralty courts provide a constant background to the history of naval activity, particularly in respect of piracy and privateering, but they belong to the civilian and not to the military administration. There was no institutional link between the courts and the Council for Marine Causes, except through the person of the Lord Admiral. The subject of this study is the growth of the navy as a fighting force – its administration, personnel, funding, policy, strategy and tactics. It threads its way between foreign policy, commerce and war, with constant sideways glances at other aspects of government. Naval history is not an isolated subject in its own right, but is an integrated aspect of the general history of the period.

The main feature which emerges from this treatment is continuity. In place of the picture of boom and slump, which tends to come from concentrating on periods of war when evidence is plentiful, we

[1] W. Laird Clowes, *A History of the Royal Navy*; J. S. Corbett, *Drake and the Tudor Navy*; Alfred Spont, ed., *Letters and Papers relating to the war with France, 1512–13*; Michael Oppenheim, *The History of the Administration of the Royal Navy*, and other works.

[2] 'The administration of the Royal Navy under Henry VIII; the origins of the navy board', *EHR*, 80, 268–286.

[3] 'The navy in Philip and Mary's war'; 'The maturing of naval administration, 1556–1564'; 'The Royal Navy at the start of Elizabeth's reign'; 'The navy in the first undeclared Elizabethan war'.

[4] C. Martin and G. Parker, *The Spanish Armada*; I. A. A. Thompson, 'The Invincible Armada', *Royal Armada*, 160–89; Fernandez-Armesto, *The Spanish Armada; the experience of war in 1588*; Mia Rodriguez-Salgado, 'Introduction' to *Armada*, the catalogue of the NMM exhibition. In this connection also, note *The Expedition of Sir John Norris and Sir Francis Drake to Spain and Portugal, 1589*, ed. R. B. Wernham.

find a profile of remarkably steady growth. If a conscious decision was ever taken to establish a standing navy, then it must date from the very early days of Henry VIII's reign, or even from those of his father. There was more activity during war time, and several identifiable administrative developments took place during those years, but by no means all. The establishment of the Council for Marine Causes was not a sudden revolutionary move; it grew naturally out of the slow multiplication of earlier offices, and the example of the Ordnance Office. The Ordinary decreed in 1557 was a commonsense conclusion from the changes which had been taking place in funding arrangements over the previous thirty years. Similarly, although the use of gun ports to mount heavy cannon below the main deck was a change of revolutionary potential, it was to be another thirty years before such firepower began to be translated into tactics. The broadside as a tactic was not so much invented as evolved, and it took another whole generation of experiment before the logical conclusion of a line ahead formation was arrived at. Sir John Hawkins may have grasped the possibilities of lower and slimmer hull design more effectively than his predecessors, but he did not invent the galleon. On the other hand there was no time when, to use Tom Glasgow's dramatic phrase, the fleet was 'rotting at its moorings'; certainly not the years 1551–4, to which he applied it.[1] Glasgow long ago disposed of the idea that Elizabeth had rescued a navy in terminal decline, but his own view that it was Philip who performed that rescue act is no more substantial. The evidence for Philip's role in initiating a fresh phase of naval development boils down to a report of one irritated letter to the English council some two months after he had left England. In fact the level of activity in the dockyards and anchorages seems to have fluctuated more in the first twenty years of Elizabeth's reign than it had at any time since the outbreak of Henry VIII's last war in 1543. Most of the men involved, both at sea and ashore, were deeply conservative, and accepted change only slowly and reluctantly. Sir William Monson was still arguing the virtues of high charged carracks in the 1620s, just as Roger Ascham was still defending the longbow against the arquebus in the 1570s. The real innovators were not the policy makers, but the practical seamen and gunners, who suddenly found themselves with unexpected problems to solve. It was almost certainly some overmatched privateer, who, in order to avoid a grapple, first fired its guns at its enemy below the

[1] 'The maturing of naval administration, 1556–1564', *MM*, 56, 1970.

waterline. When Sir John Hawkins invented his double skin to keep out wood-boring beetles, it was as a captain with experience of tropical seas, not as Treasurer of the Admiralty.

Until 1547 a steady growth in the number and variety of ships to be provided for kept up the pressure for new facilities, and the development of proper schedules for repair and maintenance. After that date, with the main services and administrative structure in place, the size of the fleet remained remarkably constant, and the emphasis shifted to the more efficient use of plant and resources. Commercial enterprise drew the royal ships out of home waters, and gradually introduced a totally new strategic concept, that of the blockade. A fleet 'circling the realm' for defensive purposes had been envisaged in the fifteenth century, and was a reality by the end of Henry VIII's reign, but the idea of lying off an enemy coast for months on end to intercept his trade arose from the activities of ambitious privateers during Elizabeth's war with Spain. Such a strategy required more seaworthy ships than the old *Mary Rose*, and proper arrangements for victualling at sea. The need created the ships, and the necessary skills, so that by 1603 such a strategy was feasible, although not upon the scale that the ambitious projectors envisaged. Similarly it appears that no one 'invented' the drydock, or planned the growth and staffing of harbour facilities. They arose, grew, and sometimes declined, in response to the needs of the moment. Once established, there were changes of emphasis between Chatham/Gillingham, Deptford, Woolwich and Portsmouth, from year to year according to the type of service most required. Each had its own special function by the middle years of Elizabeth's reign, but that had happened gradually and not, it seems, deliberately. Plymouth and Newcastle, although both used as advanced bases in wartime, never acquired any permanent plant.

In spite of the slow and unplanned nature of most of the specific changes which took place during the sixteenth century, the contrast between the navy of 1485 and that of 1603 was dramatic. At the beginning of Henry VII's reign we are still in the world of Chaucer's shipman, and of the Warwick Roll; by the time of Elizabeth's death a 'blue water' strategy is already in place, and the pattern of fighting tactics has been set for the next 150 years. A single clerk on a part time basis has been replaced by a whole department of state, and the vast 'increase of governance', so typical of Tudor England can be illustrated to perfection by this development. Even to the ordinary seaman much had changed. Life was no more comfortable aboard the *Merhonour* than it had been aboard the *Mary Rose*;[1] the pay was, if anything, worse, and the victuals were much the same. But voyages were longer, and more likely to lead to distant and exotic places; the chances of plunder were probably rather better, and the risks of working the more efficient guns rather less. There might be one of the newly invented hammocks to reduce the risk of a hard and damp bed, and there was even the prospect of a pension at the end of the day if you were unlucky enough to lose a limb at sea, and lucky enough to survive the experience. To the officer, and particularly to the master, both the demands and the rewards had increased. Sailing a great ship was a highly technical operation, and navigating it across the ocean even more so. Gone were the rule-of-thumb methods, the lead line and the portolan. The navigator of 1600 needed charts, tables of declination, tide tables, and instruments such as the backstaff and the boxed compass. He was at very least literate and numerate, and probably a man of some education. The sea had always been a way of life; by 1600 it was rapidly becoming a profession, and service on the royal ships occupied a respected place in that profession. It is often said that the Tudors made England a modern state. That is only true with certain serious qualifications, but they created a modern navy out of the office of the king's ships.

Henry VIII's navy expressed the honour of the King. Elizabeth was no less the personification of the realm than her father had been, but to the patriotically inclined her navy was 'England's glory'. The growth of national self consciousness was promoted and demonstrated by the hybrid, semi-private, nature of the sea war against Spain. A policy which the queen had been forced to adopt, and which had many disadvantages, nevertheless carried with it that bonus. The privateers and the gentlemen adventurers gave the political nation of the 1590s the same sense of active participation as was conveyed in a broader political context by the steadily increasing importance of the House of Commons. At the same time these tough-minded and often brutal seamen became in the eyes of their fellow countrymen, and sometimes in their own eyes, the champions of a Godly cause. The compatibility of genuine religious zeal with greed and cruelty had been demonstrated in the 1520s and 1530s by the Spanish *conquistadores*. Sir Francis Drake was a man in the same

[1] The work of Margaret Rule and others under the auspices of the Mary Rose Trust and the establishment of the ship as a permanent exhibition, has not only added greatly to specialist knowledge of early Tudor ship construction and rigging, it has also raised public awareness of the early Tudor navy, particularly the circumstances of life on board ship.

mould, and the observer who wrote of the attack on Cartagena in 1585

> The two galleys and galleasse, with the other fort, did so ply their ordnance against us that it was wonderful; their calivers, muskets and harquebuses did play their parts. But God is all in all, by whose good help we made them fly into the town like sheep . . .[1]

was typical of the new breed of protestant warrior. Just as Philip II took the crusading aspect of his great Armada with total seriousness, so some of those who fought against him at sea perceived themselves as doing the work of God. Because of the hazardous nature of their calling seamen had always been prone to appeal to the supernatural, but this was something much more specific and motivating. It also had tangible strategic implications. When Richard Hakluyt wrote his 'Discourse of the Commodity of taking the strait of Magellanus' in about 1580, he was arguing the importance of a global strategy against Spain, with permanent colonies and naval bases all over the world.[2] Hakluyt's specific objective on that occasion was to frustrate Philip's attempt to take over Portugal and her Empire, but his obsession was at least as much religious as political. The Counter-Reformation was a world-wide threat, and must be confronted wherever it appeared. Neither the Earl of Essex nor the Earl of Cumberland were zealots on quite that scale, but Essex took an army of preachers with him to Cadiz, and Cumberland sternly rebuked those of his captains who did not appear to take the spiritual welfare of their men with sufficient seriousness. Every ship of the navy above the burthen of about 100 tons enjoyed the ministry of its own chaplain, and it is often from these men that we derive our knowledge of their exploits. Richard Maddox who accompanied Edward Fenton on his ill-starred voyage in 1582/3 not only kept a journal, but also drew places of interest on the way.[3] By 1603 England's own *conquistadores* were ready to begin their Imperial task, and the navy had developed to the point at which such ambitions had become feasible. But the whole machinery of the English state was strained and stuttering after a century of remarkable growth and achievement, and the Admiralty's own house needed setting in order before further major demands could be made upon the navy.

[1] J. S. Corbett, ed., *Papers relating to the navy during . . . 1585–7*, 18–20.
[2] L. B. Wright, *Religion and Empire; the alliance between piety and commerce in English Expansion, 1558–1625*, 41.
[3] E. G. R. Taylor, ed., *The Troublesome Voyage of Captain Edward Fenton, 1582–83.*

2
THE MEDIEVAL BACKGROUND

In December 1480 Edward IV appointed Thomas Rogers, an experienced seaman previously in the service of the Earl of Warwick, to be Clerk, or Keeper, of his ships.[1] The office was an ancient one, which had originated in the thirteenth century, but it had been in abeyance for almost thirty years. Richard Clivedon, the previous Clerk, had presented his last account in 1452, showing a profit of £56.19s.6½d. on the sale of such stores and equipment as then remained in a rented warehouse at Southampton.[2] During the intervening years the king had owned ships, which had been operated on his behalf, but there had been no office with responsibility for their management, and consequently no naval administration. The reasons for that unusual situation lay partly in the disturbed domestic politics of the period – the so-called Wars of the Roses – and partly in the nature of the medieval navy itself. It could be said that the navy of the thirteenth or fourteenth century was like the parliament – less an institution than an event. The word itself was used, not to describe the royal fleet but the entire maritime resources of the realm. When a 'navy royal' was assembled, it was for some specific military purpose (usually an invasion of France) and consisted to only a very small extent of the king's own ships. In 1347, for example, Edward III had assembled a massive flotilla of over 700 vessels, of which 50 were fully equipped fighting ships, but his own

[1] *CPR, 1467–1485*, 242; C. F. Richmond, 'English naval power in the fifteenth century', *History*, 52, 1967, 10.

[2] PRO Exchequer LTR E364/86; Susan Rose ed., *The Navy of the Lancastrian Kings*, 55.

contribution was less than 30 – of all sizes.[1] Such a fleet was put together partly by 'ship service', and partly by commissions of impressment, similar to the commissions of array which were used to assemble an army. Ship service was a quasi-feudal arrangement whereby a port, or a group of ports, enjoyed specified jurisdictional and commercial privileges in return for providing a given number of ships, fully manned and equipped, when called upon for the king's service. The best example of this arrangement was the Cinq Ports, whose position had evolved from an early date, and who, by the thirteenth century were bound by charter to provide 57 ships for 14 days at their own expense,[2] and for as much longer as they might be required at the king's expense. Ships 'taken up' by impressment were hired at a fixed rate, known as 'tonnage' from the moment of their requisitioning, and the crews were paid direct by the treasurer of the war. During the reign of Edward III, according to a subsequent parliamentary petition, the standard rate was 3s.4d. per ton for three months; at which time a seaman was paid 3d. a day, plus his victuals, and a master 6d.[3] According to the same petition, this arrangement could provide the king with up to 150 fighting ships, in addition to the necessary victuallers and transports.

Such a system was feasible only because custom-built warships were virtually unknown. A fighting ship was created by taking a standard trading cog of between 100 and 300 tons, and building prefabricated wooden castles onto her stem and stern. A fighting top would also be added to her single mast. This work was carried out by teams of carpenters hired by the king for the purpose, when the impressed ships reached the port of assembly. When the service was completed, these additions were removed in the same way, and probably stored for future use. The majority of the king's own ships were indistinguishable from these same merchantmen. When not needed for warlike purposes they were used to transport the king's messengers and officials, and to bring Bordeaux wine or other goods for the use of the royal household.[4] They might also be leased out

[1] BL Harleian MS 246, f. 78; Cotton MS Titus E iii, f. 262; W. Laird Clowes, *The Royal Navy; a history*, 265.

[2] Hastings, Romney, Hythe, Dover and Sandwich, T. Rymer, *Foedera, Conventiones, Literae . . . et Acta Publica*, I, 53.

[3] Oppenheim, *A History of the Administration of the Royal Navy, 1509–1660*, 8. Tonnage was a measure of displacement, not weight, and was based upon an estimation of the number of tuns of Bordeaux wine with which a ship could be laded. The formula used for the estimate was probably 'depth of hold, multiplied by keel length, multiplied by main beam, and divided by 100'; M. W. Prynne, 'Henry V's Grace Dieu', *MM*, 54, 1968, 123.

[4] Laird Clowes, *The Royal Navy*, 120.

to private traders, and were converted for fighting in the same way. Until the late fifteenth century, when the Portuguese began to mount heavy guns in the waists of their long-distance carracks, there were no weapons at sea capable of damaging the structure of a large ship. Primitive breech loading guns of light calibre began to be used in the middle of the fourteenth century, and the first record of their deployment at sea refers to a fight between ships of Denmark and Lubeck in 1362,[1] but these were short range anti-personnel weapons. They were also extremely inaccurate and hazardous to use. No English ship carried more than seven or eight such guns before the death of Edward IV. The standard missile weapons, at sea as on land, were longbows and crossbows, and the standard method of sea fighting was hand to hand by a simple tactic of grapple and board. Naval tactics in the later sense were unknown, a single mass formation being the most effective method of bringing maximum force to bear. Manoeuvering in formation was impossible because of the poor handling qualities of the ships, and the only advantage which it was possible to seek was the 'weather gauge' – that is, to get upwind of the enemy. The larger the ship, the more difficult it was to board, and the bigger the advantage enjoyed by its archers, shooting down onto the crowded decks below them.[2] But large ships tended to be slow and cumbersome, and were particularly vulnerable to being driven ashore if a battle was being fought in coastal waters, as was usually the case.

One type of ship stood apart from all these generalizations. The galley was a custom-built warship, adapted from the classic fighting ship of the Mediterranean, by way of the Viking longship. It was lightly constructed, much longer in proportion to its beam than the cog or dromond, and propelled chiefly by oars. In the 1240s Henry III may have had as many as a dozen of these vessels, when they were kept in 'great sheds' at Rye, Winchelsea and Shoreham.[3] Their size was not measured by tonnage, as they had little cargo carrying capacity, but by the number of oars. By the thirteenth century galleys were virtually a royal monopoly, and were of little use against large sailing ships, particularly in open water. The last

[1] There may have been a few ship-board guns at Sluys (1340), and the earliest reference dates from 1338. P. Padfield, *Guns at Sea*, 11.

[2] In 1416 a Genoese carrack was attacked in the channel by six English balingers carrying (allegedly) 1 500 men, but escaped because the English were unable to scale her towering sides. B. Williams, ed., *Gesta Henrici Quinti*, 97; see also some of the drawings in BL Cotton MS Julius E iv, 'The Life of Richard Beauchamp, Earl of Warwick, by John Rous'.

[3] Laird Clowes, *The Royal Navy*, 120.

recorded royal galley before Henry VIII revived the genre, was the enormous *Jesu Maria* of 240 oars, which appeared briefly in 1410–11.[1] Her length must have made her extremely fragile, and there are no references to her use. Earlier galleys had mostly carried between 20 and 100 oars. They were almost twice as expensive to operate as comparable sailing ships,[2] and that factor as much as their lack of seaworthiness must have contributed to their disappearance. The main use of the medieval galley was for coastal and estuary patrols, and for swift, small-scale raiding in time of war. Barges and balingers were also propelled by oars in appropriate circumstances, but were principally small and handy sailing ships. When used for military purposes they were not fortified like the larger merchant ships, but were used either for scouting, or for skirmishing, in the manner of small galleys.

The 'navy royal' was an occasional event; but whenever there was war on the Marches of France, the King of England needed fighting ships. The Channel was not a frontier in the sense that it became after the loss of Calais in 1558, but rather a means of communication between one part of the king's dominions and another. Nevertheless the coasts of Normandy and Brittany were frequently hostile, and English shipping, both civil and military, needed protection, as did the ports of the south coast, which were always vulnerable to French raids. It was therefore normal for small fleets of armed ships to be assembled in March or April to 'keep the seas' until the end of the campaigning season in October. By the early fourteenth century such fleets were sometimes under the command of a single admiral (a term first used in 1297), but more usually in separate squadrons for the North Sea and the 'Narrow sea'. Occasionally a third fleet operated from the Severn estuary to the Isle of Man. For the most part the ships which made up these fleets were impressed in the same manner as for a 'navy royal'. Even when there was no official war, there might still be a need for naval defence. In April 1404, during the truce which lasted throughout the reign of Henry IV, a French squadron attacked the Welsh towns of Caernarfon and Harlech, and five Bristol ships were hastily mobilized and

[1] R. C. Anderson, *Oared Fighting Ships*, 50–51.

[2] In the late thirteenth century it was estimated that a sailing ship of 180 tons would cost £100 a year to hire, whereas a galley would cost £240 in 'Money of Morlaas'. This Aquitainian currency was worth about three fifths of the value of sterling. Laird Clowes, *The Royal Navy*, 129; P. Spufford, *Handbook of Medieval Exchange*, 209. A galley of 100 oars was considered to need a crew of 20 over and above the rowers.

equipped to repulse them.[1] In the same year another enterprising Frenchman endeavoured to extract a ransom from the inhabitants of the Isle of Wight, but retreated when an English fleet appeared on the scene. Not to be outdone, the English then raided the coasts of Brittany and Picardy, causing (it was alleged) great loss of life. To all this activity the king's ships themselves never made more than a small contribution. The king might have a 'great ship', such as the cog *Thomas* which Edward III used as his own flagship, or he might provide the admirals' flagships for his lesser fleets, and some galleys for scouting and skirmishing, but he did not have anything remotely resembling a standing navy.[2] Both ship service and impressment were of ancient origin, going back at least to the eleventh century; letters of marque, authorizing the holder to 'go upon' the king's enemies at his own expense under certain conditions, first appear in 1243;[3] and by the fifteenth century indentures and licences were also being used as means of providing for defence and law enforcement at sea. An indenture was essentially a contract, whereby the holder agreed to serve the king at sea with so many ships and men for a specified period, at the king's expense and in return for an agreed payment. A licence empowered the holder to keep the seas at his own expense in return for the bulk of any prize value taken, and was similar to a letter of marque, except that the enemy was not necessarily specified.

Consequently the Clerk of the King's Ships was a rather less important official than might be supposed. He had no responsibility for the king's ships when they were at sea, irrespective of whether they were on royal business or on lease.[4] If they were operating in the king's service they were the responsibility of their individual masters and pursers, and were funded directly by special warrant. The Clerk was responsible for ships which were out of commission, and for their equipment. He organized repair and maintenance work, constructed docks when these were needed, built or rented storehouses, and provided shipkeepers. In the reign of John, William de Wrotham had been responsible for a substantial fleet of royal

[1] N. H. Nicolas, ed., *Proceedings and Ordinances of the Privy Council of England*, 1834–7, I. 220.

[2] Rose, *Navy of the Lancastrian Kings*, 29–30.

[3] Granted by Henry III to Geoffrey Pyper, master of Le Heyte; the King retained a right to half the prize money. Laird Clowes, *The Royal Navy*, 129.

[4] As with all generalizations, exceptions can be found to this rule. John Chamberlain did pay the crews for voyages in 1401, 1404 and 1405, probably as a matter of convenience rather than because it was a function of his office. PRO Exchequer, Accounts various, E101/44/20

galleys, and had also handled the impressment of merchant ships, working through bailiffs and deputies in the various ports. In 1208 he organized the King's expedition to Normandy, and handled all naval payments out of the Exchequer.[1] Wrotham was not styled Clerk of the Ships, and his functions clearly transcended those of the later office. By 1250 the galley fleet had dwindled, and the Clerk proper had emerged, performing the humdrum functions which were to characterize the office down to the middle of the fifteenth century. Identifiable accounts first appear in 1344 on the Pipe Rolls, and later among the enrolled foreign accounts of the Lord Treasurer's Remembrancer.[2] The money seems to have been provided as it was needed, by occasional warrant out of the Exchequer, and the Clerk (or Clerks, there were sometimes two) recorded his disbursements in considerable detail. The accounts of John Chamberlain, who was Clerk from 1398 to 1405, show him to have been responsible for eight ships during that period, varying from the *Trinity* of 300 tons to a river barge for use on the Thames. One of these vessels was purchased for £100 from the Mayor of King's Lynn, and another was specially built for the King's use.[3] They seem to have been based in the Pool of London, which was why their names were all given the suffix 'de la Tour'; but in the winter they were removed to Greenwich, where they were drawn up on the mudflats. This process was misleadingly called 'docking', when a fence or some other temporary enclosure was built around the beached ship to facilitate work on her hull.[4] At such times the vessels were unrigged, and there must consequently have been some storage facilities at Greenwich, although these are not specifically mentioned in the accounts. Chamberlain was active, and disbursed rather more than £4 000 in six years, but his successor, John Elmerton needed only £300 for his four years in office. By the end of that time there were only two ships on the books, and it seems clear that Henry IV

[1] Rose, *Navy of the Lancastrian Kings*, 29.

[2] Ibid.

[3] The *Katherine*, which was purchased, was originally Portuguese, but had been built for northern waters. PRO Exchequer, Warrants for issue; E404/15/32. Details of the ship which was built appear in Exchequer, Accounts various, E101/43/6.

[4] The best account of this process is given in William Soper's account for the 'dokking' of the *Grace Dieu* in 1434: '. . . money paid Thomas at Hythe, and 29 men labourers, for working about making and constructing anew of a fence called a hedge, by the advice and ordinance of discreet and wise mariners, that is to say on the Wose near Brissleden aforesaid for the safe keeping and government of the King's ship . . . and also that the said King's ship shall be kept more safely and easily in its said bed called dok within the said enclosure . . .'; Oppenheim, *A History of the Administration of the Royal Navy*, 29.

was very uncertain of the value of having any ships of his own, despite the constant efforts which he was compelled to make to 'keep the seas' against French freebooters and pirates of all nationalities. If the king so willed, the Clerk of the ships could be responsible for the nucleus of a royal fleet, but he could equally be a very minor official whose function had virtually no connection with the mobilization of ships for military purposes.

If Elmerton belonged to the latter category his successor William Catton, Henry V's first appointment, clearly belonged to the former, and his activity reflected a major change of royal policy. Not only was Henry bent on war with France, he clearly intended from the start to use his own ships for that purpose, and was the first king since John to follow a naval strategy which transcended the normal *ad hoc* arrangements. By the end of July 1413, two weeks after his appointment and four months into the new reign, Catton had seven ships in his charge, and had undertaken a complete rebuilding of the old royal flagship, the *Trinity*. This he completed within his first accounting year, at a cost of £1 686.15s.11¼d.,[1] during which time two more ships were also added to the royal fleet. The first two years of the reign were quiet from a military point of view, and the King's ships were energetically deployed on private commercial voyages, which produced an income of over £2 000 in freight charges, and the loss of one vessel, the *Cog John*, which sank off the Breton coast in October 1414.[2] The major military deployment of 1415 was not Catton's responsibility, but the build-up of the royal fleet continued, and reached a climax during his second accounting period, from 1416 to 1419. During those four years, in spite of having no role in the military operations, he spent over £12 300, and had at one point as many as 36 ships on his books.[3] This must have placed a major strain upon Catton, as he seems to have been assisted only by a single clerk, and his operations extended far beyond the Thames estuary, to Rye, Dover, Southampton and Portsmouth. Apart from the *Trinity* he seems to have been personally responsible for building only two new ships, the *Jesus* and the *George*, but a considerable number of other ships were built or rebuilt by specially commissioned shipwrights during this period – not from any lack of confidence in Catton, but simply because of the burden of the work. These vessels fall into two main categories, Great Ships and balingers. The latter were small vessels of between 50 and 120 tons,

[1] PRO E28/31. Rose, *Navy of the Lancastrian Kings*, 34–5.
[2] Ibid.
[3] PRO, E364/59.

propelled both by oar and sail, as we have seen, which had come into use gradually over the previous hundred years. Four were built between 1416 and 1418, and a further seven or eight acquired by capture or purchase.[1] The Great Ships were constructed on a scale seldom seen in England before, and represent a new departure in naval strategy. The *Trinity* displaced 540 tons, the *Holigost* 760, the *Jesus* 1 000, and the *Grace Dieu* (laid down in 1416 but not completed until 1420) a massive 1 400 tons. Although their armament – a mere handful of light guns – was puny by comparison with their bulk, these were the dreadnoughts of their generation, and their appearance signified a new, although short-lived, period of English maritime ambition.

The naval operations which accompanied Henry's French war were broadly of two kinds. The invasion of France, launched on 11 August 1415, was conducted on strictly traditional lines, with an armada of 1 400 vessels and over 30 000 men. No more than 100 of these would have been fighting ships, of which perhaps 10 belonged to the King.[2] Similarly the relief of Harfleur in 1416 involved over 200 ships under the command of Sir Walter Hungerford. In this case, because of the circumstances, a sea battle was actually sought, but it was a very traditional type of action, fought in the narrow channel opposite the town. The English were more numerous and better organized, so that the siege was raised, and four large Genoese carracks in French service were captured.[3] After repair and some modifications, these modern and highly effective ships were added to the growing royal fleet. In addition to these large-scale actions, however, the King set up a regular pattern of naval patrols. These commenced early in 1415, when five ships were stationed between Plymouth and the Isle of Wight, four between Wight and Orfordness, and three on the East coast. In 1417 the Earl of Huntingdon 'swept' the channel with 40 ships, spearheaded by five royal warships, in order to clear the way for the King to cross to Normandy. Not only did Henry cross unmolested in the wake of this operation, but four more carracks were captured.[4] From then until the end of the war in May 1420, the English command of the sea was maintained by regular forays of this kind, and by keeping small numbers

[1] Oppenheim, *Administration*, 12; The table compiled by Colin Richmond shows only ten balingers in this period, of which two are noted as having been acquired, and eight built. C. Richmond, 'The keeping of the seas during the hundred years war', *History*, 49, 1964, 286–7.
[2] Laird Clowes, *The Royal Navy*, 373.
[3] A. Guistiniani, *Annali della Republica di Genova*, 277; Williams, *Gesta Henrici Quinti*; Rose, *Navy of the Lancastrian Kings* 48–9.
[4] *CPR, 1416–1422*, 142; T. Hearne, ed., *Vita Henrici Quinti*, 30.

of armed ships at sea for considerable periods on strategic stations, such as the Downs. Some of these ships were privateers, and some were impressed in the traditional way, but by 1419 the King had enough ships of his own to sustain such a presence without calling upon the resources of his subjects. The big drawback with impressment was that, during a war of any duration, it meant taking commercial ships out of service frequently and for considerable periods of time. The merchants always complained that their ships were 'taken up' long before they were needed, to the great detriment of their businesses,[1] and if they were to be called upon for regular service in the keeping of the seas, it might cost the king dear in terms of his relationship with the mercantile community. A standing navy offered a possible solution to that problem.

As long as the war lasted, Henry seems to have followed such a policy, but despite his awareness of the perennial problem of piracy, he made no effort to continue it on a permanent basis. Between 1415 and 1420 three men were receiving money for naval expenditure, Catton on a regular basis, and Robert Berde and William Soper occasionally. During that time they received altogether some £20 000. Soper took over from Catton as Clerk in February 1420, and over the next two and a half years his income totalled £5 500. The extraordinary payments ceased altogether, so naval expenditure declined by nearly 50 per cent.[2] Such an oversimplified picture does not do justice to the complexities of what was actually happening, but the impression of significantly reduced activity is generally accurate. The *Holigost*, the *Jesus*, the *Trinity Royal* and the *Grace Dieu* were all laid up on a care and maintenance basis in the Hamble by 1422, and several of the smaller ships had begun to deteriorate. When the King died in August 1422 he left instructions in his will that his ships were to be sold to discharge his debts, and the following March his son's Regency Council authorized the sale.[3] With the benefit of hindsight such a decision looks like gross dereliction of duty, but in fact it was simply a return to the *status quo ante*, and all that it really demonstrates is that Henry V, for all his purposeful activity, did not in fact transcend his predecessors, or entertain any new vision of naval strategy. Between 1423 and 1425 William Soper and his fellow commissioners disposed of 22 of the 30 ships of which

[1] J. Strachey et al., *Rotuli Parliamentorum*, IV, 79. The complaints were particularly loud against Henry V, but his consistent military success took some of the sting out of them.

[2] Rose, *Navy of the Lancastrian Kings*, 39.

[3] *Proceedings of the Privy Council*, III, 53.

the late King had died possessed. One of these was given away to discharge a debt, and eight others were described as 'debilis', fetching between £1.6s.8d. and £20 each.[1] The remainder realized some £925, the purchasers being mostly merchant syndicates, although some were individuals and three were described as 'king's mariners'. By 1427 the *Mary Barton*, the *Philip*, the *Little Trinity*, the *Redcog*, the *Andrew*, the *Mary Hampton* and the *Gabriel Harfleur*, although not specifically mentioned as sold, had disappeared from the records. Only the four Great Ships remained, and of the £750 which Soper received from the Exchequer during the five years 1422–27, £650 was spent on their upkeep.[2]

Such an outcome does not seem to have been the original intention. The *Grace Dieu* was not actually completed until 1420, and Soper was paid a salary of £40 a year – double that of his predecessor.[3] A forge and a permanent storehouse were built at Southampton, and the anchorage in the Hamble estuary was fortified. Probably Henry himself had envisaged a small nucleus of administration and plant which could be rapidly expanded when circumstances required – resources which had existed intermittently since the early thirteenth century, and could be described as entirely traditional. What actually happened, however, was a good deal more radical. When Luca degli Albizzi, the captain of the Flanders galleys, inspected the *Grace Dieu*, the *Holigost* and the *Trinity Royal* in January 1430, he described them as laid up but serviceable. Indeed he was particularly impressed with the *Grace Dieu*, describing it as the largest and most beautiful ship he had ever seen.[4] Albizzi was an experienced and widely travelled professional seaman, so he is unlikely to have been gullible; but the *Trinity Royal* had been described as 'debilis' in the previous year, and later in 1430 both she and the *Holigost* had been 'docked', that is beached and fenced around. By that time the only ship in commission was the balinger *Little Jesus*, specially built for the royal service. The *Jesus* and the *Grace Dieu* were both docked by 1434, one at Southampton and the other

[1] Richmond, 'The keeping of the seas', 285–8.
[2] PRO E364/5; Rose, *Navy of the Lancastrian Kings* 61–131 (Roper's Accounts).
[3] *CPR, 1416–1422*, 169, 256. An assistant was also provided for. For a full discussion of Soper's career, see Rose, *Navy of the Lancastrian Kings* 6–27.
[4] Albizzi's diary of his visit to Southampton has been edited by M. E. Mallett in *The Florentine galleys in the fifteenth century*, 259. Richmond believed that the *Grace Dieu* was a 'white elephant' – too large and clumsy ever to have been operational – but more recent research by Susan Rose has demonstrated that it was at sea, captained by William Payne, before the end of 1420. S. Rose, 'Henry V's Grace Dieu and mutiny at sea', *MM*, 63, 1977, 3–9.

at Bursledon.[1] None of the Great Ships had actually been used since 1422, and very little was spent on their maintenance after 1427, so by 1435 they would have required almost complete rebuilding. In that year, thanks to the political crisis in France, a flicker of life returned to the almost moribund office of Clerk of the Ships. The *Little Jesus* was rebuilt, and a barge and a balinger (named the *Jacquet*) were purchased for the defence of Crotoy.[2] However, the appearance of reprieve was deceptive. A large force was raised and shipped across for the relief of Calais in the summer of 1436; but although the Duke of Gloucester commanded over 500 vessels, no more than two or three of these belonged to the king, and the Clerk's function was marginal. In 1438 the *Little Jesus* and the *Jacquet* were still in service, and were still owned by the king, but they were no longer the responsibility of the Clerk of the Ships. Probably they had been handed over to individual masters in royal service on a contract basis. Between 1437 and 1439 Soper received no money at all from the Exchequer, and spent only £8.9s.7d., mostly on the storehouse at Southampton. By the time he was replaced by Richard Clivedon in 1442 he had become no more than a minor storekeeper.[3]

Over the next few years the Great Ships finally disintegrated and disappeared. The *Grace Dieu* was struck by lightning in January 1439, and burned to the water-line; the *Jesus* was sold in July 1447 to servants of the Bishop of Winchester at scrap rates; and the *Holigost* sank at her moorings early in 1452.[4] When the last piece of salvage had been sold, the office of Clerk was discontinued, and England was entirely bereft of naval administration – probably for the first time since the late twelfth century. Nevertheless Henry V's short-lived burst of creative activity had not been without its long-term significance. In the first place English shipwrights had been given the stimulus and opportunity to develop their skills. The balinger was developed as a vessel with considerable military potential, particularly with the building of the *George* and the *Anne* in 1416. These were both large (120 tons), two masted, and propelled by oars *modus*

[1] PRO E364/69, Soper's accounts for the years 1427–32. For the *Holigost*, see W. J. Carpenter Turner, 'The building of the Holy Ghost of the Tower, 1414–16, and her subsequent history', *MM*, 40, 1954, 270.

[2] PRO E404/52 152. Richmond, 'The keeping of the seas', 290.

[3] PRO E364/76. Richmond, 'The keeping of the seas', 291. Rose, *The Navy . . .*, 55.

[4] PRO E364/81, 86. The reason given for the loss of the *Grace Dieu* was that there were no shipkeepers on her at the time. She must therefore have been refloated after her docking in 1434, because shipkeepers would only have been provided for a ship at anchor. Soper paid £18.6s.3d. to Jurden Brownynge and four other shipkeepers on the *Holigost* from September 1426 to June 1427.

unius gallee (in the manner of a galley); they must have been rather like the galleasses of the next century.[1] When used for patrolling they carried crews of between 130 and 143 men, 'watching for enemies at sea', and when used for transport duties between 60 and 100. Similarly the Great Ships, built as an answer to the Genoese carracks, stretched technical resources and ingenuity to the limit. The *Trinity*, the *Holigost* and the *Jesus* were two masted (probably carrying a square rig on the mainmast and lateen on the mizen), but the *Grace Dieu* was three masted. Apart from being constructed in the traditional northern mode of 'clinker', or overlapping planks, instead of the southern 'carvel' (edge to edge) mode, she was one of the most advanced, as well as one of the largest, ships afloat.[2] England's capacity to build a substantial number of large and effective ships in a short space of time, and to crew, supply and maintain them efficiently, had been amply demonstrated. Three naval squadrons had operated simultaneously and with great success in the summer of 1417, and the sea had been better 'kept' for the nine years of the reign than for many years before. A successful naval strategy was therefore not a question of capability, but of political will and priority.

By 1430 that will had largely disappeared. In strictly military terms a low naval priority was justified before the Congress of Arras, however, the English council knew perfectly well that the sea had to be kept. There was only one surer way to annoy the merchant community than by continually requisitioning its ships, and that was by doing nothing at all to protect it from pirates and hostile neighbours. Moreover the war in France was going from difficulty to disaster between 1435 and 1450, and since the priority was consistently given to the need for reinforcements and rescue operations in Normandy and Gascony, there were few resources to spare for more mundane operations. Tried and traditional methods were perfectly adequate for a major military effort like that of 1436, but even when they were available, were no longer entirely satisfactory for dealing with marauders. Single masted cogs of 150–200 tons, designed to carry a maximum cargo could not cope with the balingers and carracks that such hit-and-run raiders were now likely to use. Conse-

[1] PRO E364/59. Rose, *The Navy . . .*, 42. R. C. Anderson, *Oared fighting ships*, 207.
[2] English carpenters did not have the necessary skills for carvel building, and when he wanted to repair the captured carracks, Soper endeavoured to import foreign craftsmen for the purpose. Rose, *The Navy . . .*, 45 and n.153. All these great ships seem to have been straight keeled, and to have had a straight stern-post and stern post rudder. Morton Nance, 'The ship of the Renaissance', *MM*, 41, 1955, 180.

quently, a variety of expedients were tried, none of them new or original. One was indenture, or contract. Sometimes the men and the ships were separately provided, but the intention seems to have been to encourage certain captains to specialize in such mercenary service, and to acquire or build ships suitable for the purpose. By 1449 some form of bounty had been introduced, and although the scale of payments cannot be reconstructed with any certainty, the object was to improve the size and quality of privately-owned vessels.[1] Indentured ships were used for patrolling, but to what extent is not clear. In 1435–6 a number of sums of up to £200 were paid to named individuals *pro salva custodia maris*, (to maintain the security of the sea) which suggests expeditions of limited range and brief duration.[2] The trouble with indentures was that they cost money whether they were effective or not, whereas licences cost nothing, and gave the holder the additional incentive of unlimited profit. The merchants may have petitioned for such licences in 1435, as they had done on occasions in the past, because the recent hostility of the Duke of Burgundy had closed many of their normal markets. The temptation to take their profits from the Flemings by a different route must have been considerable. Between February and July 1436 licences were issued to groups of merchants in London, Dartmouth, Ipswich, Hull, Bristol, Lynn, Winchelsea, Orwell and Barnstaple.[3] About 30 ships were involved altogether, and they were organized into a single fleet under the command of two elected Admirals, John Scot of Calais and John Milbourne of London, who received commissions of authority from the King.

Just what this force achieved is not known, but as several of the licences were renewed late in 1436, and occasional new ones issued down to 1444, there must have been some perceived gain from its operations. However, licences also had their disadvantages, the main one being that the Crown had no direct control over them. Two of the licensees at this time, John Vache and Hugh Dene, unlawfully took the *Christopher* of Danzig, and there was a similar complaint against Scot and Milbourne. As Sir John Fastolf pointed out in a memorandum of September 1435, it was very important that ships operating in the King's name '. . . bee not suffred to take nere robbe the kingis verray trew friedis and auncien allies instede of

[1] Oppenheim, *Administration*, 19.
[2] Over £1 000 was expended in this way; PRO E403/724 (28 and 29 August). Richmond, 'The keeping of the seas', 292 and n.
[3] *CPR, 1429–36*, 509, 510, 512, 515, 608, 609.

thennemies.'[1] The licensee, like the privateer, could not be expected to return without a prize, lawful or not. Too strenuous an attempt to discipline such offenders would simply dry up the supply of volunteers. Nevertheless such operators could be both expensive and embarrassing to the government which had authorized them. In 1449 one Robert Winnington, who must have deployed several large ships, captured the entire Bay fleet of over 100 Hanseatic, Dutch and Flemish vessels. English goods in Danzig were seized, English merchants in the Low Countries arrested, and relations with the Hanseatic League strained to breaking point. Eventually the Council had to pay out £4 500 in compensation, and there is no evidence that effective action was taken against Winnington.[2] By contrast, the indentured captain presented no such risk. His fee could always be withheld if the performance had not been satisfactory. Consequently indentures were reintroduced in 1440. The immediate cause was the decision to launch a major expedition for the recovery of Harfleur, lost in 1435. Between May and September a series of indentures were issued to Sir John Speke of Heywood, Devon, to serve the King upon the seas with forces of 420, 600 and 1 000 men.[3] Speke received three payments from the Exchequer during the summer, and although his role in the attack on Harfleur is not chronicled, it must have been effective. The town fell towards the end of October, and the blockade by sea had certainly repelled at least one attempt to relieve it. Nevertheless, for the general purpose of keeping the seas, indentures soon proved to be no more satisfactory than before. In 1442 and again in 1454 attempts were made to establish regular patrols on that basis, but although on each occasion the intention was for the arrangement to run for three years, the reality was failure after a few weeks. This was certainly not the result of any lack of maritime resources. Even the French author of *The debate between the heralds of England and France*, a tract probably written between 1458 and 1461, thought it was plausible for the English to claim that they were '. . . more richly and amply provided at sea with fine and powerful ships than any other nation in Christendom';[4] and the particulars of ships taken up in connection with the war between 1435 and 1453 bears this out. The problem was the government's

[1] J. Stevenson, ed. *Wars of the English in France during the reign of Henry VI*, II, ii, 583.

[2] PRO, E403/784 (28 May 1451); E28/81 (29 May 1451); Richmond, 'The keeping of the seas', 295–6. Winnington gave his own account of his exploit in a letter to Thomas Daniel of 25 May 1449; *The Paston Letters*, ed. J. Gairdner, I, 84–6.

[3] PRO E101/53/30.

[4] Ed. London, 1870, 50.

insolvency. In 1450, a year of consistent military and political failure, the bill for tonnage and payments on indenture came to £13 000 – about a quarter of the ordinary revenue – and the money was simply not available. Richard Greyle of London 'and others' were therefore commissioned '. . . to labour and entrete the seyd maistres, possessores, and maryners for agreement of a lasse sume . . .'[1] The seamen agreed to settle for £6 200, but even that was too much to be found in cash. Eventually £2 884 was handed over, and the balance was assigned on the customs. Since Henry VI's council was notorious for making double, and even treble, assignments, it is doubtful whether some of the creditors were ever satisfied. Perhaps we need look no further for an explanation of the consistent failure of the English Crown to keep the seas during these years.

Once the war had ended in 1453, with the loss of all Henry V's French possessions except Calais, domestic difficulties increased rapidly. After the first battle of St Albans in 1455 armed conflict was never far below the political surface, private armies multiplied, and what was left of the King's control disintegrated. Richard Neville, Earl of Warwick, was Captain of Calais and Admiral of the Narrow Seas, positions which he used to build up a powerful private fleet of 10 or 12 ships. He also seems to have had custody of a ship called the *Grace de Dieu*, which theoretically belonged to the King. This ship had been originally built in 1440 for one John Taverner of Hull, and had been rebuilt, partly at the King's expense, in 1446. When Taverner died (probably in 1457) she became the property of the Crown, and was handed over to Warwick because there was no Clerk of the Ships to assume the responsibility.[2] On Trinity Sunday 1458 the Earl's ships attacked (apparently without either warning or justification) a combined Genoese and Hanseatic convoy in the Channel, taking five ships and driving many others ashore. The booty was alleged to have amounted to £10 000.[3] An outraged Government dismissed him from his post and appointed the Duke of Somerset in his place. However, by that time the Duke of York had challenged Henry VI for the Crown, and Warwick sided with York. The campaign of 1459 had not gone well for York, but Warwick refused to surrender Calais, and in January 1460 attacked the fleet which was being assembled against him at Sandwich, capturing several ships and scattering the rest. In May of the same year, when returning from Ireland to Calais, he outfaced a larger royal fleet under

[1] Oppenheim, *Administration*, 21.
[2] R. C. Anderson, 'The *Grace de Dieu* of 1446–1486', *EHR*, 34, 1919,584–6.
[3] Laird Clowes, *The Royal Navy*, 386.

the Duke of Exeter, which had been sent to intercept him, but refused to fight. Unimpeded, he then landed his forces in Kent on their way to the Yorkist victory at Northampton.[1] Warwick's achievements during these months demonstrated several important truths. Firstly, that a fleet at sea has a significant advantage over any opposing fleet which is being prepared against it, unless the latter is protected in a fortified anchorage. Second, that a fleet on a permanent footing can operate effectively at any season of the year; and thirdly that a small fleet under a unified command and accustomed to operating together enjoys a major advantage over an *ad hoc* assembly of ships, however numerous.

Not only did the logic of events indicate the urgent need for a new naval policy by 1460; many voices had also been raised to argue the same cause. The earliest and best known was the anonymous *Libelle of Englyshe Polycye*, directed to the Duke of Gloucester as Lord Protector, in about 1436.[2] Not only did the author spell out in great detail the advantages of keeping the sea in general, he also made it clear that such action should be the king's responsibility. Dover and Calais were the king's 'two eyes' to maintain control over the Channel, and to enforce that *superioritas maris* which the English Crown had claimed in theory since the thirteenth century, and enforced in practice whenever it was sufficiently strong.[3] Ten years later John Capgrave echoed the same sentiments:

> . . . if the sea were kept by our navy many good results would follow – it would give a safe conduct to merchants, secure access to fishers, the quiet of peace to the inhabitants of the kingdom, to our king himself a large measure of glory.[4]

The Duke of York not only shared these sentiments, he also had some practical suggestions to make about how such maritime supremacy could be achieved. A permanent organization was required

[1] Charles Ross, *Edward IV*, 20–25; Oppenheim, *Administration*, 27–8.
[2] Edited by Sir George Warner, 1926; see also G. A. Holmes, 'The Libel of English Policy', *EHR*, 76, 1961, 193–216.
[3] Laird Clowes, *The Royal Navy*, 135, 141. These claims were always controversial, and the documents cited in such works as Selden's *Mare Clausum* and Sir John Borough's *The Sovreignty of the British Seas* are often of uncertain authenticity. However a Flemish petition of 1320, asking Edward II for redress '. . . quod ipse est dominus dicti maris, et depraedatio praedicta facta fuit supra dictum mare infra potestatem suam', and reproduced in Rymer (Foedera, ii, 434) seems to indicate that some such claim was acknowledged.
[4] F. C. Hingeston, ed., *Liber de Illustribus Henricis*, 134; cited Richmond, 'English naval power', 1.

> . . . to th'entent that all your Navire bee redye togedirs, and of power for to assemble in such place as is most convenable for th'assemblyng of thaim, for to breke the puissance of the Navire of the seid Adversarie, before thaeire assemblyng . . .[1]

Assembling a fleet piecemeal, by requisition or indenture, was always a slow business. The fleet should exist as a unit, in one place where it could be rapidly and conveniently mobilized. Whoever got his navy to sea first should be able to destroy his enemy while the latter was still endeavouring to complete his preparations. That was how the English had won their great victories at Damme in 1214 and at Sluys in 1340. That was also how Warwick destroyed Lord Rivers and Sir Gervase Clifton at Sandwich in 1460. It might be easier and more congenial to mount raids upon the enemy coast, which was frequently done by both the English and the French in the latter stages of the war, but the real secret of the command of the seas was an unexciting matter of administration and logistics. It was no use having great resources of ships and men if they could not be concentrated and deployed when and where they were needed.

Consequently, when a Yorkist victory was finally assured at Towton in March 1461, it might have been expected that these lessons would be speedily applied. York's son, Edward, Earl of March, had become King Edward IV, and Warwick was a key figure in his government. However, there was little sign of immediate or dramatic change. Edward was at least as impoverished as his predecessor had been, and that may well be sufficient explanation for his inaction. Fleets operating in the King's name were at sea in the summers of 1461 and 1462, against the Lancastrians and their French backers.[2] These seem to have been organized by the Earl of Warwick, who in February 1462 entered into an agreement very much like one of the earlier indentures, contracting to keep the seas for three years at £1 000 a year.[3] In 1463 the Earl of Worcester was appointed 'captain and keeper of the seas', but his activity in that capacity is shadowy, and it seems that Warwick continued to supply the majority of the ships for the King's service, as well as to lead them. Edward did, in fact, begin to acquire ships of his own, three (including the *Grace de Dieu*) in 1461, and three more (all by purchase) in 1463; there is even a single reference to Piers Bowman as 'clerke of

[1] J. Strachey et al., *Rotuli Parliamentorum*, V, 254–5.

[2] *CPR, 1461–7*, 99–100; Ross, *Edward IV*, 48–9.

[3] *CPR, 1461–7*, 100–101; Oppenheim, *Administration*, 31. Warwick also contributed ships to the fleets sailing under other commanders, Richmond, 'English Naval Power', 8–9.

oure shippes'.[1] However, no such officer was either operational or paid, and it seems likely that the Earl of Warwick's entrepreneurial activity was one of the factors which inhibited a return to such methods. Control of the fleet was a powerful weapon in Warwick's political armoury, and one which he did not hesitate to turn against Edward when their relations cooled after 1467. When the King's ships were not operating under Warwick's control, they were leased out to merchants, in accordance with the old custom. As Warwick became less reliable, Edward turned instead to another naval entrepreneur, Sir John Howard, and it was Howard who organized the passage of the King's sister Margaret to her marriage with the Duke of Burgundy in 1468.[2] Howard was also commissioned to 'take certaine rovers that lie in the Tamyse mouth' in August 1470, but he did not have Warwick's resources, and when the latter went over to the Lancastrians he was able to land his forces at Dartmouth unopposed in October of the same year.

Warwick's death at the battle of Barnet in April 1471 ended Henry VI's readeption, but it did not give Edward IV a navy. Most of the Earl's ships passed to an illegitimate kinsman, Thomas Neville, known as the Bastard of Fauconberg, who had been serving as his lieutenant. Thomas endeavoured to maintain the Lancastrian cause by landing a force in Kent in May 1471. He failed to find sufficient support, but the fact that he was able to operate with such impunity merely re-emphasized the lesson of the previous year. Captured, he was pardoned and entered the King's service for a time, but Edward never acquired the ships which he had inherited from Warwick. After 1471, although the King continued to call upon Howard occasionally, he also purchased more ships of his own; the *Anthony*, the *Peter* and the *Trinity* in that year, the *Falcon* in 1475 and the *Mary of the Tower* in 1479.[3] These vessels were not leased, but were operated by experienced mariners directly in the King's service. The influence of the City of London may well have been behind this change of policy. London had played a large part in Edward's victories, both in 1461 and in 1471, and its merchants were the principal sufferers from the activities of the pirates who had become ever bolder and more numerous during the years of civil

[1] Bowman was actually appointed in July 1464 (*CPR, 1461–7*, 335), but there is no record of his having discharged the functions of the office.
[2] B. Botfield, ed., *Manners and Household expenses of England in the Thirteenth and Fifteenth Centuries*, 488, 512–32, 568–80; Howard had about six ships in 1470; G. V. Scammell, 'Shipowning in England, 1450–1550', *TRHS*, 5th series, 12, 1962, 119.
[3] Richmond, 'English naval power', 12–14.

strife. The merchants argued that they paid customs duties to the King specifically to be protected against such pests, and they did not see why they should have to pay twice, or be expected to protect themselves.[1] Consequently, after 1470 the King gradually revived the practice of patrolling, sometimes using his own ships, and sometimes indentures. In the summer of 1472 William Fetherstone, one of the King's mariners, led a squadron of royal ships against the Hanse, and in 1474–5 it was again the King's ships which 'wafted', or convoyed, the fleet of the Merchant Staplers to Calais.[2] On the other hand, when the French were raiding the coast of Wales early in 1475, two Bristol merchants were called upon to provide five ships to send against them, a service for which they were paid £190. When war with France threatened in 1474, the traditional machinery of mobilization was put into effect. Members of the King's household were issued with commissions to locate and 'take up' suitable ships and crews in all the ports and creeks of the south coast; the Warden of the Cinq Ports was ordered to equip and put in service all those ships for which the Ports were traditionally liable, and the King's own ships were armed and fitted out to provide the core.[3] Lord Dinham as Admiral hoisted his flag in the *Grace de Dieu* in April 1475 and set out with a vanguard of nine ships and 3 000 men to clear the Channel for the King's passage to France, an operation which was successfully completed later in the summer. The commercial interests of the merchants were spared as much as possible by hiring a substantial proportion of the transports needed for the crossing from abroad, mainly in the Low Countries.[4]

By 1480, with another war looming against Scotland, Edward IV had restored the navy to what might be described as an active traditional level. He had an effective Clerk of the Ships, storehouses at Southampton, Portsmouth and (possibly) Greenwich, and some fifteen or sixteen ships, nearly all of them purchased. Some of these were small, but others, such as the *Peter* or the *Holy Ghost* were carracks of 400 tons or more. Little is known about their armament, but they would all have carried guns like those illustrated in the Warwick Roll, which was compiled in about 1490.[5] Some of these

[1] Tonnage and poundage was originally levied in 1347, by royal prerogative; from 1373 it was a parliamentary tax, which became customarily granted to each king for life on his accession. In 1406 it had been briefly handed back to a committee of merchants as part of a sea-keeping contract. Oppenheim, 10.

[2] *CPR, 1467–77*, 340, 355; Richmond, 'English naval power', 10.

[3] Ross, *Edward IV*, 218–20.

[4] Ibid., 219.

[5] BL Cotton MS Julius E iv, f. 201 et seq.

were built up breech loaders, of which two specimens survive at Woolwich, with bound iron barrels and bronze breeches. These examples are 8ft. 6in. long, and weigh 8½ cwt; they would have cast an iron ball of 9–10lb. a distance of about half a mile, but their effective range would have been much less.[1] Others might have been small swivel guns, firing a 2–3lb. shot, although these are not actually recorded until the following decade. The number of guns carried was not large – 6–8 on a large carrack – so they could not be described as principal armament, but they were a symbol of power, not least because they were expensive. The king's ships, so equipped, did not in themselves constitute an impressive navy, and were not sufficient to keep the seas unaided against pirates, or to provide protection against the casual hostility of neighbouring princes, but they did constitute a focus for mobilization and a quick response force of modest dimensions. The brief and troubled reign of Richard III saw no change in this policy. Thomas Rogers continued to act as Clerk of the Ships, and to carry out a programme of maintenance and refitting. It seems likely that Sir Edward Woodville defected with the *Trinity* and the *Falcon* to Brittany, but Richard purchased at least three ships, and already owned two as Duke of Gloucester.[2] Royal ships patrolled successfully against the Bretons in 1483–4, and defeated the Scots in the North Sea in the latter year. Richard was able to deploy ten or eleven ships of his own in his efforts to intercept Henry of Richmond in the summer of 1485, and although he failed, that was not through neglect of his naval establishment. During the last ten years or so of Yorkist rule, it would not be unreasonable to conclude that the kings had heeded the advice offered by Sir John Fortescue in *The Governance of England*;

> And though we have not alwey werre uppon the see, yet it shalbe nescessarie that the kynge have alway some ffloute apon the see, ffor the repressynge off rovers, savynge off owre marchauntes, owre ffishers, and the dwellers uppon owre costes, and that the kynge kepe alway some grete and myghty vessels ffor the brekynge off an armye when any shall be made ayen hym apon the see.[3]

Edward had eventually accepted the responsibility – not unknown in the past but urged in vain upon his predecessor in the 1440s and

[1] P. Padfield, *Guns at Sea*, 21; see also G. F. Howard, 'Early ships guns I; Built up breech loaders', *MM*, 72, 1986, 439–52.

[2] Dominic Mancini, *The Usurpation of Richard III*, ed. C. A. J. Armstrong, 103–7; Richmond, 'English naval power', 11 and ns 53, 54.

[3] Edited by C. Plummer, 1885, 248.

1450s – to provide himself the leadership and the mechanism for the maritime defence of England.

The most important ingredient in naval power was therefore political will; but it was not the only one. A financially exhausted government was always tempted to cut this type of optional expenditure at the end of a period of war, and substantial resources of skilled manpower were needed to provide the masters and crews for the royal ships. The south and east coasts of England had always been populated with flourishing maritime communities, but their seamen for the most part ventured no further than the Low Countries, Northern France or Ireland, voyages for which the traditional rule-of-thumb navigational methods were sufficient. Most seamen were illiterate; their standard equipment extended no further than a compass and a lead-line; and their skills were learned by practical methods of apprenticeship.[1] The merchants who were the principle ship owners were, however, becoming more enterprising, and by the middle of the fifteenth century their regular trade routes extended from Portugal and Andalusia in the south to Iceland in the north. Such voyages called for larger ships, and when reinforcements were sent to Aquitaine in 1439 35 ships of over 100 tons (of which 12 were over 200 tons) were obtained from 18 or 19 ports.[2] A similar expedition twelve years later – the last desperate attempt to save Gascony – took up 47 such ships, of which seven were over 300 tons. These certainly represented only a proportion of what was available, and we may conclude that trading ships of 300, and even 400 tons were by no means uncommon. New routes and opportunities were also being explored. In 1446 a Bristol merchant named Robert Sturmy laded his ship, the *Cog Anne*, with wool and tin and sent her into the Mediterranean, where she was wrecked on the Greek coast. In 1457 he tried again, and on this occasion his ships were attacked and destroyed by the Genoese, an act of piracy which eventually cost the Genoese community in London £6 000 in compensation.[3] In spite of these misfortunes, English ships continued to find their way into the Mediterranean, and some of them were lucky enough, or powerful enough, to return with a profit. The first English merchants to appear in the Azores were recorded in 1479, operating with

[1] Dorothy Burwash, *English Merchant Shipping, 1460–1540*, 15–24. The portolan, or rutter, a crude coastal chart was also widely used towards the end of the period, having been adopted from the Mediterranean.

[2] Oppenheim, *Administration*, 19–20.

[3] *CPR, 1452–1461*, 517; E. Carus Wilson, 'The overseas trade of Bristol' in *Studies in English Trade in the Fifteenth Century*, ed. E. Power and M. M. Postan.

Portuguese partners in a jointly owned vessel.[1] By 1500 there was a regular trade between Madeira, Bristol and Plymouth. The English were both less enterprising and less skilful than the Portuguese, who by 1480 had explored most of the West Coast of Africa, set up a string of trading posts there, and established a fully fledged navigational academy at Sagres. However, they were not altogether lacking in the same spirit. In July 1480 a ship belonging to the Bristol merchant John Jay set out on what seems to have been a voyage of discovery, searching for the fabled island of Hy-Brazil.[2] The voyage was unsuccessful, but returned safely, and may have been repeated by Jay and others in subsequent years. There was certainly a tradition of Atlantic seafaring in Bristol, which is why the Cabots decided to base their voyages there in the following decade. England was well supplied with mariners who were skilled in the ordinary crafts of seamanship, but lacking in scientific navigators, a situation which was not remedied until the second half of the sixteenth century. Similarly her shipwrights, although possessing all the traditional skills, had lacked a major challenge since the days of Henry V, and do not seem to have kept abreast of the latest developments in ship design. The terminology is extremely confusing, but although the English seem to have been extensively influenced by the Low Countries in small ship design, Portuguese and Mediterranean developments in larger ships do not seem to have been followed. Two and three masted carracks were being built in England by the 1480s, but it is probably significant that the majority of ships so described in English ownership appear to have been purchased abroad.

The king's ships were manned and operated in exactly the same way as their mercantile contemporaries. When the laws of Oleron were compiled, probably in the twelfth century, only two grades of officer had been recognized, the master and the 'lodesman', or navigator;[3] but by the fifteenth century a large merchantman normally carried a master, boatswain, purser, steward and cook; and frequently a pilot, coxswain, master's mate and boatswain's mate.[4] The crewing levels varied to some extent with the nature of the voyage, but the norm was one man to every four tons of burthen,

[1] G. V. Scammell, 'The English in the Atlantic Islands *c.* 1450–1650', *MM*, 72, 1986, 294.
[2] William of Worcester, 'Itinerarium', *Itineraria Symonis Simeonis et Willelmi de Worcestre*, ed. J. Nasmith, 267; Burwash, *English Merchant Shipping*, 22.
[3] The Laws of Oleron were a code of maritime law and practice, originating in Aquitaine and introduced to England by King Richard I. A complete text is printed in *The Black Book of the Admiralty*, ed. Sir Travers Twiss, I. See also A. B. Wood, 'The Laws of Oleron', *MM*, 4, 1914, 196.
[4] Burwash, 36–7.

except on vessels below 60 tons, where it was rather higher. So a ship of 240 tons carried 60 men (inclusive of officers); and one of 200 carried 50, but one of 60 tons carried 21.[1] The soldiers who were carried on a fighting ship were quite separate from the crew, except in one important respect: the captain, whose prime responsibility was to command the soldiers, also had overall responsibility for discipline on board ship. As the commission granted by Edward III to John Pavely, Prior of the Knights of St John, put it

> We constitute the said Prior captain and leader of the said army, and all the men serving therein, granting him full and sufficient power to muster, rule and govern all the ships of the whole army aforesaid, and to supervise all their munitions, and all the men recruited to serve in them, whether mariners or any others whatsoever . . .[2]

Pavely was Admiral, with jurisdiction over many ships, but similar powers were exercised by the captain on any ship of war. It was the master's responsibility to sail the ship, and to direct the seamen in the execution of their duties, but the captain was in command. Inevitably there were many grey areas of jurisdiction, as when military duty conflicted with the safety of the ship, and disputes were frequent, but since the captain was of superior social status to the master, and responsible to the King, his will normally prevailed.[3] The officers and crews of royal ships were also differently paid from those of merchantmen. The latter might be hired by the voyage for an agreed cash sum, or they might be given a share of the cargo space for their own, or someone else's, goods. Often the two were combined, so that a mariner working between Newcastle and London (for example), customarily received 4s. hire and the portage of two quarters of coal.[4] On royal ships all ranks were paid by the

[1] Laird Clowes, *The Royal Navy*, 136–7.

[2] '. . . constituimus ipsum priorem capitaneum et doctorum armatae predictae, omnibum hominum in ea existentium, dantes eidem plenam, tenore praesentium, potestatem arraiandi, regendi, et gubernandi omnes naves totius armatae predictae, et supervivendi omnes munitiones earundem, as singlos homines in eisdem ad vadia retentos, tam marinarios, quam alios quoscumque . . .', T. Rymer, *Foedera, Conventiones, Literae . . . et Acta Publica*, III, i, 479.

[3] The Laws of Oleron provided that, when any question of the ship's safety arose, the master should consult the mariners and be guided by their advice. If he failed to do so, then he alone became responsible for any misfortune to the ship. This principle, which became deeply embedded in seafaring custom, was directly contrary to the autocratic disciplinary powers exercised by the captain, and was a source of constant conflict and uncertainty.

[4] Burwash, *English Merchant Shipping*, 53.

day, or by the week, an ordinary seaman receiving 3d. or 4d. a day from the mid-fourteenth century to the end of the fifteenth. Victualling in both cases was the responsibility of the operators, and was calculated at 1s. 6d. per head per week on the royal ships of Henry VI. The whole pattern of payment and reward could become extremely complicated, particularly on private ships, where wages were not only combined with portage, but might also be paid in more than one currency. There was also the question of prize. Taking prizes was not supposed to be the business of ordinary merchantmen, but most merchants ran a sideline in piracy, and a generous distribution of shares among the crew sometimes explains terms which in other respects appear to be meagre.[1] Licensees and privateers normally kept all proceeds except the Lord Admiral's 20 per cent, and even that was sometimes waived, with the soldiers and sailors often receiving as much as 50 per cent. On royal ships the pattern does not seem to have been standard at this time, but a larger proportion was retained by the officers. Broadly speaking a seaman in the king's service was regularly and moderately well paid, but had few opportunities to enrich himself; a merchant seaman was poorly paid, but had reasonable opportunities to make a profit; while a privateer might make a fortune – or he might get nothing but his victuals.

Victualling was always a problem because of the perishable nature of most food, and the poor storage facilities available on board ship. Royal ships on the whole suffered less, simply because they were less likely to be sent on long voyages, or to be at sea for more than a few days at a time. A merchantman bound for Andalusia would carry supplies for the outward journey only, replenishing at her destination for the return. Victualling a man of war was the responsibility of the purser, who drew money for that purpose from the treasurer of the fleet; the food was stored and distributed by the steward, and prepared by the cook. Details are hard to come by before the sixteenth century, but most large ships would probably have followed the same pattern as the *Margaret Cely*, whose accounts for a voyage to Zealand in 1487 have survived.[2] The bulk rations were salted and dried herring and cod, salt beef, biscuit, butter, eggs and beer. Fresh fruit and vegetables were occasional delicacies, and wine would certainly have been drunk, although it does not appear in the accounts. Most ships of any size would be fitted with a special galley

[1] Burwash, *English Merchant Shipping*, 51.
[2] PRO C47/37/14, mm. 1–6, 7–12.

for cooking purposes, consisting of a solid brick-built oven and firebase low down in the hold. These galleys not only guaranteed hot food under all but the most adverse conditions, they also provided additional ballast, which would not shift in a heavy sea. In spite of this, life on a medieval warship must have been cramped, cold and wet. Even when there were not two or three times their number of soldiers on board as well, the seamen had no proper sleeping quarters, but merely a space in which to unroll their bedding. There were no uniforms, and the seamen provided their own clothing, but there is some evidence to suggest that the practical demands of their calling had led to considerable standardization. Sir John Howard's men wore specially made 'jackettes', and there are a few drawings showing sailors wearing garments resembling hooded anoraks, and long loose trousers.[1] Such clothing was no doubt warm and robust, but it was not waterproof, and could not be easily dried. Above all, the necessity of going barefoot on wet and slippery decks must have produced some of the physical ailments and deformities observable in the remains of the crew of the *Mary Rose*, which went down a century later. The officers undoubtedly fared better, although only large ships had cabins for anyone except the captain and the master.

For men who were accustomed to earning their living from the sea, and were familiar with its hardships and uncertainties, service in the king's ships towards the end of the fifteenth century had much to commend it. The ships themselves were seaworthy and properly maintained, the wages regular and adequate; and the food and accommodation no worse than on any other vessel. The risk of injury or death in combat was slight – only a fraction of the hazard from disease or shipwreck which was common to all seafaring. Consequently there are few references to any reluctance to serve, or to desertion from the colours, both common problems during the Tudor period. As long as the king had no more than half a dozen ships at sea on an occasional basis during a normal summer, he was not, in any case making excessive demands upon the seafaring community. At the same time, he was providing only a skeleton protection. More protection meant more ships, more men, and perhaps more arduous conditions of service, but the implications of that were still in the future when Richard III fell at Bosworth.

[1] Burwash, *English Merchant Shipping* 79; Cotton MS Julius E iv, f.6.

3
EARLY TUDOR DEVELOPMENTS, 1485–1520

The turbulent years from 1483 to 1485 saw no break in the continuity of naval administration. Thomas Roger received a general pardon from Richard III in 1483, and one from Henry VII in November 1485, retaining his office throughout. Although his patents of appointment are dated March 1485 (from Richard) and February 1486 (from Henry),[1] he had already taken charge of some of the King's ships in October 1485, and there seems to have been no break in his activity. He died in harness in January or February 1488, and the accounts which his widow Joanne later submitted commence in August 1485, immediately after Henry's accession.[2] The picture which these accounts present is fuller than any which can be derived from the equivalent submissions of John Starlyng or William Soper, and show the Clerk's duties at this date to have been varied and somewhat ill-defined,[3] but hardly arduous. Henry VII appears to have inherited six ships. Of these, two, the *Falcon* and the *Trinity*, do not appear in Roger's account at all, and must have been in other hands throughout the two and a half years. A third, the *Martin Garcia*, he held for only four days in December 1485, before the king gave it to Sir Richard Guildford. There can hardly have been time to compile the inventory of rigging and tackle which was handed over with the ship.[4] Consequently the record relates mainly to the management, maintenance and disposal of the

[1] *Naval Accounts and Inventories of the Reign of Henry VII*, ed. M. Oppenheim, xvi–xvii, 3–5.

[2] Ibid., 3.

[3] Alan Moore, 'Accounts and Inventories of John Starlyng, Clerk of the King's Ships to Henry IV', *MM*, 4, 1914, 20–26, 167–73; for Roper, see Susan Rose, *The Navy of the Lancastrian kings*.

[4] *Naval Accounts*, 67–70.

other three, the *Grace Dieu*, the *Mary of the Tower* and the *Governor*. Each was formally taken over 'in a dokke at Hamill (Hamble) on the hoke in the Countie of Southampton', the *Grace de Dieu* on 10 October and the others on the 11th. The contents of each was inventoried, and these inventories form a substantial proportion of the whole account.[1] A week after receiving her, Roger moved the *Governor* from the Hamble to Bursledon, where she needed only four shipkeepers instead of the previous twenty-two. Over the next five months he expended £115.18s.2d. upon wages, victuals and maintenance work; and then on 18 February 1486 he handed her over 'apparailed and tackled' to Ralph Astry and Thomas Grafton, merchants of London. This must have been a sale or a gift rather than a rental, because the *Governor* never reappears in the records, but the purchase price, if any, was credited elsewhere. The *Grace de Dieu* was elderly and much rebuilt. Although she was the largest ship owned by the King, her future was in doubt from the start. John Haster, a London shipwright, was brought down to Southampton to inspect her, and the decision to dispose of her seems to have been taken before the end of October.[2] Her masts were felled, and the ballast removed; and the last shipkeepers were paid on 11 March 1486. Then, or shortly after, she was handed over to Sir Reginald Bray 'to be broken spent and emploied for and upon the makyng of (the King's) ship cald the Souveraine'.

Consequently by the end of March 1486 Roger was responsible for only one ship, the *Mary of the Tower*. Like the *Governor*, she was moved from the Hamble to Bursledon within a few days of being taken over; and there she remained upon a care and maintenance basis until she was leased on 28 February 1486 to Sir William Capell and William Heriott of London for a voyage to Lombardy. On her return in July 1487 she was carrying certain cables and other ropes which were impounded by the customers of London, and for which Roger was constrained to rent storage space in the city.[3] She was also somewhat weather-beaten, and a team of carpenters and mariners had to be employed for several weeks in August, shifting her ballast and repairing the leaks. In October of the same year the *Mary* was brought into dock at Erith, and most of her rigging and other fittings put into store at Greenwich. Only two shipkeepers were employed upon her during the last few weeks of the account. Nevertheless, the impression of decline conveyed by such a profile is

[1] *Naval Accounts, 36–73.*
[2] Ibid., 16–17.
[3] Ibid., 32.

in many ways misleading. The storehouse at Greenwich, although rented rather than owned by the king, became a miniature arsenal under Roger's supervision. There were 26 guns and 160 chambers in the store when he took it over. To these were added eight serpentines and 23 chambers from an unknown source, and 55 guns taken out of the *Mary of the Tower*.[1] Altogether Roger received 90 guns and 319 chambers, along with bows, arrows and gunpowder, and distributed 32 guns, 95 chambers and 400lb. of powder to three different ships and the captain of the *Isle of Guernsey*. He also performed some of the functions later discharged by the Treasurer of the Navy, paying out £715 for the wages and victuals of six ships taken up for the King's service in the spring of 1487.[2] Henry Palmer, who was probably Roger's clerk, was paid riding expenses for several journeys undertaken at the same time in connection with the arresting of a ship called the *Mary of Portsmouth*, and with the payment of seamen's wages in Portsmouth, Weymouth and Sandwich. When certain Spanish ships were detained in the Thames for the King's service, and then not used, Roger was instructed to pay them £20 in compensation for their wasted time.[3] Altogether his declared account showed receipts of £1 864.11s.4d., mostly on a variety of warrants from the Tellers of the Exchequer, and expenditure of £1 869. 11s.11d. – about £800 a year. This was small-scale activity by later standards, and not as great as that of the peak years of Henry V, but most of the elements of the developed naval administration of the following reign were already present.

Henry VII was no innovator in administrative matters, as we know from other aspects of his government, and he did not set out to develop the office of Clerk of the Ships. Roger did not pay all the wages of ships at sea in the King's service, and there was sometimes confusion over exactly which transactions had passed through his hands. His widow disclaimed responsibility for over £700 which he had allegedly paid out to ships commanded by Thomas Brandon at Harwich in 1487, on the grounds that the money 'never come unto thandes of the said Thomas Roger ne any of his deputees'[4] but was paid direct to Brandon by William Page, one of the Tellers of the Exchequer. Her claim was allowed. Similarly she pointed out that

[1] The serpentine was the favourite ships gun of the period, weighing (on average) 300–320 lb. with the chamber. At this time such guns were not provided by the Master of the Ordnance, and Roger bought seven serpentines from Philip Loker of Southampton in June 1486. *Naval Accounts*, 19, 77–9.

[2] Ibid., 28–30.

[3] Ibid., 32.

[4] Ibid., 34–5.

£40 received by Henry Palmer 'towards the makyng of the Souveraine' was no part of her husband's account 'because he as yet kepith the hole Accompt & Rekinnyng of the newe makyng of the said Ship', presumably under the supervsion of Sir Reginald Bray to whom the task had been entrusted. Another new ship, later called the *Regent*, had also been laid down before Roger's death, under the supervision of Sir Richard Guildford, but of this there is no trace at all in the Clerk's account, and he clearly had nothing to do with it, even inadvertently.

It is the building of these two ships which constitutes Henry's chief claim to the attention of naval historians. Such a decision, taken within a few weeks of his accession, when urgent business of all kinds was pressing upon him, is worthy of consideration. They were to be Great Ships – the *Sovereign* of about 450 tons, the *Regent* of 600 – of a sort which neither Henry VI nor Edward IV had attempted to build. When Edward or Richard wanted a large ship, they bought it, and no such vessel had been laid down on the King's orders since 1418. The *Regent*, we know, was intended to be 'like unto a ship called the *Columbe* of France', but the thinking behind the instructions can only be deduced.[1] The *Sovereign* was built at Southampton, and was sufficiently advanced for the King to be 'aboard' of her in August 1488, so she may have been launched at about that time. The *Regent* was built at Reding, on the river Rother in Kent, and was probably about six months behind her sister ship in construction. Both were four masted carracks of the latest design, with the most sophisticated rigging available, although, like all English ships, they were clinker rather than carvel built. Payments of over £950 can be traced for the building of the *Regent*, but it is not known what proportion of the whole that sum represents, and Palmer's accounts for the *Sovereign* have disappeared completely. Nevertheless it is clear that these two ships constituted a heavy investment at a time when the Crown's finances had not even begun to respond to Henry's therapeutic treatment. Perhaps the king saw them as a commercial investment at a time when the demand for very large ships was increasing. The lesson of Mediterranean ventures in particular was that the larger and better armed the vessels were, the better the prospect of success. The *Mary of the Tower* had been armed to the teeth for her voyage to Lombardy in 1486–7. Perhaps the main consideration was prestige. A few Great Ships, worthy to carry the royal banners of a king, were not only a military

[1] M. Oppenheim, *A History of the Administration of the Royal Navy, 1509–1660*, 36.

asset in time of war, but also a symbol of the king's claim to authority at sea which would have been readily understood by contemporaries. Sir John Fortescue had been thinking along those lines, and Henry was always keenly aware of the importance of sending out the right signals – which was why he spent so lavishly upon the magnificence of his court.[1] As Michael Oppenheim pointed out a century ago, the *Regent* and the *Sovereign* were not revolutionary in design, merely unusual in size.[2] They were also unusual in the weight of their armament. Before 1480 even fighting ships had carried only a small number of guns, but six years later thinking was changing. The *Mary of the Tower* had carried 55 guns on a private trading voyage, so it is not surprising to find that the *Sovereign* was armed with 141 serpentines, and the *Regent* with no fewer than 225.[3]

The disposition and mounting of these guns can be partly reconstructed from the inventories. Field artillery by this time was mounted on wheeled carriages, but guns at sea seem to have been secured to solid wooden stocks, which may have been fastened to the deck, or may have been roped to allow for some movement on recoil. The fact that elm wood, which is resistant to splintering, was used for such stocks, suggests that some movement was expected. Serpentines were breech loaders, some cast in bronze, but most built up of iron bands. Each gun was equipped with three chambers, which indicates that a rapid rate of fire could be achieved.[4] All the guns were deployed in the forecastle and the poop, where they seem to have been fired through open portholes. Although a serpentine could weigh up to two tons, they should be classed as light weapons, designed to destroy an enemy's rigging and clear his decks, rather than to sink or disable the ship itself. There was no such thing as a gun deck, and Oppenheim believed that both ships would have lain low in the water in order to carry their top-hamper. However, part of the effectiveness of a carrack lay in the fact that its height made it difficult to board, and we should probably conclude instead that the collective weight of over 200 small guns would not have been sufficient to destabilize a vessel of 600 tons. Whether these ships should be described as 'custom built' men of war, and thereby distinguished from the royal ships of an earlier age, seems highly debatable. Henry V's *Grace Dieu* had never been used for commercial purposes,

[1] D. Loades, *The Tudor Court*, 24–5.
[2] Oppenheim, *Administration*, 40.
[3] Ibid., 41.
[4] P. Padfield, *Guns at Sea*, 57.

and to that extent was a specialized fighting ship, but she had had a very short working life, and differed only in size from the design of a normal merchantman. The *Regent* and the *Sovereign* were somewhat different in that their castles were built to carry guns, which required a stronger structure and more portholes, but such modifications were relatively minor. Guildford and Bray, who were responsible for the building, were friends and confidential servants of the King, with no known experience of ship design, but Bray was clearly a man of many talents, who was also responsible for the royal chapels at Windsor and Westminster. The *Sovereign* was used for only one commercial voyage during the period covered by the existing accounts – by James Finch of London to the Levant early in 1497 – but she was clearly available in the same way as other royal ships.[1] The *Regent* may have been thought of differently, as she is not known to have been used for any private purposes. She was in a special sense the King's Great Ship, invariably the Admiral's flagship, but such vessels had existed in the past, and there was probably no intention of departing from tradition when she was commissioned.

Nevertheless, the existence of these large and expensive warships did have some implications which may not have been foreseen. The *Grace Dieu* had been built for a particular war, and once laid up had never been used again, in spite of the fact that hostilities had continued. The *Regent* and the *Sovereign* were not built for a particular war – indeed when they were laid down there was no war in prospect – and never became redundant. Consequently they needed to be maintained at a high level, and the somewhat casual beaching and docking which sufficed for smaller vessels was not adequate. In 1496 a special dock was constructed at Portsmouth for this purpose, together with a storehouse and a forge. Over £2 000 was also spent on fortifying the harbour, so it is not an exaggeration to describe it as an embryonic naval base.[2] Quite a lot is known about the dock because the full building accounts survive, but there are also some puzzling features which must affect any assessment of its importance in naval history. Although it is described by Oppenheim and others as the first known dry dock in England, there is no contemporary indication that anything unusual was being attempted. Excavation started on the site of the later No. 1 basin on 14 June 1495 and continued until 29 November. Work was then suspended until 2

[1] *Naval Accounts*, 218.
[2] Ibid., xxxiv.

February 1496, when it was resumed until 17 April. During the first period of 24 weeks an average of 35 labourers and carpenters were employed every week, at an overall cost of £124.2s.3d.[1] The basin so created was lined with timber, and closed with a double wooden gate. No similar structure can be adduced from earlier references to docks, but some degree of excavation was common, and references to timber props being used to shore up vessels in dock make it clear that water was normally excluded. Oppenheim believed that these older docks were no more than shallow scrapes at the high water mark, with earth and rubble piled across the front to keep out the top of the tide. If that had been the case, then the contrast with the structure at Portsmouth would have been very marked. However, it seems likely that the differences were less obvious than Oppenheim believed. In the first place, in spite of the gates, it was necessary to 'fortify' the dockhead with large quantities of stone and rubble. This must mean that the space between the gates was filled in, an interpretation confirmed by the fact that every time a ship was taken out of the dock subsequently a gang of workmen had to be employed at low tide to dig out the dockhead.[2] No doubt the excavation at Portsmouth was larger and deeper than usual, and may have been sited to take account of the fact that both ships drew a lot of water. The structure was probably more elaborate, and references to a pump for extracting the water also suggest a higher degree of sophistication, but neither the principle nor the practice of dry-docking was new, and it seems unnecessary to speculate where the King's engineers could have found such a revolutionary idea.

Henry VII reigned for twenty-four years, and during that time he disposed of all the ships which he had inherited. Joanne Roger handed over *The Mary of the Tower* to her husband's successor, William Commersall, in February 1488, but after 1496 the ship disappears from the records, although whether sold or broken up is not clear. The *Falcon* and the *Trinity* similarly disappear in 1503. In place of these vessels appeared not only the *Regent* and the *Sovereign*, but also the *Sweepstake* and the *Mary Fortune*, which were built in 1497, the *Carvel of Eu*, which was bought after having been hired for a period, the *Margaret*, captured in 1490, and the *Bonaven-*

[1] *Naval Accounts*, 143–48.

[2] e.g. 'Also the sayd Robert Brygandyne hath payed for the wages of xxti workemen laboryng abought the brekyng up of the dokke hede at Portesmouth weyng ut of the piles & shorys And dyggyng of the clay and other Rubbysh bytwene the gates for having oute of the Soueraigne laboryng abought the seid bisynes at every tyde both day and nyght . . . by the space of iiii wekes . . .'; Ibid., 170–1.

ture.[1] In 1489 the King tried to buy a Spanish ship called the *Juan de Hoyo*, but in spite of considerable pressure he was unsuccessful, perhaps because of the reluctance of Ferdinand and Isabella to allow their subjects to sell ships abroad.[2] The *Mary Fortune* is described as a bark, and cost £120.17s. to build and rig. The *Sweepstake* was about the same size, and cost £75.3s.2d., without the rigging. Each was equipped with 52 oars or sweeps, and must therefore have resembled the balingers of an earlier generation. There is not a great deal of evidence as to how any of these ships were used. The operations of the summer of 1487, which lasted about two months involved six hired ships, one of which was the *Carvel of Eu*. The reason for this modest mobilization was probably the invasion from Ireland in support of the pretensions of Lambert Simnel, but there was no fighting at sea. Sir Edward Woodville's expedition to Brittany in 1488 was a strictly private affair, and it was not until 1489 that the King's ships saw any further service. In April of that year a small official force was sent to Brittany, and 18 ships (including the *Regent* and the *Sovereign*) were involved, under the command of Lord Willoughby; but again there was no sea battle.[3] There was action in the summer of 1490 against the Scots, but both the circumstances and the details are unclear. James IV of Scotland eventually built up a powerful navy, including the *Michael* constructed at Culross by French shipwrights, which was larger than the *Regent*, but these were the early days of his reign, and how far the fighting involved royal ships on either side is uncertain. Sir Andrew Wood of Largs allegedly captured five English ships, and it was at this time that the *Margaret* was captured by the English.[4] The fact that she was added to the King's fleet suggests that it was ships in the King's pay which took her, but there was no open war and the operations should probably be classed as 'keeping the seas'. In December 1491 the Duchess Anne of Brittany married Charles VIII of France, and Henry found himself bound to honour the pledge which he had made at the treaty of Redon to protect Breton independence. This was not entirely a matter of honour, as the establishment of French control over the harbours and shipping of the Duchy posed a considerable threat to English interests in the Channel. In the summer of 1492, therefore, with the nominal alliance of the Emperor Maximilian, Henry mobilized against France. On 2 October, very late in the

[1] Oppenheim, *Administration*, 35.
[2] *Naval Accounts*, xxxi.
[3] Ibid., xxviii, 103; J. D. Mackie, *The Earlier Tudors*, 96–7.
[4] Laird Clowes, *The Royal Navy*, 444.

year for campaigning, he landed at Calais with 25 000 men, and laid seige to Boulogne.[1] The seriousness of his military intentions had always been doubted, and by early November a peace treaty had been agreed at Etaples. Henry allowed himself to be bought off for 745 000 gold crowns [about £185 000], which was quite a good bargain, considering that the Emperor had failed to support him, but did not resolve the problem of French naval power.

The fleet which had brought the English army to France consisted of 500 vessels raised in the traditional manner, but the landing was not resisted, and most of the ships saw no action. Because of Henry's reluctance to bring matters to an issue, they had been on standby since the early summer. Some of them had made a sweep of the Channel in June without encountering any opposition, and the only fighting involved 12 ships under Sir Edward Poynings, which helped to dislodge the count of Ravenstein from Sluys. Ravenstein was in rebellion against the Emperor, and had seized the port early in 1492, turning it into a destructive pirate stronghold. In August the town was beseiged by an Imperial army commanded by Albert of Saxony. English assistance was by no means disinterested, as Ravenstein's ships had captured many English traders, but it was decisive. Sluys fell on 13 October, and Poynings secured control of the castle.[2] The English expeditionary force returned in mid-December, and if there was any military activity at sea during the following three years, the records of it have not survived. In 1494 Charles VIII launched a long-prepared invasion of Italy, and thereafter French attentions were concentrated south of the Alps. This should have meant that the Scottish Borders were also quiet, and perhaps they would have been if it had not been for the activities of Perkin Warbeck. This young man was a native of Tournai, who bore a striking physical resemblance to King Edward IV, and was induced to impersonate Edward's younger son, Richard of York, who had disappeared in 1483 and was almost certainly dead.[3] Warbeck appeared in Ireland in the autumn of 1491, but attracted very little support. However, as the risk of hostilities with England mounted in the summer of 1492, Charles VIII invited him to France with the obvious intention of using him against Henry. The treaty of Etaples brought that project to an end, but Warbeck was immediately able to turn to his putative 'aunt', Margaret of Burgundy, who was willing to take up any cause which promised embarrassment to the

[1] S. B. Chrimes, *Henry VII* 282; Mackie, *The Earlier Tudors*, 108.
[2] Laird Clowes, *The Royal Navy*, 445.
[3] Chrimes, *Henry VII*, 81–2 and n.

Tudors. Thanks to the countenance which Margaret gave him, Warbeck was able to stir up a conspiracy in England which cost the head of Sir William Stanley, the King's Chamberlain and former confidant, but when he attempted to land a force in Kent in July 1495, he was repulsed with contemptuous ease. Nevertheless, despite the excellence of Henry's intelligence service, Warbeck was not intercepted at sea on that occasion, which suggests that there was no system of regular patrols, even when a threat was known to exist. Unmolested by the King's ships, the pretender withdrew again to Ireland, but finding no better welcome there than before, moved on to Scotland, where James IV received him with some warmth in November 1495.[1]

Henry had consistently wooed the Scots since his accession, starting with a three year truce in 1488. That truce had been renewed for seven years in April 1494, and Henry was seriously attempting to interest James in a marriage alliance. However, the latter soon found Warbeck an attractive proposition. Whether he was really deceived, or was merely hoping to use 'the prince of England' to secure some territorial advantages in the borders is not clear. After entertaining him generously for nearly a year, and attracting a good deal of diplomatic interest from the courts of Europe, in September 1496 he crossed into England for the ostensible purpose of restoring his guest to his rightful inheritance. The result was almost as big a fiasco as the raid on Kent. Warbeck had no following in England, and after about three weeks the Scots retreated, having broken the peace for nothing.[2] Although he probably realized that the threat had evaporated, Henry could not ignore the provocation. In January 1497 he obtained a grant of about £150 000 from parliament, and set about preparing an expedition to the north. In the event the Cornish rebellion set off by the taxation turned out to be more violent than the campaign, but Henry did not allow his preparations to be interrupted. Sixteen or seventeen ships were taken up in February, armed and equipped, while the *Regent*, the *Sweepstake* and the *Mary Fortune* were also prepared for service. Shipments of ordnance, weapons and provisions to the north began in early May, and the fighting ships had set off by the middle of June.[3] Realizing that a confrontation was inevitable, James again crossed the border and laid siege to Norham castle. However, there was an element of shadow boxing about the whole episode. The Earl of Surrey, with a

[1] Chrimes, *Henry VII*, 86.
[2] Mackie, *The Earlier Tudors*, 140.
[3] *Naval Accounts*, xlv–vi, 82–132.

substantial force of about 10 000 men, raised the siege of Norham in August, and then set about destroying a number of minor Scottish fortifications just north of Berwick with unnecessary thoroughness. James retreated from Norham without a fight, and did not allow himself to be tempted into interrupting these operations. The fleet, under the command of Lord Willoughby, probably got as far north as the Firth of Forth, and managed to expend a modest amount of ammunition, but how is not clear since there was no recorded fighting. The *Regent* was at Berwick from 21 to 29 June, and back at Sandwich by 9 September, so the army was probably disbanded at about that time.[1] The 'fforen and petye costes' of the King's flagship during these weeks of service came to £266.5s.7d. – without counting the wages, victuals or munitions.[2] The King, however, achieved as much by this costly show of strength as he would have done by victory. When peace was finally concluded between the Kingdoms in January 1502, James committed himself to marry Henry's daughter Margaret. Warbeck had been expelled from Scotland before the campaign was over, and had made one final attempt by landing in Cornwall in September 1497. Defeated and captured, he had eventually been executed in 1499.

The second half of Henry's reign saw plenty of maritime activity, but nothing of a military nature. Treaties with Spain and the Low Countries encouraged trade; another with France in 1497 was designed to curb piracy by agreeing that the seamen of each country should be systematically subjected to bonds and recognizances to desist from molesting the shipping of the other.[3] In matters of this kind, however, the King was reactive rather than pro-active. The navigation acts which were passed in his reign to promote the shipping of wine and Toulouse woad in English 'bottoms' were the result of his favourable response to lobbying by the mercantile community rather than of his own initiative. Merchants were good taxpayers, and their interests merited a measure of promotion when it was diplomatically convenient to do so, as was demonstrated at Medina del Campo in 1489, and in the treaty called the Magnus Intercursus of 1496. About 20 commercial statutes were promoted in the House of Commons by petitions from particular groups, and the King's hand can only be detected when his own financial interests were directly involved, as when he insisted that aliens who became

[1] *Naval Accounts*, 241.
[2] Ibid.
[3] Laird Clowes, *The Royal Navy*, 447.

denizens should continue to pay customs at the aliens' rate.[1] Similarly his support for the Bristol based voyages of discovery, sometimes claimed to have represented the first dawning of Imperial ambitions, was neither spontaneous nor particularly generous. John Cabot, a native of Genoa but a citizen of Venice, came to England in 1490 after unsuccessfully seeking patronage in both Lisbon and Seville. It was not until 1496 that his applications to the King finally bore fruit, when he was granted a patent of privilege for a voyage of discovery. This empowered him, his sons, and their heirs or deputies, to sail with five ships under the English flag to all parts of the eastern, western and northern seas, and to annex any lands hitherto unknown to Christians.[2] They were to be exempt from customs on any goods which they might bring back, and were to enjoy a monopoly of trade with the lands which they discovered. Such gains were hypothetical, however, and the sober reality was that the Cabots were to bear all the costs of the expedition themselves, and to pay the King 20 per cent of any profit they might make. The significance of the King's grant lay less in any evidence of enlightened commercial thinking than in the fact that it implicitly rejected the recent Bull of Pope Alexander VI, dividing the world into Spanish and Portuguese spheres of influence.

In the event, Cabot set off from Bristol on 2 May 1497 with one small ship, the *Mathew* of about 40 tons, which was presumably all he could afford. He made a landfall, probably in Newfoundland or Nova Scotia, and was back in Bristol by 6 August believing that he had discovered a new route to the land of the Great Khan. Henry was sufficiently impressed to give him a gratuity of £10, a pension of £20 a year for life, and a second patent to undertake a further voyage.[3] The Bristol merchants were sufficiently impressed to put up the capital for this second attempt, which set off in May 1498 with five ships. One of these had been provided by the King, although whether it was a royal ship in the proper sense, or one which he had hired, is not clear. Very little is known about this second voyage. One of the captains, Lancelot Thirkill, received a loan of £30 from the Crown, and certainly returned because he is mentioned again in a document of 1501.[4] But of John Cabot there

[1] Statute I Henry VII, cap, ii; *Statutes of the Realm*, 2, 501. The treaty of Medina del Campo was with Spain, and the Magnus Intercursus with the Netherlands.
[2] J. A. Williamson, *The Cabot voyages and Bristol discovery under Henry VII*, 49–50, 203–5.
[3] Ibid., 86; doc. 27.
[4] Laird Clowes, *The Royal Navy*, 608.

is no further mention and he probably died on the voyage. There is reason to suppose that some, at least of the ships reached America, because when the Spanish pilot Juan de la Cosa produced his map in 1500, he marked an extensive portion of the coastline of what is now the north eastern United States as 'Sea discovered by the English', which would be a considerable exaggeration of the achievement of the first voyage. For some years thereafter the King's interest was maintained at a modest level, and the merchants of Bristol were sufficiently encouraged to persist in their attempts. In 1501 an Anglo-Portuguese syndicate was granted a patent in similar terms to Cabot's, and in the following year the same group received a second patent which seems to have envisaged establishing actual possession by settlement.[1] No settlement was established, but the voyages certainly continued. In 1502, according to a London chronicler, three 'wild men' from the New Found Lands were brought to the court at Westminster, and by 1506 some kind of a company of Adventurers to these same lands had been formed in Bristol.[2] There seems to have been little tangible result from this activity, and Henry was not disposed to make any substantial investment. The north Atlantic lacked the glamour of New Spain, and the prospect of instant riches, but enough was done to demonstrate that the English possessed both the ships and the skills necessary for oceanic enterprise when the social and economic climate was right. John Cabot's son, Sebastian received a patent of his own in 1505, which he also executed from Bristol, probably in 1508. He explored a considerable stretch of the American coastline, and returned in 1509 convinced that he had found the beginning of the north west passage. However, by that time Henry VII was dead, and the new King's warlike ambitions, which were to be so stimulating to the navy, left little interest or energy to spare for trans-Atlantic adventures.

The dramatic contrast between Henry VIII and his father is a commonplace of historical writing, and was much commented upon by contemporaries. But of course the young man was to a large extent what his father had made him. Quite apart from the exaggerations of flattery or propaganda, he was a very good jouster and tennis player, but only because the elder Henry had subjected his raw athleticism to the instruction of the finest tutors. His enthusiasm for guns and warships is usually supposed to have been in marked

[1] Williamson, *The Cabot Voyages*, 116–44; docs. 43, 45, 46, 47, 49.
[2] Mackie, *The Earlier Tudors*, 227.

contrast to his father's irenic and commercial tastes, but in fact Henry VII showed a considerable interest in artillery. From the beginning of his reign he employed a number of French gun-founders, who were probably casting bronze cannon, and by 1489 he had 30 gunners in his service at the Tower of London – German and Spanish as well as French.[1] In 1496 he issued commissions for the manufacture of ordnance intended for the Scottish campaign; and a certain Pierre Robertes was making wrought iron guns and iron shot in Ashdown Forest in the same year. There had been an iron foundry at Buxted, just to the south of Ashdown, since about 1490, although it is not known who was operating it.[2] By 1497 he had 49 gunners in his service, and as we have seen, his ships were far more heavily armed than those of the previous reigns. The first attempt to cast iron guns in England was made in Sussex in 1508, and by 1510 breech loaders with separate chambers were being successfully cast. These were of moderate size (714lb. for the gun and 425lb. for the chamber) and may well have been intended for naval use. Henry VIII was consequently not innovating when he established the Hounsditch foundry in 1511, but continuing an established tradition of patronage. Similarly the first ship known to have been designed to carry heavy guns on a gun deck above the orlop was the *Mary Rose*, but it is not clear whether the *Mary Rose* was laid down before or after Henry VII's death in April 1509. According to G. F. Howard the idea of firing guns through ports cut in the side of the ship was developed 'between 1505 and 1509', but nobody knows exactly whose idea it was, or whether there had been experiments before the *Mary Rose*.[3] The invention of the porthole has been credited to one Descharges, a shipbuilder of Brest, but it is not at all clear what he is supposed to have invented. Both the *Sovereign* and the *Regent* mounted guns firing through open ports in their castles, and the Warwick Roll shows the same technique at least a decade before Descharges' alleged invention. Perhaps he was the originator of the closed or lidded porthole, which would be necessary on a lower deck, but used it for loading or access rather than for gunnery. The *Mary Rose* almost certainly had lidded gunports from the beginning, and thus marked a revolution in warship design,[4] but it

[1] H. Schubert, 'The first cast iron cannon made in England', *JISI*, 146, 1942, 131.
[2] Ibid.; The account of the first successful cast guns can be found in the Duchy of Lancaster Receiver's accounts for Sussex (454 nos. 7329–7331).
[3] G. F. Howard, 'Gun port lids', *MM*, 67, 1981, 64.
[4] PRO E36/13 f.23. G. F. Howard 'Early ships' guns I; Built up breech loaders', 439–52.

may well have been Henry VII's shipwrights rather than those of his son who were responsible for this major advance.

Thomas Roger was succeeded as Clerk of the King's Ships by William Commersall, who held the office until the end of April 1495. Not very much is known about Commersall, except that he was an experienced seaman, but his accounts do not seem to have survived and there is some suspicion that he may have been dismissed for incompetence. His successor Robert Brigandyne, was a much more substantial figure, and it is with him that the story of Tudor naval administration really begins. Brigandyne was a Yeoman of the Crown from a well established but not particularly wealthy Kentish family. He had received several marks of favour from the King before his appointment, including an annuity of £10 in 1490, and was briefed personally by Henry about his new duties on 1 May.[1] His patent, dated 19 May, was drawn up in the traditional form, and his emoluments were the same as Roger's – 12d. a day for himself, 6d. a day for a clerk, 3s. a day when travelling on official business, drawn on the customs of Exeter and Dartmouth. Like Roger he was also authorized to obtain the necessary writs and warrants for the discharge of his duties from the Chancery upon the exhibition of his patent. The Treasurer and Tellers of the Exchequer were to honour warrants so obtained without requiring further authorization. An interesting appendix to the patent, however, went somewhat beyond precedent in referring to 'prests' or advances of money authorized by special royal warrants for the particular works intended at Portsmouth, and

> . . . for the Reparacion Rygging Apparalyng Kepyng and Amendyng of diverse and soundrie shippes of our seid souveraigne lorde the Kynges & provision of tackle and apparell for the same with the severall accomptes of stuff tackle and apparell ordinances Artillarie and Abillamentes of Warre to the Kynges shippes the Kynges house calld the Blokkhouse or the Kynges dokke at Portesmouth . . .[2]

Whether this represented an extension of the Clerk's duties or merely an additional emphasis upon his accountability is not clear. Unlike Roger, Brigandyne does not seem to have been involved in the payment of either wages or victuals during active service, and did not record any expenses involved in the 'taking up' of other ships.

[1] *Naval Accounts*, 138.
[2] Ibid.

On the other hand he seems to have been entirely responsible for the storehouse and dock at Portsmouth, and for the maintenance, repair and servicing of four ships. There is no further reference to the rented storehouse at Greenwich, but whether it had been abandoned or placed under other management is not clear. Ships were still sometimes kept in the Thames, and £18.2s.2d. was expended in January 1497 for the construction of a barrier to protect the *Sovereign* from 'the yse in Thamys',[1] but for the most part they were at Portsmouth, where both the *Regent* and the *Sovereign* – but particularly the latter – spent far more time in dock than would have been required for their maintenance. As had been the case in earlier generations, docking was a form of short-term storage.

During the two and a half years covered by his surviving account, from May 1495 to the end of 1497, Brigandyne expended £2 061.18s.8d., of which the dock cost a little over £193, the *Sovereign* £595 and the *Regent* £1 042.[2] This represents a higher level of 'normal' activity than Roger's, because it does not include any extraordinary payments to ships at sea, but the account raises almost as many questions as it answers. Where, for example, were the *Trinity* and the *Falcon*, which were owned by the King until 1503, but not Brigandyne's responsibility? Was there a dock at Portsmouth before the new work began, as the wording of the patent seems to suggest? Did Brigandyne account for the ordnance used in the Scottish war, or is there no connection between the two documents? Roger's last remaining ship, the *Mary of the Tower*, had been duly handed over to William Commersall, but never came into Brigandyne's hands. Instead there are two notes which indicate that she had been either given or sold to Sir Ralph Astry (who had also obtained the *Governor* in 1486), complete with all her tackle and over 60 guns.[3] Brigandyne repurchased all this equipment from Astry's executors in 1495 for £680.14s.11d. Did Henry make a habit of allowing artillery to come into private hands, or is some exceptional event concealed behind these bland figures? There were only five guns in the Blockhouse at Portsmouth when Brigandyne took it over, so the guns which Roger had held at Greenwich must have been bestowed elsewhere. The Clerk of the Ships supplied gunpowder, shot, bows, arrows and bills to the ships going north against the Scots in 1497 but not (apparently) the guns themselves. When equipment of this kind was placed in one of the king's own ships the

[1] *Naval Accounts*, 164.
[2] Ibid., 344.
[3] Philip MacDougall, *The Royal Dockyards*, 21; *Naval Accounts*, 186.

Clerk remained accountable, although its use was out of his control, but when it was placed in a hired ship, then the master became accountable to the Clerk. Despite the complexities and uncertainties, it is possible to see some progress in the definition of the Clerk's duties. By 1497 it is clear that his main responsibility was servicing. He hired and paid the shipwrights, caulkers, carpenters and painters who were employed by the day or the week on repair and maintenance work; the shipkeepers and other mariners who looked after the ships when they were not in service, who moved them and docked them when necessary, or sailed them between Portsmouth and the Thames. He was also responsible for labouring work on the dock, and for the building of the storehouse. He purchased timber and other materials, particularly cables, and the canvas which the mariners themselves probably made into sails. He provided lodging and food for all the men working on the ships, and food for the shipkeepers. As we have also seen, he stored and issued munitions. On the other hand, he was not responsible for ships at sea on the King's service, and no longer seems to have played any part in hiring ships for such service. Brigandyne kept the accounts for the building of the *Sweepstake* and the *Mary Fortune*, but not for the *Mary Rose*, the *Peter Pomegranate*, or any of the other big ships laid down on the King's orders between 1509 and 1523 when he died or retired.

Henry VII's naval policy can be partly reconstructed from this evidence. He appreciated the necessity to own and operate his own ships, and realized that the really big fighting ships necessary to provide the core of a navy royal were hard to find from private resources. He revived and made more systematic the earlier payment of bounties for the building of large ships, but the effect of this is very hard to determine. In 1502 Ferdinand and Isabella of Spain introduced a fixed bounty of 100 marevedis a ton up to 1 500 tons (Spanish tuns were somewhat smaller than English), and then forbade their subjects to sell ships to aliens, under severe penalties.[1] Henry never went so far, but seems to have paid between one and five shillings a ton from about 80 tons upward. Whether such payments were general, or only made in special circumstances, is not clear. In 1488 he allowed Nicholas Browne of Bristol £26.13s.4d on a new ship of 140 tons, which is about 3s.10d. a ton; while in 1491 the builders of a ship of 400 tons were allowed 5s. – perhaps it depended upon the size.[2] Even those who purchased medium-sized ships

[1] Oppenheim, *Administration*, 37.

[2] Ibid., 38; see also B. Dietz, 'The Royal bounty and English shipping in the sixteenth and seventeenth centuries', *MM*, 77, 1991, 5–21.

could expect some consideration. In 1502 three Bristol merchants who had purchased a French ship of 120 tons were allowed £20, on the understanding that the ship was to be available to the King 'at all tymes at oure commaundement'.[1] For the most part Henry hired ships, as his predecessors had done – one shilling per ton per month from the English, and two shillings from aliens. He seems to have particularly liked Spanish and Low Countries vessels, or perhaps they were the most available. His own subjects were not particularly pleased by this disparity of payment, but were not in a strong position to argue with a king who in other respects looked after their interests well. They would have preferred a fixed rate rather than one based on tonnage, and said so in a petition of 1487, but do not seem to have been heeded.

Without making any major changes or innovations, Henry nevertheless handed on to his son a more active and more firmly based naval administration than had existed for many years. It had a base at Portsmouth, with improved facilities, a small number of good ships in seaworthy condition, and a programme for expansion. Naval armament had been developed, and an experienced Clerk of the Ships was given adequate resources to keep his storehouses stocked. The King was sufficiently interested to talk to Brigandyne about his duties on a number of occasions, and probably decided the deployment of individual ships himself. Whether he conceived of a standing navy with a regular peacetime function, is however, a different matter. Regular patrols for the keeping of the seas are nowhere referred to, and if occasional expeditions were sent out against pirates they must have been separately organized. Only the taking of Sluys in 1492 could be so construed, and that was in the context of war. Complaints about piratical depredations, although they can be heard, were neither as numerous nor as vociferous as they had been half a century before. Perhaps there was less piracy, or perhaps merchant ships were better able to take care of themselves. If the *Governor* and the *Mary of the Tower* could mount 50 guns when sailing under private colours, other masters may have been able to buy or hire guns from the well-stocked royal arsenals – or perhaps Henry's favourite expedient of recognizance actually worked in this context. Whatever the reason, these seem to have been relatively peaceful and prosperous years for seagoing merchants. Nor does it seem to have been difficult to recruit seamen for

[1] This must have constituted a specific commitment, because the king could 'take up' any ship without such a prior arrangement. Oppenheim, *Administration*, 38.

the king's service, in marked contrast to later periods. An ordinary seaman's pay was about 5s. a month, which was less than the 3d. a day which had been normal in the fourteenth century, but that was over and above his victuals which were costed at the same rate.[1] The pilot of a big ship like the *Sovereign* could be paid over 50s. a month, and the master only a little less. There were also many other officers on such a ship; purser, steward, boatswain, coxswain, master's mate, cook, and a number of others, each paid above the basic seaman's rate.[2] Although opportunities for royal service were limited, both the certainty of the reward and the relative comfort of a large ship seem to have proved attractive. The harbour rates were lower – 3s.4d. a week for the master and 1s. a week for a seaman, but again victuals were provided and the work must have been fairly safe and undemanding. The king's ships cannot have provided permanent employment for more than a handful of men, but the Clerk was regularly hiring skilled workmen of all kinds on a daily or weekly basis – for example, 28 shipwrights and caulkers from 21 August to 30 October 1497, or two sawyers from 21 January to 5 February in the same year.[3] There must have been many shipwrights and carpenters in the Portsmouth area for whom the royal dockyard was the main source of employment during these years, and the beginnings of a regular establishment can be glimpsed. Probably no conscious decision was ever taken that this should be so, but more ships and a higher level of activity tended to make an intermittent function continuous, and that was increasingly the case over the years which followed.

Henry VIII continued Robert Brigandyne in his service, just as his father had continued Thomas Roger. His first act as Clerk of the Ships in the new reign was an indenture dated 4 May 1509, but no accounts survive to present a coherent picture of his responsibilities at this time. He shared with John Dawtry, one of the customers of Southampton, and with John Hopton, the costs of repairing the *Sovereign*, and of 'new making' the *Regent* between 1504 and 1512.[4] On 28 October 1509 the *Sovereign* was in dock at Portsmouth, and Brigandyne received £1 175.14s.2d. for work already

[1] Oppenheim, *Administration*, 41. Victuals were actually costed at 1s.2d. a week or 4s.8d. a month (the month being computed at 28 days). Shipkeeping in harbour was paid at 1s. a week.

[2] 'Wages of maryners with lodemanage', *Naval Accounts*, 166.

[3] Ibid., 178.

[4] 'Indenture between Thomas Thomas of Southampton and Robert Brygandyne clerk of the king's ships on one part, and Harvey Halbeard, master of the king's ship the Regent on the other part'. *Letters and Papers of the Reign of Henry VIII*, I, 16. PRO SP1/2 f. 149, *L and P*, I, 1393.

carried out on her. On 18 November he received on the King's behalf an unnamed ship, which seems to have been the *Regent*, loaned to an Italian merchant named Ludovico de la Fore for a voyage to the Levant in July 1508. On 9 June 1510 he wrote from Woolwich to Richard Polshide, another customer of Southampton, about money received for the new making of the *Mary Rose* and the *Peter Pomegranate* – the first time those famous ships appear in the records.[1] In October 1511 he received £1 600 for rigging two new barks, and two newly built rowbarges are also mentioned at this time. As Dr Davies observed several years ago, Brigandyne was only one of a number of agents used by the King about his maritime affairs, 'not a one man department of state'.[2] Like other Clerks before him, he had no budget, but was paid by specific warrant for specific purposes. Like his father, Henry VIII was sufficiently interested to make policy decisions about the navy himself, and often to sign the warrants, so there was little chance for the Clerk to develop a semi-autonomous department, even if he had had the status to do so.

Such evidence as there is suggests that there was considerable continuity between the two reigns, and that Henry VIII took over a building and maintenance programme in full swing. Some sort of dockyard seems to have existed at Woolwich as well as at Portsmouth, and it is somewhat misleading to say that only five ships were actually handed over. A set of accounts deriving from Sir John Heron, the Treasurer of the Chamber, and commencing on 1 May 1509, show that an enhanced level of naval activity antedated the outbreak of war in 1512.[3] Ships were prepared and rigged for the safeconduct of the Merchant Adventurers in June 1511; in the following month three armed ships were sent out to 'waft' unnamed merchants to Zeeland, and in August arrearages were paid for 'defending the merchants against rovers'.[4] By 3 February 1512, before the build-up to the summer campaign began, Heron had spent £4 617.19s.9d. on maritime affairs since the opening of the account, and that did not include any of the routine expenses for which the Clerk was responsible. There had also been some action at sea which indicated the King's willingness to respond to challenges and opportunities, even on a small scale. According to a versified

[1] PRO SP1/2 f. 149; *L and P*, I, 1393.
[2] C. S. L. Davies, 'The administration of the Royal Navy under Henry VIII; the origins of the Navy Board', 268–88.
[3] PRO SP1/3 f. 6; *L and P*, I, 1416.
[4] Alfred Spont, *Letters and Papers relating to the war with France, 1512–13*, ix and n.

account written long after the event, Henry was petitioned by the merchants of London to protect them against the depredations of the Scottish pirate Andrew Barton.[1] The King then swore 'a great oath', and vowed that he would have Barton's head, calling upon his noblemen who stood by for a volunteer to undertake the task. The challenge was taken up by Charles, Lord Howard, and a detailed account of the battle then follows. In fact there was no Howard named Charles in that generation – it was Sir Edward Howard who fought against Barton – and the circumstances in which the action was launched are not known, but the chivalric aura of the knight sallying forth to protect the innocent seems to be authentic. Howard hired two (or possibly three) ships at the King's expense in July 1511, intercepted Barton, of whose whereabouts he must have been very accurately informed, and defeated him, capturing both his ships.[2] Barton himself was killed in the action, and there were prolonged diplomatic repercussions. James IV claimed that Barton was his servant, holding letters of marque against the Portuguese, and demanded the return of his main ship, the *Lion*.[3] The second ship, the *Jenett of Purwyn*, belonged to the King of Denmark, having been illegally purchased by Barton in Copenhagen, and the Danes also made representations. Howard's exploit cost the Exchequer £200, and both prizes were added to the growing royal fleet, but significantly the King's own ships were not used. The *Regent*, the *Sovereign*, the *Mary Rose* and the *Peter Pomegranate* were all at sea within a month of the engagement, and must therefore have been available, but would not have been sufficiently nimble to catch Barton's ships of 120 and 70 tons. The *Mary and John* had been leased to a merchant group in April 1511, but the king had at least three other ships which could in theory have been used, the *Sweepstake*, the *Gabriel Royal* and the *Mary James*. Presumably they were either not ready for the sea, or not deemed suitable for some other reason.

Two small military expeditions were also sent overseas in 1511; some archers to assist the Emperor against the Duke of Gelders, and 1 000 men under Lord Darcy to accompany Ferdinand of Aragon against the Moors.[4] Darcy was instructed to embark his men at Portsmouth, and not to allow them to disembark at the other end until he had instructions from Ferdinand. In the event, by the time

[1] 'The ballad of Sir Andrew Barton', C. H. Firth ed., *Naval songs and ballads*.
[2] Spont, *Letters and Papers*, viii, quoting Holinshed's Chronicle.
[3] BL MS Royal 13B II, f. 646; *L and P*, I, 1070.
[4] Instructions for Lord Darcy, May 1511; *L and P*, I, 730.

they arrived at Cadiz Ferdinand had no use for them, but Darcy allowed them to land, and two weeks of drunken indiscipline sent the expedition home in disgrace and demonstrated the wisdom of Henry's original order. It is not known which ships were used for these operations, but they were probably 'taken up' or hired in the traditional way. By the time that England joined the Holy League in December 1511, and the war against France which Henry had been seeking became imminent, he had some 13 ships in his own possession – the largest royal fleet since the days of Henry V – and the build-up was continuing rapidly. In the course of 1512 five ships were certainly built for the King, a further three probably were, and six more were acquired by purchase. These varied in size from 80 to 700 tons, and three of them are described as galleys.[1] The purpose of this development was soon apparent. Henry intended to wage war both by sea and land, and did not see his fleet simply as a means of escorting troop transports. The key to his naval strategy was the same alliance with Spain which was supposed to result in a combined invasion of Guienne, and on 7 April 1512 this strategy was set out in the instructions issued to Sir Edward Howard, who was appointed to succeed the Earl of Oxford as Lord Admiral. Howard was an active and effective commander at sea, of a sort which had not been seen since the early days of the previous century, and his brief was explicit:

> Amongst other articles contained in a treaty made and concluded between the king's highness and his father [in law] the king of Aragon, it is provided that the king's highness for his part shall before the end of this instant month of April put in rediness and actually send to the sea the number of 3000 men, well and sufficiently harnessed, in ships apparelled, dressed and furnished with habillements of war apt and necessary for battle on the sea, to keep and defend the sea after their policies, strengths and powers, from the mouth of the Thames to the Trade, against the courses of outward enemies. Like as the king's said father, the king of Aragon, is by the said treaty semblably bound to defend the sea with like number of men and ships beyond the said Trade. The said

[1] The ships certainly built were; the *Lizard* of 120 tons, the *Swallow* of 80 tons, the *Kateryn Galley* of 80 tons, the *Rose Galley* and the *Henry Galley*, both of unknown tonnage. Those probably built were the *Dragon* of 100 tons, the *Great Bark* of 400 tons, and the *Less Bark* of 160. The purchases were the *Anne Gallant* of 140 tons, the *John Baptist* of 400 tons, the *Great Nicholas* of 400 tons, the *Christ* of 300 tons, the *Katherine Fortileza* of 700 tons, and the *Lesser Barbara* of 160 tons. Oppenheim, *Administration*, 49.

> armies to continue in such defence and tuition of the sea by the space of six months . . . After the fleet shall come to the sea, the Admiral shall take his course, if wind and weather will serve, towards the Trade, for the defence of the sea on that coast, according to the tenor of the said articles, and from thence return scouring the sea, to and fro, as the case shall require . . .[1]

In the spirit of these instructions, Howard's fleet conducted its own campaign, quite independently of the army which set out for Guienne in July under the Command of the Marquis of Dorset. Dorset's expedition was a fiasco, largely because Ferdinand once again failed to produce the promised support, and tried to divert his allies to assist his own attack on Navarre. Howard did not wait for the promised Spanish fleet (which never arrived) but set out in April, as soon as his preparations were complete. Thanks to the indenture which he made with the King on 8 April, we have a very detailed knowledge of how his fleet was organized; the names and tonnage of all his ships, the rates of pay of his officers and men, and the mustering and victualling arrangements.[2]

He was provided with 18 ships '. . . in such manner rigged, equipped, tackled, decked and furnished with ordnance and artillery as to such a voyage and service (is) for the honour of our said Sovereign Lord'. Six or seven of these were the King's own vessels, including the *Regent*, *Mary Rose* and *Peter Pomegranate*, although the *Regent* was not ready in time for the first foray. Why over half the royal ships, including the *Sovereign*, were left behind and a similar number 'taken up' is not clear. The onset of an expected war would have led to the cancellation of all commercial leases. Perhaps they could not be prepared in time, or perhaps they were retained for deployment elsewhere. By the terms of his indenture, Howard and his men were instructed to make their musters before the King's commissioners, and having done so, were then entitled to their wages, rewards and victualling money in accordance with the rates laid down. They were then to return and re-muster every three months, as long as their service lasted.[3] The scheduled muster of 18 captains, 1 750 soldiers and 1 233 mariners and gunners was held at Blackheath on 16 April, and John Dawtrey was then issued with £6 000 to pay for the 'necessaries' of the first three months.

[1] T. Rymer, *Foedera, conventiones . . . etc.*, 6, 30b. The Trade was the entrance to the harbour of Brest.

[2] Rymer, 6, 31; *L and P*, I, 1132; PRO E101/61/12.

[3] Rymer, 6, 31. At the end of the campaign Howard accounted for £14 111.10s.10d. PRO E351/210.

Seventeen of the officers were gentlemen of the King's new band of Spears, and their wages were not charged to Dawtrey, but paid by the King direct.[1] The impression given by the documentation is one of brisk efficiency and thoughtful planning. A careful memorandum drawn up in February noted many of the necessary steps to be taken, from matching the quantities of shot and powder to the number of guns to listing the 'places wherein provision of beer shall be made'; two yeomen of the guard were deputed to record the allocation of every man to his ship, and each purser was allocated money to provide fresh victuals while the ships were still within the Thames estuary.[2] It is not known who had overall charge of the arrangements, but the systematic mind of the King's almoner, Thomas Wolsey, can probably be detected.

At first it seemed that Howard's fleet would achieve little '. . . chasing the French fishing boats and plundering every trading ship he met' as Alfred Spont put it,[3] but it soon became apparent that his speedy mobilization had taken the French completely by surprise and given Henry a decisive initiative at sea. Having returned briefly in May to collect the *Regent* and two new rowbarges, he then escorted Dorset's transports down the Channel as far as Brest between 3 and 6 June. Having discharged this duty, he attacked the Breton coast near Bertheaume, landing forces on four successive days and causing widespread damage. According to Lorenzo Pasqualigo, the Venetian consul in London, Howard also captured 26 Flemish hulks and 40 small Breton vessels in the course of this operation. So unprepared did the French appear to be at sea that early in July Louis' ambassador to Scotland, Charles de Tocque, narrowly avoided capture by English ships lying in wait off Berwick, and one of his two Scottish escorts was taken.[4] Late in the same month Howard returned again to Portsmouth, where the fleet was visited by the King himself, and reinforced with five additional ships, including the *Sovereign*. By August the French response was at least beginning to gain momentum, and serious fighting was in prospect. A fleet of 22 men of war drawn from Normandy and Brittany was assembled at Brest, and the Mediterranean Admiral, Prégent de Bidoux was instructed to take his galleys to the same rendezvous. At

[1] The band of Spears had been created in 1511, in imitation of the French model. SP1/5 f. 48; *L and P*, I, 1414, payments by John Dawtry at Portsmouth, October 1512.

[2] PRO SP1/229 f. 43, 46; *L and P*, I, 1080, 1134.

[3] Spont, *Letters and Papers*, xv, 17–18.

[4] Ibid., xvi–xvii. On 18 July James IV complained vigorously to Lord Dacre that the captured seaman, David Falconer, was not a pirate but was on official business, and Dacre advised Henry not to have him executed. *L and P*, I, 1298, 1302.

the same time a swarm of privateers was unleased from the Breton ports, anxious to take their revenge on any English ship which was not protected by Howard's guns. Nevertheless, the initiative remained with the English. On 10 August Howard's fleet arrived off Brest, several days before it was expected and while the French ships were still scattered, with many of their officers ashore. The action which followed was scrappy and inconclusive. The two sides were evenly matched in Great Ships (22–25), but the French did not want to fight at a disadvantage and the English were unable to pin them down. The French Admiral, Rene de Clermont, was subsequently accused of cowardice, but his main concern seems to have been to keep his fleet in being.[1] In this he would have been almost entirely successful, if it had not been for the courage (or foolishness) of Hervé de Porzmoguer, Captain of the *Cordelière*. Porzmoguer decided to stand and fight, and after taking a heavy pounding from several English warships, was grappled by the *Regent*. What then happened is not entirely clear. According to English accounts the *Cordelière* was about to be overrun, and some zealot fired the magazine rather than surrender, but other observers thought that the fire was a pure accident. For whatever reason, the magazine exploded, and both ships were engulfed in flames. Both were destroyed with enormous loss of life, and the incident was recorded by every chronicler and correspondent of the period.[2] Although it had suffered an equal loss, the English fleet retained command of the sea and Howard renewed his depredations on the Breton coast. For about a fortnight he continued to capture French ships at will up and down the Channel, and then returned to Portsmouth at the end of the month.

Although it could hardly be described as a great victory, Henry had every reason to be pleased with this expedition, and rewarded Howard generously. If the *Mary Rose* and the *Peter Pomegranate* had been the first warships to mount heavy cannon, then the French had certainly caught up quickly, and there is no indication of any marked English superiority in firepower. Nor does it seem that the heavy guns carried at this early stage were particularly effective. According to one account a second French ship, the *Admiralda*, was also sunk, but there is no suggestion that it was destroyed by gunfire.[3] On the other hand, by superior organization and swifter deployment, the English had retained the initiative at sea through-

[1] He was accused by one of his captains, Rigault de Berquetot; Spont, *L and P*, 65–7.
[2] e.g. Wolsey to the Bishop of Worcester, 26 August 1512; Spont, *L and P*, 49–50.
[3] A letter to the Cardinal of England, 27 September 1512, *L and P*, I, 1403.

out the summer against an enemy with far greater resources. That initiative they also retained after the end of the campaigning season. In early October the fleet was reduced and reorganized. Six ships, including three of the King's, were brought round from Southampton to the Thames estuary; six others were 'discharged and delivered to their owners' at Southampton, while a further 15 were probably released at the same time.[1] On the other hand 12, of which six or seven belonged to the King, were 'appointed to keep the seas this winter', headed by the *Great Bark* under the command of Sir Weston Browne.[2] This fleet was divided into three squadrons – Westward, Northward, and Dover and Calais – and the whole 'army' was to be victualled and paid for two periods of two months, from the end of October to the end of February. Financially, this operation was kept separate from the summer campaign. In mid-October John Dawtry at Portsmouth accounted for £649.7s.7d. spent in discharging captains, seamen and gunners, paying tonnage charges (still at 12d. per ton per month) and issuing conduct money home. On 28 October Howard completed his own account, showing a total expenditure of £13 903.9s.9d. for the seven months from April to October.[3] At the same time John Heron, one of the customers of London, accounted for £758.15s.6d. spent mostly upon the wages and victuals of ships which had been deployed upon the coasts of Norfolk and Suffolk to protect the herring fleet against French marauders. On 12 November Sir Edward Howard reported to Wolsey from Harwich that there had been no interruption to the North Sea fishing. 'There will be no Frenchman over 60 or 80 tons this side of the Trade', he declared with satisfaction, 'If the king will let the *Lizard*, the new bark of Stephen Bull and one good ship lie in the Camber, and another in the Solent, no Frenchman will stir.'[4] There was nothing to be feared from Great Ships 'which dare not keep the Narrow Seas these winter nights'. His own ships were victualled and paid for a month, and he was about to transfer his flag from the *Mary James* to the *New Bark* as the former needed to return for repairs.

It is clear that Henry did not confine his naval operations during 1512 to military support in the narrow sense. No mention has yet been made of the shipping which conveyed the Marquis of Dorset to Guienne, or brought him home with his tail between his legs at the

[1] PRO SP1/3 f. 157; *L and P*, I, 1413.
[2] Ibid.
[3] PRO E351/210.
[4] PRO SP1/3 f. 6; *L and P*, I, 1416. SP1/229 f. 92; *L and P*, I, 1480.

end of October, but that was also a substantial fleet, for his army was over 12 000 strong. There were also naval operations against the Scots, which resulted in the capture of David Faulkener, and led to a further acrimonious diplomatic exchange, although James did not eventually 'put forth his strength' at sea as expected. Much of this activity was of a traditional nature; escorting troopships, 'wafting' merchants and fishermen, intercepting messengers at sea, and skirmishing with privateers. However the main operation conducted by Howard was significantly different. He was not supporting land forces, nor relieving and besieging coastal fortresses, but waging war upon the sea with the objective of harrying the enemy's coast and destroying his shipping, both military and civilian. Perhaps it was the unexpected nature of this strategy which caused the French response to be so delayed. Moreover, the spectacular conflict beteen the *Regent* and the *Cordelière* was something new in sea fighting – closer to the world of the *Chesapeake* and the *Shannon* than to that of the *Grace Dieu* or the *Cog Thomas*. Nor did the King's efforts relax during the winter. In addition to the standing patrols, this was a period of intense activity. Ships were repaired at Woolwich, Erith and Greenwich. The new Great Ship, at first called the *Henry Imperial* and later the *Henry Grace a Dieu*, was probably launched in February or March 1513, and several other large vessels were purchased; the *Katherine Forteleza*, the *Gabriel Royal*, the *John Hopton* and the *Great Nicholas*.[1] By the time that his main fleet was ready for the sea again, in mid-March, Henry had revised the list several times in consultation with Wolsey. Eventually Sir Edward Howard seems to have taken command of 23 royal ships and 27 others, plus a similar number of victuallers.[2] Six of the hired fighting ships were Spaniards.

However, this time the initiative was less easily won. Prégent de Bidoux had arrived in Brittany with six galleys at the end of October 1512. He was a very skilled and experienced sea fighter, and each of his galleys carried a single heavy gun, known as a basilisk, in the prow, which was reputed to be able to sink any man of war. Prégent's reputation, and perhaps his energy, stirred Louis XII into action. By early March he had fitted out 11 ships in Brittany, and another 15 or 16 in Normandy, and had appointed a new Admiral,

[1] Oppenheim, *Administration*, 49. A list of ships, captains and numbers of seamen for the new campaign, drawn up in February or March 1513 starts with the *Henry Imperial*; Spont, *Letters and Papers*, 79–85. The *Chesapeake* and the *Shannon* fought a celebrated duel off the North American coast in 1813.

[2] Spont, *Letters and Papers*, 86–7; *L and P*, I, 1661.

Guyon le Roy, in place of the uncertain Clermont. However, little use seems to have been made of this advantage. In February it was believed that Prégent would raid Plymouth or Falmouth, but galleys were at their most effective in calm weather and in shallow coastal waters. The English Channel in March exposed their limitations, and nothing happened. By the end of March the Norman squadron had moved to Brest, but no aggressive action had been attempted and the advantage had been wasted. It took Howard almost a month to move his fleet from the Thames to the Breton coast, because of the adverse weather, and by the time he arrived there, his victuals were almost exhausted.[1] The French retreated into the harbour of Brest without offering battle, and Prégent was cut off at St Malo. The English now had the tactical advantage, as they had had in the previous year, but on this occasion time was not on their side. Howard decided upon a bold frontal attack, but the strength of the French defensive position within the harbour, and the sudden wreck of one of his own ships upon a hidden rock caused him to pull back.[2] By this time some victuallers had arrived, giving the Admiral a little more time to consider his next move. For a few days he kept his men occupied in raiding the coastal villages, and while he was still undecided, was counter-attacked by Prégent's galleys, who sank one of his ships and badly damaged another. This manoeuvre seems to have made up his mind. Unable to tempt the main French fleet to battle, he left his own Great Ships to blockade Brest, and mustered his smaller vessels for a decisive attack upon the galleys. However, the English did not have any galleys to match Prégent's force, only small sailing ships and rowbarges. During the previous winter Henry had considered hiring six galleys from the Venetians, but the asking price of 1 000 ducats a month each seems to have deterred him.[3] So Howard faced this action at a considerable disadvantage, and William Sabine, one of his most experienced captains, endeavoured to dissuade him. Bidoux had drawn his galleys in among the rocks, where they were very difficult to get at, and positioned guns on the shore to cover them. With more courage than discretion, Howard took his rowbarge straight in to the attack,

[1] Report sent by Thomas Spinelly to Henry VIII, 21 March 1513, BL Cotton MS Caligula D vi, f. 88; Spont, *Letters and Papers*, 90–94. Sir Edward Howard to Henry VIII, Spont, 94–8. Howard to Wolsey, 5 April 1513, *L and P*, I, 1748.

[2] Howard to Henry VIII, 17 April 1513, Spont, *Letters and Papers* 126–9; *L and P*, I, 1786. The ship lost was probably the *Nicholas of Hampton*, commanded by Arthur Plantagenet.

[3] Andrea Badoer to the Doge and Senate, December 1512, *L and P*, I, 1522. Four of these were 'subtle' and two 'bastard'.

and got aboard Bidoux's own vessel. What then happened is not entirely clear; whether his own men cut and ran in the face of such daunting odds, or were driven off by the fire of the shore batteries. For whatever reason, Howard was cut off and killed, and the English ships retreated in confusion. Demoralized by Howard's death, and once again running out of victuals the whole English fleet returned to Plymouth on 30 April, just a week after the action with the galleys.[1]

The King was angry, believing, perhaps rightly, that his captains had shown a distinct lack of both courage and enterprise. However, his indignant letter, sent as soon as the news reached him, only made the situation worse. When Lord Thomas Howard, appointed to replace his brother as Lord Admiral on 4 May, reached Plymouth, he found '. . . more than half the armye on lande, and I fere me, by hering say, there is a grete nomber stolen away'.[2] He took immediate steps to round up the deserters, and begged Wolsey to persuade the King to send some message of encouragement. 'Never man saw men in greter fere than all the masters and maryners be off the galies, insomuch that in amaner they had as leve go into Purgatory as to the Trade . . .' Howard's intention was to have his fleet back on station within a week, but it proved impossible to revictual in such a short time, especially in a remote port like Plymouth. Wolsey and Edward Fox did their best, and Howard appointed his own clerk controller, one William Symons, to oversee the distribution of the victuals to the ships, but shortages of casks and of transport vessels made delays inevitable.[3] On 9 May Wolsey ordered the mobilization of another 4 000 men under Sir Charles Brandon, to be at Southampton by the 18th for the purpose of reinforcing the fleet, and on 13 May Howard drew up instructions for Brandon to lead a further 'enterprise' against Brittany.[4] Howard's intention seems to have been to send some of his own ships back to Southampton, and to launch this fresh attack from there in order to get round the victualling problem. However the winds were

[1] The fullest account of the action, and of the manoeuverings which preceded it, is given by Prégent himself in a letter of 28 April; Spont, *Letters and Papers*, 132–40; see also William Sabine to Wolsey, 30 April 1513; BL Cotton MS Caligula E i, ii, iii, f. 1; Spont, 141–4.

[2] Edward Echyngham to Wolsey, 5 May 1513, *L and P*, I, ii, 1844; Lord Thomas Howard to Henry VIII, 7 May 1513, BL MS Cotton Caligula D vi f. 104; Spont, *Letters and Papers*, 154–61.

[3] 9 May 1513, *L and P*, I, ii, 1855. John Dawtry to Wolsey, 11 May 1513, *L and P*, I, ii, 1859.

[4] *L and P*, I, ii, 1869.

adverse, and Brandon's men were soon consuming pay and victuals to no purpose. On 4 June the King decided to suspend independent naval operations, and to concentrate his resources upon his own planned invasion of France. The hired Spanish ships were diverted to this new service, and within a month the whole fleet together with 132 victuallers of between 60 and 100 tons were engaged in getting the King, much of his household, and 10 000 fighting men across the narrow sea to Calais.

Louis made no attempt to exploit the tactical and psychological advantage which the withdrawal of the English fleet had given him, and Guyon le Roy seems to have had no more concept of aggressive naval warfare than Clermont had had. Instead of pursuing their enemies, and blockading Plymouth in the same way as Howard had blockaded Brest, the French fleet dispersed. The Norman ships returned to Honfleur and disembarked their ordnance, while the galleys were put out of action for several weeks when sickness in Brest laid low most of the rowers.[1] When Henry landed at Calais on 30 June he was supported by a fleet which included 21 of his own ships, 26 hired English ships and 6 Spaniards; there was no opposition upon the seas. However, after hesitating most of the summer, once Henry was safely in France, James IV of Scotland began to show his hand. A fleet of 13 large ships and 10 smaller ones left Leith on 25 July, and on 11 August a Scottish herald appeared in the English camp at Therouanne to issue a formal declaration of war.[2] A part of the English fleet, led by the *Mary Rose* and the *Katherine Fortileza*, had been lying in the Downs for about two weeks in anticipation of such a move, but the Scots evaded them and arrived at Brest early in September. By that time the French had also remobilized. Bidoux's galleys were supplied with fresh rowers and re-armed, while a number of Breton and Norman ships were paid and victualled for two months. The intention seems to have been to intercept Henry on his return to England, although it is hard to see how the number of ships implied by the scale of the preparations (six to eight, apart from the galleys and the Scots) could have given battle to the English fleet. In the event the whole Scottish war effort was shattered by the defeat at Flodden on 9 September, and the death of James IV. The Franco-Scottish fleet stayed together until October, but was then scattered by a storm and achieved nothing.

[1] Spont, *Letters and Papers*, 169, 175. See also the report by Robert Acciajuoli from Blois, 7 May, 1513, ibid., 161.

[2] Spont, *Letters and Papers*, 171–2; P. F. Tytler, *History of Scotland*, 2, 138; Spont, 176 n. i; J. J. Scarisbrick, *Henry VIII*, 37.

Three of the largest Scottish ships remained in French service, and the rest returned to Leith in November. Flushed with the capture of Tournai and the total defeat of Scotland, by the end of October Henry could look back on an expensive but successful summer, even if his navy had achieved nothing as an independent military arm. By 1 November 1513 John Heron's account as Treasurer of the War showed a total expenditure of £173 058, of which £63 879.10s. had been spent upon the navy.[1] Between 15 March and 31 October 1513 Sir Thomas Wyndham, the Vice Admiral and Treasurer of the fleet, had spent £22 560 of that total.

During the winter of 1513/14 the majority of the great ships returned to Portsmouth or the Thames. Wyndham was instructed to keep his great ships together until the middle of October, and was authorized to pay his men 16d. a week in order to do so, because disease on board was making it difficult to recruit replacements.[2] After that, presumably the fleet went onto a winter footing of 16 ships and 1 500 men, authorized by the council. Sir Weston Browne was appointed to command this squadron, as he had done the previous winter. In January 1514 William Gonson was patrolling the narrow seas with three ships, and the Lord Admiral (who had become Earl of Surrey with his father's elevation to the Dukedom of Norfolk in the same month), was writing from Portsmouth that his ships were constantly at sea 'to learn what the Frenchmen do'.[3] In fact the French were busily preparing for the new campaigning season as early as the middle of December. Ships were being prepared at Honfleur, St Malo and Dieppe, and many French privateers were active, in spite of the English patrols. Surrey saw no immediate danger, however, and wrote that Portsmouth was well fortified and completely secure. He may have been wrong, because on 7 February Andrea Badoer reported that the French fleet had almost succeeded in burning a large number of English ships, and in April the persistent Prégent de Bidoux raided and destroyed the small village of Brighton on the Sussex coast. Henry was determined upon another major attack in the coming season, despite the fact that both Ferdinand of Aragon and Maximilian had signed separate treaties with France by the end of March.[4] Anger as much as military ambition drove him on. Forty-five ships, led by the massive *Henry Grace a Dieu* and carrying nearly 8 000 men set out at the end

[1] *L and P*, I, iii, 2479. *L and P*, I, 1463.
[2] Ibid., 2260.
[3] Thomas, Earl of Surrey to the Council, 14 January 1514, *L and P*, I, iii, 2574.
[4] *Cal. Span.* 2, 164; *L and P*, I, iii, 2743.

of April, and it was planned to send another 6 000 to reinforce the garrison at Calais.[1] Once again the French, in spite of their winter preparations, made no attempt to challenge the command of the seas, and in the absence of an enemy to fight, very little was accomplished. Sir Thomas Wyndham made a rather half-hearted attempt to cut off Bidoux's galleys at the end of May, and Sir John Wallop raided the coast of Brittany, burning, it was claimed, 21 villages in return for the destruction of Brighton.[2] Had the war continued, another attempt might have been made to corner and destroy the French fleet, and another large-scale invasion might well have been launched. Henry was reported to be determined to surpass his achievement of the previous year, but in the event, at the beginning of June, he called a halt. His reasons for doing so have never been clear. Perhaps the intercession of the new Pope, Leo X, who was anxious to bring the war to an end, carried weight.[3] Perhaps Wolsey andFox persuaded him towards a *rapprochement* with France, or perhaps he simply became alarmed at the ever-mounting cost. By September his ships were conveying his sister Mary to her wedding with Louis XII, and Bidoux's galleys had returned to the Mediterranean in an attempt to support the crumbling French position in Italy.

The war which fizzled out so unsatisfactorily in the summer of 1514 had been immensely important for the development of the English navy. When it ended Henry VIII had over 30 ships of his own, of which seven had been purchased and nine built since 1512. Several of these ships were equipped with heavy guns, as the King's interest in artillery led him to experiment with improvements in design, mounting, and ammunition.[4] His new flagship, which displaced 1 500 tons and cost over £8 000 to build, was the most powerful warship the world had ever seen.[5] His shipwrights had also at last abandoned the traditional clinker build for the stronger carvel style. The clinker built *Mary Rose* had been designed with only two gunports on each side on her lower deck, where the *Henry Grace Dieu* had six. By 1514 all these big ships were carrying brass

[1] *L and P*, I, iii, 2686, 2842; Council to Sir Edward Poynings, ibid., 2888.
[2] Spont, *Letters and Papers*, xlvi.
[3] One of the pretexts upon which Henry had entered the war had been a quarrel between Louis XII and Pope Julius II. In 1513 the new Pope, Leo X, had settled that quarrel, and set out to disperse the anti-French league which his predecessor had created. Scarisbrick, *Henry VIII*, 50–52.
[4] Oppenheim, *Administration*, 54–6.
[5] *L and P*, I, iii, 3060; J. Charnock, *History of Marine Architecture*, 44–5. One Italian reported that she displaced 4 000 tons!

curtalls, which could weigh up to 3 000lbs, and brass falcons which were only slightly smaller, while culverins also made their first appearance during this war.[1] At the same time the navy was beginning to detach itself from the 'army royal' with which it had traditionally been associated. In 1512 no army royal was mounted, and the navy operated on its own; while in 1513 such sea fighting as there was was over before Henry set out for France. Moreover, although the fighting was inconclusive, the English command of the sea was as complete as the technology of the period permitted. Only in limited galley operations did the French enjoy any success, and they seem to have been completely taken aback by the positive and aggressive tactics of both the Howards. Equally important, although much harder to describe coherently, was the development of administration and support services. There had been a forge at Portsmouth since the building of the dock in 1496, and by September 1511 another had been opened at Greenwich 'for the armourers of Brussels'.[2] New docks were constructed at Limehouse and at Erith in Kent, the latter receiving no fewer than 12 ships for repair between November 1512 and February 1513. Storehouses were constructed at Erith and Deptford to hold stocks of rope, canvas and other necessities, and to receive the tackle of ships which were laid up. The former of these, at least, was a substantial brick building, which needed modification after being flooded by an exceptionally high tide at Christmas 1516.[3] Ships not in dock were 'kept aflote' at various places along the Thames and the Medway, at Portsmouth and in Southampton water, where the wages and victuals of the shipkeepers continued to be regular items in the accounts of the Clerk Controller. This office, to which John Hopton, a gentleman usher of the Chamber, was appointed, seems to have been created early in 1512 to share administrative responsibilities with the existing Clerk of the Ships, Robert Brigandyne.[4] Hopton's first account starts on 10 February 1512. Thereafter he seems to have handled the lion's share of the traditional clerk's responsibilities, Brigandyne's operations being largely confined to Portsmouth, where he continued to account down to 1523. As Clerk Controller Hopton was paid £33.6s.8d. a year in half-yearly instalments – considerably more than Brigandyne's 12d. a day – although the

[1] Oppenheim, *Administration*, 55.

[2] PRO SP1/2 f. 149; *L and P*, I, 1393.

[3] Payments by John Hopton, Clerk Controller of the King's Ships, 26 November, 1518, *L and P*, 2, 4606.

[4] *L and P*, I, iii, 3318, 30 September 1514.

latter had generous allowances. It is not clear whether he was Brigandyne's superior in any managerial sense since they accounted separately, but he was clearly the more important of the two officials. In January 1514 that importance was further enhanced when he received the additional post of Keeper of the storehouses at Erith and Deptford, for life at 12d. a day.[1]

Once the war was over, the level of activity inevitably subsided. It also becomes harder to trace as its level of priority was reduced, but Henry VIII never contemplated disposing of his fleet in the manner of Henry V and his successor. Hopton's and Brigandyne's accounts continue to refer to sums of money spent upon rigging and caulking the big ships, which indicates that they were either in use or being maintained at a high level of readiness. The *Great Harry*, the *Gabriel Royal* and the *Katherine Fortileza* were brought out of Barking creek to be so renovated in March 1518.[2] The *Katherine* underwent further repairs during the summer, and a new dock was constructed at Erith for the *Gabriel*, but since it cost only £30 it was presumably much less elaborate than the main dry dock at Portsmouth. In August of the same year a further £100 was spent on caulking the *Mary Rose*. Much thought was clearly given to the most satisfactory method of keeping these ships in good condition when they were not in use. Even the safest anchorages were open to storms, and required keepers on every ship, while proper dry docks were expensive and could hold no more than one ship at a time. In June 1517 another device was therefore tried, and Hopton contracted with Surrey and John Heron to build a 'pond' at Deptford for 600 marks. The specifications laid down were precise:

> The Whiche ponde the forsaid John Hopton . . . shall wele surely sufficyently and substancally cause to be made and cast in a medow next adjoynyng unto the storehouse of oure said sov(er)-aign lorde at Deptford Stronde at the westend of the said storehouse a good and hable pond Wheryn shall ride at all tymes and flote thise shippes ensuyng that is to say the great Galay the Mary Rose the peter Pomegarnet the great barke and the lesser bark. And also the said John hopton covenauntith and grauntith . . . that he . . . shall wele and substancyally make or cause to be made a good hable and suffycient hed for the same ponde and also certeyn hable Slewsis thrugh the Whiche the watir may have entre

[1] *L and P*, 2617.
[2] *L and P*, 2, 4606.

> and course into the foresaid ponde aswell at Spryng tydes as at nepe tydes . . .[1]

Probably the advantages were not eventually considered to be worth the effort and expense, because later in the century this pond seems to have been used mainly for the maturing of masts and other large timbers. As far as I know no other was constructed. Deptford was the main centre of activity once the war was over. In 1516 a shed was added to the storehouse 'for keeping dry the king's ordnance', and for drying ropes and cables. By October 1517 about 22 ships were on a care and maintenance basis in the Thames estuary, at a cost of about £700 a year in shipkeepers' wages.[2]

Evidence for the use of ships during this period is scanty, but not entirely absent. The *Anne Gallant* was leased to a London merchant, and wrecked 'at Galisie in the port of Mongeoy [Mondoa]' sometime during 1516; £173.6s.8d. was spent on the hire of the *Mary James* in August 1518; and when the King was preparing for his meeting with Francis I of France in the spring of 1520, the *Mary Rose*, the *Great Bark* and the *Less Bark* were sent to 'scour the seas' in advance of his crossing.[3] Politically these were years of peace, but the seas were never entirely quiet, and it seems likely that some of the smaller royal ships continued to be used for 'wafting' and patrolling, as they were both before and afterwards. New ships also continued to be both built and purchased. The *Great Harry* and the *Great Elizabeth* were in service before the war ended, and in October 1515 they were joined by the *Great Galley*. This intriguing vessel appears to have been an enormous galleasse, of very unusual size and design. According to contemporary French and Italian descriptions she carried over 200 guns, 70 of them of brass.[4] Fourteen of these were mounted, seven to a side, on a gun deck above the rowers, and

[1] BL Additional Charter 6289.

[2] Wages paid by John Hopton to the keepers of ships in the Thames, 8 October 9 Henry VIII to 23 March 12 Henry VIII, *L and P*, 3, 1911. At this date the masters of all but the smallest ships were retained as shipkeepers, usually with 2–4 mariners. Only the *Great Harry* kept her master and 11 mariners.

[3] *L and P*, 2, 4606; ibid., 1479; *L and P*, 3, 704. The *Anne Gallant* had made several previous trips under private management, although it seems that the King placed one or more of her officers, perhaps as a safeguard against improper use. The *Peter Pomegranate*, the *Mary George* and the *Christ* were also leased out for voyages between 1515 and 1520. In 1515 the *Christ*, freighted by Hugh Clopton and other merchants of London, was taken by barbary corsairs, and John Hopton was licensed to gather alms to ransom the survivors. Oppenheim, *Administration*, 66–8; *L and P*, 2, 811.

[4] De Bapaume to Louise of Savoy, Regent of France, 6 November 1515, *L and P*, 2, 1113; *L and P*, I, iii, 2958. R. C. Anderson, 'Henry VIII's Great Galley', *MM*, 6, 1920, 274.

she was propelled by 120 oars. Four masts with topmasts gave her a sailing potential as great as the *Mary Rose*, which was generally praised for its speed and handling qualities. She was officially called the *Princess Mary*, or the *Mary Imperial*, but is usually referred to simply as the *Great Galley*.[1] The naming ceremony was performed by Queen Catherine, the first occasion, as far as I am aware, upon which a royal lady was called upon to perform such a function. One awe-struck Italian declared that she was three times the size of a first class Venetian war galley, displaced 800 tons and carried over 1 000 fighting men.[2] We have no idea how much she cost to build, but analogy with the *Great Harry* would suggest not less than £5 000. The *Great Galley* was to have a long career; as a galleasse until 1536, and then rebuilt as a sailing ship and renamed the *Great Bark*. She was still in service in 1548. Although it was reasonably successful, Henry did not repeat his experiment. Other galleys and galleasses were built later, but they were much smaller, more like the *Sweepstake* and the *Mary Fortune* of Henry VII. The King enjoyed himself immensely on her maiden voyage, dressing up in a seaman's coat and trousers of cloth of gold, and blowing on a golden whistle, but the French thought the appearance of so formidable a vessel betokened a renewal of the war, and they had to be reassured.

The *Great Galley* may have been built out of a desire to beat Prégent de Bidoux at his own game, or it may simply have been a *jeu d'esprit* like the great English pavilion at the Field of Cloth of Gold. Another minor extravagance of the same nature was the building of the *Katherine Plesaunce* in 1519. The *Katherine* was built at a cost of £323.13s.9d. solely for the purpose of carrying Henry and Catherine across to Calais for the former's meeting with Francis in 1520.[3] He had plenty of other ships in which he could have sailed, but the *Katherine* was fitted out to a special standard of luxury. One hundred wainscotts were purchased for the cabins and chambers 'in the said new bark for the king and queen'; the cabin windows were glazed (two panes with the royal arms), and the Queen's cabin was fitted with a dozen joined stools. It must have been like a very early royal yacht.[4] Three other vessels were also acquired during the years of peace, the *Mary Gloria*, purchased from John Hopton in 1517 for £500, the *Trinity Henry*, a little bark of 80 tons built in 1519, and the *Mary and John*, which seems to have been a present

[1] R. C. Anderson, 'Henry VIII's Great Galley', 274, Oppenheim, *Administration*, 50.
[2] *Cal. Ven.*, 2, 659, 662.
[3] *L and P*, 3, 558.
[4] Ibid., 1009.

from the Emperor Charles V. John Hopton's pond was the largest addition to the shore facilities at this time, but it was not the only one. Two more sheds were built at Deptford in 1520, and the storehouses at Deptford and Erith were fitted with new locks. A few ships also disappear from the records at about this time, but there was no deliberate attempt to reduce the number of the King's ships once the war was over – and this was in marked contrast to the practice of all earlier periods.

Consequently we can say that by 1520 the standing navy has come into existence. Henry has a peacetime fleet of about 30 ships, varying in size from Great Ships to rowbarges, of which six to eight are in use at any given time. He also has two dockyards, one at Portsmouth and the other at Deptford, with other facilities at Erith, Woolwich and Southampton. All this is administered by two permanent officials, the Clerk Controller, based at Deptford, and the Clerk of the Ships, based at Portsmouth. Of these the former was by far the more important, but it does not appear that Brigandyne was answerable to Hopton. Indeed, there was no 'management structure' in the modern sense at all. The Lord Admiral had a general responsibility or oversight. He was, for example, a party to the contract for Hopton's pond, but he did not exercise any routine control.[1] The King made the decisions, as his father had done, and the Clerks carried them out; even the ubiquitous Wolsey does not seem to have been much involved, except in time of war. The Clerks purchased timber, ropes, canvas, ironwork, and all other necessities for the maintenance of the ships; they also paid the shipwrights, caulkers and other workmen, both on the ships and in the shore establishments, and the wages of the shipkeepers. Victualling, on the other hand, seems to have been separately contracted both in war and peace, and gunsmiths like Cornelius Johnson were also paid direct, either out of the Exchequer or the King's Chamber. Similarly when the ships were in service the money for wages, emergency repairs, and the 'topping up' of victuals was paid to the master or the purser. These distinctions were not new, but they do seem to have been more systematically observed than in the past. In time of war all such expenditure passed through the accounts of the Treasurer of the War, although they were often handled by one of his deputies or agents. In peacetime, however, there was no overall control, and the level of spending is very hard to compute. The various officials

[1] Thomas Howard, like his brother, was an active Admiral, but only in war-time. Strictly there were three permanent officials, since the Keepership of the storehouse was separate from the Clerk Controllership, but there were only two men.

received their money mainly from John Daunce, one of the Tellers of the Exchequer, or John Heron, the Treasurer of the Chamber.[1] There does not seem to have been any settled pattern of payment. Brigandyne's original patent had specified the payment of his own wage and allowances out of the customs of Exmouth and Dartmouth, and he may have continued to receive money by assignment on that source, or from Southampton. Probably a warrant or assignment was drawn on whichever account had (or was thought to have) money available, consideration also being given to the physical whereabouts of the specie which was to be used. Management, in fact, had not kept up with the development of the navy itself. Apart from the two Clerks there was no permanent structure. Craftsmen and mariners alike were hired by the day, week or month, according to the job. There was no unity of control, except in the hands of the King, and no budget. Had the peace continued this situation might have been gradually resolved, or the fleet might have dwindled again to a level for which it was adequate. But in August 1521 Henry signed a new treaty with the Emperor, intended to lead to renewed war with France, and in that war the English navy was to play a crucial role. The King toyed briefly with the idea of an immediate strike against French shipping. Wolsey dissuaded him, but the Emperor recognized that English control of the Channel was going to be a necessary condition for the success of their proposed joint operations, and by the spring of 1522 the English fleet was back on what might be described as an ordinary war footing. No major expedition had as yet been planned, but in April three squadrons, each of four ships were appointed to keep the seas between the Tweed and the Channel Islands, and the Earl of Surrey issued a fresh set of general orders.[2]

[1] e.g. PRO SP1/3 f. 6; *L and P*, I, 1416. *L and P*, 2, 68.
[2] *L and P*, 3, 2296.

4
ADMINISTRATION, EQUIPMENT AND SERVICES, 1520–1547

In the spring of 1523 Robert Brigandyne retired. On 22 March he was granted the usual release (or pardon) for any embezzlements or misdemeanours committed in office, and was succeeded by Thomas Jermyn.[1] Although he remained active to the end, and his account for 1522–3 makes a substantial book, he was no longer as important as he had been in 1495, and his successor is an obscure figure. It appears that Jermyn continued to manage the facilities at Portsmouth, but unlike Brigandyne (who had been involved in a subordinate capacity with shipbuilding at Woolwich) he was not active elsewhere.[2] Indeed the phrase which was added to his title in his patent of appointment 'custos de le Doke apud Portismouth' indicates that such was the intention. John Hopton died in 1524, and the two offices which he had held were then clearly separated. William Gonson became Keeper of the Erith and Deptford storehouses by patent of 25 September 1524, and Thomas Spert became Clerk Controller by warrant dormant to the Chamber.[3] Each received the same emoluments as Hopton. Spert was an experienced sea captain, who had been the first master of the *Henry Grace a Dieu*, while Gonson was a man of many parts. Variously described as 'gentleman usher of the king's chamber', 'Teller of the Exchequer' and 'Grocer of London', he was assessed under the latter title in 1535 (probably for a subsidy) at £1 000 and was one of the wealthiest citizens. It may have been for this reason, or because he was a man

[1] *L and P*, 3, 2992. Oppenheim, *Administration*, 84.

[2] *L and P*, 3, 3690; PRO E36/6; C. S. L. Davies, 'The administration of the Royal Navy under Henry VIII', 268–88.

[3] PRO C66/674 m. 13. *L and P*, 4, 1, 309; PRO C66/700 m. 32 (Osborne's patent of reversion); Davies, 'The administration of the Royal Navy under Henry VIII'.

of exceptional energy and ability, that Gonson steadily outstripped Spert in importance during the later 1520s and 1530s. The Clerk Controller was paid almost twice as much as the Keeper of the Storehouse, and both that fact and the nature of his title would seem to indicate a superior role. But it was Gonson rather than Spert who took over Hopton's occasional role of transmitting money from the Crown's financial officers to the men who were actually paying the bills. For example it was he who issued, jointly with Lord Lisle, one of the vice-admirals, the warrants upon which Sir John Daunce (by then the General Surveyor) paid money to Thomas Jermyn for the wages of the shipkeepers at Portsmouth.[1] By contrast, the original Clerkship diminished. Edmund More succeeded Jermyn in 1538 on the same terms, but both seem to have been mere functionaries. The King did not call upon them for advice, as Henry VII had called upon Brigandyne.

After the death of the Earl of Oxford in 1512, the office of Lord Admiral was occupied for 13 years by effective military commanders, but on 16 July 1525 Henry apparently reverted to the earlier tradition by naming his seven-year-old illegitimate son, Henry Fitzroy. Fitzroy had recently been created Duke of Richmond, and was also named as Lieutenant of the North.[2] The King may have been considering some means of including him in the succession – increasingly in doubt after 1520 – but his important offices probably had a different significance. His household and council as Lieutenant were vehicles for the influence of the Lord Chancellor, Cardinal Wolsey, in the North, and it may well be that Wolsey had designs on improving the administration of the navy. The Earl of Surrey (who became Duke of Norfolk on the death of his father in 1525) continued his service as Vice-Admiral, and Lord Lisle[3] was appointed to the same rank; but Lisle can only occasionally be seen acting in an administrative capacity, and Norfolk not at all. Gonson reported directly to Wolsey, and referred to him rather than to the vice-admirals for instructions. Both he and Spert were active sea-captains as well as administrators, but it was Gonson who conducted the correspondence, first with Wolsey and later with

[1] *L and P*, 4, 2, 3656; 12 December 1527. 17 warrants are listed altogether, covering the period 17 March 1526 to 12 December 1527.

[2] H. Miller, *Henry VIII and the English Nobility*, 20.

[3] This was Arthur Plantagenet, an illegitimate son of Edward IV, the second of three men to hold the title during Henry's reign. The first was Charles Brandon, who was Viscount Lisle for one year (1513–14) before becoming Duke of Suffolk, and the third was John Dudley, who was created in 1542. Arthur Plantagenet was created in 1523, and died in 1542.

Cromwell. In March 1528 he reported that he was endeavouring to 'waft' Imperial merchantmen '. . . out of the Frenchmen's danger', and sought for guidance in dealing with ships out of Spain.[1] By August 1532 his stature seems to have grown further, and he could tell Cromwell that he had sent his clerks and other messengers to Harwich and along the East coast 'to seek the king's ships of war, with money and commissions for fulfilling all things according to the king's pleasure'. This was the letter of a man in a position of responsibility, and over the next few years his was always the first name to be called on when the King needed ships for any purpose.[2] He not only handled the bulk of the money issued for the navy, but arranged for the purchase of cables and other equipment, for routine repairs, and for the manning and victualling of ships for special missions. In October 1536 he was placed in charge of the Duke of Suffolk's ordnance when the Duke went north against the Pilgrimage of Grace. On 14 November Henry wrote to Suffolk asking that Gonson be returned to his service, which was apparently done, because on 4 December Suffolk appealed to Henry 'Let us have William Gonson again; we lack him both for putting things in order and for counsel . . .'[3] Clearly his was an administrative talent of no common order.

Richmond died in July 1536, and was succeeded as Lord Admiral on 16 August by Sir William FitzWilliam. FitzWilliam, who was to become Earl of Southampton in the following year, had served at sea as a young man in both 1513 and 1523, but he was never called upon to command a fleet.[4] His name appears occasionally in connection with naval affairs, as when he wrote to Cromwell in April 1539 about the potential hiring of Florentine and Venetian ships, but he was not actively involved with either policy or administration. The same was true of his successor, Lord John Russell, who held the office from July 1540 to January 1543, and whose previous experience seems to have been confined to a single voyage in 1522.

[1] *L and P*, 4, 2, 4066; 13 March 1528.

[2] *L and P*, 5, 1228; 15 August 1532. Gonson also reported that he had transmitted the King's command to the ships in the Thames that they remain at sea, and had provided both money and victuals; See also Cromwell's remembrances, 1 April 1534, *L and P*, 7, 420.

[3] Gonson to Cromwell, 10 October 1536, *L and P*, 11, 638; Henry VIII to the Duke of Suffolk, 14 November 1536, ibid., 1061; Suffolk to the King, 4 December 1536, ibid., 1239.

[4] A war fleet, that is. He was responsible for assembling the King's ships at Portsmouth in April 1539, and for the escort which brought Anne of Cleves to England in January 1540. *L and P*, 14, 1, 726; Southampton to Cromwell, 9 April 1539, *L and P*, 15, 14.

Henry's last Lord Admiral, however, John Dudley, Viscount Lisle, was an altogether different proposition. As Sir John Dudley he had served from 1537 as Vice-Admiral, and had been an active commander. In March of that year he had been instructed to 'keep the seas between the Downs and Poole', and in July those instructions had been extended to the Severn estuary.[1] He had been at sea through most of the summer of 1537, and had been actively involved in the mobilization of 1539. As Admiral he was to command the King's navy during his last war with France, and the fleet orders which he issued in August 1545 show him to have been a student of contemporary Spanish tactics. Like the Howards in the previous generation, he took his duties seriously, and became interested in the strategy of sea power, but he left the day by day running of the navy to his subordinates, of whom the most important was William Gonson. By the time that Gonson died in 1544 the need for a more sophisticated management structure had become apparent, and it may well have been his death which provided the occasion for such a reorganization. If so, it is reasonable to suppose that Dudley, as Lord Admiral played a leading part in the deliberations which must have lain behind the memoranda of early 1545 which outlined the future 'Council for Marine Causes'.

Before 1525 the administration had been running hard to keep up with the rapid expansion of the navy, and coming to terms with the fact that, like the office of the king's works or the ordnance office, it was going to make permanent (albeit fluctuating) demands upon the financial and management resources of the Crown. After 1525 there followed eighteen years of peace, and for most of that time (1525–9 and 1532–40) the administration of the realm was controlled by two outstanding royal servants, Wolsey and Cromwell, whose highly personal style of management discouraged the growth of institutional structures which they could not control. Consequently both seem to have been content to run the navy through a small group of officers who had no clearly-defined relationship to each other, and the definition of whose duties was partly a matter of custom, and partly of convenience. As early as December 1525 Gonson was paying the wages, victuals, deadshares and tonnage of two ships, the *New Bark* and the *Barbara Vincent* of London, which had been hired for royal service earlier in the year. At the same time Christopher Coo, who held no office but was frequently employed as a

[1] *L and P*, 12, 1, 601; ibid., 2, 393.

captain, was discharging the same function for two other ships.[1] In April 1528 Gonson was patrolling the narrow seas in command of two ships, and reporting to Wolsey on the deployment of other ships, which he had carried out on the King's orders. In 1529 he sailed in command of a squadron of ten ships, with the title of Admiral – hoisting his flag in his own ship, the *Mary Gonson*.[2] In 1530 we find him paying money to Thomas Jermyn at Portsmouth to cover the Clerk's routine expenses upon repairs and maintenance, and by 1533 he was already receiving large round sums (£300, £900) from Sir Brian Tuke, the Treasurer of the Chamber, for vaguely defined purposes such as 'rigging and apparailing the king's ships'.[3] Gonson was both more and less than a treasurer during these years. Less because Thomas Spert was regularly receiving money which did not pass through his hands, and some direct payments were also made to Henry Huttoft (who contracted to build a new ship for the King in 1538), and others, particularly for victuals. He was more because Cromwell, in particular, used him as an all-purpose agent in maritime affairs. In addition to the variety of tasks which we have already noticed, a note in Cromwell's remembrances for 10 April 1535 reveals Gonson contracting directly with Richard Cavendish to provide ropes and cables from the Baltic. On 3 September in the same year he was borrowing money on his own credit in London to pay for 'the king's causes', and in June 1537 he was negotiating for the return of an English crayer taken by Frenchmen from Boulogne.[4]

By contrast, Thomas Spert's role was both more limited and less responsible. He received money directly from the Treasury of the Chamber, but usually specific sums for specific jobs – £71.13s.4d. in August 1529 for rigging and trimming the *Minion* and the *Mary Guildford*; or £168.4s.0d. for the victuals and wages of the keepers of the King's ships in July 1530.[5] As Clerk Controller, Spert was usually linked with Gonson when general orders were sent out for the mobilization of ships, or when the state of the navy was under

[1] *L and P*, 4, 1, 1853.

[2] *L and P*, 4, 3, App. 247; in which squadron Christopher Coo commanded the *Margaret Bonaventure*.

[3] Jermyn's accounts, 5 January 1530, *L and P*, 4, 3, 6138; Tuke to Cromwell, 17 August 1533, *L and P*, 6, 992.

[4] *L and P*, 8, 527; ibid., 9, 260; ibid., 12, 2, 149. Gonson frequently complained of being owed large sums of money; for example in April 1538 his account showed a 'surplusage', or deficit, of £2 142.10s.5d. on an expenditure of £15 589.3s.5d., *L and P*, 13, 1, 777.

[5] *L and P*, 5, 314–5; ibid., 321.

investigation. Like Gonson, he was an active sea commander, being at one time in charge of the *Mary Rose*. In July 1535 he was actually referred to as 'Master of the king's ships', in a letter which implied that he had a specific brief to oversee the sailing qualities of the ships, and to carry out modifications if necessary. His report to Gonson on an inspection of the *Great Nicholas* of Bristol in 1539 shows that he had skill and judgement in technical matters, but the evidence is too scanty to say more. From 1538 he was also Captain of Portsmouth, and was responsible for the new fortifications at Gosport which were put up during Henry's crash programme of coastal defence works in 1539 – referred to later as the 'bulwark of Mr. Sperte's building'.[1] He was knighted in 1535 or soon after, but by 1540 age and ill-health were impairing his effectiveness. His name disappears from the records, and in July of that year his office was granted in reversion to John Osborne, who was described as a Gentleman of the Household. Spert died in September 1541. Osborne spent most of that year in the Low Countries buying copper for the King, and in January 1542 was also appointed to the office of Principal Marshall of the Court of Admiralty. How seriously he took the duties of either of these positions is open to doubt. The Marshallship he held jointly with Thomas Warner, and in 1543 it was noted that 'Warner exerciseth and paieth Osborne V^{li} by yere'.[2] As Clerk Controller he is mentioned on a number of occasions, but usually in connection with the payment of his fees. It is not clear what he actually did, and reasonable to suppose that he was much less active than Spert. It was perhaps for that reason, rather than because of the actual pressure of work, that a new clerkship was created in March 1542, to be assistant to the Clerk Controller. Richard Howlett was appointed to this position at a wage of 8d. a day.[3] Osborne died early in 1545 and when the naval administration was formally reconstructed in that year, William Broke was appointed to the office of Controller.

Thomas Jermyn remained Clerk of the Ships until February 1538, when he was succeeded by Edmund More, and his accounts constitute one of the most informative sources relating to the maintenance of the King's ships during this period. Between October 1518 and March 1522 John Hopton had looked after 21 ships at Deptford and Woolwich 'aswell in their dockes as aflote', at a cost of £1 481; but

[1] *L and P*, 13, 1, 1242; ibid., 19, 719; H. M. Colvin, *The History of the King's Works*, 4, 409.
[2] PRO HCA 25/1.
[3] *L and P*, 17, 220.

with the mobilization of the fleet in the spring of 1522 the main focus of activity shifted to Portsmouth, where it seems to have remained after the war ended in 1525. Between November 1524 and June 1530 Jermyn received £4 421, mainly via William Gonson, and spent £3 691.5s.0½d. on 'wages and vitaylles of maisters boatswains and maryners keeping the Kings shippes'.[1] The *Great Harry* spent ten months in dock during this period; she was unrigged, and carpenters were paid for 'wollyng and terryng' her masts and spars. The *Mary Rose, Peter Pomegranate* and *John Baptist* were also docked and refitted; the *Gabriel* was moved from Portsmouth to Southampton, and docked at Bursledon. A new dock was constructed, and the existing dry dock enlarged so that the carpenters could have easier access to the keels of the ships.[2] A capstan or windlass was constructed to wind the ships into dock, and the dock itself repaired where the sea had broken in. Storehouses were built for the new dock, and the existing buildings repaired, both those at the old dock and the 'long house' in Portsmouth itself. In March 1528 labourers were paid £14.17s.6d. for removing the guns from the walls into store on the orders of Lord Lisle.[3] Jermyn was based at Portsmouth, and most of his accounts relate to that port, but he also paid some bills relating to ships in the Thames. One account records a number of small sums paid to the shipkeepers of 12 ships for short periods between March 1526 and January 1530, amounting to about £103, and for some repairs to the *Minion*, the *Sweepstake* and the *Swallow*.[4] All the vessels referred to in this account were medium or small size, and some of them seem to have been in regular use. There is no evidence that Jermyn worked at Deptford or Woolwich, and why this account should have been kept by him rather than by Gonson is something of a mystery. In April 1541 Charles de Marillac, the French ambassador, reported that the King of England's ships were being caulked and repaired 'as is done every two years'.[5] Probably he meant that each ship was renovated on a two-year cycle, rather than that the whole fleet was taken out of commission every second year. When such a regime was introduced is not known, and it is unlikely that it was ever strictly adhered to, but some such pattern is certainly consistent with the evidence of Jermyn's accounts, and indeed with Hopton's earlier. It may well have

[1] *L and P*, 4, 3, 6138; PRO E315/317 f. 41.
[2] PRO E315/317 f. 58.
[3] Ibid., f. 72.
[4] Ibid., ff. 84–6.
[5] *L and P*, 16, 762; 27 April 1541.

been introduced, as a sensible working practice, after Henry's first French war, when it had become clear that the maintenance of a standing navy was going to be a requirement for the foreseeable future.

Edmund More, described as a Groom of the Chamber, who followed Jermyn as Clerk, has left little trace in the records. His accounts do not appear to have survived, and he held the post for less than three years, being replaced in December 1540 by William Gonson's brother-in-law, Edward Water 'Gentleman usher of the Chamber'. Water was closely associated with Gonson, with whom he purchased Assheling wharf in the parish of St Dunstan, London, but little is known about his activity as Clerk of the Ships.[1] After Gonson's death, in February 1545, he surrendered his patent and was appointed instead as a Sergeant at Arms. At about the same time, in January 1545, Richard Howlett, John Osborne's clerk, was appointed to succeed Gonson as Keeper of the Deptford Storehouse.[2] In spite of, or perhaps because of, the fact that England was again at war with France, the whole question of naval administration was re-examined early in 1545. It would have been apparent to a much less astute man than John Dudley that Gonson's position had been anomalous, and that references to him as 'paymaster' of the King's ships had been nearer the mark. Nor had it been very satisfactory to have the Clerk Controller doubling as Captain of Portsmouth, or as a commercial agent in the Netherlands. An undated memorandum, probably of February or March 1545 listed seven officers. Three of these already existed, the Clerk Controller, the Clerk of the Ships, and the Keeper of the Storehouse. The four additional posts were Lieutenant (or Vice-Admiral), Treasurer, Surveyor and Rigger, and Master of the Naval Ordnance.[3] Vice-Admirals had also been appointed before on a somewhat casual basis, but the intention on this occasion was not casual. Although his duties were not laid down in any set of instructions which has survived, he was intended to be the chairman of what was already being referred to as 'the Kinges majesties counseall of his mareyn' in a letter dated 11 March.[4] How quickly the new structure was implemented is not quite clear. John Winter, named as Treasurer, died in November or December 1545, and the role of William

[1] More's patent was dated 5 February 29 Henry VIII; *L and P*, 14, 1, 384; ibid., 16, 1056, licence to Sir Anthony Knyvett to alienate.

[2] *L and P*, 20, 1, 58, 14 January 1545.

[3] *L and P*, 20, 2, App. 27.

[4] *Literary Remains of Edward VI*, ed. J. G. Nichols, ii, 288.

Gonson's son, Benjamin is uncertain. In a duplicate set of accounts covering the period 5 August to 29 November 1544 he is described as 'appointed to act as treasurer of sea causes after the death of his father William Gonson, and by virtue of letters issued by the Queen and Council from Hampton Court the 17th August 36 Henry VIII'[1] during the King's absence on campaign in France. The accounts are subscribed by Edward Water and by Robert Rigge, the Cofferer of Prince Edward's household. The younger Gonson had been named as Surveyor and Rigger, a post to which he was formally appointed in the following April, and the new Treasurer was Robert Legge, originally named as Controller. Dr Davies was probably right when he suggested that Gonson's treasurership was of an interim or acting nature, but it may also indicate that there was some disagreement about the division of responsibilities.[2] Probably the final form of the Council was not settled until the patents of appointment were issued in 1546, when Sir Thomas Clere became Lieutenant, Robert Legge, Treasurer, Benjamin Gonson, Surveyor and Rigger, William Broke, Controller, Sir William Woodhouse, Master of the Ordnance and Richard Howlett, Clerk of the Ships.[3]

The significance of this reorganization can hardly be emphasized too strongly. For the first time there was 'line management', officers with clearly differentiated functions, and a committee exercising collective responsibility. For the first time, too, those officers were adequately, indeed generously remunerated. Before 1545 the Clerk Controller had received 50 marks (£33.6s.8d.) and 3s.4d. a day travelling expenses; the Clerk of the Ships and the Keeper of the Storehouse had each received 1s. a day, 6d. a day for a clerk, and 3s. a day travelling expenses. Like most officers of the Crown, they gained their principal rewards from prerequisites, or from the advantage which their position gave them for the exercise of their private affairs. After 1545 the Lieutenant was paid a fee of £100 a year, 1s.8d. a day for two clerks, 10s. a day travel expenses, and £10 a year for 'botehire', which if fully utilized would have given him an income of over £275 a year.[4] The second best paid, although not the second in terms of responsibility, was the Master of the Naval Ordnance, with a fee of 100 marks (£66.13s.4d.), 2s.4d. a day for three clerks, 6s.8d. for travel, and £8 for boathire – a total of £238. The Treasurer, who was probably the most important officer after

[1] PRO E351/2193.
[2] Davies, 'The administration of the Royal Navy', 273.
[3] PRO C66/788 mm. 27–30.
[4] Davies, 'The administration of the Royal Navy', 288.

the Lieutenant, was also paid 100 marks, but as he was only provided with two clerks, his total came to £220. The Controller's fee was £50, for a total of £155; the Surveyor's £40 and £145; and the Clerk of the Ships £33.6s.8d. and £100. Whoever devised this scale of fees certainly intended to remove all temptations to corruption, and to concentrate the officers' minds and energies upon the tasks in hand.[1] It has been suggested that these reforms were modelled on those of the Ordnance office, but it would probably be more true to say that the Ordnance and the navy developed along parallel lines and for similar reasons. In 1509 the Ordnance already had a Master, a Clerk and a Yeoman, while the navy had only a Clerk with one humble assistant. By 1540 a Surveyor had been added to the Ordnance, and the navy had grown to three officers and two clerks. By the time the Council for Marine Causes was formed, the Ordnance had a highly paid Master (200 marks), a Lieutenant and a Treasurer, in addition to the Surveyor, Clerk and Yeoman. The two establishments were very comparable and both indicated the high priority which the King gave to military technology. Less than a year before his death, Henry's lifelong interest in ships and guns was translated into management structures which were remarkably sophisticated for their time. The French, with a similar need, created a number of subordinate offices – controleurs, commissaires, trésoriers de la marine – headed by a special secretary of state.[2] This was a system which certainly had centralized coherence, but lacked the most distinctive feature of the Council of Marine Causes; that it was a team of men skilled and experienced in the affairs of the sea, and enjoying considerable autonomy within the limits of its competence.

It is not clear who was responsible for these important steps. Thomas Cromwell had certainly maintained a consistent pressure upon Gonson and Spert to keep the King's ships in good order, and had brought about some minor improvements. He had been responsible for the appointment of Stephen Vaughn as the King's agent in the Low Countries in 1538, and had given him a brief which included the purchase of military and naval stores as well as financial affairs.[3] He may also have established a 'King's merchant' in Danzig in 1539 for the specific purpose of bypassing the Hanseatic monopoly of pitch, tar and cordage. The first beginning of a permanent workforce in the dockyards may also be traced to the payment

[1] Davies, 'The administration of the Royal Navy', 273.
[2] For a discussion of parallel French developments in this period, see Gaston Zeller, *Les Institutions de la France au XVIe Siècle*, 333.
[3] W. C. Richardson, *Stephen Vaughn*.

of an annuity at the rate of 4d. a day to the shipwright James Baker in 1538.[1] However, Cromwell had gone to the block in 1540, and there is no evidence that any plan for comprehensive naval reorganization existed before that date. The King's personal interest may have been the inspiration, but can hardly have been the effective cause when his most energetic and creative years were well behind him. Given both his previous and subsequent record, to say nothing of his authoritative position during these years, the most likely candidate is John Dudley, Viscount Lisle; and that likelihood is increased by the fact that he had also had a hand in the Ordnance office (albeit indirectly) as Master of the Armoury.

The only aspect of naval administration which was not controlled by the Council for Marine Causes was victualling. The reason for that omission was probably the strength of custom, based upon the fact that all foodstuffs were highly perishable, and that demands needed to be met immediately upon a local basis. In wartime, or during periods of heightened naval activity, such as 1539–40, the general management of victualling was placed in the hands of special commissioners; Bishop Fox and the Southampton customers in 1513, William Paulet, Lord St John, Richard Southwell and John Ryther in 1545.[2] Victuals for the King's ships (like those for his household) were subject to purveyance, and the commissioners set the rates. They might also decide which brewers and bakers were to be used at the major ports of assembly. The commissioners and their agents were responsible for getting the provisions to the quayside, but they were not responsible for actually getting them onto the ships. That was the task of the pursers, who were provided with money at the rate of about 1s.3d. per man per week, and who purchased their supplies from the agents. This was a system open to considerable abuse, and it was reported during the crisis which struck Sir Thomas Howard's fleet in 1513 that 'the pursers will deserve hanging for this matter'.[3] The food provided on the King's ships was simple, and the diet by modern standards monotonous and ill balanced. The staples were a specially baked ships biscuit, beef and beer, with cod or herring (for the mandatory fish days required by the church) butter and cheese. However, getting this food from the producers to the consumers was less simple, and offered many opportunities for sharp practice. The first links in the

[1] Davies, 'Administration', 276, Baker's annuity was increased to 8d. a day in 1544, signifying his recognition as a master craftsman.

[2] *L and P*, I, 2, 1845, 1858–9; ibid., 19, 1, 141 (26), 610 (1); 20, 1, 215. PRO E101/62/40.

[3] Fox and Dawtry to Wolsey, 21 May 1513, *L and P*, I, 2, 1912.

chain were the county purveyors, appointed by warrant to take up a given quantity of one or more of the staple commodities in a given county or counties – like John Risbyche and William Rede 'purveyors of oxen for the seas' from Kent, Surrey and Essex, who accounted eventually in 1551 for their activities during 1545 and 1546.[1] Such purveyors delivered their produce to the agents or contractors in the port towns, whose job it was to convert grain into loaves or biscuit, and oxen into pipes of salt beef, and it was from their stores that the pursers supplied the ships. The controlling commissioners were responsible for ensuring that sufficient quantities were purchased in the first place, and that all the food was made available in an appropriate form while it was still fresh enough to eat. These were delicate equations when there were 15 000 or 20 000 mouths to feed for six weeks or three months. Inevitably mistakes were made, and complaints were endless. In April 1544, when the Earl of Hertford and Lord Lisle were leading the army against Scotland, they wrote directly to the King that they were 'somewhat encumbred with the order of victuals . . . wherein your highness's great charge consisteth and as it appears to us your majesty has been not a little deceived in the same . . .'.[2] They had, they claimed, caused the victualling record of every ship to be checked, and had discovered major discrepancies between the records and the reality. The main thrust of their accusation was that the agents had been defrauding the pursers by selling them short weight beef and mouldy bread, and that Bishop Stephen Gardiner, who was the chief commissioner, was too incompetent to prevent such things from happening under his nose. Hertford and Lisle were political enemies of Gardiner, who were anxious to discredit him, and his reply to their charges was convincing as far as his own competence was concerned.[3] Nevertheless it seems that on this occasion, as so often when large forces were assembled either by land or sea, the commissariat was the least satisfactory part of the preparations.

Victuals for shipkeepers, shipwrights, labourers and other dockyard workers were provided by the manager of that particular place or enterprise – the Clerk of the Ships at Portsmouth and the Clerk Controller or the 'paymaster' elsewhere. This provision would include what might be termed 'handling crews', that is mariners and pilots engaged to move ships from one place to another, even if they were as far apart as Portsmouth and Deptford. Before 1520 ships in

[1] PRO E351/2193.
[2] *The Hamilton Papers*, ed. J. Bain, 2, 346.
[3] *L and P*, 19, 1, 411; Glyn Redworth, *In Defence of the Church Catholic*, 213.

service during peacetime were provisioned directly by their pursers (who presumably knew the right middlemen to approach), without recourse to purveyance. But increasingly after 1525 William Gonson assumed an overall responsibility for victualling ships which were in service, but not part of a major military enterprise.[1] In September 1535, for example, he reported to Cromwell that he had prepared victuals for the voyage of the King's agents Stephen Vaughn and Christopher Morris to the Low Countries, and that he would be able to divert some of that provision into the royal ships which were now to be despatched to Bordeaux. He was, however, likely to be left with a considerable quantity on his hands which he would have to get rid of quickly.[2] As far as can be ascertained from the accounts, Gonson used his own servants or agents to purchase these supplies, which were then allocated to the ships without any further financial transactions. Such a system must have been both more efficient and less subject to abuse than funding through the pursers, and provided the model for the method which subsequently came into general use when a Controller of Victuals was added to the Council for Marine Causes in 1550. The pursers did not cease to handle money, because they still had to be able to purchase stores direct in the event of accident or emergency, and also to provide dietary supplements, such as fresh fruit and vegetables, which did not come within the scope of the victuallers' activities.[3] The cash for such supplements came normally from Gonson via local agents such as Edward Baeshe in London or William Johnson in Portsmouth, who also hired the victualling boats which might be necessary to convey provisions to ships which had to be revictualled at a distance.

The purchase of timber, pitch, ropes, canvas, ironwork, and the various other materials necessary for the repair and maintenance of ships presented fewer problems, largely because such commodities were not perishable. Some timber was provided from royal forests, such as the New Forest, but most was purchased – as close as possible to the relevant dock or shipyard because transport cost twopence per ton per mile. In June 1536 Thomas Cromwell noted that he had purchased woods 'beside Portsmouth' sufficient for the

[1] *L and P*, 9, 234, 260, 418.

[2] Ibid. Gonson also complained on this occasion that he had had to find £600 out of his own pocket to victual the ships for Bordeaux, which had 'undone' him.

[3] Such commodities never appear in the victuallers' accounts, but we know that they were carried and used from the archaeological evidence of the *Mary Rose*. The use of citrus fruit as an anti-scorbutic does not seem to have been understood before 1600. D. W. Waters, 'Limes, lemons and scurvy', *MM*, 41, 1955, 167–9. No doubt on short voyages, individuals often provided their own.

new making of the *Henry Grace a Dieu* and the *Great Galley*.[1] Rough and unseasoned oak cost about 1s. a ton, seasoned oak 1s.8d., and ready squared 3s.4d. Ash was 1s. a ton, and beech 6d. There was already concern in the south of England about the shortage of suitable timber for ship-building, and in Elizabeth's reign an Act of Parliament was passed to restrict felling.[2] Pine and fir for masts and spars was largely imported from Scandinavia. Before the sixteenth century most of the cables and cordage used on the king's ships came from Bridport in Dorset, but by the 1530s Bridport had fallen on hard times, and the town authorities sought the protection of parliament against interlopers who, it was claimed, were undermining the trade.[3] Perhaps Bridport ropemaking declined for that reason, and the king's officers purchased abroad because Bridport could not supply in sufficient quantities for the expanding navy. But it seems equally likely that the Dorset town, which had enjoyed a virtual monopoly for many years, had gradually priced itself out of the market. For example, Gonson contracted in April 1535 with Richard Cavendish 'for the provision of ropes and cables in Estland' (that is, the Baltic), claiming that by doing so he could save the equivalent of the rigging of one ship. Cavendish seems to have had a kind of roving commission from Cromwell, because in August 1535 he was paid £400 on a direct warrant to purchase ropes and cables in Denmark.[4] In February 1536, however, he reported to Cromwell that he had been unable to obtain the necessary ropes in Hamburg (or, presumably, in Denmark), and that he had spent part of the £400 on pitch and tar – four lasts of pitch and 42 barrels of tar – which he was sending home in the *Minion*. By then he had received further instructions from Gonson to obtain cables, yarn and hemp, which he had been unable to do in Hamburg, France, or Flanders. Eventually he had been able to obtain a supply from 'a man of Rye', which had so far cost £600, and would cost another £400.[5] He had borrowed the extra money in Hamburg, and sent Cromwell the bills of exchange.

It is unlikely that Cavendish's activities were unique, because the opportunistic style of these transactions was typical of Cromwell's method. Cables were expensive. Measuring anything up to 17 in. in circumference, they averaged £12 a ton in 1515, and appreciably

[1] *L and P*, 10, 1231.
[2] 1 Elizabeth cap. 15.
[3] 21 Henry VIII cap. 12, 'An Acte for the true making of great cables . . .'
[4] *L and P*, 8, 527; Cromwell's remembrances, 10 April 1535. Ibid., 9, 217.
[5] Cavendish to Cromwell, 3 February 1536; *Letters and Papers*, 10, 240.

more by 1545, so it was worthwhile making special arrangements for large-scale purchase. Similarly the best canvas came from France, as the names of the various types – Olron, Vitery, Poldavys – suggest, and the large quantities required also necessitated special commissions.[1] Substitutes could be obtained from the Baltic, particularly Danzig, if war or political conflict made trade with France impracticable. Pitch and tar was better and cheaper in Hamburg or Stockholm than it was in England, although the price of a barrel of pitch doubled from 4s. to 8s. in the thirty years after 1514. On the other hand ironwork such as shovels and nails, like timber, was normally purchased locally, in the vicinity of the dockyard. More mundane necessities, such as tallow, oakum, rosin and reeds, bricks for the ships' ovens and tiles for the storehouse roofs, were bought as required, also from local suppliers. How much all this cost in a typical year can only be judged very approximately. Between 1 October 1534 and 7 December 1535 – just over fourteen months – Gonson received about £3 500 from Cromwell for 'apparalling and rigging' the King's ships, plus another £500 for other expenditure. This was not a crisis year, and Gonson was not handling all the expenditure, so a total budget of at least £5 000 for a twelve month period would seem to be indicated.[2] In the twelve months from 21 August 1533 to 25 August 1534 Gonson also recorded payments of £4 444.8s.6d., which points to the same conclusion. In June 1539 (which was a crisis year), it was estimated that 36 ships assembled at Portsmouth, with 1 613 officers and men, would cost £1 425.0s.10d. for one standard month of 28 days.[3] It therefore seems reasonable to conclude that by 1540 normal peacetime naval maintenance and routine operations were costing the Crown approximately £5 000 a year, while the additional preparations caused by the threat of war would double that figure without any actual fighting taking place. The extra money spent in fees and allowances to the officers of the new Council for Marine Causes would be well bestowed if they could improve the efficiency of an operation which had become large and complex as well as permanent over the preceding thirty years.

By 1547 Henry had nearly 60 ships, varying in size from the *Great Harry* to rowbarges of 20 or 30 tons, and such a fleet required extensive dockyard facilities. It is, however, very difficult to be precise about the size, number and location of these docks, because the term seems to have been used very flexibly. The existing dry dock

[1] Oppenheim, *Administration*, 98; Howard, 'Early Tudor rigging', *MM*, 68, 277–8.
[2] *L and P*, 7, 1564.
[3] Ibid., 12, 2, 1028; ibid., 14, 1, 1097.

at Portsmouth was refurbished and extended in 1527, when the surrounding land was also purchased and enclosed.[1] A second timber-lined dock, which appears to have been of similar construction, was provided in 1522–3 at a cost of £553.[2] There is also a reference to a 'new dock' for the grounding of the *Mary Rose*, the *Peter Pomegranate* and the *John Baptist*, also at Portsmouth, in 1527.[3] Whether this was equally elaborate, or merely what would later be called a 'mud dock' is not clear. The original brewhouse and bakery dated back to 1492, and there had been a major building programme in April 1512, which had cost over £2 000. By 1544, when there was a further expansion and rebuilding, Portsmouth had at least two large storehouses, a forge and workshops, and no fewer than five breweries, which were leased to private traders except in wartime. No ships of any significance were built at Portsmouth, but all the King's Great Ships seem to have been docked there at one time or another, and both the facilities and the skilled labour existed for comprehensive repair and maintenance. Other docks and storehouses were scattered along the south bank of the Thames between Deptford and Erith. Apart from the 'pond' at Deptford, docks are also referred to there, at Woolwich and at Greenwich, although it is not known what sort of constructions these were.[4] Some belonged to the King, others were rented from private owners. In December 1534 a certain Walter Wilcokkes wrote to Cromwell complaining that two of the King's ships had been laid up in a dock belonging to him between Rotherhithe and Greenwich, a service for which he should have received 8d. per ship per week, but in fact he had been paid nothing, in spite of the fact that the ships (which were probably small) had been there for two years.[5] An inspection of the King's ships in the Thames, carried out in January 1539, raises almost as many questions as it answers. The investigators reported that four ships, the *Great Galley*, the *Less Bark*, the *Jennet* and the *Lion* were 'new made and ready to sail in 30 days'; the *Trinity* would be ready in 40 days, while the *Primrose* and the *Sweepstake* could be available in 20 days. At the same time the *Mary Rose*, the *Peter* (*Pomegranate*) and the *Minion* were 'new made, standing in their docks'; their masts were ready, but not yet set up, and it would be three months

[1] PRO E315/317 f. 58.
[2] PRO E36/6 ff. 4–5, 35–46.
[3] PRO E315/317 f. 58.
[4] Oppenheim, *Administration*, 69–71. Small ships were still beached for minor repairs, and these docks were intended mainly for larger vessels.
[5] *L and P*, 7, 1662.

before they could be ready for the sea. 'As to the keeping of all these ships', the writer went on, 'there is no keeping them after their removal from the docks they are now in, but only for three of them . . .' To keep them afloat would cost £1 000 a year in cordage and wages, and they would also be in danger from 'great frosts'. Either they must be kept in use, or out of the Thames, or else provided with docks before the following winter.[1] This only makes sense if the docks referred to were purely temporary structures, which were demolished or allowed to decay as soon as the ships for which they had been provided were removed.

On 9 December 1533, during a period of acute tension in Anglo-Imperial relations following Henry's marriage to Anne Boleyn and the birth of Elizabeth, Eustace Chapuys, the Imperial ambassador, reported the extreme nervousness of the English council. They had 'lately called those who have the management of the King's ships, commanding them to get them ready, and desiring to know if the whole could be in a readiness by 1 May. But they have been given to understand that it would be impossible to do it within twelve or thirteen months . . .'[2] If this report is accepted at face value, then it represents a very rapid deterioration over the previous two or three years. But Chapuys had every reason to exaggerate English weakness, since he was endeavouring to persuade his master to intervene in support of the rejected Catherine of Aragon. He had himself reported only a few months earlier that Henry had sent four ships north to 'stop the trade' of the Scots.[3] There are no surviving accounts for the years 1531–3, so it is possible that the maintenance programme which can be reconstructed for the years before and after was not functioning properly between the fall of Wolsey and the rise of Cromwell, but given the King's personal interest in the navy, this seems unlikely. Probably the key lies in the phrase 'the whole'. No doubt some of the King's ships were in need of virtual rebuilding, and Chapuys exaggerated a state of relative unpreparedness for his own purposes. If there had been any significant lapse, the programme had certainly recommenced by August 1533. However, a note among Cromwell's memoranda for April 1534, to call upon Gonson, Spert and others to provide for the repairing of the ships, suggests that the minister was not satisfied with the state of affairs at that date, and provides some support for Chapuys's picture. Just

[1] *L and P*, 14, 1, 143; 26 January 1539.
[2] Ibid., 6, 1510. Chapuys had made several references over the previous weeks to the King's anxiety to have his ships prepared.
[3] *L and P*, 6, 142, Chapuys to the Emperor, 9 February 1533.

over two years later, in June 1536, Cromwell reminded himself with some satisfaction that since 1532 he had caused the *Mary Rose*, the *Peter Pomegranate*, the *Lion*, the *Catherine Galley*, the (*Great*?) *Bark*, the *Minion* and the *Sweepstake* to be rebuilt, and had provided for the 'new making' of the *Henry Grace a Dieu* and the *Great Galley*.[1]

Unlike maintenance, the building of ships for the King's service was not a virtually continuous process, being associated mainly with war or the preparation for war. Four ships of modest size were completed during 1522, when the country was committed to war, but not actually fighting, and a further five during the war years 1523–4. There was then a ten-year gap before the *Lion* and the *Mary Willoughby* were laid down, followed by a new *Sweepstake* in 1539, and the *Jennet* in the same year. Five years later, after the start of the last war of the reign, and more or less simultaneously with the creation of the Council for Marine Causes, a programme of unprecedented scale was launched, which produced 18 new ships of between 30 and 450 tons in the space of three years, as well as 13 rowbarges of 20 tons apiece.[2] In most cases we do not know where these ships were built, or who was responsible for them. In January 1535 Chapuys arranged a rendezvous with the Duke of Norfolk 'at the place where the king's ships are built, halfway between London and Greenwich'. Such a description more or less fits Deptford, and it is possible that there were royal ships under construction there at that date, but most evidence, particularly for the later period, suggests that a variety of yards along the Thames were used, as well as others as far away as Hull and Southampton.[3] A few of the smaller vessels, such as the *Katherine Pleasaunce* (1518) and the *Galley Subtle* (1544) were built by direct labour – William Gonson was responsible for the latter – but most seem to have been constructed on contract in private yards. James Baker, the King's first shipwright, enjoyed an excellent posthumous reputation, but whether he had any say in the design of these ships, either in general or in detail, is uncertain. The King's personal interest in his ships is frequently attested. He visited Portsmouth on several occasions, dining on board the *Great Harry* in September 1535 after one of her numerous refits, gleefully showing off three newly equipped vessels to the

[1] *L and P*, 10, 1231.

[2] Oppenheim, *Administration*, 50–1.

[3] Smalhithe and Woolwich are specifically mentioned, as well as Deptford. The *Brigandine* was probably built at Dover. There were several yards along Southampton Water, and the origins of about half the ships built are unknown. Oppenheim, loc. cit.

French ambassador in April 1538, and playing pilots at the launching of the *Great Galley* in 1515. In July 1541 Chapuys informed the Emperor that Henry had sent to Italy for three shipwrights skilled in the making of galleys, but he would probably not employ them because he was building galleys to his own design. This was almost certainly a reference to the *Galley Subtle*, for which the first payment was recorded in December 1541; but the very small galleys known as rowbarges also seem to have been a particular enthusiasm of his.[1] The fact that they were rapidly disposed of after his death suggests that his enthuasism was not shared by his marine officers.

After the *Henry Grace a Dieu* Henry's interest in great ships seems to have waned. Perhaps the cost was felt to be prohibitive, but more likely they were thought to be of limited usefulness. Only three ships of 400 tons or more were built for the King's service in the remainder of the reign – the *Pauncey* in 1544 and the *Grand Mistress* and the *Anne Gallant* in 1545. Rather more were purchased; the *Matthew* of 600 tons from William Gonson, and the *Great* and *Less Bark*, of 500 and 400 tons respectively from Hamburg – all in the difficult year 1539. 1544 saw three more large purchases, the *Mary Hamboro* of 400 tons, the *Jesus of Lubeck* of 600, and the *Struse of Dawske* (Danzig) also of 400. The *Marian* of 400 tons was bought in 1545, and the *Christopher* of the same size in 1546.[2] Eleven prizes were also taken in the two wars after 1520, but the largest was the *Salamander* of 300 tons captured in 1544. In time of war or emergency the traditional practice of taking up privately owned ships, both English and foreign, on a temporary basis continued, but represented a much smaller proportion of the total navy than in times past. Henry continued to pay bounties, as his father had done, for the building of ships over 100 tons. These usually took the form of remission of customs dues, but sometimes payments were made in cash. Thomas Cromwell managed to arrange two such payments for himself. Of the twenty or so ships known to have been built with a bounty during the reign, seven were constructed between 1540 and 1547. During the tense spring of 1539, and again in the autumn of 1540, the reports of the French ambassador Charles de Marillac provide some interesting observations upon the strength and organization of the English fleet. At the beginning of April he noticed

[1] *L and P*, 17, 258; J. E. G. Bennell, 'English oared vessels of the sixteenth century', *MM*, 60, 1974, 169–85.

[2] Oppenheim, *Administration*, 51. On the payment of bounties, see B. Dietz, 'The royal bounty . . .'

many warlike preparations; the King's ships were ready to leave the Thames for Portsmouth, all trade was interdicted, and English subjects summoned home.[1] He estimated that the whole fleet would number 150 sail. A fortnight later 'not less than 80 ships of war' were fully ready. By 20 May the sense of urgency was evaporating, although the preparations continued. A Venetian ship of 700 tons and a Ragusan of 500 had been requisitioned by the English government.[2] The whole fleet numbered 120 sail. On 9 June he lowered his estimate again to 90, but noted that artillery was still being loaded into ships in the Thames. Seven or eight Venetian, Ragusan and Florentine ships of 400–500 tons had been purchased, presumably inclusive of the two already mentioned.[3] By 12 August the alarm was over, and fewer than a dozen ships remained at Portsmouth. On 1 October 1540, in response to a request from Francis I and in somewhat cooler circumstances, Marillac assessed England's naval strength. The King had 30 or 40 ships of his own 'at most', of which three, then lying in the Thames, were Great Ships – the *Great Harry* of 1500 tons, and the *Mary Rose* and *Peter Pomegranate* of 900 or 1000 tons. The rest were of no great size, although all were well-furnished, thanks to the panic of the previous year.[4] One or two replacements were also being fitted out. For the rest, the whole kingdom could not produce more than seven or eight ships of over 400 tons, and three of those were owned by the former Lord Admiral, Sir William FitzWilliam. The remainder were 'little ships of 50–80 tons'. Seventy or 80 sail was all that could be assembled, and when more than that were needed, the English resorted to hiring Venetians, Genoese or Ragusans. Marillac was clearly not a very systematic or accurate observer, and his reports contain several inconsistencies, but he was close to events, and deserved to be taken seriously. Although he overestimated the size of the three great ships in the Thames in October 1540 he can hardly have been wrong about their number. In theory Henry should have had seven or eight other Great Ships at that time, but either they were unserviceable or they

[1] Marillac to Montmorency, 2 April 1539, *L and P*, 14, 1, 670.

[2] Marillac to Francis I, 15 April 1539, *L and P*, 14, 1, 769. Same to same, 20 May, ibid. 988; same to Montmorency, 20 May, ibid., 989. These were still being hired at 1s.3d. a ton, and their crews paid 7s.6d. a month (as against the English rates of 1s. and 5s.).

[3] Marillac was probably wrong about these purchases; there are no other records of so many large ships being purchased, and his first thought that they were hired was almost certainly correct.

[4] *L and P*, 16, 110.

had already been disposed of.[1] The ambassador may also have been right in claiming that there were very few English merchantmen of over 400 tons. Where he was most obviously wrong was in his assessment of the supporting vessels. An optimistic count would give the King 47 ships of his own in 1539, and of those all but 10 were over 100 tons.[2] As far as I am aware there is no census of English merchant ships from this period, but during the war of 1512–14 Henry had been able to take up 57 English ships of over 100 tons, of which 12 had been over 200; and an Elizabethan census of 1582 listed no fewer than 177 vessels of 100 tons or more belonging to all the principal ports.[3] Within five years Marillac's parsimonious estimate of the number and size of the ships which the King of England could muster was to be dramatically demolished. Nor is there any sign in other records of the large foreign ships which Henry is alleged to have purchased, and it seems that the ambassador was better informed in 1540 than he had been in 1539.

The quantitative changes which took place in the English navy between 1520 and 1547 do not seem to have been matched by comparable technical developments. Both the *Great Harry* and the *Mary Rose* were described by enthusiastic contemporaries as exceptionally good sailing vessels, but the verdict of modern seamen upon the latter, as now retrieved, is a good deal less flattering.[4] Although the bowline had been developed before the end of the fourteenth century, it seems unlikely that any sixteenth-century ship was capable of working closely to windward. Most ships, except the very smallest, had four masts, of which at least three would be fitted with top masts. Larger ships would also have top-gallants on two or three of their masts; but the only innovations seem to have been the increased use of spritsails, and the introduction of spankers (or lateen sails) on the main and bonaventure mizzen masts (the third

[1] It is often hard to be sure when ships were sold or broken up, but of the Great Ships (over 400 tons) listed by Oppenheim, the *Sovereign*, the *Gabriel Royal*, the *John Baptist*, the *Great Nicholas*, the *Katherine Fortileza* and the *Great Elizabeth* do not appear in the lists of 1539. The *Sovereign* was probably broken up in 1525, but the fate of the others is unrecorded. T. Glasgow Jr., 'List of ships in the royal navy from 1539 to 1588', *MM*, 56, 1970, 299–308.

[2] Oppenheim, 49–51; this figure would almost certainly be too high, because of the losses noted above, which would equally apply to smaller ships. Glasgow's figure, on the other hand, at 9 is certainly far too low. Marillac's estimate was intended to be disparaging, but was probably about right.

[3] Dorothy Burwash, *English Merchant Shipping, 1450–1540*, 183; PRO SP12/156, ff. 88r–90v.

[4] A Mary Rose Trust lecturer, responding to the question of how the ship would have handled, compared her to a wet haystack. For a more academic judgement, see A. Moore, 'Rig in Northern Europe', *MM*, 41–2, 1955–6, 42–6.

and fourth masts). These changes should have made large ships easier to steer, and reduced the effect of the very tall forecastles which were characteristic of most fighting ships. A more significant development may, however, lie concealed in the uncertainties of contemporary terminology. The same ships could be described in one list as galleys, in another as galleases, and in a third as barks. In some cases this seems to have been the result of rebuilding. By 1540 the *Great Galley* had been rebuilt as an ordinary sailing ship, and was called the *Great Bark*.[1] In other cases, however, it was probably the result of genuine doubt about the classification of a vessel which was, for most purposes, a sailing warship, but which could be moved by sweeps in an emergency, or if becalmed. The *Grand Mistress* and the *Anne Gallant*, for example, were essentially large four masted galleons of 450 tons, with two gun-decks, but because they could also be moved by oars, they were correctly described in 1546 as galleases.[2] Such vessels probably suffered from most of the disadvantages of the carrack, without much mitigation, and were rapidly becoming obsolete. Other galleases, such as the *Hart, Antelope, Tiger* and *Bull*, were much more genuine hybrids. As portrayed in the Anthony Roll they appear as flush-decked ships, without the high castles of the carrack, and with but a single gun-deck; they were consequently much closer in profile to the genuine galley, and also seem to have been longer in proportion to their beam. However, like the *Grand Mistress* and the *Anne Gallant* they do not seem to have been capable of normal propulsion by oars, but to have used sweeps in the same manner. As sailing ships, because they had finer lines and less top-hamper, they were probably both faster and more manoeuvrable than the great ships, and were the direct ancestors of the galleons of the next generation. In 1546 they were described as 'fast wingers', and it has been suggested that they were specifically designed to counter the threat from the French galleys, although their effectiveness remained untested because peace was concluded not long after they were launched.[3] Apart from the rowbarges, the only genuine oared warships in the English navy at the end of the Henry's reign were the *Galley Subtle* and the *Galley Blanchard*, a prize taken in 1546.

The English navy consequently enjoyed no great advantages over its rivals in the construction or performance of its ships; but in

[1] This confusion is compounded by the fact that there seem to have been two *Great Barks*.

[2] Magdalene College, Cambridge, Pepys MS 2991, f. 51 'Abstract of the second roll'.

[3] T. Glasgow, 'Oared vessels in the Elizabethan navy', *MM*, 52, 1966, 371.

gunnery it had a distinct edge. During the war of 1512–14 the serpentine had been the standard gun at sea, with a small number of curtalls, and the culverin beginning to make its appearance. By 1540 English ships were equipped with no less than 14 different types of gun, seven of brass and seven of iron, ranging from cannons to fawconnettes and from port pieces to quarter slings.[1] The *Mary Rose* at that date carried 96 guns, of which six could be classed as heavy, but there was no standardization, and the weight and calibre of guns in the same classification seem to have varied widely. All guns by this time, except the very smallest, were mounted on wheeled carriages which enabled them to be run back inboard for loading, and the elevation was adjusted with chocks inserted between the gun and the carriage.[2] Even quite small ships were heavily armed. The *Lion* of 160 tons carried 33 guns, of which eight were heavy; the *Jennet* of 200 tons carried 42 guns; the *Great Bark* of 500 tons 87 guns; even the *Roo* of 80 tons mounted two demi-culverins.[3] Just how these guns were used is a matter of some controversy. The increased use of iron rather than stone shot, and some improvement in the quality of the gunpowder used gave the culverins of the 1540s considerably more penetrative power than the curtalls of the 1520s. Lisle's fleet orders of 1545 do not suggest any concept of using synchronized gunfire to inflict maximum damage upon the enemy's ships, but a Spanish author writing in 1574 gives a rather different impression;

> . . . the ordnance flush with the water should be at once discharged broadside on and so damage their hull and confuse them with smoke. This is their own (the English) way of fighting, and I have many times seen them do it to the French thirty years ago . . .[4]

It is possible that the broadside, which was to be the basic method of sea fighting for the next three centuries, was invented during Henry VIII's last war with France.

Even if this was so, however, naval battles were not expected to be resolved by such methods. Warships carried soldiers whose business

[1] From an inventory of guns carried in 10 of the King's ships, dated 13 February 1540, analysed in the *MM*, 6, 1920, 281–2.

[2] Margaret Rule, *The Mary Rose*, 159–62. For a tabulation of average gun weights and calibres; see also K. H. Tomlin 'The influence of the introduction of heavy ordnance on the development of the English navy in the early Tudor period'. (University of West Michigan M.A., 1980)

[3] Oppenheim, *Administration*, 55–6.

[4] C. Fernandez Duro, *La Armada Invencibile*, I, 382; cited by A. H. Taylor, 'Carrack into Galleon', *MM*, 36, 1950, 144.

was hand-to-hand fighting, and the broadside, even if used, was only preliminary to the serious business of grapple and board. The standard weapons with which these soldiers were equipped were the longbow, the bill and the morrispike, although arquebuses were just beginning to put in an appearance by 1545. Over the half century or so which separated the first of Henry's wars from the early years of Elizabeth's reign, the balance of manning and armament changed, no doubt reflecting the gradual advance of gunnery in the priorities of naval tactics. In 1513 the *Great Harry* of 1 000 tons carried 700 men – 400 soldiers, 260 seamen and 40 gunners – and was armed with 2 000 bows, 1 500 bills and 1 500 morrispikes.[1] In 1575 the *Triumph*, of the same burthen, also carried 700 men – 450 mariners, 200 soldiers and 50 gunners – and was armed with 250 arquebuses, 50 bows, 200 pikes and 200 bills.[2] These figures are revealing, because the *Triumph* did not really require nearly twice as many seamen as the *Great Harry*, and she carried far more heavy guns than is reflected in a 20 per cent rise in the number of gunners. The inference must be that by 1575 it was the mariners who were manning the guns, no doubt under supervision of the professional gunners, and the soldiers were already retreating towards the secondary role later occupied by the marines. The enormous number of hand weapons carried by the *Great Harry* can probably be explained by her role in support of an invasion force rather than by anticipated use at sea, and the virtual replacement of bows by arquebuses in the *Triumph* is simply a reflection of developing military technology. The same pattern can also be seen in the smaller ships. In 1513 the *Great Bark* of 400 tons carried 150 soldiers, 88 seamen and 12 gunners; the 350 ton *Swallow* in 1565 carried 120 seamen, 60 soldiers and 20 gunners. The manning levels on warships were always very much higher than on merchant ships of similar burthen, because a merchantman was trying to operate as economically as possible, so the numbers of mariners listed in 1513 were probably an accurate reflection of the numbers actually needed to work the ships, while the numbers for 1565 reflect the fighting role which they had by then taken over.[3]

[1] *L and P*, I, 3977, 4379. The tonnage of the *Henry Grace a Dieu* is given variously between 1,000 and 1,500.

[2] Bodleian Library, Rawlinson MS A 297, ff. 15v–16v. In 1546 the *Henry Grace a Dieu* carried 249 soldiers, 301 mariners and 100 gunners; Pepys MS 2991, ff. 2–3.

[3] The *Elizabeth* of Newcastle operated during Henry's last war both as a victualler and as a fighting ship. In the former capacity she carried 40 men, in the latter 100. G. V. Scammell, 'War at sea under the early Tudors', *Archaeologia Aeliana*, 39, 1961, 179–205.

In the early part of his reign, Henry seems to have had no difficulty in recruiting seamen, although the rates of pay had remained unchanged for many years. In May 1514 the main battle fleet was manned by 3 982 seamen and 447 gunners, in addition to the soldiers. However by 1544 the situation was becoming more difficult, and there begin to be references to shortages, and even to desertions.[1] In 1545 it was estimated that 5 000 men would be needed, which 'wilbe some diffycultie', and the King raised the basic seaman's wage from 5s. a month to 6s.8d.[2] In 1546 the projection drawn up in March for the summer required a minimum of 6 400 seamen, soldiers and gunners, probably nearer 7 000 with the North Sea fleet.[3] Part of the problem was caused by the increased size of the navy, and part by the rival attraction of the privateers, which do not seem to have featured largely in the earlier years, but which were out in strength in 1544 and 1545. It was alleged at the time that the difficulty was caused by the decay of the port towns and of the fishing fleet, driving seamen to seek other work. The truth of this is hard to judge. Some ports were certainly in decline; Southampton, for example, did not recover from the loss of most of its Italian trade to London in the late fifteenth century. The Cinq Ports were in decline because their harbours were silting up. On the other hand Newcastle upon Tyne was flourishing. In 1544 50 ships belonged to the port, of which 25 were reported as suitable for use in the King's service.[4] Many of the lamentations were connected with attempts to promote protectionist legislation, and need consequently to be treated with caution – like complaints of urban decay in general. The Iceland fishing trade was certainly a great nursery of seamen. In response to an Admiralty court inquisition in 1536–7, the villages of Blakeney, Wyston and Cley in Norfolk reported that they had 'lx saylyng men, and x men able to be masters into Iseland and the quoste hereabowte'.[5] This trade may have passed its peak by 1545, but many of the complaints came from those who, in the next reign,

[1] On 24 January 1545 the death penalty by martial law was proclaimed for desertion from the king's ships; P. L. Hughes and J. F. Larkin, *Tudor Royal Proclamations*, I, 346. In 1568 James Humphreys noted that desertion was 'felony by statute'; Pepys MS 1266, 49.

[2] Hughes and Larkin, I, 347; 24 January 1545. Part of the problem seems to have been the relative attractiveness of privateering; Oppenheim, *Administration*, 94–5.

[3] *L and P*, 21, 498.

[4] G. V. Scammell, 'War at sea under the early Tudors', *Archaeologia Aeliana*, 38, 1960, 73–.

[5] PRO HCA 13/1 (unfoliated); cited Burwash, *English Merchant Shipping*, 28.

were trying to persuade a protestant government to retain the 'fish days' of the catholic church.[1]

The basic pay may not have been much of an inducement to seamen who could make much more through the profit-sharing system of a private voyage, but it had the great advantage of being regularly paid, and there were well-established supplements. Not only were victuals provided, and conduct money to and from the port of embarkation, it was also common to supply jackets or 'coats' as a type of uniform, often in the Tudor colours of green and white. Sir Edward Howard in 1512 charged for 1616 seamen's coats at 1s.8d. each, and 1 812 for his soldiers. By 1545 the cost had risen somewhat to 2s.[2] Another source of profit, although one largely confined to the officers, was the distribution of 'deadshares' or rewards. These seem to have been based upon the established military custom of allowing every captain pay for more men that he was actually leading, these 'ghost' wages being his own additional profit. Militarily this could be dangerous as an avaricious captain might deliberately keep his band below strength into order to increase his profit, but at sea deadshares were very specifically allocated. In 1513, for example, the *Trinity Sovereign* received 38 such shares of 5s. each; of these the master received seven, his mate two, the boatswain two and his mate one. Altogether 11 officers received 23 shares between them; seven mates or assistants received nine, and six were distributed among the pilots. A similar distribution pattern was followed on the smaller ships, some of which received 20½ shares, some 17½ and some 16.[3] The ordinary seamen were not included at this stage, but later in the reign it seems to have been usual to divide a certain number of shares between the rest of the crew. A similar pattern was also followed with the distribution of prize money, an area in which royal crews fared noticeably worse than the privateers, where a less hierarchical system was followed, and where it was much easier to avoid paying the Lord Admiral's 20 per cent. Large warships also carried surgeons and physicians, and although the evidence which we have of their ministrations fill the modern mind with dread, they were the best available at the time, and well in advance of anything which was available on civilian ships. Whatever we may think of his equipment, the surgeon of the *Mary Rose* in 1545 was a member of the barber surgeons company, and thus had

1 These efforts persisted into the reign of Elizabeth. See, for example, 23 Elizabeth cap. 7, 'An acte for the increase of mariners and for the maintenance of navigation'.

2 Oppenheim, *Administration*, 74–5.

3 PRO E101/61/12.

the highest professional qualifications.[1] The King could also be generous to mariners who became sick or were injured in his service. Sick men were often landed, both to give them a better chance of recovery and also to check the spread of infection on the ships, but they continued to be paid – at least in theory – until the end of their period of employment. Gratuities were also sometimes paid to the disabled, although this does not seem to have been done regularly, and pensions were not introduced until much later.[2]

Discipline was based upon the ancient laws of Oleron, which had a universal currency in northern Europe, and there was no special code for the king's ships. A written version of these laws was supposed to be 'set in the mayne mast in parchement to be rid as occasion shall serve', although this can have been only a gesture of promulgation, since most seamen were illiterate, and the weather would soon have disposed of a document so displayed. The essence of the code was rough justice; a murderer was to be tied to the body of his victim and thrown overboard; a seaman who struck the master lost his right hand, or paid a fine of 5s.; a thief was towed ashore behind the ships boat and dismissed.[3] Much of the original code dealt with payments, and with the share rights of seamen, and was not relevant to the Tudor navy, but the main disciplinary practices showed extraordinary durability. The position originally accorded to the master (and taken over by the captain on the larger warships) was a curiously ambiguous one. On the one hand his power could be arbitrary, extending to life or death in certain circumstances; yet in other matters he was circumscribed by the consent of the crew. Frequently it was specified that the whole ship's company should participate in disciplinary action, and if the master set sail, or entered an unknown port, without the consent of his men, or against their advice, then he was alone responsible for any damage or loss which might ensue. It must often have been difficult to know when a captain was acting within his powers, and when not, which is why Michael Oppenheim declared that discipline 'in the modern sense' was unknown.[4] In 1513 when mutiny threatened on a ship com-

[1] James Watt, 'The surgeons of the Mary Rose', *MM*, 69, 1983, 3–19. The first reference to an organized naval medical service appears in BL MS Cotton Galba BIII, f. 154.

[2] Oppenheim, *Administration*, 76–7; Statute 35 Elizabeth c.4, 'An acte for the necessarie relief of Souldiers and Maryners'.

[3] The best edition of these laws (and there are many) is in *The Oak Book of Southampton*, ed. Paul Studer. There is also a text in James Humphries' book of 1568 (Pepys MS 1266, 25–49), confirming the code's continued use in the navy. By the sixteenth century the original fine of 5s. had risen to 100s.

[4] Oppenheim, *Administration*, 79.

manded by Sir Weston Browne, the Admiral was advised to replace the captain if he could not pacify the discontent; and in 1545 Sir George Carew ascribed the disaster which overtook the *Mary Rose* to the disorderly conduct of 'a sort of knaves I cannot rule'. On the other hand there was an actual discipline to working the ships, which was part of a mariner's professional skill, and without which disasters would have been of much greater frequency. About this discipline we know very little. A station list for the *Henry Grace a Dieu* has survived, of unknown date, indicating the positioning of 516 men around the ship. However, according to the manning tables of 1513, she was supposed to carry 260 seamen and 400 soldiers. Presumably, therefore, this list is of battle stations and includes most of the soldiers, although which was which can only be deduced.[1] Probably the 100 men in the forecastle and the 120 in the waist were soldiers, while the four at the helm or the eight at the mainsail ropes would have been sailors. In time of war seamen and soldiers alike were subject to the law martial, and that law was sometimes extended ashore, particularly to deal with deserters, but how the boundaries were drawn between the martial law and the much more communal customary law, we do not know. It is perhaps not surprising that complaints about what Dr William Knight called 'the ungodly manners' of the seamen were frequent, and became more so as the century advanced.

To reinforce his authority, the captain of a Tudor warship could usually fall back upon his social status. Whereas the master was normally an experienced seaman of yeoman rank, captains were gentlemen, either by birth or by attainment. Admiralty officers, like William Gonson, Sir Thomas Spert and Sir William Woodhouse were captains before they were administrators, and often merchants before they were captains, but they were all accepted as gentlemen. The supposedly rigid distinctions of Tudor society look remarkably flimsy in the case of a man like Gonson – merchant of London, gentleman of the household and sea commander, all at the same time. As the navy gained in importance there were more gentlemen willing to serve at sea. In 1513 several of the captains were members of the King's elite bodyguard, the band of Spears, and others were noblemen, like Walter, Lord Ferrers.[2] By 1545, when the King's warfleet numbered over 100 vessels, Lord Lisle reported a shortage

[1] Ibid., 80.
[2] Ibid., 77; A. Spont, *Letters and Papers relating to the war with France, 1512–13*, 8–9 etc. See also John Webb, 'William Sabyn of Ipswich', *MM*, 41, 1955, 209–221, for the view that gentlemen officers were always hard to find.

of captains, and regretted that some of the smaller ships might have to make do with captains of lower status;

> As concernynge the meane shippes I know noon other waye (I meane those that come out of the west parties and such of London as were victuallers that want captaignes) but to place them with meane men to be their captaignes as serving men and yeomen that be most mete for the purpose.[1]

Clearly fighting ships, even small ones, were normally commanded by gentlemen, while victuallers, transports, and the other auxiliary vessels which had always made up the largest number in any medieval fleet, were not. It was the unprecedented assembly of 104 warships which had caused this embarrassing and temporary situation. Thanks to Henry's personal interest in his navy, the 'honour' of service at sea had increased markedly, and thanks partly to the example of his court an intelligent interest in navigation and cosmography was now considered a suitable part of a gentleman's breeding. Only the galleys still failed to find favour, and in 1546 a Spaniard had to be retained as captain of the *Galley Subtle*, even although this meant providing him with an interpreter so that he could communicate with his crew.[2]

It would be an exaggeration to claim that by the end of Henry VIII's reign sea fighting had taken over from land fighting as the priority of the English military aristocracy, but it had certainly moved much nearer to parity. The navy was still a long way from being a professional service in the eighteenth-century sense, but it had a professional core. There was a navy in a sense that there was not an army. There was an Ordnance office, garrisons in Calais and Berwick, and numerous fortifications around the south and east coasts, but there was no military equivalent of the Council for Marine Causes, with its dockyards, storehouses, workshops, and stock of warships to be maintained and deployed alike in war and peace. The days of naval improvisation were not yet past, but it had become a fringe activity, a supplement to the main maritime strength, which now lay in the King's ships.

[1] *State Papers of Henry VIII*, 7 August 1545; cited Oppenheim, *Administration*, 78.
[2] *APC*, ed. J. Dasent, I, 14 April 1546.

5
THE NAVY IN ACTION, 1520–1547

After spending over two years endeavouring to preserve the peace achieved through the treaty of London in 1518, by the summer of 1521 England was moving uncertainly towards renewed war. The tangled diplomacy of these years need not concern us here, but throughout 1520 relations between the King of France and the newly elected Emperor, Charles V had continually deteriorated.[1] Francis was the aggressor, and Charles angled strenuously for an English alliance. In May 1521 he obtained it at the secret treaty of Bruges, but Wolsey continued to hope for a mediated settlement, and managed to deflect Henry's enthusiasm for an immediate campaign. There was talk of an invasion, and of the destruction of the French fleet, but no effective mobilization was ordered. The King lost interest and went off hunting, leaving Wolsey free to resume his tortuous diplomacy. By August he was using the threat of an open break to bring the French to the conference table, but that was the limit of his effectiveness; he could not bring about a settlement. On 24 November he signed a second treaty at Bruges, committing England to war against France. A naval campaign was to be conducted in the summer of 1522, and in 1523 the Emperor and the King of England were to co-ordinate a double invasion.[2] The autumn of 1521 was consequently a somewhat tricky time. During September, Henry for some inexplicable reason suddenly became concerned that the French would suspect what was intended and impound the considerable assets of the English merchants in Bordeaux. Wolsey endeavoured to reassure him, arguing that if the

[1] For a discussion of the politics following Charles's election as Holy Roman Emperor in 1519, see R. J. Knecht, *Francis I*, 105–8.
[2] *Cal. Span.*, 2, 365; *L and P* , 3, ii, 760.

English ships did not appear as usual, the likelihood of suspicion would be much greater. Their correspondence became quite acrimonious before the King was eventually persuaded – or again lost interest. At that time, and for some months thereafter, no warlike preparations would have been visible. The majority of the King's ships, 22 in number, were docked or anchored along the Thames from 8 October to 23 March. Routine winter patrols were maintained. On 3 November Richard Pace reported to Wolsey that both John Hopton and Robert Brigandyne had been forced to bring their ships into harbour by bad weather, and that Brigandyne's – the *Katherine Fortileza* – had been badly damaged.[1] It was not until April that new orders were issued to the fleet, and that active preparations commenced; which was no way in which to seize the initiative for an aggressive stroke.

The main reason for this delay was Wolsey's search for a diplomatic solution. Throughout the winter of 1521–2 he continued to stall on the Emperor's demands for action, and to call upon both sides to return to the conference table. John Stuart, Duke of Albany, the heir presumptive to the Scottish throne, had returned to Scotland out of France, and a resurgence of French influence in the northern kingdom threatened England with a war on two fronts. By the spring English policy was completely ambiguous. The fleet was mobilized, commissions were sent out to assess the number of men available, and preparations were made for large-scale taxation.[2] It was not clear whether France was the enemy, or Scotland, or both, and Wolsey continued to issue his appeals to Francis to negotiate. However, at the end of May this elaborate charade was brought to an end by a personal visit from the Emperor, who landed at Dover on 28 May, and stayed until 6 July. If Wolsey still wished to dissuade his King from war, he stood no chance against Charles, who knew exactly how to play upon Henry's vanity and ambition. By the time that he left an English herald had delivered the formal declaration of war to Francis, and the Vice-Admiral, Sir William FitzWilliam, was at sea with 28 sail. Perhaps as a studied compliment, and perhaps because he recognized that England's most significant contribution to the war would come at sea, on 8 June the Emperor issued a patent from London appointing the Earl of Surrey Lord Admiral of the combined Anglo-Imperial fleet.[3] A flurry of naval activity quickly developed. By the end of April, well before FitzWilliam sailed, and

[1] *L and P*, 3, 1911, 1744.
[2] Scarisbrick, *Henry VIII*, 94–5.
[3] Laird Clowes, 458; Hall, *Chronicle*, 461.

before war was certain, ships had been appointed to keep the seas; three from Jersey to the Camber; three from the Camber to the Tweed; and an extra four between Dover and Calais. More than half of these were hired ships, rather than the King's own, and were probably small. Their purpose was not to wage war, but to cope with the detritus of piracy and maritime lawlessness which always flourished under the cover of a major conflict.[1] During May a squadron of seven ships was also sent to the Firth of Forth where they attacked and burnt (apparently without warning) as many Scottish ships as they could take. But the main fleet was that commanded initially by FitzWilliam, and no sooner had Surrey received his joint command than he went down to Southampton to take over. A French attack upon the Channel Islands was threatened, and a squadron was detached to cover them. After a few days of enforced inactivity caused by contrary winds, Surrey sailed at the end of June, announcing that he intended to scour the Channel to secure the Emperor's safe departure.

In reality his purpose was far more aggressive, and on 1 July he landed a small but well-equipped force near Morlaix, on the coast of Brittany. The town was assaulted, taken and burned; an action in which Nicholas Carew, Francis Bryan, and several of the King's other gentlemen distinguished themselves.

> And the next day with honor they tooke their shippes, and when all men were shipped and fewe or none missed. The lorde Admirall commaunded xvi or xvii shippes small and great liying in the haven to be brent . . .'[2]

From Morlaix the English fleet proceeded to Brest, destroying villages and shipping on the way, and entered the haven almost unopposed. Surrey, however, wisely decided that he lacked the strength to attack the great castle there, and withdrew after a destructive raid on the town. Before the end of July Henry called his warships home, and the Lord Admiral was warmly received at court. Apart from some skirmishing around Calais, the harrassing of Brittany, 'wherewith all the duchy . . . was sore troubled' was the only fighting to take place in 1522. In September it seemed that a major attack was about to be launched from Scotland, as a result of the Duke of Albany's activity there, and the Earl of Shrewsbury was sent to the north with a large force. It was rumoured that 80 000 Scots, backed

[1] *L and P*, 3, 2296, Orders for the fleet.
[2] Hall, 462.

by 500 French handgunners and a train of artillery were advancing on Carlisle, and the whole of the north was mobilized against them.[1] The rumour was not so much false as exaggerated. The Scottish campaign was not pursued with energy in the face of the English preparations, and Lord Dacre succeeded in negotiating a truce, much to Albany's chagrin. The chronicler Edward Hall noted that

> . . . the Scottishe king did muche for the Frenche kynges pleasure to draw the lordes of England with their powers toward that partie & to put the kyng of England to charges so that he should not invade France . . .

If that was the intention, it was wasted effort, for Henry had no intention of invading France that year; but it demonstrated the need for substantial French stiffening if the Scots were going to constitute a real second front. The memory of Flodden was fresh in the minds of the Scottish lords.

By October the fleet had retreated to its winter quarters at Portsmouth and in the Thames, leaving a squadron of eight ships to keep the narrow seas. Between the end of that month and the end of February £2 418 was spent at Portsmouth on repairing and refitting the ships, and a further 1 000 marks upon the fortifications of the harbour.[2] The whole cost of the winter preparations both naval and military, covering the same period, was £70 995 because England was bound by her treaty with the Emperor to make a major effort during the following summer.[3] That effort was, however, slow to develop. In June a substantial army was sent to the North under the command of the Earl of Surrey, which raided across the border and burned the town of Kelso, but even this provocation failed to produce a major Scottish response, and Surrey was apparently under orders to tempt the Scots into the field rather than to launch a full scale invasion. There was some fierce skirmishing, for the second successive summer, between Calais and Boulogne, and the French made a futile attempt to block the entrance to Calais harbour at Rysbank, but it looked as though a second summer was going to pass without large-scale fighting. The development which changed that situation was the quarrel between Francis I and the

[1] Ibid., 469.

[2] *L and P*, 3, 2073; estimates of expenditure, 28 February 1523; ibid., 2935, Wolsey to Sir John Daunce, 8 April 1523.

[3] PRO E36/5, f. 156; Scarisbrick, 125.

Duke of Bourbon, High Constable of France. The dispute was private rather than political in origin, but Bourbon was so incensed by the King's behaviour that he entered into secret negotiations with the Emperor and the English. By the end of July he had signed a treaty, agreeing to support them in arms, and suddenly there seemed to be the prospect of a decisive victory. The main English fleet was already prepared and mustered, and Wolsey's energetic administration produced enough transports for an expeditionary force of 10 000 men in less than a month.[1] One of the main reasons for the lack of action during the summer had been the Cardinal's continued search for a diplomatic settlement, but his enthusiasm to capitalize upon Bourbon's treason as, if anything, greater than the King's. The original objective of the army led by the Duke of Suffolk had been the capture of Boulogne, but by the middle of September Wolsey had become convinced that such an enterprise would be protracted and expensive. The campaigning season was too far advanced, and only a bolder stroke would stand any chance of forcing the French to make a favourable offer of terms before the winter.

The King's more orthodox mind needed convincing, but Wolsey's powers of persuasion were famous, and by the end of September Suffolk and his army were advancing rapidly on Paris. At the end of October they were within 50 miles of the French capital, the speed and unexpectedness of the attack having wrong-footed the French authorities at every stage. However, the momentum could not be sustained, and the supporting strikes by Charles and Bourbon fizzled out – the latter without a blow being struck. In the event Suffolk was defeated by the weather rather than by Francis. Heavy frost was followed by a sticky thaw; his Burgundian supporters deserted, and the news of Bourbon's collapse was the last straw. By Christmas Henry was consoling himself with plans for a new and victorious expedition in the spring, although the tattered remnants of Suffolk's army, stuck in the Pas de Calais, should have been a more immediate subject for concern.[2] In the north the Earl of Surrey made no similar attempt to seize the initiative. The Duke of Albany was in France, and the campaign appeared to be stalled. However, Francis needed to reactivate the Scottish front in order to take pressure off himself, and mobilized a force of about 5 000 men to accompany the Duke back to the north and inject a little much needed stiffening into his allies.

[1] S. J. Gunn, *Charles Brandon, Duke of Suffolk*, 75–7; Scarisbrick, 128.
[2] S. J. Gunn, 'The Duke of Suffolk's march on Paris in 1523', *EHR*, 101, 1986, 596–634.

> The King of Englande, hearyng that the Duke of Albany should passe into (Scotland) to make warre on his realme, thought to have him met on the seas, and therefore he prepared a flete . . . and made Admirall of that jorney Sir William FitzWilliam, and with him Sir Francis Brian, Sir Anthony Pointz, Seriant Rot, John Hopton, William Gonstone, Anthony Knivet, Thomas West & other, whiche with great diligence, laie in waite to mete with the said duke of Albany . . .[1]

Unfortunately, FitzWilliam's 'great diligence' did not extend to resisting the temptation to attack Tréport. After burning the suburbs of the town, and several ships in the harbour, the English were repulsed and FitzWilliam had some difficulty in extricating his forces without serious loss. He then returned to England, probably to revictual and to dispose of his plunder. Albany, taking advantage of the temporary absence of the English fleet, swiftly embarked his force, which had been awaiting such an opportunity, and sailed north. After coasting Wales he landed at Kirkudbright on 21 September, and the Scottish lords rallied to him. Henry's expensive naval preparations had failed in one of their chief objectives, and he was 'not a little displeased' by the news; but it was too late to do anything about it, and early in October the main fleet returned to its anchorages for the winter.[2] In the event the harm done by FitzWilliam's little diversion was less serious than it might have been, because in spite of the warm welcome which they accorded him, the Scots had no desire to follow Albany into England at such a late season of the year. Consequently his expensive French troops remained for the time being unused; but their mere presence on Scottish soil constituted a threat which kept English forces in being and affected the diplomatic thinking of the winter months.

At the beginning of 1524, as in 1522, Henry was pursuing two lines of policy simultaneously, or at least appearing to do so. On the one hand he was boasting that he would lead his army to Paris, and on the other angling cautiously for a settlement, and declaring that any renewal of hostilities would be conditional upon the Emperor moving first. This double stance may have been partly due to a difference of opinion, or at least of priority, between the King and the Cardinal, or it may have been due to a reluctance to rebuff the peace initiative coming from Pope Clement VII. During the early summer the Duke of Bourbon again became a force to be reckoned

[1] Hall, 660–1.
[2] Ibid., 665.

with, and Richard Pace, sent by Henry to evaluate his strength, urged the King strongly to support Bourbon's invasion of Provence with a fresh incursion into Picardy.[1] But at Westminster, apart from a few brief flickers of bellicosity from the King, caution prevailed. Bourbon was not the Emperor, and it was a campaign by Charles which was really looked for as the cue for English action. Meanwhile, the absence of an army royal did not altogether mean a cessation of hostilities. Both sides kept patrols at sea during the winter months, and on 19 January six French ships caught the *Katherine Galley* off Sandwich, and in spite of a strenuous resistance, took both her and a ship of Sandwich which came to her aid. At the end of February another French patrol attacked a small fishing fleet out of Rye, but were caught in their turn by the English warships, which took two of them; so the skirmishing honours were about even.[2] April and May saw raiding and counter-raiding between the garrisons of Calais and Boulogne, and in the latter month a squadron of royal ships commanded by Christopher Coo supported a sustained attack upon Boulogne with an amphibious operation which also seems to have involved a bombardment of the fortifications of the harbour.

As far as England was concerned, the summer of 1524 saw little more than 'phoney war'. There was more skirmishing in Picardy in July, and some fierce affrays on the Scottish border, involving as many as 4 000 men at a time. Edward Hall gives us a blow by blow account of these little battles, with the casualties on each side, but he mentions no sea fights during this time, and the activities of the navy are largely a matter of conjecture. It is almost certain that some of the King's ships were at sea because of the need for protection against French raids, but we do not know which, or exactly where they were. England would almost certainly have concluded a separate peace in the spring of 1525, if it had not been for the crushing defeat inflicted upon Francis by the Emperor at the battle of Pavia on 14 February. Suddenly the prospect was not that of another hard fought campaign of uncertain outcome, but of a victorious parade through a conquered country. Francis had been captured at Pavia, and his army destroyed. Within a fortnight of receiving the news, Henry was making overtures to his ally for joint action and a subsequent division of the spoils. He had also sent out commissioners to raise a new fiscal levy, optimistically entitled the Amicable

[1] Pace to Wolsey, *L and P*, 4, 442.
[2] Hall, 674.

Grant, which would enable him to take advantage of this heaven-sent opportunity. However, neither Charles nor Henry's subjects saw the matter in the same light. The Emperor knew that Wolsey had been making quiet overtures to the French before Pavia. He found the King's change of heart unconvincing, and his vaunting ambition ridiculous. The English had contributed nothing to the war effort since the end of 1523, and had no right to a share in the fruits of his victory. Moreover, he had no desire to dismember France, being satisfied with a quick peace on favourable terms. Neither he nor the King of England would be able to hold on to sizeable parts of France for any length of time. At the same time, the Amicable Grant was a fiasco. Faced with widespread defiance and near rebellion, Henry retreated, using Wolsey as a scapegoat to cover his discomfiture.[1] Unable to afford a major campaign, even in collaboration with Charles let alone on his own, he allowed negotiations to resume in June, and on 30 August Wolsey successfully concluded the treaty of the More.

During the period of this war, from 1522 to 1525, and immediately thereafter, the *Great Harry* was anchored at Northfleet when not in use, at a cost of about £40 a month for shipkeepers wages and replacement rigging.[2] Most of the remaining ships were kept at Portsmouth – 16 of them in the winter of 1523–4 – although Surrey had expressed a preference for Dartmouth as an advance base.[3] To judge from the accounts some, such as the *Mary Rose* and the *Great Galley*, must have remained in harbour throughout the winter. But others were clearly there for shorter periods, and these were the smaller vessels, such as the *Less Bark*, which were used for the patrols which we have already noticed. During the period 2 September 1524 to 16 March 1525 21 of the King's ships spent varying periods at Portsmouth, at an overall cost of £3 691.5s.[4] The patchy nature of the evidence makes it virtually impossible to trace the deployment of individual ships, but we can catch a few instructive glimpses. On 24 May 1523 FitzWilliam reported to the King that his ships were becalmed at Portsmouth, although in other respects ready for action. He had sent two barks (unnamed) to ferry ordnance to Berwick, and was expecting the return of the *John Baptist* and the *Mary George* from a reconnaissance mission to the Seine

[1] *L and P*, 4, 1243, 1260, 1266; Scarisbrick, 139.
[2] PRO E315/317, f. 84.
[3] Surrey to Henry VIII, 30 June 1522; *L & P*, 3, 2355.
[4] PRO E315/317, f. 45v.

estuary.[1] He had also received the King's instructions to send a ship of 400 tons to support Sir Anthony Poyntz 'in the west seas', although there is no mention of which ship he was planning to send. Poyntz must have been cruising in the Irish Sea most of that summer for the purpose of disrupting communications between France and Scotland, because on 20 August a further order was issued to dispatch two ships, one of 400 tons and the other of 200. These were to support his attempt to intercept the Duke of Albany, which, as we have seen, was unsuccessful. By the end of August FitzWilliam was anxious to recall the fleet to Portsmouth, pleading a lack of victuals, but Wolsey insisted that it remain at sea, and provided supplies for two further weeks.[2] The result, as we have seen, was the attack upon Tréport. Thereafter, when the main fleet retired for the winter, an unspecified number of ships under the command of John Hopton took over the 'keeping of the seas'.

Thomas Jermyn's accounts for the keeping of ships on the Thames also provide information about use, some direct, some indirect. Over a period of five years, commencing on 17 March 1525, 15 ships, mostly small, were in and out of the Woolwich and Deptford anchorages.[3] Individual vessels might stay for as long as six months, but the average duration was much shorter. Three ships, the *Minion*, the *Sweepstake* and the *Swallow* were 'based' on the Thames during these years. In May 1527 Jermyn recorded that they had been repaired there, and went on to note '. . . all such stuff bought and delyvred by me Thomas Jermyn to the Mynyon the Sweepstake and the Swallow which did kepe the narrow sees at all tymes when nede required.' They were not the only ships used for such a purpose, but were clearly the ones most regularly called on. Similar information can be gleaned from other accounts. For example in March 1525 William Gonson was provided with wages and victuals for 150 mariners, gunners and soldiers aboard the *New Bark* and the *Barbara Vincent* of London, for service unspecified; and Christopher Coo was similarly furnished for the *Margaret Bonaventure* and the *Margaret Prowe*. Probably these were voyages in pursuit of pirates, and it is interesting to note that three out of the four vessels named must have been specifically hired for the purpose. Similarly in November 1526 when an abstract of charges for the King's ships was drawn up, it was noted that the *Minion* and the *Mary Guildford* were 'not yet come from Bordeaux', where they had gone on a trading

[1] *L and P*, 3, 3046.
[2] Wolsey to Henry, 20 August 1523; *L and P*, 3, 3256.
[3] PRO E315/317, ff.41–45.

venture.[1] Whether this was on the King's behalf or on lease to private merchants is not clear. The same ships had been to Bordeaux in 1524, and two others were to go in 1533. Large ships presented something of a problem in peacetime, because they were not suitable for routine patrolling, and were expensive to maintain. A survey conducted in 1526 classified 21 of the King's ships under three headings: the *Gabriel Royal*, the *Katherine Fortileza*, the *John Baptist*, the *Barbara*, the *Mary Gloria*, the *Mary John*, the *Mary George* and the *New Bark* were described as 'fit for merchant voyages to Spain, the Levant, Bordeaux, Iceland and Flanders, if they might be set on work; and if not they will be in a few years spoiled for lack of caulking and trimming.'[2] The *Great Galley*, the *Mary Rose*, the *Peter Pomegranate*, the *Great Bark* and the *Less Bark*, on the other hand were classified as 'good for the wars, or else for the King's pleasure', although their overlops, summer castles and decks were in urgent need of attention. The *Sovereign*, the *Great Nicholas*, the *Mary James* and the *Mary of Hampton* were unserviceable, and needed 'new making' before they could be used again.

Scotland had not been included in the treaty of the More, but a three-year truce was signed in January 1526, and the following summer was the first since 1521 which saw no warlike preparations. However, as relations with France improved, the Emperor became increasingly estranged. Wolsey played a large part in creating the anti-Imperial League of Cognac in May 1526, aimed at forcing Charles out of Italy; and the Emperor finally abandoned all pretence that he would wait for Henry's ten-year-old daughter, marrying Isabella of Portugal in the spring of the same year. Henry was annoyed, if not particularly surprised, by this rebuff, and the Emperor was extremely dilatory about repairing his fences. So although England did not actually join the League of Cognac, she was definitely on the French side of the great diplomatic divide by the beginning of 1527. As that year advanced, the situation became increasingly complex. At the end of April a new Anglo-French treaty was signed, whereby the two countries agreed to make a joint approach to the Emperor for peace – a peace which would secure the release of Francis' sons, still held in Spain. England's role was officially that of mediator, but the clear implication was that if Charles were to refuse reasonable terms, then England would enter the war on the French side. At almost exactly the same time a

[1] *L and P*, 4, i, 1853; 4, ii, 3634.
[2] BL Royal MS 14 BXXII D; *L and P*, 4, ii, 2635.

mutinous Imperial army sacked Rome, and confined the Pope to the Castel San Angelo. This not only took him out of the League of Cognac, it left the church temporarily leaderless. Moreover Henry had very recently, it is not known exactly when, resolved to end his eighteen-year-old marriage to the Emperor's aunt, Catherine of Aragon.[1] Fortunately the King's Great Matter lies outside the scope of this study, but it was being considered by a secret tribunal in England at the same moment that the Pope was virtually Charles's prisoner, and Wolsey was making ambitious plans to set up an alternative Curia in Avignon. By the end of the year these plans had collapsed, and Henry and Wolsey were beginning to work at cross purposes. Wolsey above all wanted peace between the Emperor and the League of Cognac, but the King's main purpose was now best served by keeping the war alive, and using whatever leverage the military situation might offer to prise a favourable response out of Rome. The King's will inevitably prevailed. Wolsey's Anglo-French peace initiative having been rebuffed in July 1527, on 21 January 1528 England formally declared war on the Emperor.

The intention, however, was not to conduct any active operations. There was no mobilization of English forces, because Henry's war effort was to be confined to financial and moral support. This was quickly emphasized by the conclusion of a commercial truce with Margaret of Savoy, the Regent of the Netherlands, and by the issuing of highly selective orders to the English fleet. On 13 March William Gonson, who was commanding the squadron then operating in the narrow seas, reported to Wolsey that he was using his best endeavours to make sure that Imperial ships sailing Eastward were 'wafted out of the Frenchmen's danger'.[2] On the other hand his instructions also required him to keep the peace between French and Imperial warships, both strange positions for one who was theoretically a belligerent on the French side. Only if fighting actually broke out was he to 'take the Frenchmen's part' with all his power. But if the English were held to an equivocal position by their agreement with Margaret, this did not cover the Spaniards, and Gonson's report makes clear that he was expected to 'go upon' any Spaniard that he could reasonably expect to overpower.[3] Not surprisingly,

[1] There are many discussions of the circumstances surrounding this decision. The most recent, and one of the best, is contained in the introduction to *The Divorce Tracts of Henry VIII*, ed. Edward Surtz and Virginia Murphy, i–xxxvi.

[2] *L and P*, 4, ii, 4066.

[3] Ibid. 'That if they see any ships of Spain, or men of war sailed by Spaniards . . . they shall do their best to take them'.

he asked Wolsey for some clarification. Between April and June Gonson remained at sea, and two further reports, written on board the *Minion* 'betwixt Dover and Calais' chronicle some of his actual activities. At the beginning of April he sent two ships to Harfleur to escort four French vessels to the Thames, and remained at sea throughout the month 'wandering up and down the Narrow Seas' with the *Minion* and another ship.[1] Both the French and the Dutch were at sea seeking prizes, and about the 20th of April he retrieved two French ships which had taken refuge in Rye, much to the chagrin of the pursuing Dutchmen. A few days later he was escorting grain ships from Boulogne to London, and seems to have continued this activity throughout the two succeeding months, in spite of periodic shortages of victuals. On 23 June he was instructed to remain at sea, but for how much longer is not clear. Gonson was not involved in any fighting, and as far as we know did not take any Spaniards, but the English merchants in Antwerp enjoyed an exceptionally good year, and the delicate balancing act of policing the Channel during a phoney war seems to have been carried out with considerable success.

Over the next eighteen months Henry was almost totally preoccupied with the search for a solution to his matrimonial problem. From his point of view war and diplomacy alike were primarily methods of bringing pressure to bear upon the Emperor to relax his formidable grip. We can infer from the rigging and victualling accounts that his ships were at sea – irregularly and in small numbers – but we can only guess what they did.[2] Meanwhile Wolsey's subtle foreign policy, designed to smooth the King's path by reviving the prestige of 1518, fell apart in the early months of 1529. A settlement between France and the Empire was indeed in prospect, but it owed nothing to English initiative or pressure. Bilateral talks at Cambrai made steady progress, and in July Wolsey suddenly awoke to the fact that, while he had been bogged down in the divorce proceedings at Blackfriars, a peace had been negotiated which took no account of England's interests. Not only would England not be a party, and thus face diplomatic isolation, but Henry would also lose what little leverage the French alliance had given him against Charles. The Emperor and the Pope were about to be formally reconciled. Wolsey managed to scramble in at the very end of the 'Ladies peace', which was signed on 5 August, and thus avoid complete ignominy, but he

[1] Gonson to Wolsey, 23 April 1528. *L and P*, 4, ii, 4193.
[2] PRO E315/317, ff. 58–94.

could not avoid losing the bargaining counters which the war had given him. Coming on top of the total failure of the Blackfriars court, and Clement's renewed intransigence over the 'Great Matter', this fiasco spelt the end of Wolsey's political career. His fall left a significant gap – not in power, because the King had always been the master in his own house – but in administrative control. The instructions which Wolsey had still been sending to Gonson in the summer of 1528 disappeared, and no equivalent can be found until Cromwell had taken up the threads at the end of 1532. In the interval, the accounts continue to provide scraps of information. The master of the King's Barge, for example, puts in an appearance, conveying the French ambassador from Greenwich to London in a boat with ten oars; and in August 1530 the *Minion* and the *Mary Guildford* were despatched to Bordeaux for the time-honoured purpose of fetching wine for the royal household.[1] Spert and Gonson were active 'rigging and trimming' both at Portsmouth and in the Thames, but the next specific reference to a naval operation came in August 1532, when Gonson reported to Cromwell that he had conveyed the King's orders to his ships of war that they were to remain at sea, and had provided the necessary money and victuals.

Although there was no war, there was probably more to this activity than an occasional hunt for pirates. As he continued to pursue his hopeless quest for an annulment, Henry was beginning to contemplate a more radical solution, and was again looking to France to provide him with diplomatic support to outface papal and Imperial hostility. At the beginning of September he created Anne Boleyn Marquess of Pembroke in order to prepare her for an encounter with the French court, and in the middle of October they crossed together to Calais on board the *Swallow* – a journey for which William Gonson was paid £240.[2] On 20 October Francis and Henry met halfway between Calais and Boulogne, and there then followed ten days of expensive entertainment and revelry, reminiscent of the Field of Cloth of Gold. When the celebrations were over, Henry and Anne remained stormbound in Calais for a further fourteen days, while the ships of those who had had the temerity to set out were scattered along the Flemish coast. It may have been while they were lodged together in the old Exchequer building, that Anne finally yielded to Henry's importunities; convinced, perhaps, that Francis's ecclesiastical muscle would succeed where Henry's

[1] Each rower in the royal barge was paid 8d. a day, and the master 16d., *L and P*, 5, 310; accounts of the Treasurer of the Chamber, *L and P*, 5, 321.

[2] E. W. Ives, *Anne Boleyn*, 208–9; *L and P*, 5, 1600.

had failed. By January 1533 Anne knew that she was pregnant. Henry secretly married her, and the die was cast. A summer of high drama and inevitable political tension followed, but it took some time to convince either the Pope or the Emperor that the King of England was really serious in his pretensions. In July Clement ordered Henry to return to Catherine under pain of excommunication, giving him until September to comply. On 14 August Cromwell reminded himself to brief the King on the state of the navy, but the September deadline passed uneventfully, thanks largely to the intercession of Francis, who persuaded the pope to postpone sentence for a further two months. It would not have been characteristic of Charles to attack England in support of a papal excommunication, even if it had been in his interest to do so, and in November 1533 it was not in his interest. On 24 November Chapuys reported that Henry had ordered a mobilization of the fleet, 'This shows they are beginning to be afraid . . .' he added hopefully.[1] However, there was nothing much to be afraid of. The papal sentence was indeed issued, but not promulgated, and Catherine was bitterly convinced that her nephew was doing nothing to help her cause.

Chapuys's stories about the unpreparedness of the English navy in the winter of 1533–4 need to be treated with caution, as we have seen, but he may well have been right in reporting the Duke of Norfolk's opinion that Henry's navy would, in any case be no match for that of the Emperor, and that it was high time to be fortifying the coasts.[2] The ambassador tried assiduously to spread alarm and despondency in London in the hope of frightening Henry's courtiers into a more Imperialist frame of mind, and he had some success; but neither the King nor Cromwell was moved, and the crises of these years were almost entirely domestic. In April 1534 the fleet was again surveyed, and routine repairs and maintenance carried out, but there was no mobilization and only routine patrols seem to have been sent out during the summer. Nominally there was still war with Scotland, but the last mention of any action at sea was a report in February 1533 that four ships had been sent north. A truce was concluded in the following May, and converted into a peace treaty in May 1534.

A low level of activity was maintained over the two following

[1] Chapuys to the Emperor, 24 November 1533, *L and P*, 6, 1460. Chapuys's information (as distinct from his opinion) is confirmed by a Council memorandum of a few days later, *L and P*, 6, 1487.

[2] Chapuys to the Emperor, 9 December 1533, *L and P*, 6, 1510.

years. In May 1535 there were rumours of 'certain rovers' in the Channel. Sir William FitzWilliam investigated, and reported a false alarm. There was a further heightening of political tension following the execution of More and Fisher during the summer, and at the end of September Henry visited Portsmouth, where he ordered the *Great Harry* and certain other ships to be equipped, but this was simply a precaution, and there is no evidence that they ever left harbour.[1] Two royal ships went to Bordeaux in September, and the *Minion* was sent to Hamburg for a supply of pitch and tar, but it was not until November 1536 that there was any action of a military nature. The death of Catherine in January, and the fall of Anne Boleyn in April had aroused the hopes of Cromwell's enemies at court, but he had outmanoeuvred them and his grip on power had remained unshaken. Disillusionment with this outcome, combined with popular discontent over taxation and the dissolution of the smaller monasteries produced rebellion, first in Lincolnshire and then, by the end of October, in Yorkshire and other parts of northern England. On 6 November a report reached Cromwell that Robert Aske and Robert Constable, two of the leaders of this Pilgrimage of Grace, as they called it, were fitting out a ship at Hull. William Gonson was sent to Grimsby to cover any move which they might make. Gonson certainly took some of the King's ordnance with him to Grimsby, but whether he used a royal ship or hired one locally is not clear. There were certainly ships available, both at Portsmouth and in the Thames, but in the event the Pilgrims never put to sea, and received no outside support. At least one royal ship later visited Hull, and landed guns there for the defence of the town, but there was no fighting at sea.

In August 1536 Henry had solemnly announced his neutrality in the continuing struggle between France and the Empire, but the removal of both Catherine and Anne, followed by the partial rehabilitation of Mary in July had improved relations with Charles, and English policy began to return towards a more normal orientation. On 16 February 1537 Henry Huttoft reported to Cromwell that French pirates were again active around the Isle of Wight, and suggested that some of the King's ships 'now ready to set forth' should keep the sea between the Needles and St Helen's point, that is, in the Solent and Spithead.[2] By 24 February Sir John Dudley

[1] Sir William FitzWilliam to Cromwell, 25 May 1535, *L and P*, 8, 760; Richard Towris to Lord Lisle, 28 September 1535, *L and P*, 9, 467.

[2] On the changes in Henry's policy following Anne's fall, see Scarisbrick, 248–53; *L and P*, 12, i, 438.

and Thomas Seymour had set out with four ships. At the same time FitzWilliam warned that Flemish pirates were operating off the Camber, and the *Minion*, which was already on patrol, was reinforced with two other ships, one of them commanded by Baldwin Willoughby. Their instructions were to escort any threatened English shipping safely into the Thames estuary. In March Dudley was formally commissioned as Vice-Admiral to command the four ships which he already had at sea, and he and Seymour sent back periodic reports of their progress, but they seem to have enjoyed little success, and the complaints continued.[1] In June William Gonson wrote to Lord Lisle at Calais to inform him that an English crayer had actually been taken by a French man-of-war, and the matter had been taken up with the ambassador. Warned of Dudley's presence in the Solent, the pirates, both French and Flemish, seem to have shifted their attention to the straits of Dover. At the end of March there were rumours in France that Henry had armed a great many ships for the purpose of intercepting James V of Scotland as he returned home with his new French bride, but there seems to have been no foundation for such reports, beyond the patrols of Dudley and FitzWilliam. It was not until April that a full mobilization of the fleet was ordered, as a part of a general scheme of defence preparations.[2] As the reality of the English schism was understood all over Europe, Henry began to fear the prospect of diplomatic isolation. On 10 July John Husee reported to Lord Lisle that the *Great Bark*, the *Minion*, the *Jenet* and the *Sweepstake* were about to sail, but the *Minion* and the *Sweepstake* had been at sea before, and this probably represents a redeployment rather than a significant reinforcement. Dudley's instructions were renewed on 31 July to cover the whole coast from the Downs to the Severn. This time his second in command was Sir Gawain Carew, and on 18 August their report to Cromwell was full of frustration. Carew's ship was a leaky tub, and they had accomplished nothing.[3] A few days later Henry Huttoft in Southampton complained bitterly that the King's ships were still in the Solent, and that the depredations of the pirates continued unabated. However, just when it had been decided to withdraw the patrol, and Dudley was expected back in the Thames, there was a late flurry of activity. Two Breton ships, lurking off St Helens, were taken on 22 August, and a few days later there was a sharp engagement in Mount's Bay, which resulted in the capture of

[1] Dudley's orders, *L and P*, 12, i, 601, dated 7 March; Ibid., 602, 8 March.
[2] Council memorandum, *L and P*, 12, i, 815–6.
[3] Dudley's second instructions, *L and P*, 12, ii, 393; Ibid., 535.

at least one French ship.[1] So the English Council got some return for its expenditure, and could truthfully claim that it had made a genuine effort to protect the interests of its merchants.

The year 1538 was only a few days old when Cromwell received a petition from certain merchants of St Malo for the return of one of the ships taken by Dudley. The distinction between a legitimate trader and a pirate might be no more than one of occasion, and the records of the High Court of Admiralty are full of disputes over the lawfulness of particular captures, but the speed with which this one reached the highest level suggests either a powerful sense of outrage or the desire to create a diplomatic incident.[2] Cromwell was well aware of the difficulty of walking the tightrope between two little zeal and too much when it came to dealing with piracy. In the same month as the French petition he sent a special envoy, one John Hutton, to placate the Regent of the Low Countries, who thought him to have erred on the side of too much zeal. He was instructed to explain to Mary that the King's armed ships were patrolling in response to the complaints of his own subjects, and with no aggressive intent towards her. As evidence of Henry's goodwill, Hutton was to hand over a captured Flemish pirate known as 'the Admiral of Sluys', to be dealt with by the Emperor's jurisdiction.[3] The year ahead was to be an ominous one for England, not because of piracy (although that continued unabated) but because of the steady improvement in relations between Charles and Francis. Henry, a widower since the death of Jane Seymour in the previous year, did his best to keep them apart by negotiating simultaneously for a marriage treaty with each side, but failed ignominiously. On 17 December 1538 Paul III ordered the execution of the Bull of excommunication which had been drawn up afresh in 1535, and on 12 January 1539 the Emperor and the King of France signed the treaty of Toledo, each agreeing to make no new alliance with England without the other's consent.

In the circumstances two courses of action were prudent, a search for new allies and the preparation of military defences. The former, a scrappy affair which resulted in the unsatisfactory Cleves marriage in January 1540, lies outside the scope of this study, but the latter caused the highest level of naval activity since the last war had ended

[1] Dudley, Carew and William Nicholson to the King, 22 August 1537, *L and P*, 12, ii, 563; Sir William Cadogan to Cromwell, 28 August 1537, ibid., 595. On 9 September Castillon, the French ambassador, reported that all four had been taken, ibid., 670.
[2] Jehan Bertre to Cromwell, January 1538, *L and P*, 13, i, 186; Books of Acts of the High Court of Admiralty, PRO HCA3, nos. 1–12.
[3] *L and P*, 13, i, 191.

in 1525. As early as 26 January the French ambassador reported that Henry was arming and equipping his fleet, buying fresh sailcloth and ordnance; a report which is substantiated by the survey taken at the same time, which estimated the readiness of different ships from 20 days to 3 months.[1] On 2 April Marillac reported that the ships in the Thames were ready to leave for Portsmouth, and they had gone by the 15th. On the 9th the Earl of Southampton wrote to Cromwell asking for a fresh commission, declaring that he expected to have his whole force mustered within 15 days. As we have seen, French estimates of the number of ships involved ranged from 80 to 150, at a time when the King had about 40 of his own. On 15 April Marillac thought that 60–70 of the assembled fleet exceeded 200 tons, and that 90 were fully armed, the rest being victuallers and support ships.[2] However, on the 25th Thomas Cromwell received a report to the effect that only 20 ships had so far reached Portsmouth. Some were still at Bristol, and the remainder presumably assembling at other ports. The next month saw the invasion scare peak and begin to recede. Beacons were erected on the southern and eastern coasts, and round-the-clock watches maintained, while 'five or six ships' did 'nothing but circle the kingdom' to provide instant warning of the approach of any foreign navy.[3] In spite of Marillac's estimates, it seems clear that the whole fleet was never assembled in one place. On 10 June, while the full alert was still on, there were 37 ships in pay at Portsmouth, of which four of five were the King's own, two Venetian, and the remainder belonging to various English ports. An unknown number were still in the Thames when the merchantmen began to be discharged on 22 June. The only known victims of this mobilization were six Portuguese pirates who, according to Marillac were caught and executed within fifteen days of being complained of – a noteworthy achievement which showed what could be done when the seas were crowded with armed warships. They were also among the first recorded victims of the statute of 1536 which had removed piracy from the jurisdiction of the Admiralty court, and placed it under the common law.[4]

[1] Castillon to Montmorency, Constable of France, *L and P*, 14, i, 144; The muster and state of the King's ships in the Thames, ibid., 143.

[2] *L and P*, 14, i, 670; ibid., 726; ibid., 770.

[3] Richard Abbes to Cromwell, 25 April 1539, *L and P*, 14, i, 855. Marillac to Montmorency, 15 April 1539, ibid., 770.

[4] Marillac to Francis I, 20 May 1539, *L and P*, 14, i, 988; Statute 28 Henry VIII, cap.15. The maritime law was basically Roman law, which required either confession or first hand testimony to secure conviction. Under the common law it was only necessary to convince a jury.

After the end of June naval activity returned to what seems to have been its normal summer level. Four royal ships were at sea during July, and in mid-August seven or eight were still on stand-by at Portsmouth. In mid-September an unknown but probably small number were patrolling between Portsmouth and the Downs, and there were rumours of French galleys at sea. On 19 September John Winter was victualled and paid for one ship during two months, and Cromwell was enquiring whether Edward Waters in the *Mary Guildford* was also required. At the same time two unnamed barks of 120 and 90 tons 'well manned and ordnanced' were sent out against pirates.[1] By the end of the month Gonson's thoughts were beginning to turn to the lighter task of escorting the King's new bride. Four ships, including the *Great Harry*, were brought round from Portsmouth to the Thames, and estimates were drawn up for flags, pennants and streamers, which it was expected would take at least 80 days to produce. According to Edward Hall Anne of Cleves was escorted by 50 sail when she left Calais on 27 December, and the King's ships *Lion* and *Sweepstake* fired off 150 pieces of ordnance by way of salute.[2] Gonson's end of the celebrations cost almost £2 000. The fear of war had not entirely disappeared, but there was no repetition at the beginning of 1540 of the hectic preparations of the previous year. Continuing concern was most clearly to be seen in the programme of coastal defence works, which had been initiated in the spring of 1539, and continued throughout that year and for the remainder of the reign. Portsmouth had been fortified since the mid-fifteenth century, and major works had been undertaken there in 1494 and again in 1522. In 1539 castles were commenced on Calshot spit and at East and West Cowes, while another was planned for Hurst point, and built two years later.[3] By 1552 the works at Portsmouth and Southampton Water had cost £53 117, and the result was one of the most heavily defended sea approaches in Europe. According to H. M. Colvin, 'Henry VII had initiated and Henry VIII had confirmed an entirely new concept in English warfare, the defensible naval base on which the seapower of subsequent centuries was in large part to rest.'[4]

The original defence plan drawn up by the commissioners in 1539

[1] *L and P*, 14, ii, 194.

[2] Hall, 832–3; Gonson to Cromwell, 23 September 1539, *L and P*, 14, ii, 213; *L and P*, 15, xiv; ibid., 642.

[3] B. M. Morley, *Henry VIII and the Development of Coastal Defence*, passim; H. M. Colvin, *The History of the King's Works*, 4, 370–1.

[4] Colvin, 410.

represented the first concerted attempt at coastal fortification, but it soon turned out to be too expensive and ambitious. Apart from the artillery forts along Southampton Water, the main works to be completed in Henry's lifetime were Sandgate castle, guarding the entrance to Dover harbour; similar forts at Walmer and Deal; and Pendenis and St Maws at the mouth of the Fal. All were built to a similar design, with immensely thick walls and semicircular artillery bastions. Only Sandown, on the Isle of Wight, commenced in 1545, showed signs of the new Italian influence in design which was to make all these immensely expensive works out of date within ten years. Nevertheless, to be out of date was not to be useless, and it was the strength and security of Portsmouth which made it the most favoured base for war operations for the remainder of the century. Small forts at Gravesend, Milton and Tilbury improved the security of the Thames estuary, but even after the building of a more substantial bulwark at Upnor in 1559, the anchorages were still more open and vulnerable to attack than those of Portsmouth. Elizabeth did not waste money, and she continued the building programme there throughout her reign.

Fears of attack from the continent may have subsided in the early months of 1540 – so much so that Henry felt able to repudiate his German bride and destroy his invaluable chief minister – but there were still enough suspicions and uncertainties to provide work for fighting ships. In May Marillac reported that the English believed James V of Scotland was about to intervene in Ireland, 'to make himself lord of those who refuse this king', and had sent 20 or 30 armed ships to the north-west to forestall any such attempt.[1] The French ambassador reported what he had been told, and this military gesture may have been conceived by Henry as part of a new initiative in the north. In February he had sent Sir Ralph Sadler to Scotland to try and persuade James into following his lead against the papacy. It was not a subtle move, and would have been typical of Henry to inject a hint of military threat. If such was the case, it produced no effect, but the King seems to have believed that he was making progress. In 1541 Sadler was able to take advantage of the absence of Cardinal Beaton in France to persuade James into agreeing to a meeting with Henry at York. The latter made a significant progress north – further north than he had ever been in his life – and reached York on 18 September, but James did not come. On the 29th he set out again for the south with a strong and dangerous sense

[1] Marillac to Montmorency, 21 May 1540, *L and P*, 15, 697.

of having been made a fool of. This futile excursion made for a quiet summer in other ways. There had been some talk of sending the King's ships to sea before Easter, but apart from the usual two or three escorts for the Calais wool fleet, they went back to their anchorages. Probably Marillac, who was always a bit jumpy about the English navy, had misinterpreted a routine exercise. The English set great store by Calais, he wrote, and believed that the command of the seas was necessary to retain it, so their fleet was a matter of great concern and attention.[1] At some point during the autumn two of the King's ships were sent from the Thames to Hull and back, probably inspired by reports of Scottish pirates.

In July 1542 the steadily deteriorating relations between Francis and Charles again erupted into war, and the treaty of Toledo was finally buried. However, instead of heaving a sigh of relief, Henry immediately began angling for an Imperial alliance. This may have been connected with his desire to put pressure on Scotland after his rebuff of the previous year. Relations were certainly strained during the summer, with frequent border raids and an exchange of recriminatory letters, but Henry was clearly the aggressor, and James was guilty of nothing more than a pointed refusal to follow his uncle's lead against the Pope. In August 1542 Sir Robert Bowes raided Teviotdale, and was defeated at Haddon Rig. Provoked further by this failure, Henry then sent the Duke of Norfolk on a brief but immensely destructive foray through the lowlands. At last, in November, James was sufficiently angered to launch a major counter-attack, which may have been what Henry was angling for. On the 23rd the Scottish army was decisively beaten at Solway Moss, and a number of important prisoners were taken. James's death three weeks later was probably unconnected with this defeat except in romantic fiction, but two such blows in rapid succession left Scotland extremely vulnerable to the aggressive intentions of her southern neighbour. Important as they were, these hostilities did not constitute a war, and left few marks on the records of the navy. On 4 April Marillac dutifully reported the annual launching of the King's ships, merely noting that it was a little later than usual.[2] He speculated upon the possibility of an 'enterprise', but a month later the preparations (if such they were) had been discontinued. However

[1] Marillac to Francis I, 27 April 1541, *L and P*, 16, 762.

[2] In military terms, Solway Moss was not much of a battle, but the English made the most of it for propaganda purposes. 'This was only the handstroke of God, for the Cardinal of Scotlande promised them heaven for destruccion of England.' Hall, 856. Marillac to Francis I, *L and P*, 17, 235.

on 10 June something more purposeful seems to have been in the air. The *Great Harry* and eight or ten other ships were being armed and equipped. Because there was no general mobilization Marillac suspected a bluff, but it may well have been that they were intended to contribute to the intimidation which was soon to be applied to Scotland.[1] General mobilization, either of troops or ships, would have meant a continental war, and for that Henry was not yet ready. He seems to have hoped, for reasons which lay within his personality rather than in the political situation, to launch himself against France in alliance with the Emperor in the summer of 1543, but the treaty was not eventually signed until February, and Scottish affairs were still demanding a good deal of attention.

The Earl of Arran, Governor of Scotland for the infant Mary, led Henry to believe that he would be co-operative. He arrested Cardinal Beaton and made hostile noises about the Pope. Henry, meanwhile, extracted from the prisoners taken at Solway Moss an oath to work for a marriage settlement between Prince Edward and their young Queen, and sent them home. But neither Arran nor the 'assured' Scots were reliable. Beaton was released and a pro-French party rapidly gathered round him. A Papal legate was despatched to Scotland, and evaded the naval patrols which were by this time a normal and unremarked feature of English policy, in spite of Henry's explicit instructions to intercept. Scotland was taken into Papal protection, which clearly in the circumstances meant French. For the time being Arran continued to pretend that he was the leader of a pro-English party, and in July signed the treaty of Greenwich, committing his country to the desired marriage alliance. The treaty contained no adequate safeguards for fulfilment, and in truth was not worth the ink expended upon it, but it deceived Henry into thinking that he could now move against France without the risk of Scotland becoming a second front.

As usual when serious fighting was in prospect, naval preparations began early in 1543. Lisle and Bryan were appointed in early January, and Sir William Woodhouse as Admiral of the North Sea in February.[2] Gonson and Osborn were instructed to take up a ship called the *Mary Harford* for convoy duties, and four Newcastle ships, the *Trinity, Anthony, John Evangelist* and *Mary Grace* were appointed to keep the North seas between the Humber and the Tweed.[3] Although this was only February, their instructions were

[1] Marillac to Francis I, *L and P*, 17, 392.
[2] *L and P*, 18, 19; ibid., 225.
[3] Commission to Gonson and Osborn, 4 January 1543, *L and P*, 18, 6; ibid., 225.

to take all Scots and Frenchmen as good prizes, but not to touch Flemings, Spaniards or Portuguese. The King's new treaty with the Emperor was supposed to be secret, but its effects were already becoming visible. By the middle of March a second squadron was stationed in the Downs, commanded by Andrew Flammock, and later a third in the western approaches, under John Arundel and Nicholas Poyntz.[1] Their instructions were presumably similar to those given to Woodhouse, and proved to be easier to issue than to observe. At the end of April one Richard Brooke, a captain under Flammock, was specifically reprimanded by the Council for 'staying both friends and foes'. In June, when Henry briefly thought that things were going his way in Scotland, his instructions to Sir Rice Mansell as Vice-Admiral of the West were to take French ships, but not Scots.[2] Considering that England was still technically at peace with all its neighbours, the situation must have been highly confusing to those actually at sea. 'Neither perfite peace nor open warre . . . but Shippes were taken on bothe sides and Mercauntes robbed' as Edward Hall observed. As far as France was concerned, clarification was not far away. On 20 June Lord Lisle reported that the King had been to Harwich to view the havens, and that war was imminent. The very next day Henry delivered an ultimatum to the French ambassador, and when that expired three weeks later, war was declared. This was not formally proclaimed in England until 2 August, '. . . and lycence geven to the Kynges subiectes to seaze upon the Frenchemen and their goodes as in lyke cases before had ben accustomed.'[3] At the beginning of July Rice Mansell with six ships encountered eleven Frenchmen in the Narrow Sea, and had a 'great fight', as Lisle reported, but the modest outcome was the capture of a French hoy by the *Less Galley*. On 10 July Chapuys wrote that fresh ships would be ready in two to three days, and again on the 27th that Henry was stepping up his naval preparations.[4] No great enterprise was planned, so this was probably in connection with the despatch of Sir John Wallop and 5 000 men to Calais for the defence of the Netherlands. According to Chapuys he had 'bought' six or seven ships to reinforce 12 of his own. As there seems to be no record of such a purchase until the following year, these had probably been hired, or 'taken up' in the usual way.

[1] Council instructions to William Gonson, 14 March 1543, *L and P*, 18, 276.
[2] *L and P*, 18, 712.
[3] Hall, 860. P. L. Hughes and J. F. Larkin, *Tudor Royal Proclamations*, I, 320–21.
[4] Lisle to Henry VIII, 11 July 1543, *L and P*, 18, 867; Henry VIII to Sir Ralph Sadler, 22 July, ibid., 935; Chapuys to Charles V, 27 July 1543, *L and P*, 18, 954.

By this time things in Scotland were going irretrievably wrong. Beaton's communications with France were being stepped up, and on 13 August Sadler reported that a squadron of French ships was lying off Holy Island.[1] By the end of August the English party had almost collapsed, and Henry decided to send an army to support the Earl of Arran. Before any move could be made, Arran himself had defected to the French side, and a furious Henry declared that he considered himself to be at open war with Scotland, because the treaty had been 'annihilated' by their failure to observe it. It may have been for this reason that a somewhat mystified Chapuys reported on 6 September that fresh ships were still being equipped, as though the King were intending some enterprise at sea of which he, the ambassador, was unaware.[2] If such was the intention, it was not carried out, and although the King continued to talk of using force, he actually confined himself to endeavouring to fabricate a new English party out of the affinity of the Earl of Angus. This did not work either, and on 11 December the Scottish parliament repudiated all treaties with England. Four days later it formally renewed its links with France, and after a year of blundering and misconceived diplomacy, Henry had lost all the gains of Solway Moss. So far the navy had been only partially deployed; a higher level of activity than during a normal year of peace, but nothing like a full mobilization. Sterner times lay ahead. On 25 August it had been proclaimed that no seamen or mariners should be conscripted for shore service, but that they should be left '. . . to serve us when war shall otherwise dispose them at our pleasure . . .'[3] A major reorganization of naval administration was taken in hand, and a massive ship-building programme was launched. 1544 was intended to be a year of major action. Henry was committed to launching 42 000 men against France by 20 June, and the naval preparations would have to be on the same scale.

The King's first thought for dealing with the ancillary problem of Scotland was to launch a series of punitive raids across the border, but it was pointed out to him that the principle sufferers from such a tactic would be his few remaining allies. Also, he had attracted the useful allegiance of the young Earl of Lennox, Matthew Stewart, and hoped that the combination of Lennox and Angus would prove strong enough to wrest control from Arran and Beaton. As late as March he was still pursuing this strategy, but then suddenly became

[1] Sadler to Suffolk, 13 August 1543, *L and P*, 18, ii, 42.
[2] Chapuys to Charles V, 6 September 1543, *L and P*, 18, ii, 134.
[3] Hughes and Larkin, I, 322.

convinced of its futility, and reverted to violence of a somewhat different kind. Instead of raiding across the border, he would send an army by sea to Leith to sack Edinburgh and devastate the Eastern lowlands *pour encourager les autres*. Edward Seymour, Earl of Hertford, who was to command the expedition, endeavoured to persuade him that the occupation and garrisoning of Leith would be more constructive, but was overruled. The force was assembled in haste and anger. By 20 April 200 transports from London, Ipswich, King's Lynn and Hull had assembled at Newcastle, escorted by an unknown number of the King's men of war.[1] The whole force, with the fleet commanded by the Lord Admiral, reached the Firth of Forth on 3 May, and landed near Leith on the 5th. Having defeated a Scottish army estimated at 6 000 men, and taken a number of ships including the *Salamander* and the *Unicorn*, which were lying in the harbour, they secured control of the town and proceeded to Edinburgh. There, mindful of his instructions, Hertford refused an offer to surrender on terms, took the town by storm and sacked it. The castle held out, but the remainder was burned to the ground. Returning to Leith, he then served that in the same fashion, destroying both the pier and the haven. By this time the English had taken so much plunder that it filled the waiting ships, which were then despatched south. The army returned to Berwick overland, destroying everything in its path – 27 towns and villages according to Hall's account[2] plus another three coastal villages burnt by the fleet in passing. Later in the year the helpful Earl of Lennox led a similar, but much smaller raid with a dozen ships on Arran, Bute and Argyll, taking his plunder back to Bristol. Politically, nothing had been achieved by this gratuitous violence. The Scottish problem had become more bitter and intractable, and the Queen Dowager, Mary of Guise, replaced Arran as Regent. What had been demonstrated was the efficiency and speed with which Henry's naval officers could mobilize and transport a medium-sized expeditionary force by sea. Given that the King had only made up his mind in the middle of March, to have the fleet and the army ready by 20 April was a remarkable achievement, and if it was under victualled, as was alleged, that in no way impeded the operation.

By contrast the main campaign into France, although it resulted in the capture of Boulogne, was an unmitigated shambles and led directly to another quarrel with Charles, who was disgusted with the

[1] Laird Clowes, 460. Hall, 860.
[2] Ibid., 860–1.

antics of his ageing and egocentric ally. For this state of affairs Lord Lisle and his fleet were in no way to blame. In May and June they transported over 30 000 men across to Calais, including some who had come straight from Hertford's campaign in Scotland.[1] The siege of Boulogne began, both by land and sea, on 19 July, and the navy contributed not only by blockading the harbour, but also by bombarding the seaward defences. 'The toune was so beaten withe ordinaunce that there was not left one house whole therein' as one contemporary commented. Boulogne surrendered on 14 September, and Henry entered on the 18th, playing the conquering hero for the last time in his life. At the end of the month he returned to England. By that time the fighting was virtually over. The Duke of Norfolk, who had been unsuccessfully besieging Montreuil, managed to extricate himself from an extremely menacing situation, and got his troops back to Boulogne before the King left. However, it was one thing to take an important town, and quite another to hold it. Boulogne needed to be both supplied and reinforced before the winter arrived, and at the end of October Sir Thomas Seymour was appointed Vice-Admiral and instructed to convey a quantity of stores to the newly conquered (and extremely battered) fortress.[2] Having completed this assignment, he was then to remain at sea to carry out harrying raids in the estuary of the Canche and along the Normandy coast. He duly set out from Portsmouth, and by 6 November was lying off Dover. However, at that point the weather took over. Easterly gales prevented him from reaching Boulogne, and he discovered that 17 French men of war were lying at Etaples, making the Canche too strong to attack. He requested, and obtained, permission to divert his attentions to Brittany, but hearing *en route* that another 17 Frenchmen were in the estuary of the Seine, decided to attack them instead. This plan too was disrupted by a gale, and Seymour eventually struggled back to the Solent, having failed to carry out any part of his orders, and equally failed to detach the 14 ships which he was supposed to provide for the defence of the Channel.[3] The King was highly displeased, but eventually accepted that this sequence of failures was due to circumstances beyond Seymour's control.

It had been a year of more aspiration than achievement, and Henry's determination to maintain a command of the seas showed signs of over-stretching his resources. For the first time there are

[1] Scarisbrick, 446–8. Hall, 861–2.
[2] *L and P*, 19, ii, 281, 29 October 1544.
[3] *L and P*, 19, ii, 580, 9 November; Laird Clowes, 461.

signs that mariners were hard to find, and were reluctant to serve in the King's ships. On 8 August the common crier of London was sent round the city to rout out those seamen who had received their coat and conduct money, but who had not reported for duty.[1] They seem to have been part of the 1 000 or so who were supposed to be serving under Sir William Woodhouse in the Narrow Seas. On 24 January following, a fierce proclamation painted a dismal picture of dereliction of duty:

> . . . contrary to the most just laws of his Grace's realm the said mariners and soldiers do run and steal away from the said ships, taking the King's wages, prests and conduct money to their most extreme perils; by which means, contrary to the King's majesty's expectation and trust, his said ships are constrained for want of men to lie still in the harbours and docks, neither being able to do any enterprise themselves nor yet to defend the King's majesty's people travelling in the seas . . .[2]

Inflated rhetoric was customary in such pronouncements, but the fact that the executive clause of the proclamation then went on to prescribe death by martial law for such desertion indicates that the problem was a genuine one. On the same day the carrot was added to the stick in a second proclamation, which raised the monthly wage of an ordinary seaman from five shillings (where it had rested since the previous century), to six shillings and eightpence.[3] Part of the trouble was caused by the increasing number of the King's ships. By building, purchase and capture 11 vessels had been added to the fleet in a single year, all but three of them over 200 tons. Even so, many of the regular duties continued to be performed by hired ships. William Bullyn, owner and captain of the *Martin* of London, was appointed on 31 August to waft the wool fleet to Calais, and on 6 November the Earl of Shrewsbury was informed that the King's 'great navy' could not be divided up to protect distant ports like Newcastle and Bristol, presumably because it was fully occupied in guarding the Narrow Seas, and following Sir Thomas Seymour in abortive strikes against France. The King was sorry to hear from Shrewsbury that the people of Newcastle were suffering upon the seas, but their best remedy was to imitate the western ports, or Rye,

[1] From Benjamin Gonson's accounts, 6 August to 28 November 1544, *L and P*, 19, 674.
[2] Hughes and Larkin, I, 346–7.
[3] Ibid., 347–8.

which had sent out numerous privateers at their own expense, and made a considerable profit.[1]

By the end of 1544 privateering had become something like a regular policy. In September William Hawkins and two companions had been commissioned, upon their own petition, to 'go upon' the King's enemies at sea.[2] They were to do this at their expense, but were authorized to take up victuals, men and artillery in Devon, Cornwall, Somerset and Dorset in the King's name. On 20 December a general proclamation invited other citizens to follow suit, offering exemptions from the Lord Admiral's customary share of the spoils, and commissions similar to those issued to Hawkins and his friends. The response seems to have been satisfactory, because in April 1545 one John of Calais was appointed to be 'captain of all such adventurers as shall serve his majesty in this war', and all those who wished to serve under him (provided that they were not already committed to some other service) were instructed to report to the sign of the gun in Billingsgate before the 23rd of the month.[3] How successful this 'auxiliary navy' turned out to be is problematic. There was certainly plenty of privateering activity over the next two years – so much so that it seems to have aggravated the problem of recruitment to the King's own ships, but John of Calais remains a shadowy figure, and probably exercised little authority. The main problem, as always with such adventurers, was to prevent them from plundering friend and foe alike, a habit which each official pronouncement deplored, but for which there proved to be no effective remedy.

If 1539 had seen a potential crisis, 1545 saw a real one. Offended with his ally and needing peace for his own purposes, the Emperor had signed the treaty of Crespy with France, and withdrawn from the war. England was thus left to face the undivided attentions of both France and Scotland, where the last remains of English influence had finally succumbed to Henry's unique blend of duplicity and violence. The battle of Ancrum Moor on 27 February provided the Scots with a rare victory in open battle, albeit a small one, and major French forces were expected on both the East and West March during the summer. For his part, Francis was determined to recover Boulogne, and not having an Imperial army to occupy him,

[1] Privy Council to the Earl of Shrewsbury, 6 November 1544. The western ports had (it was claimed) sent out 14–16 armed ships, and Rye 3 or 4. *L and P*, 19, ii, 560.
[2] Grants in September 1544, *L and P*, 19, ii, 340 (6). '. . . with 4, 6, or 8 barks of your retinue'.
[3] Hughes and Larkin, I, 348.

to carry the war to the English. In March and April arrangements were made to despatch part of the Mediterranean galley fleet from Marseilles to Etaples, where they arrived, 25 in number, about the middle of May.[1] Francis had the services of two distinguished galley commanders in Antoine Escalin and Leo Strozzi, and seems to have placed a great deal of faith in this particular arm, as Louis XII had in 1513. Six new galleys were building at Rouen, and six others were stationed in Scotland.[2] During May and June Claude D'Annebaut, the Admiral of France, assembled a large fleet, variously estimated between 123 and 300 vessels of various kinds, at Le Havre, Harfleur, Honfleur and other ports on the Seine estuary. Of these, between 50 and 150 were sailing warships of different sizes.[3] The main object of this great armament was the siege of Boulogne, but the navy was ready before the army, and Francis consequently decided to use it for a direct attack upon England, while he completed his other preparations. The English were well aware of this developing threat. Commissions of array were issued on 7 May and 14 June, and regional military commands were set up under the Dukes of Norfolk and Suffolk, Lord Russell and the Earl of Southampton. Small numbers of ships had been patrolling throughout the winter, and between February and April there was full-scale mobilization. By early June Lord Lisle had 160 ships and 12 000 men at sea, over a month before the French were ready to sail.[4] About the middle of the month he tried to capitalize upon this tactical advantage, entering the Seine estuary in the hope of being able to cripple the French preparations before they were complete. Unfortunately his ships got becalmed, and found themselves exchanging fire at a disadvantage with the French gallies, which were on guard. The wind then rose strongly, which forced the gallies to run for shelter, but also threatened to drive the English onto the shoals, so they stood out to sea with their mission unaccomplished, and returned to Portsmouth. The French were in no position to take advantage of this withdrawal, being both unprepared and weatherbound, but they were not molested further, and on 6 July were able to sail. After a skirmish near Alderney, they entered the Solent unopposed ten days later, the English fleet being confined to Portsmouth by adverse winds.

Taking advantage of this situation, D'Annebaut sent a number of

[1] *L and P*, 20, Introduction. Laird Clowes, I, 461–2.
[2] Ibid., 462.
[3] Hall says 200 sail and 26 gallies, 863. Laird Clowes, 462.
[4] Hall, 863. *L and P*, 20, i, 823.

gallies forward to reconnoitre, and landed men at various points on the Isle of Wight from whence, according to Edward Hall, they were 'to their greate loose and payne driven again to their Galies'.[1] These were mere aggressive gestures, not serious actions, and although the gallies did succeed in tempting a squadron of about a dozen English ships to venture out on the lightest of airs, the subsequent manoeuvring was inconclusive. On the night of the 18th D'Annebaut reorganized his fighting ships, by this time 128 in number, into four squadrons. The 26 gallies formed the vanguard, and the sailing ships were divided into three 'battles' of approximately equal size.[2] The intention seems to have been for the gallies to carry out probing attacks, particularly if the wind continued to be light or non-existent. Later, if the wind gave the English any momentum, they were to fall back and support D'Annebaut's main battle, possibly in a single co-ordinated formation. If this deduction from the scanty evidence is correct, it represents advanced tactical thinking, but not beyond the level which both French and Spanish admirals are known to have achieved. On the English side, Lord Lisle's fleet orders also show a knowledge of up-to-date tactical thinking. The previous known orders, issued by Thomas Audley in 1530 while the Duke of Richmond was Lord Admiral, had shown no tactical appreciation of the possibilities of gunfire, concentrating mainly upon the protocol of hand combat.[3] At that stage, although port firing guns had been in use for twenty years, conservative tacticians still saw their main use in terms of confusing the enemy with noise and smoke. Lisle, on the other hand, like D'Annebaut, intended to marshall his ships in three squadrons, and added

> It is to be considered that the ranks must keep such order in sailing that none impeach another. Wherefore it is requisite that every of the said ranks keep right way with another, and take such regard to the observing of the same that no ship pass his fellows forward or backward nor slack anything, but (keep) as they were in one line, and that there may be half a cable length between every of the ships.[4]

Although this instruction could be read to imply a line ahead forma-

[1] Hall, 863.
[2] Lapeyrouse Bonfils, *Histoire de la Marine Francaise*, 25.
[3] 'A Book of Orders for the War both by Land and Sea, written by Thomas Audley at the command of King Henry VIII'; BL MS Harleian 309, f. 42; extracts printed in *Fighting Instructions, 1530–1816*, ed. Julian S. Corbett, 15–17.
[4] Lord Lisle's instructions, from the Le Fleming MSS, printed in *Fighting Instructions*, 20–23.

tion of the later kind, the rest of the orders suggest that line abreast was intended, and that the guns would have been brought into play only after the front line had 'passed through' the front rank of the enemy. Nevertheless the main purpose of a tightly controlled formation was to co-ordinate the use of gunfire to the maximum effect, so that 'laying aboard', which was still the ultimate objective, could be carried out with a better chance of success.

In the event, no serious engagement resulted from D'Annebaut's massive incursion into the Solent. On the morning of 19 July, there still being no wind, the French gallies moved in to attack, firing their single heavy guns. Henry had only four or five galleys and galleasses with which to oppose them, supported by 13 small galleys or 'row-barges'. These put up a worthy resistance, but would have been overwhelmed if the wind had not risen at that point, enabling the main English fleet to move out to attack. Thereafter the weather was more important than the intentions of either combatant. For most of the day the wind was too fickle to enable either the English warships to press home their attack on the gallies, or the French warships to come to their support. Towards evening a freshening breeze favoured the English, but the onset of darkness prevented any serious attack. The following day, the weather continuing to be unhelpful, the French landed more raiding parties on the Isle of Wight, with the same result as before. On the 21st, unable either to obtain a secure landing or a decisive encounter with the English fleet, D'Annebaut withdrew. So far the campaign at sea had proved unproductive to both sides, D'Annebaut leaving the Solent as empty handed as Lisle had left the Seine. Each side had suffered loss, but neither as a direct result of enemy action. On 6 July, before the fleet set out, Francis' flagship, the 800 ton *Caraquon*, had burned out at her moorings as a result of an accidental fire, and the almost equally large *Maitresse* was forced to return to Le Havre on 18 July because she was taking in so much water. On the English side the *Mary Rose* had foundered on 19 July, with the loss of her captain, Sir George Carew, and about 500 soldiers and seamen.[1] There has been a great deal of speculation about the reason for this disaster, which can probably be ascribed to a combination of overloading and poor crew discipline. The French claimed at the time that she had been sunk by gunfire from their gallies, but English sources always denied this, and the recovery of a substantial portion of the hull by marine

[1] Laird Clowes, 462–4; Hall, 863; Knecht, *Francis* I, 372, names D'Annebaut's flagship as *Le Philippe*. A. McKee, 'The complement of the Mary Rose', *MM*, 72, 1986, 74.

archaeologists in recent years seems to have confirmed the English view. No sign of structural damage prior to the sinking has been found. The *Mary Rose* was an old ship, but had been rebuilt in 1536, and there had been no complaints about her safety or handling qualities. It seems that overloading had brought her lower gun deck too close to the waterline, and when a rare gust of wind caused her to heel over, with her gunports open ready for action, the water rushed in. The heavy loss of life has been attributed to the fact that the anti-boarding netting was in place, and many men were trapped on and below the decks. The whole incident lasted only a few minutes, leaving the King an aghast spectator, and the topmasts of the sunken ship forlornly projecting from the water.[1]

Having abandoned his attack on Portsmouth, D'Annebaut did not immediately return to France. He sailed along the English coast as far as Dover, landing small forces near Brighton and Newhaven, which were quickly repulsed. Thereafter he crossed over to Boulogne and put ashore 4 000 soldiers and 3 000 pioneers. It may then have been his intention, according to the original plan, to blockade the harbour as part of the siege operations. If so, the weather again frustrated him, and by 10 August an easterly gale had left his fleet once more upon the Sussex coast. This time Lisle was at sea with about a hundred ships, and looking for a fight. He issued a fresh set of battle orders, apparently intending to engage at once, but it was the 15th before he finally made contact with the enemy. D'Annebaut then had the better of a complicated day of manoeuvring, and having gained the weather gauge sent in his galleys to the attack. Had this first thrust been properly supported, it might have inflicted considerable damage, but before the French could bring their main battle into action a rising wind and sea forced the galleys to run for cover. A desultory exchange of artillery fire continued until dark. By morning both fleets had decided to disengage, the English returning to Portsmouth and the French to Le Havre. Disappointed with his lack of success, and with 12 000 men still under arms, on 2 September Lisle crossed to Normandy and launched another attack on Tréport, taking and burning the town, with 30 ships in the harbour.[2] Militarily this exploit served no useful purpose whatever, but at the end of a campaigning season which had seen enormous efforts on both sides, it was the nearest thing to a victory which either achieved. The French were particularly frustrated.

[1] As shown on the Cowdray engraving, M. Rule, *The Mary Rose*, 36–8.

[2] Peter Padfield argued, on somewhat slender evidence, that Lisle's ships fired 'the first broadsides fired in anger', during this engagement on 15 August. *Guns at Sea*, 33.

Having caught England for once without her protective Imperial alliance, they had failed to exploit the situation, either by invading England or by recovering Boulogne. The English were correspondingly relieved. By the middle of September, 13 of Lisle's ships were infected with plague, and a rapid demobilization began. The demands of the navy had reduced the fishing fleets of Devon and Dorset to a shadow – a few inshore boats crewed by women and children – according to Lord Russell.[1] But the Admiral had acted in time and the majority of the seamen were able to return home without bearing the deadly infection with them. Fortunately the French had no appetite to seize an opportunity so late in the season.

The success of the navy had been largely negative, but informal operations had proved far more productive. English privateers had operated in the Channel like a swarm of wasps since the beginning of the war. Their letters of marque were sometimes directed against the Scots and the French, and sometimes against the French alone, but the records of the Admiralty court are full of complaints from Flemish, Spanish and Italian masters and merchants that these limitations were not respected.[2] As long as the King and the Emperor were allies, some attempt was made to provide remedy for these complaints and to keep the privateering captains under control. But once the Emperor had withdrawn from the war in September 1544, Henry made no serious effort to give his subjects satisfaction. So bad had the situation become by January 1545 that Charles arrested all the English ships that he could lay his hands on by way of retaliation, and embargoed further trade. The English complained in turn that Flemings and Spaniards were taking advantage of their neutrality in the continuing war, and were transporting increasing quantities of French goods.[3] By the laws of the sea such goods were legitimate prize, and neither the arrests nor the embargo were justified. It is against this background that the exploits of Robert Reneger have to be seen. Reneger was a merchant of Southampton who, according to Hakluyt, not only traded regularly to Spain and the south of France but also, from about 1540, to Brazil.[4] He had complained frequently about the loss of his goods to French pirates, and was one of the first to be granted Letters of Marque in 1543. Operating jointly with Henry Huttoft, who we have

[1] *L and P*, 20, ii, 190, 346. Laird Clowes, 465–6.
[2] G. Connell-Smith, *Forerunners of Drake*, 132 et seq. quotes several cases from HCA Examinations and Libels for these years.
[3] *Cal. Span.* 7, 4.
[4] Connell-Smith, *Forerunners of Drake*, 137.

already noticed on the fringes of the Admiralty administration, he is known to have taken several prizes over the next two years, and also to have suffered some loss of his own ships. Then on 1 March 1545, lying off Cape St Vincent with four small ships, he took the *San Salvador*, inward bound from San Domingo in Hispaniola. The pretext later offered was that the Spaniards had unjustly detained one of his own vessels at San Lucar. In any case, he claimed, much of the cargo was French owned. The incident soon became of major significance because the bulk of the lading consisted of gold from the Indies, to the enormous value of 7 243 075 marevedis (about £4 300), which Reneger claimed had never been declared to the Emperor's officials, and was therefore unprotected.[1] His story was imaginative and unconvincing, but Henry's Council accepted it, and the King received a large proportion of the loot. Repeated attempts by the aggrieved Spaniards to secure legal redress were unsuccessful. The treaties between England and Spain were appealed to in vain, and by the middle of April Reneger and three of his ships were serving in Lord Lisle's fleet in the channel.[2] English commercial operations in Spain had been getting more difficult for years, thanks largely to the tendency of the Inquisition to regard all Englishmen as heretics, on account of the Royal Supremacy. Reneger's exploit poisoned the atmosphere still further. Regular contacts dwindled, and by 1553 when the question of a marriage treaty between Mary and Philip arose, the two nations cordially detested each other. On 7 April 1546 Lisle wrote to Lord Paget that 'Every Spaniard, Portugall or Fleming that comes from the south is robbed by our adventurers, some calling themselves Scots, some wearing visors (masks) . . .'.[3] It is not surprising that Henry's diplomatic attempts at a new relationship with the Emperor made no progress, and that England looked like facing another campaigning season on her own. The political price for this undisciplined reign of terror could be very high.

Despite mounting financial difficulties caused by the enormous cost of the war, Henry entered 1546 apparently determined upon another massive effort. Somewhat half-hearted attempts at peace negotiations, mediated by the German Lutherans (who had their own reasons for hoping that Francis would soon be free to turn his attentions to the Emperor again) failed during December. By the

[1] Archivo General de Indias, Contratación, Legajo 2439, Ramo 6, no. 2; PRO SP1/200, ff. 95–6, quoted Connell-Smith, 141.
[2] PRO SP1/200, ff. 25–8.
[3] *L and P*, 21, 563.

middle of January it had been decided to raise an army of 20 000 and a fleet of 45 sail.[1] Fresh musters were ordered, and agents sent to Antwerp, Middleburg, Bremen, Hamburg and Danzig in search of corn, naval stores and munitions. In March two ships, the *Trinity* and the *Mary Fortune*, were sent from London to the coast of East Anglia to be 'continual wafters' of supplies to Calais and Boulogne. By the beginning of April two others had been appointed to join them, but Lisle was still worried about the lack of protection, claiming that a French privateer had done considerable damage before the English warships came on the scene.[2] The King, however, was at last losing his enthusiasm. At the end of March tentative feelers went out, and on 24 April peace negotiations began. It was by no means certain that they would succeed, because the English at first took a tough line, and in the meantime the fighting continued. A French attempt on Ambleteuse, near Boulogne was frustrated, and there were several inconclusive naval skirmishes. One of these took place on 18 May, three days after the peace of Cercamp had been successfully concluded, when eight English men-of-war encountered a similar number of French ships in the Channel, and captured one galley – the *Blanchard*.[3] On 7 June peace was formally concluded. Although he was now an old and sick man, Henry was still very much in command of his policies, and in spite of the fact that Scotland was supposed to be comprehended in the treaty with France, he made it clear that he intended to keep up his pressure upon the northern kingdom. At the end of May Cardinal Beaton had been murdered and his castle of St Andrews seized by a group of protestant rebels, who naturally looked to England for assistance. As long as Henry lived this support was continued, and in mid September a small fleet of six ships, the *Pauncey*, the *Minion*, the *Hart*, the *Jennet, Dragon* and *Lion* was detailed to go to their relief, and instructed to take a passing swipe at the Firth of Forth on the way past, just in case the Scots had forgotten the damage which his displeasure could do.[4]

This was the last naval action of the reign, and it was left to the minority government of his son to count the cost. According to an account drawn up in 1549 the cost of the naval war alone between 1543 and 1547 had been a little short of £200 000;[5] of which

[1] *L and P*, 21, 85, 91, 122, 124, 218, 221, 251, 272.
[2] Lisle to the Council, 4 April 1546. *L and P*, 21, 538.
[3] Laird Clowes 466.
[4] *L and P*, 21, 123; 18 September 1546. Ibid., 134, 20 September 1546.
[5] PRO SP10/15, ff. 23r–24v.

£45 230 had been spent on cables, timber, canvas and other stores; £2 415 on coat and conduct money; £127 846 on wages; and £559 on the costs of endeavouring to salvage the *Mary Rose*. The Venetian experts who had undertaken that task had managed to recover some guns, but otherwise had succeeded only in snapping the masts off the wreck. The ordnance written off as unrecoverable was valued at over £1 700. The victualling of the navy, costed separately because it was not under the direct control of the Council for Marine Causes, had during the same period, amounted to over £100 000. It has been estimated that the total expenditure on these wars by land and sea was in the order of £2m, so it could be argued that the navy was good value for money, but these accounts demonstrate in a very striking way the price which had to be paid for the greatly increased size of the establishment, both in ships and facilities, and for the improved technology in which the old King had always shown such an interest.

6
THE NAVY AND SEAFARING POLICY, 1547–1558

The death of Henry VIII on 28 January 1547 brought swift and radical political changes, but they could hardly be described as unexpected. With the disappearance of its architect and resolute defender, the Royal Supremacy over the church could have been rescinded or quietly forgotten, and the element of ideological confrontation in England's relations with her neighbours removed. However, during the last five years of Henry's life the politics of his own court had made such an outcome increasingly unlikely. After his last marriage, to Catherine Parr, in July 1543 the Reforming party originally associated with Thomas Cromwell gradually recovered the ascendancy which it had lost with the minister's fall in 1540. These men – Archbishop Cranmer, Edward Seymour Earl of Hertford, and John Dudley Viscount Lisle in particular – were not Protestants during these years, but they were wholehearted supporters of the King's anti-papal policy and simplified Church order.[1] The new Queen (who was not at all the intellectual she is sometimes represented to have been) shared many of their views, and they secured control over the education of the young Prince Edward. At the same time they outmanoeuvred and eventually defeated the Conservative party led by the Howards, and by Stephen Gardiner, Bishop of Winchester. Gardiner and Norfolk did not always see eye to eye, and both made mistakes which played into the hands of their rivals. Consequently, after a series of factional skirmishes in which fortunes had varied, by the end of 1546 Gardiner had lost the King's

[1] M. Dowling, 'The gospel and the court; reformation under Henry VIII' in *Protestantism and the National Church in sixteenth century England* ed. P. Lake and M. Dowling, 36–77.

confidence and retired to his diocese.[1] At the same time the Howards were more dramatically destroyed by the extraordinary indiscretions of the Earl of Surrey, which led to Surrey's own execution a few days before Henry's death, and to the attainder and imprisonment of his father. The Regency Council provided for in the old King's will, to rule in the name of his son during the latter's minority, was therefore dominated by the Reforming party. That will, the final version of which was completed only a few days before Henry's death, was authenticated by the use of a dry stamp. This procedure was perfectly lawful, but because the dry stamp was controlled by Sir Anthony Denny, the Principal Gentleman of the Privy Chamber and a member of the Reforming party, doubt has been cast upon the validity of the will.[2] Changes were undoubtedly made from the penultimate draft, but it has never been conclusively proved that these were made without the King's knowledge and consent – and no such suggestion was made at the time – so it is reasonable to assume that the Regency Council as finally composed, represented Henry's authentic intention.

However, not even Henry VIII could rule from beyond the grave, and within a few days the Executors (as the Regency Council were officially styled) had sought a new commission from the young King, and were reconstituted as the Privy Council of King Edward VI. For the time being all the officers of state were confirmed in their posts. Edward was nine, and his minority was therefore likely to last for almost a decade. Sooner or later a single executive head to act in the King's name would be essential, in spite of the fact that no such position had been provided for in the late King's will. On 1 February it was decided to create two offices, Protector of the Realm and Governor of the King's Person, and to bestow both upon Edward Seymour, Earl of Hertford, the King's uncle.[3] Given the balance of power in the Council, and the fact that Hertford had previously secured the support of Cranmer, Dudley and Sir William Paget, this was not a surprising outcome. By 15 February the new regime had consolidated itself with a distribution of honours. Hertford became Duke of Somerset, Thomas Lord Wriothesley Earl of Southampton, and Viscount Lisle Earl of Warwick. There may have been individuals who were disgruntled by this virtual *coup*, but there was no

[1] G. R. Redworth, *In Defence of the Church Catholic; a life of Stephen Gardiner*, 231.
[2] L. B. Smith, 'The last will and testament of Henry VIII; a question of perspective', *J. British Studies*, 2, 1962, 18–19. W. K. Jordan, *Edward VI, The Young King*, 54–5 and note.
[3] *APC*, 2, 4–5.

opposition.[1] Charles V was deliberately vague in responding to the news of Edward's accession. In his eyes the young King was illegitimate, because the English schism had already begun when Henry and Jane Seymour had married. To all strict Catholics Mary was Henry's only legitimate child, and therefore his lawful heir. But Mary herself gave no sign of sharing that view, and after a few weeks the Emperor accepted that the new regime in England was not going to be challenged. The French had been less scrupulous in according recognition, because they regarded Mary as a Habsburg puppet, but the new Protector could not look for assured friendship from either of the major powers. On 31 March 1547, only a few weeks into the reign, Henry's long time sparring partner Francis I of France followed him to the grave, and the new King, Henry II, regretted the treaty of Cercamp, and cast hungry eyes on Boulogne.[2]

The Protector's international position was rendered even more uncertain by the policies which he deliberately chose to follow. He inherited the unresolved struggle with Scotland, in which he had been a principal agent, and it was reported that the dying Henry had specifically enjoined him to pursue that war to a victorious conclusion. Moreover, by the summer he had also made it clear that he intended not only to uphold the independence of the English Church, but also to move its doctrine and worship in a Protestant direction. In July 1547 there were developments on both these issues. Archbishop Cranmer published a series of Homilies, or model sermons, one of which taught the Protestant doctrine of Justification by faith alone – in contravention of the Act of Six Articles of 1539, which had laid down the current standard of orthodoxy. And on the 21st of the month a French fleet commanded by Leo Strozzi bombarded St Andrews castle into surrender.[3] English warships were at sea in the spring and early summer of 1547, but they were too few and in the wrong place. On 17 February the Earl of Warwick had been replaced as Lord Admiral by the Protector's brother, Lord Seymour of Sudeley. Seymour was experienced, but he may have been less energetic than his predecessor, and he may have been concentrating his attention upon the invasion which Somerset was already preparing. On 27 February Andrew Dudley, Warwick's younger brother, was given the command of the *Pauncey*, with

[1] The story of Wriothesley's opposition, based upon Bishop Burnet's account of 1679, is not substantiated by contemporary sources. Gilbert Burnet, *The History of the Reformation of the Church of England*, 2, 40.

[2] R. J. Knecht, *Francis I*, 422–4.

[3] W. K. Jordan, *Edward VI; the young King*, 245.

instructions to cruise in the North Seas. Since he was dignified as Admiral, he probably had some lesser vessels with him as well.[1] Early in March the *Pauncey* was in action, probably capturing the *Lion*, which was subsequently lost with all hands before it could be brought to harbour, but neither Dudley nor any other English captain seems to have been in the vicinity to impede Strozzi's action. Seymour himself had probably gone to the Scilly Isles to retrieve certain unspecified royal ships and return them to Portsmouth. Meanwhile, in April or May, estimates were drawn up for the forthcoming campaign; £22 810 per month to transport an army of 15 000 to the Firth of Forth by sea, and £24 113 for 14 000 foot and 4 000 horse by land. Victuals would cost between £5 and £6 000, and the hire of 9 000 tons of shipping a further £2 000. It was normal to budget by the month, but the absence of any multiplier in these estimates suggests that a short, sharp campaign was intended.[2]

That intention was realized. In the event the Council compromised, sending the army overland, and the bulk of the supplies by sea, with a substantial number of warships to provide supporting firepower. When Somerset marched north from Berwick at the end of August he was accompanied by a fleet of 65 sail, including 34 fighting ships under the command of Edward Fiennes, Lord Clinton. By that time Robert Legge, the Treasurer of the navy, had received £20 690 on 12 separate warrants from the Council since the beginning of March.[3] Not all that money was devoted to Clinton's fleet, but as the navy was to absorb another £7 000 before the campaign was over, it is clear that the earlier estimates were well short of the mark. Sir Ralph Sadler, the Treasurer of the war, later accounted for £45 912 for the army alone, so the total cost must have been of the order of £65 000 for a campaign which lasted about five or six weeks.[4] Militarily, the operation was a complete success. On 10 September the main Scottish army was defeated with great slaughter at Pinkie Cleugh, near Musselburgh; the town of Leith and a number of villages and fortresses were captured and destroyed. On 13 September a seaborne attack was made on Kinghorn and the island of Inchcolm was captured. Two days later Lord Clinton, with one galley and four or five smaller vessels, attacked the harbour and castle at Blackness, recapturing the *Mary Willoughby* and the

[1] W. K. Jordan, *The Chronicle and Political Papers of King Edward VI*, 5–6; PRO SP10/1/23, 23 February 1547.
[2] PRO SP10/3/22. Jordan, *Edward VI; the young King*, 250–51.
[3] *APC*, 2, 60–120.
[4] Arthur Clifford, ed., *The State Papers and Letters of Sir Ralph Sadler*, I, 355–64.

Anthony of Newcastle, which had been lost to the Scots in the previous year, and burning several other ships.[1] On 18 September Somerset ordered a general retreat, but established a garrison on Inchcolm to command the Firth of Forth, and despatched Lord Seymour and Sir Andrew Dudley with a small naval force to capture Broughty Crag on the north shore of the Firth of Tay. When that had been successfully accomplished, Dudley remained in command of the garrison, while Inchcolm was entrusted to Sir John Luttrell. Politically, these victories achieved nothing. The French were taken by surprise, and made no immediate attempt to intervene, but it would have taken more than such a defeat to alter the policy of the Scottish Government. There was no recovery of the Anglophile party of the early 1540s, and the only hope of long-term advantage to England lay in the establishment and maintenance of military garrisons in sufficient number and strength as to act as a virtual army of occupation. Such a policy was to prove tactically difficult, financially exhausting, and in the end politically futile.

Many of these garrisons lay inland, along the borders, and their fortunes do not directly concern us here, but such as were on the coast depended upon the navy for supplies and reinforcements, and provided a constant focus for activity and expenditure over the following months. The most distant and exposed of these outposts was Broughty Crag. The neighbouring town of Dundee submitted to Dudley without resistance at the end of October, and agreed to supply provisions at reasonable prices, but Dudley was keenly aware of the fragility of his position, having neither enough men nor secure fortifications. Late in November, in spite of the apparent friendliness of the surrounding country, he was besieged by a strong Scottish force. Without relief, Broughty would certainly have fallen, but Sir Thomas Wyndham from his base in Newcastle was able to reach the Tay in time.[2] Wyndham seems to have had two men-of-war, the *Lion* and the *Tiger*, and a number of smaller ships. He brought supplies and reinforcements, raised the siege, and landed 300 men above Dundee, receiving a second submission from that town. It was, however, a temporary relief. Before the end of December Somerset had decided to withdraw Wyndham and concentrate the main English power on inland Haddington, controlling the approach to Edinburgh. This left Dudley with a single ship and less than 200 men – enough (just) to hold Broughty, but quite insuf-

[1] William Patten, *The Expedition into Scotland, 1547*, 138

[2] *Cal. Scot., 1547–1603*, I, 35, 45–6, 48–9.

ficient to defend Dundee as well. The Protector ignored his pleas, although they were strongly reinforced by Lord Grey, the Captain of Berwick, and by the end of January 1548 Dundee had again been lost. Grey in Berwick and Lord Wharton in Carlisle between them disposed of about 10 000 men during these winter months, but the cold weather kept them largely inactive.[1] Meanwhile the naval and diplomatic initiatives were lost. On 24 December Robert Heyland, one of Wyndham's captains, wrote directly to Somerset complaining that the King's ships were stranded at North Shields, without either money or victuals.[2] There seem to have been no patrols on the west coast, and by the middle of January 7 French ships had reached Dumbarton, bringing a military mission, and the young Gerald FitzGerald, Earl of Kildare, who was reported to have designs on marrying the Queen of Scots and uniting Scotland and Ireland against England. The French were by then working hard to redeem their negligence of the previous autumn, promising full aid and a declaration of war in return for a marriage alliance between Mary and the young Dauphin, Francis.

By February French influence was clearly in the ascendant, but they were not finding it easy to motivate the Scots towards a renewal of full-scale war, and the English fleet was already preparing for the sea. A survey of available ships in north-eastern ports was taken, and estimates drawn up, as in the previous year, for an invasion army both by land and sea. By March Wyndham was again in the Tay with four ships, and although he complained bitterly of being short of money and tackle, his mere presence restored confidence in the viability of Broughty, and demonstrated that the English navy had not shortened its reach.[3] At the end of the month he returned to the Tyne, and despatched an urgent plea for 200 more men on account of sickness in the fleet. In spite of Sir Andrew Dudley's persistent complaints, Broughty was by this time reasonably strong, having been reinforced with 300 soldiers and 80 mariners despatched by Lord Grey from Newcastle. New fortifications had also been constructed under the guidance of Sir Thomas Palmer, and although a renewed attempt to control Dundee had failed, Broughty was, after Haddington, the strongest and most strategically important of the English garrisons. At the end of March Sir John Luttrell was instructed to abandon Inchcolm, raze its fortifications, and transfer

[1] Jordan, *Edward VI; the young King*, 270.
[2] PRO SP10/2/23, 24 December 1547.
[3] PRO SP10/4/4; *Cal. Scot.*, I, 84; Jordan, *Edward VI; the young King*, 272–3; PRO SP10/3/20-21.

himself and his small force to the Tay. This was done, and Luttrell was soon complaining as vigorously about Broughty as Dudley had done, but as the spring turned to summer he was able to hold out without much difficulty against a light Scottish siege, continuing to be supplied (and sparsely reinforced) by sea. The navy, however, failed in its main assignment. In May Lord Clinton arrived in the Tyne with the main fleet of about 70 sail, where he was joined by Wyndham. His instructions were to proceed to the Forth, to destroy any Scottish shipping which he might find there, and to prevent any communications between Scotland and France. His resources should have been adequate to accomplish the task of interception. The French had given plenty of warning of their intention, and on 5 June the Council had ordered beacons to be prepared and a watch to be kept on the English coast in anticipation of French raids.[1] There was no state of war, but there were ominous signs of French movement against Boulogne, and Mary of Guise had been negotiating for military assistance since before the defeat at Pinkie. Nevertheless, when the French fleet was spotted off Dunbar on 12 June, Clinton was in no position to impede it. With a favourable wind about 30 transports, three warships and 16 galleys reached Leith on 18 June, and disembarked 6 000 seasoned troops, some French, some German and some Italian, under the command of Andre de Montalembert, Sieur d'Esse.[2]

The arrival of this formidable army transformed the complexion of the war. D'Esse immediately deployed his whole force to the siege of Haddington, and D'Oysel the French ambassador was in a position to dictate the terms of the agreement between the two countries which was drawn up virtually under the noses of the besieging army. By the Convention of Haddington, submitted to the Scottish parliament on 7 July, Mary was to be betrothed to the Dauphin immediately, and a full union of the Crowns was to follow in due course.[3] At the end of July Mary left Scotland by the western route, and arrived safely in France a few days later. If English ships made any attempt to intercept her, no record of the fact has survived, and in less than a month the whole basis of Somerset's Scottish policy had been destroyed. He was, however, too far committed to withdraw with honour, and the siege of Haddington became a war of attrition which was to last for almost a year. In that war the navy continued to play a full part. Almost as soon as

[1] PRO SP10/4/9; Ibid., 12, 5 June 1548.
[2] *Cal. Scot.*, I, 121–2. *Cal. Span.*, IX, 274.
[3] Jordan, *Edward VI; the young King*, 283.

the Convention of Haddington was signed an English army of over 10 000 men under the Earl of Shrewsbury was assembled at Berwick to dislodge D'Esse. Meanwhile Clinton, having retreated south to revictual at Ipswich and Harwich, had returned to Holy Island where he picked up an advance force of 1 000 men to transport to the Forth by sea.[1] The French fleet was still at Leith, and this time the Admiral was given the unusual instruction to seek it out and destroy it. On 10 August he reported that he had found 12 French supply ships at anchor and burned them, but the fighting ships had again eluded him. For the time being the Forth was under total blockade, but the horse had already bolted before the stable door was locked. In the face of Shrewsbury's advance D'Esse withdrew from Haddington, but the English campaign was not pursued with any vigour. In early September he retreated to Berwick and began to disband his army, under direct orders from a Protector who was becoming acutely conscious of the cost of the war. At the end of the month the French reinvested Haddington, and Clinton, faced with deteriorating weather conditions, sailed south.

There was little activity at Broughty after the French forces had been committed to the siege of Haddington. Luttrell replaced Dudley in command, but the Scots seem to have been too apprehensive of Clinton's fleet to press home an attack. A small number of reinforcements were sent in August, and more in October. But late in November, when Luttrell complained in the same vein as Dudley about shortage of supplies and flimsy fortifications, Somerset withdrew his German mercenaries before revictualling the diminished garrison for six months. Neither the English nor the French at this stage wished to widen the field of hostilities beyond Scotland. Some threatening gestures were made against Boulogne in August, which resulted in exchanges of artillery fire, but neither side wished to proceed beyond threats. More serious, because much harder to control was a noticeable increase in what might be described as licensed piracy. It could not be correctly described as privateering, because in the absence of war no letters of marque could be issued. However, the constant French traffic with Scotland, and the fact that English privateers were operating against the Scots, made the whole situation very amorphous, and Lord Seymour was particularly prone to encourage private enterprise. Eight or nine English ships were taken during the autumn of 1548, and in retaliation Seymour authorized an attack by West Country ships on the French

[1] *Cal. Scot.*, I, 149–51; PRO SP10/6/391, 20 July 1548.

Newfoundland fishing fleet.[1] On 7 September John Graynfyld reported to the Admiral that an engagement had been fought off the coast of Brittany, which had resulted in ten French ships being captured, and several driven ashore.[2] Surveys of Henry VIII's coastal defences, made at about the same time, revealed that many of these hastily constructed fortresses, although less than a decade old, were crumbling as rapidly as they had been built, but there was little that could be done in the overstretched condition of the Government's finances. Both the Danes and the Swedes complained about the unrestrained depredations of English pirates, but Somerset was either unable or unwilling to offer any effective redress. Perhaps the accusations shortly to be made against the Lord Admiral, that he was colluding with pirates and receiving a share of their spoils, were true. Or perhaps the confusing nature of the Council's own orders encouraged the lawlessness which it theoretically deplored.

The arrest of Lord Seymour in January 1549, and his execution in March, encouraged the French to hope that England might become paralysed by civil war, and that her positions both in Scotland and in Boulogne would collapse. Henry II was finding Scotland an expensive and unco-operative ally, but could not disengage as long as the English threat remained. In the short term he was disappointed. In spite of his problems, Somerset was determined upon a new campaign in the North. Fresh musters were ordered in April, to assemble at Berwick by 20 May, and Lord Grey was replaced as Warden of the East March by the youthful Earl of Rutland. The fleet was mobilized as usual, although not, apparently, to its full strength. Eleven ships were detailed for the Irish Sea and the western approaches, and 18 for the Channel and the North Sea.[3] Broughty was revictualled in April, and Wyndham was ordered to remain in or near the Tay estuary with a squadron of unknown size. Luttrell complained bitterly and continually of his lack of men, money and munitions, but he held on, and although the siege of Broughty was tightened, no attempt was made to storm the fort in the face of the English ships lying offshore. However, Somerset's new campaign came to nothing. During June there was desultory raiding, and fragmentary fighting with more ferocity than sense of purpose, and by July the growing civil disorders in England made any coherent

[1] PRO SP10/4/39, 41, 44.
[2] PRO SP10/5/3, John Graynfyld to Seymour, 7 September 1548.
[3] PRO E351/2353, accounts of Edward Baeshe and Richard Wattes, 1 July 1547 – 28 September 1550.

strategy in the borders impossible. Seizing the opportunity which had come six months later than expected, at the beginning of August the French began to mount increasing pressure upon Boulogne. Meanwhile an outbreak of plague in Haddington, and a realistic report upon the expense of continuing its defence, persuaded Somerset to evacuate his forces on the same day that the French finally declared war – 14 August.[1] By the middle of September the war in Scotland had virtually been abandoned, but the Scots had no appetite to take advantage of the situation. Haddington was evacuated without loss, and the French commander de Thermes remained inactive in Edinburgh while his ill-disciplined forces skirmished with their ostensible allies. In the north there was no will to take advantage of the paralysis which overtook English government during the weeks which led up to Somerset's overthrow early in October; but in the South Henry was gathering an army royal at Montreuil for the attack on Boulogne and an amphibious assault was mounted against the Channel Islands.

This latter consisted of 12 galleys commanded by the veteran Italian Leo Strozzi and a similar number of transports carrying about 2 000 troops. The English fleet was under the overall command of Sir Thomas Cotton, and was divided into three squadrons by this time. One, as we have seen, was in the north east under Sir Thomas Wyndham, and was operating out of Newcastle; the second, under Cotton himself, was operating out of Dover; and the third, commanded by William Winter, was operating out of Portsmouth. It was this third squadron which engaged Strozzi off Jersey early in August, and inflicted a decisive defeat upon him, the light French gallies proving to be no match for Winter's heavy guns.[2] So the only battle honours of this distracted summer belonged to the navy. The Earl of Warwick, who was the effective leader of the councillors who had overthrown Somerset, and succeeded him as *de facto* Regent, also resumed his former office as Lord Admiral on 28 October 1549. By this time Boulogne was closely invested, and only the English command of the seas enabled it to be defended at all. Three thousand reinforcements, victuals and munitions were brought in by sea towards the end of the year, but by that time Warwick was coming to the conclusion that the town was not worth the enormous cost of defending it. The Emperor Charles V, who had guaranteed English possession of Calais by his last treaty with

[1] BL Cotton MS Caligula B vii, 176, Holcroft's report, 2 August 1549; Jordan, *Edward VI; the young King*, 298.
[2] Laird Clowes, *The Royal Navy*, 469.

Henry VIII, refused to extend his protection to the 'new conquest', and in February 1550 negotiations were opened for its surrender. By the treaty of Boulogne, signed on 14 March 1550, Henry II achieved his objective at a cost of 400 000 crowns (about £133 000).[1] Many contemporaries considered the treaty dishonourable to England, but in fact it was a good financial bargain, given the cost of the garrison and fortifications. Scotland was comprehended in the same treaty, the remaining English strongholds were evacuated, and for the first time since the reign began over three years earlier, there was peace.

The management of the navy during this war has to be reconstructed from somewhat fragmentary evidence. The first ship list of the reign is dated 5 January 1548, and contains the names of 52 vessels, displacing over 11 000 tons.[2] Since 1546 the *Artigo* had been sold, the *Great Pinnace*, the *Mary James*, and the *Mary Thomas* had disappeared from the record, the *Mary Willougby* had been retaken from the Scots and the *Bark Ager* captured. No new ships appear to have been built or purchased during 1547. Forty-two ships of all sizes were listed as being at Portsmouth in January 1548, six at Deptford and four in Scotland. Only the *Great Harry* was at Woolwich. Robert Legge's last surviving account runs from 25 December 1546 to the same date in 1547, and shows an expenditure of £41 000.[3] Recorded Privy Council warrants from 8 March to 11 December 1547 show him to have received £32 800 during that somewhat shorter period, so the available figures are consistent.[4] Legge's account is organized by categories of expenditure, e.g. 'Timber, boards and planks', 'pitch, tallow and rosen', with totals under each heading for Deptford, Woolwich, Gillingham, Harwich, Colne and Portsmouth. During this year 'sea charges', which covered the wages of officers and crews at sea, accounted for £6 926; £484 was spent at Colne, £1 211 at Portsmouth, £1 631 at Harwich, £3 439 at Woolwich, £4 167 at Gillingham, and a massive £18 824 at Deptford.[5] In spite of the fact that nearly three-quarters of the navy was at Portsmouth in January 1548, the great majority of the ships were normally based in the Thames and the Medway. It was there that they were serviced and repaired, and kept on a care and maintenance basis when not in use. To these costs should be added a proportion, probably as much as half, of the £31 234.11s.3d. that

[1] W. K. Jordan, *Edward VI; the threshold of power*, 121.
[2] Bodleian Library MS Rawlinson 846, ff. 85–92.
[3] PRO E351/2588.
[4] *APC*, 2, 60–151.
[5] PRO E351/2588.

Edward Baeshe and Richard Wattes, Surveyors of the Victuals, spent between 1 July 1547 and 28 June 1550.[1] Rather surprisingly, there is no record of expenditure at Newcastle, in spite of the fact that a squadron was based there throughout the summer. The death of Henry VIII had not been followed by any noticeable change either of personnel or policy in the administration of the navy, although the presentation of a single consolidated victualling account makes it clear that the decision had already been taken to bring that activity under the central control of the Council for Marine Causes. Until 1547 Edward Baeshe had been only one of a number of purveyors and agents, but his joint commission with Richard Wattes was an exclusive one, and foreshadowed an appointment by Patent on 28 June 1550 (the terminal date of his account with Wattes) to be General Surveyor of the Victuals for the Seas, with a fee of £50 a year and 5s.4d. a day for expenses. With this appointment the logical structure of the Council was complete.[2]

By 1547, as we have seen, there was a considerable amount of plant, particularly at Portsmouth, Deptford and Woolwich, but apart from the single appointment of James Baker as King's Shipwright in 1538, no record of any permanent staff establishment below the level of the officers themselves. Common sense would suggest that there must have been something very like a regular workforce, at least at Deptford, but the first acknowledgement of persons 'in ordinary wages' does not come until 1548. At some point during that year a list was drawn up of 19 named and 14 unnamed men in regular receipt of wages, expenses and victuals, at a total cost of £386.18s.10d.[3] Seven of the named men are not located. Two of these, William Holstocke and Thomas Morley, are not designated by function, although Holstocke is elsewhere described as an assistant to Robert Legge. They were probably clerks since they were paid at 8d. a day, but were additional to the clerks for whom the officers already claimed allowance. Of the other five men in this category, three were messengers 'ridinge in post by ye yeare', and the other two purveyors of timber. Two unnamed shipkeepers, paid 13s.4d. a month each, are also unlocated, and together these nine men probably formed a core staff who could be deployed at the discretion of the council. The others are all listed under particular ports or havens; at Deptford and Deptford Strand one master mar-

[1] PRO E351/2353.

[2] Oppenheim, *Administration*, 103.

[3] Bodleian Library, MS Rawlinson 846, ff. 135–41, 'A declaration of such persons as be in ordinary wages'.

iner, one purveyor, one victualler, three clerks and nine shipkeepers; at Woolwich two men of unidentified function paid 7d. a day each; at Harwich and Colne one man at 8d. a day, one at 12d., and one at 9s. a week who must have been a surveyor or overseer. At Portsmouth there was just one man at a humble 6d. a day, who can have been little more than a caretaker; and at Gillingham a victualler and a clerk. There is an approximate consistency between this list and the proportions of expenditure in Robert Legge's account. Deptford was clearly the most important naval base by both reckonings, and Portsmouth the least important; Woolwich and Gillingham were rougly equal; but whereas the 'ordinary' suggests that Harwich and Colne together were more important than either, the account suggests the opposite. Harwich had only been in use since the beginning of Henry's last war, and there may well have been few facilities there, in spite of the relatively large number of permanent employees.

At some point during 1548 Robert Legge died and was succeeded by Benjamin Gonson. Legge's last account terminated on 29 September, and Gonson's first commenced on the same day, so that may have been the actual date of his decease but is more likely to have been the nearest conventional accounting date.[1] The new Treasurer's patent of appointment was not issued until 8 July 1549. William Winter, the son of that Thomas Winter who had originally been named as Treasurer, succeeded Gonson as Surveyor at the same time. Both Gonson and Winter were regular sea commanders in addition to their official responsibilities, and Winter was in command of the *Minion* when her crew earned a bonus of £100 for taking a French prize (probably the *Black Galley*) in 1549.[2] In the course of 1548 most of the 20 ton rowbarges so much favoured by Henry VIII were disposed of, and three new pinnaces, the *Flower de Luce*, the *Seven Stars* and the *Moon*, were built to take their place. A fourth pinnace, the *Double Rose*, was probably purchased.[3] It was clearly not new, and by 1552 was described as 'not worth the keeping'. Three further pinnaces were acquired in 1549; one of these, the *Swift*, was probably a new ship, and a second, the *Prickshaft*, may have been. Apart from the exchange of pinnaces for rowbarges, the recovery of the *Mary Willoughby* and the capture of the *Black Galley*, the navy in May 1550, at the end of the wars, was much as Henry VIII had left it. That is not surprising considering that most of it had been built or acquired between 1544 and 1546, but there is

[1] PRO E351/2194.
[2] Ibid.: Oppenheim, *Administration*, 106–7.
[3] T. Glasgow, 'List of ships in the royal navy from 1539 to 1588 . . .', 299–307.

similarly no sign of any decline in the administration or servicing of the fleet, in spite of the undoubted delinquencies of Lord Seymour as Lord Admiral, and the fact that the office was vacant from March to October 1549.

With the return of peace some reduction in the level of naval activity was inevitable. However it was an uneasy peace, and although the country was deeply in debt the Council seems to have taken the view that it would be a false economy to cut back heavily on naval expenditure. So although the continental mercenaries were paid off and the fortifications of Calais left unrepaired, the fleet continued to be properly maintained. In 1552, when the Crown debts had reached over £240 000, only £5 000 of that was owed on the Admiralty account.[1] One of the reasons for this was that, as relations with France improved after the cession of Boulogne, the Emperor became increasingly hostile. A protracted quarrel between Edward and his sister Princess Mary over the latter's continued celebration of the mass provided the pretext. However the real reason seems to have been the desire of Charles's sister Mary of Hungary, his regent in the Netherlands and one of the main controllers of Imperial policy during his frequent illnesses, to secure control of an English port to act as a base for the Flemish fleet. In September 1551 she wrote to the Bishop of Arras, the Emperor's confidential advisor

> We must therefore have a port in that country at our disposal, either by force or through friendship. Many people are of the opinion that the kingdom of England would not be impossible to conquer, especially now that it is a prey to poverty and discord.[2]

The Emperor himself probably never intended war, but he allowed his ambassadors, first Van der Delft and then Jehan Scheyfve, to bluster and threaten, and to take instructions from Mary of Hungary. Consequently the Earl of Warwick, Lord President of the Council, could not afford a policy of disarmament, even if he had wished to follow it for reasons of economy. He handed over the office of Lord Admiral to Lord Clinton on 4 May 1550, when peace with France and Scotland was already assured, but his interest in the navy as an instrument of policy remained.

When a fresh survey of the fleet was carried out on 26 August 1552 only one ship had been disposed of since 1548, the *Marian of Danzig*,

[1] PRO SP10/15/41.
[2] Mary of Hungary to the Bishop of Arras, 5 October 1551, *Cal. Span.*, X, 377.

sold for £400 in December 1551.[1] Twenty-four ships and pinnaces were then listed as 'in good case to serve'; seven needed to be 'docked and new dubbed'; and three other were already dry-docked and awaiting new building. Four were 'thought meet to be sold', and six others, mostly small, 'not worth the keeping'; four were also mentioned with no indication as to their condition. It was pointed out that every ship needed to be grounded and caulked once a year to keep it seaworthy, and that the gallies in particular needed annual repair 'if your Lordships pleasure be to have them kept', about which there was (presumably) some doubt. The crews of the galleys had been paid off in February 1551, and they had been laid up on the grounds that they were of little use,[2] but this opinion does not seem to have been shared by the Council for Marine Causes, since two of the three were still in commission at the beginning of Elizabeth's reign. Four further ships were added to the list between May 1550 and August 1552; the *Jerfalcon* of 140 tons and a new *Bark of Bullen* some time in 1550; and the *Primrose* of 300 tons and a rebuilt *Mary Willoughby*, both launched on 4 July 1551 by the young King himself.[3] The little *Trego Reneger*, otherwise known as the *Spanish Shallop*, no longer appears, but there is no record of what happened to her. Apart from the addition of Edward Baeshe as Surveyor of the Victuals, there were two other changes among the officers of the Admiralty; on 16 December 1552 Sir William Woodhouse, the Master of Naval Ordnance, succeeded Sir Thomas Clere as Lieutenant of the Admiralty (or Vice-Admiral), and Thomas Wyndham replaced Woodhouse.

Deptford continued to be the main base. Gonson's first account, running from 29 September 1548 to 24 October 1551 shows expenditure there of £30 300, compared to £6 600 at Gillingham, £2 054 at Woolwich, and £1 157 at Portsmouth.[4] Operations at Harwich and Colne seem to have been discontinued. The whole account is for £66 250 in a little over three years, about half of which was wartime. Over the same period the Privy Council recorded individual payments to Gonson amounting to £58 948 – the great bulk of the £65 809 which his account shows him to have received.[5] Baeshe's

[1] British Library MS Harleian 354, f. 9; PRO E351/2194; Oppenheim, *Administration*, 101. This account also records the sale of 14 other prizes, mostly small, for a total of £763. Certain anchors and other items of equipment were also sold, but in small quantities.

[2] *APC*, 3, 209, 7 February 1551.

[3] Glasgow, 'List of Ships . . .'; Jordan, *Chronicle of King Edward*, 70.

[4] PRO E351/2194.

[5] *APC*, 2, 223 to *APC*, 3, 372.

first consolidated victualling account, and the only one surviving for the reign, runs from 28 June 1550 to 29 September 1552.[1] It cannot be directly compared with Gonson's account, partly because of the different period and partly because of its different divisions. Woolwich and Deptford are lumped together, costing £8 382, while £2 407 was spent at Portsmouth. On the other hand £646 was spent at Dover where there was no base, probably a reflection of the revictualling of ships at sea which is known to have taken place in the Downs. Gillingham was victualled from Rochester at a cost of £6 137. Altogether the Surveyor of Victuals spent £17 572 in 27 months and received £17 780 on warrants passed by the Privy Council. Deptford therefore continued to absorb the lion's share of the money, but there were misgivings about the scope of its anchorages. During wartime Portsmouth was the front line, but not many ships were based there and in peacetime, when the majority of the ships (particularly the larger ones) were on a care and maintenance basis for months at a time, more space was needed. It may have been for that reason that Harwich was used experimentally for a few years, but not found satisfactory. On 8 June 1550 the Privy Council made what appears to have been a policy decision, and directed that all ships, once their officers and crews had been discharged, were to be laid up at Gillingham.[2] On 14 August this was followed up with a specific order that the men-of-war currently at Portsmouth should be brought round to the Medway, where the convenient mud flats and the large tidal variation would facilitate the routine work of 'grounding and graving', which was recognized by this time as an annual requirement.[3] On 22 August William Winter was sent down to Portsmouth to organize this transfer. As we shall see, the officers of the Admiralty were to make another attempt to urge the unique advantages of Gillingham in 1559, but the dockyard and workshops remained at Deptford for the rest of the century.

Edward inherited his father's delight in ships, and paid numerous visits to Deptford, as well as recording such exploits as the capture of the *Black Galley* in his journal. £88.6s.2d. was expended on

[1] PRO E351/2353.
[2] *APC*, 3, 43.
[3] Ibid., 104. The Privy Council's concern for the proper maintenance of the navy is further demonstrated by the fact that on 4 November 1550 the officers of the Admiralty 'had access to the Lords to declare the estate of that office, where they exhibited four books, one touching the docking and repairing of certain ships, another of articles touching their pleasure in certain things necessary to be done, the third of an estimate for cables and sailcloths . . . and an account of old debts . . .', *APC*, 3, 151.

paving the high street there on one occasion, so that the King could '. . . pass to and fro to see the building of his highness's ships' without having to undergo the inconvenience of its 'noisomeness' and filth. Two Breton craftsmen were brought to Deptford in 1552 for the purpose of training local sail makers in the manufacture of 'poldavies', sail cloth of a particularly tough and durable nature.[1]

Idle ships were expensive, and only about a dozen or fifteen seem to have been in regular use for patrols or attempts to combat piracy during the three years which followed the ending of the war. For the first time for nearly a decade royal ships were available for commercial use, and the officers of the Admiralty – all of whom had their own mercantile interests – naturally had the first call upon them. There was nothing improper in such activity, nor should it be interpreted to mean that they were neglecting their naval responsibilities. William Winter and Benjamin Gonson hired two large men-of-war, the *Jesus* and the *Matthew*, for a trading voyage to the Levant, and on 6 November 1552 entered into a recognizance for £1 208 to return the *Matthew* in the same condition as she had been at the time of hiring.[2] At the same time the *Mary Willoughby* and the *Jerfalcon* were hired in the traditional manner, by London merchants for a voyage to Spain. Nevertheless, there was pressure for economies, not from Warwick himself (Duke of Northumberland from October 1551) but from the Council. The survey of August 1552 seems to have been in part a response to such pressure, and in October there were vague but ominous hints about 'discharging the Admiralty'. The special commission set up 'to consider means of increasing revenue and reducing charges', when it reported in December 1552 recommended a reduction in the 'riding charges and other extraordinary allowances' of the officers, and the discontinuance of the new office of Surveyor of the Victuals.[3] Like most of the other recommendations of that Commission, however, these comparatively modest economies were never realized. Even the sales specifically suggested in the survey were not implemented in Edward's lifetime, and in spite of the general demand for retrenchment, naval expenditure remained, as we have seen, at about £20 000 a year for the remainder of the reign.

[1] Oppenheim, *Administration*, 103.
[2] *APC*, 4, 162. Merchant ships likewise continued to be used in the royal service, although on a much smaller scale than hitherto, and a bounty of 5s. a ton continued to be paid on merchantmen of 100 tons and over. Oppenheim, *Administration*, 107.
[3] BL Harleian MS 7383 f. 67r; T. Glasgow, 'The maturing of naval administration, 1556–1564', *MM*, 56, 1970, 3–26.

The evidence of specific activity, however, is scrappy in the extreme. In April 1551 two ships were sent to Ireland, and on 11 March 1552 Gonson was paid over £3 000 for victualling and 'equipping to the seas' the *Primrose*, the *Antelope*, the *Hart*, the *Greyhound* and the *Falcon*.[1] This suggests the same type of summer patrolling as had been carried out in the early 1540s, before the outbreak of war, and that impression is confirmed by a Council letter to Edward Baeshe on 14 June 1552, instructing him to see that the ships at Gillingham, and the pinnaces 'appointed for the narrow seas' were 'furnished forth with victuals'.[2] On 29 November in the same year Gonson received another payment for 'the charges of certain the king's majesty's ships sent into Zeeland for the conduct of the English fleet', although the small sum involved (£179.13s.3d.) suggests no more than two or three ships for short period. Piracy was a major concern, and absorbed a great deal of diplomatic time and effort, as well as keeping the Admiralty courts busy on both sides of the Channel, but there is no evidence of the King's ships being involved in its suppression. Some pirates arrested in Ireland were brought over for trial in May 1549, and on 27 August 1552 William Thomas, the Clerk of the Council, sought a special commission to try pirates within the liberty of the Cinq Ports.[3] Probably the navy did make some arrests, as in earlier and later years, and the patrols had some deterrent effect, but hardly enough to make a significant impact on the problem. The same could be said of every period until almost the end of the century.

The most important maritime activity of the period, and that which was eventually to have the most profound effect upon strategic thinking and the whole concept of seapower, at the time had nothing to do with the navy. As we have seen, Henry VII had supported the Bristol merchants in their attempts to open up routes across the Atlantic, but in spite of the promptings of Robert Thorne and Roger Barlow, his son had not followed suit. Henry VIII had no thoughts to spare for distant exploits when there were French galleys to be challenged in the Narrow Seas, and his navy had remained primarily a coastal defence force. However in 1548 Sebastian Cabot returned to England. He was the son of that John Cabot who had

[1] *APC*, 3, 503.

[2] *APC*, 3, 79.

[3] PRO SP10/7/12, warrant for Sir Thomas Woodstock's expenses, 18 May 1549; SP10/14/69. In January 1549 a proclamation had specifically ordered the arrest of nine named pirates operating in Irish waters, and offered up to 1 000 crowns a head reward for their capture. Hughes and Larkin, *Tudor Royal Proclamations*, I, 437–8.

sailed from Bristol in 1497, and after 1509 he had several times attempted unsuccessfully to obtain English patronage for further voyages. Instead he had made a distinguished and lucrative career as Pilot Major to Charles V. For some reason which is not entirely clear, Cabot retained a desire to work in England, and after Henry's death, in spite of advancing years and a well-established position in Spain, he came. The Emperor was understandably annoyed, and tried to claim that his Pilot Major was being held against his will. Not only was Cabot a very accomplished navigator, he was also the master of all the secrets of the *Casa de Contratacion*, the Spanish maritime academy over which he had presided for many years. Diplomatic relations were strained in any case, and Northumberland seems to have made the most of his good fortune. Cabot was given a pension, and encouraged to impart his knowledge to English friends and pupils. He had probably brought with him from Spain the desire to seek a new route to China around the north of Russia – what was later to be known as the North East passage – and in May 1553 he became the governor of a company set up for that purpose. With Northumberland's active encouragement and support about 200 London merchants and courtiers took up shares in this company.[1] Two hundred and forty shares were issued at £25 each; not an entirely new way of doing business, but original in this context, and a tribute to the enthusiasm of the promoters, because no more cautious body of men existed anywhere than the so-called Merchant Adventurers of London. Cabot was too old to lead the expedition himself, so it was placed in the hands of Sir Hugh Willoughby as Captain General, with Richard Chancellor as his pilot. On 10 May 1553 three small ships, the largest only 160 tons, set sail from Ratcliff, carrying an investment of £6 000, and grandiloquent letters of greeting from King Edward VI to the Emperor of China. In spite of his mortal sickness the young King was carried to the window of his chamber to see them pass. Although it could hardly have been guessed, a new era of English seafaring was about to begin.

Mary's reign began inauspiciously. Although no one in England knew it, in August Willoughby and Chancellor became separated off the Lofoten Islands, and the former made the fatal decision to winter in the bay of Arzina on the coast of Lappland.[2] In London the Duke of Northumberland made the equally fatal mistake of trying to intrude his daughter-in-law Lady Jane Grey into the

[1] Sir William Foster, *England's Quest of Eastern Trade*, 8.
[2] Ibid., 9–10.

succession when Edward died on 6 July. Jane was a granddaughter of Henry VIII's younger sister, Mary, and was intended to preserve the Protestant establishment, but her position was legally and politically weak, and Northumberland's position collapsed within two weeks. The euphoria which followed the Queen's defeat of this plot was dampened almost at once by religious protests, and by the destruction of the venerable but still awe-inspiring flagship, the *Henry Grace a Dieu*. On 25 August she was burned at her moorings off Woolwich '. . . by neckclygens and for lake of over-syth' as Henry Machyn reported.[1] Since it was exactly this kind of accident that shipkeepers were employed to prevent, his judgement was probably correct, although whether the keepers had been discharged or gone absent without leave, we have no means of knowing. Since the Council allocated at least £7 000 for the ordinary expenditure of the navy between July and December 1553 there was clearly no sudden economy drive by the new regime.[2] The navy had even, in a small way, contributed to Mary's success, since the six ships which the Duke of Northumberland had sent to the Orwell to block her escape route to the continent had mutinied and contributed their guns to her army gathering at Framlingham. In spite of this, the Council for Marine Causes was under a political cloud during the winter of 1553–4. Lord Clinton had been a little too close to Northumberland for comfort, and although he had survived the crisis of the summer apparently unscathed, he was replaced as Lord Admiral for no obvious reason on 26 March 1554. His replacement was Lord William Howard. Some time during the summer of 1553 Sir Thomas Wyndham, the Master of Naval Ordnance, had died during a trading voyage to the Guinea coast, and he had not been replaced. Most serious of all William Winter, the Surveyor, was arrested, tried and condemned for his part in Sir Thomas Wyatt's rebellion.[3] On 16 December Winter had been sent with a small squadron to Ostend to escort the Emperor's ambassadors, coming to England to complete the negotiations for Mary's marriage to his son Philip of Spain. For this service Winter had been rewarded by the Emperor with a gold chain, but the marriage was generally unpopular in England, and the Surveyor may already have been involved in conspiracy against it before he undertook his mission. He seems to have played

[1] J. G. Nichols, ed., *The Diary of Henry Machyn*, 43.
[2] *APC*, 4, 339–378.
[3] D. M. Loades, *Two Tudor Conspiracies* 95–6.

no active part in the rebellion, but was arrested along with several friends and associates, on 20 February 1554.[1]

No ship list survives from the early part of Mary's reign. We know that the old *Struse* was eventually disposed of to Robert Warner for £200 during 1553, and that the *Matthew* did not return to service after her use by Benjamin Gonson in the Mediterranean.[2] If she was really worth £1 200 she can hardly have been ready for breaking up, and may have been lost on the voyage. In 1554 there were 29 men-of-war in commission, five more than in August 1552, manned by 4 034 men. Although there was political tension with France, both before and after the Queen's marriage to Philip in July, there was no war, and so it is reasonable to conclude that, in spite of the problems at the Admiralty, the level of peacetime naval preparedness was as high as it had ever been. This impression is borne out by the surviving accounts. Sir Edmund Peckham, the Treasurer of the Mint, who had exclusive control over the disbursement of all the Crown's revenue for two years after his commission on 5 December 1553, paid out £10 967 to Gonson between October 1553 and May 1554.[3] Between May and the end of September 1554 a further £15 159 went to the same destination, making a total for 12 months of £26 126. Even if we assume that this includes the money which Gonson would have to pay over to Baeshe for victualling, it still suggests a very different situation from the neglect which is traditionally portrayed for this period. Most of Gonson's detailed disbursements have not survived, but at some point during 1554 £649.5s. was paid to William Watson for delivering to Deptford a variety of masts and spars 'brought out of Dansk', including three of 31 yards in length, and seven of 30 yards, suitable for the largest ships.[4] There is consequently no need to postulate a sudden change of policy in 1555, or to speculate about the way in which Philip may have galvanized the English Council into action. Philip was certainly interested in the English fleet, rightly seeing it as England's most effective military arm, but he can have had no good reason to be disappointed with what he found when he arrived. What did happen was that some time in the summer or early autumn of 1555 a decision was taken to lay down two large new ships. The last ship built for royal service had been the *Primrose* in 1551. A large number

[1] Ibid.
[2] Glasgow, 'List of Ships . . .'.
[3] PRO E101/63/5, f.7. For Peckham's special commission, see D. Loades, *The Reign of Mary Tudor* 140.
[4] Bodleian Library, Rawlinson MS 846, f. 166.

of ships had been added to the fleet less than ten years earlier, and a gap of four years in the building programme was not particularly remarkable. This particular decision was probably prompted by the loss of the *Great Harry* and the *Matthew*, and indicates rather a desire to keep the navy up to strength than to resurrect it in the interests of the King. The *Philip and Mary* of 500 tons and the *Mary Rose* of 600 tons were both launched towards the end of 1556.

The impression that the navy was run down during the first two years of Mary's reign comes primarily from the large number of sales which took place in 1554 and 1555. Gonson's account from Michaelmas 1554 to Christmas 1555 records the disposal of no fewer than 14 vessels of various sizes.[1] However, this should be seen as good housekeeping rather than the wasting of assets. With the exception of the *Primrose*, sold to a London consortium in December 1554 for £1 800, all were old; some had been out of commission for years, and some – such as the *Shoulder of Mutton* – never seem to have been commissioned at all. The whole lot fetched £181. The sale of the *Primrose* is something of a mystery. A 300 ton ship only three years old should have been worth much more than £1 800, and she may have been damaged during a voyage to Guinea in the previous year. After refitting she sailed to Russia for her new owners in 1557, and was to rejoin the navy in 1560. During this period the Treasurer expended £26 524 – an annual rate of about £21 000 – and the breakdown enables an approximate picture of the situation to be reconstructed.[2] Deptford was still by far the most important dockyard, accounting for £6 524.5s.5d., and operations had recommenced on a small scale at Colne, where £504.13s.7d was recorded. Nothing at all was expended at Portsmouth, which probably means that the very small charges incurred in keeping the substantial plant there on a care and maintenance basis were paid out of some other pocket. Portsmouth was essentially a wartime base, and its peacetime role seems to have been reduced to virtually nothing. The 'sea charges', or wages and incidental expenses for ships actually in service amounted to almost £4 000, while Baeshe expended £11 614 on victuals. Altogether what was soon to be classified as 'ordinary' expenditure accounted during these 15 months for £10 927 – a rate of a little over £9 000 a year. In the absence of a detailed breakdown the repair and servicing programme can only be glimpsed. In November 1553 the Council auth-

[1] PRO E351/2195.
[2] Ibid.

orized a special payment (which presumably did not pass through Gonson's accounts) of £34.6s.8d. to William Stevens, a master shipwright, for the repair of the *Lion* barge.[1] In March 1556 a warrant to Gonson was specifically described as being for 'the amending, repayring and grounding of the saide shippes and their boates', which was unusual by that date, and on the same day it was resolved that '. . . the King and Queenes Majesties' Navie shulde be augmented and encreased, and that the small *Bark* and the *Peter Pomegranate* shulde this yere be repaired . . .'[2]

The activity of the navy must similarly be pieced together from a variety of sources, as the global figure for sea charges can give only a very general indication of the level. Within a few days of her accession, and before she had even reached London, Mary placed the six ships already in her hands under the control of Sir Richard Cavendish, but this seems to have been only an interim measure, until the allegiance of the existing naval officers could be established. In due course all were to be confirmed in their positions. With remarkable speed, again before the end of July 1553, the Queen began to put her ships to work. William Tyrell was appointed Vice-Admiral of the Narrow Seas, and was despatched with the *Jennet* and the *Greyhound* to the straits of Dover.[3] Anxieties about the intentions of the French probably lay behind this rapid deployment, and one part of Tyrell's instructions referred to '. . . regarde by intellygence or otherwyse' for discovering 'what power by the seas is or shalbe set forth, and to what purpose, in the Frenche Kyng's domynyons . . .'[4] However, equal prominence was given to the protection of the Queen's subjects against 'pyrates and rovers apon the seas', who were to be apprehended whenever possible. It was probably the cost of this voyage which was being met when Gonson was paid £867.1s.5d. on 24 September 'for discharge of victualling'. On 16 December Winter was instructed to escort the Imperial ambassadors who were coming from the Low Countries to sign the treaty of marriage between Mary and Philip, the Emperor's only legitimate son; and on 11 January 1554 the officers of the Admiralty were instructed to prepare the *Bark*, the *Jennet*, the *Greyhound* and

[1] *APC*, 4, 362.
[2] *APC*, 5, 258.
[3] *APC*, 4, 17–18.
[4] Henry Dudley, the Duke of Northumberland's cousin, had been sent on a mission to France to raise support for Jane against Mary. He had not succeeded but Mary's Council were fearful of belated French intervention. Loades, *Two Tudor Conspiracies*, 166; *APC*, 4, 418.

the *Phoenix* 'to be equipped forth with speed to Spain'.[1] At that point it was believed that Philip would be coming within a few weeks to claim his bride, and these ships were probably intended to escort or greet him. However, the French, whose interests were directly threatened by an Anglo-Habsburg alliance, were doing their best to stir up discontent in England, and at the end of January a widespread plot resulted in the Wyatt rebellion in Kent. The crisis passed in less than a fortnight, but the Emperor's ambassador in London, Simon Renard, was understandably apprehensive about the Prince's safety. This, combined with Philip's own dissatisfaction over the terms of the treaty which had been negotiated on his behalf, and genuine difficulties about providing for the government of Spain in his absence eventually postponed his coming for several months, and it is unlikely that this projected voyage ever took place. Much to the embarrassment of Renard, Philip's intentions throughout the spring of 1554 remained unclear. He was betrothed to the Queen *per verba de praesenti* in March, but neither Renard or the English Council had any firm knowledge of when to expect him.[2] Early in April the new Lord Admiral set out with 28 ships, and a set of instructions which were perforce vague. He was to cruise the Channel, protect trade, and arrest any pirates he could catch; but the real purpose of having such a large fleet at sea was to meet Philip and to protect him against French interception, which was believed to be a serious danger.

April became May, and May became June, and still there was no word of the Prince's coming. The ships had to return for revictualling, and some needed repair. It was almost unprecedented to have such a large fleet at sea for so long in peacetime, and the lack of action made captains and crews equally restive. It was also extremely expensive. Howard's frustration was shared in full measure by the Sieur de la Capelle, the Imperial Admiral. Repeated rumours were calling them to action stations, only to be proved false. Capelle tried to victual his ships in England, but Baeshe had had no instructions to make provision for him, and he was turned away, to his intense disgust. Capelle denounced Howard for incompetence, without any justification as far as can be seen, and Howard blamed Simon Renard, who was equally innocent of responsibility.[3] In fact Philip

[1] *APC*, 4, 380, 383.
[2] Loades, *Reign of Mary Tudor*, 81–2. *Per verba de praesenti* expressed the present tense, i.e. 'I take', rather than 'I will take', and was thus more binding.
[3] *Cal. Span*, 12, 293–5. Howard's concern that the ambassador was 'too deep' in the Queen's confidence was rather more justified.

had left Valladolid early in May, as soon as the Earl of Worcester arrived with confirmation of the betrothal ceremony, but he did not reach his point of embarkation at Coruna until the end of June. Meanwhile an English embassy led by the Earl of Bedford had been shipped direct to Coruna, ostensibly bearing a token from the Queen to her betrothed, but in reality to find out what on earth was going on. Part of the trouble, it subsequently transpired, was actually caused by the lack of a naval infrastructure in Spain. Spanish naval activity had hitherto been geared to the production of a galley fleet for the Mediterranean. Atlantic voyages had been entirely civilian, and Philip had no means of mobilizing a fleet for Atlantic service, beyond calling upon the traditional obligations of the north coast ports. It was as though Mary had still been dependent upon the Cinq Ports. Such provision was very slow, and very reluctant; Philip was still pursuing defaulters ten years later, and when he eventually set out on 12 July his ships were fewer and less well-equipped than he would have wished.[1] It did not matter because the French threat never materialized, and all the English, Flemish or Spanish squadrons did was to provide an honorific escort. English sources say that Howard insisted upon Philip striking his colours when he entered English waters; but since the Spaniards, who were profoundly suspicious and on the lookout for any slight, make no mention of such a circumstance the story is probably apocryphal.[2] The English were extremely careful to point out to Philip that he was not their King until the marriage had actually taken place, but such a gesture would have been out of keeping with the spirit of Howard's mission on this occasion.

The remainder of 1554 seems to have witnessed only routine activity. By the terms of the marriage treaty Philip was debarred from involving England in his war with France, and although he resented that provision intensely, he made no immediate attempt to evade it. From September to November the *Falcon* and the *Sun* were patrolling the Narrow Seas, and at the end of March further payments indicate that the patrols had been maintained throughout the winter. On 8 December powder was issued to the *Phoenix*, the *Seven Stars*, the *Greyhound* and the *Jennet*.[3] Similar scraps of evidence are all that have survived from 1555. In September Sir Edmund Rowse and others were licensed to fish the Bann in Ireland, and to arm ships for the protection of their activities. In return they were

[1] Archives General de Simancas, Diversos de Castilia, VI, ff. 65–8.
[2] Laird Clowes, *The Royal Navy*, 471–2.
[3] *APC*, 5, 86.

bound to seek for and apprehend one Cole and other pirates operating off the Irish coast, although there is no evidence to suggest that they ever succeeded.[1] Mary seems to have taken the fight against piracy seriously. Althought most of the references are to the licensing or arming of volunteers for the purpose, the Queen herself seems to have had a squadron of about eight ships at sea seeking for Cole and another Irish pirate named Stevenson in the latter part of 1555 and early 1556. There was more to this apparently public-spirited concern than met the eye, however. The collapse of Wyatt's rebellion in February 1554 had driven a number of disaffected gentlemen into exile in France. These men, Sir Peter Carew, Christopher Ashton, Peter Killigrew and a number of others, maintained themselves by piracy, an art in which some of them had had a lot of practice.[2] In return for the indulgence of the French naval authorities, they concentrated their attentions on English, Spanish and Flemish shipping. The English Government believed that they actually held Letters of Marque from the Admiral of France, but that was never proved. To Henry II, anxious to harrass and destabilize a country which was now firmly attached to his Habsburg enemy, these pirates were useful allies. As early as February 1554, within a few weeks of his flight, Carew was reported to be cruising with ships hired at Rouen, and largely English crews. By the end of March the Killigrews were also at sea with three ships, one of which was the 160 ton *Sacrette*, reported to have been loaned free of charge by the French King. Henry at least turned a blind eye to these activities, and responded to diplomatic representations with bland professions of ignorance. Occasionally one was captured. Nicholas Tremayne, for example, was interrogated in prison in February 1555, but with what result is not known.[3] When Henry Dudley's elaborate conspiracy to rob the Exchequer in London and launch an exile invasion from France was broken up in the spring of 1556, he and his followers also joined the pirate fleet, which had become a major hazard to trade and an important political grievance by the summer of that year. On 19 June Edward Wotton, the English Ambassador in France, reported that this fleet was at sea and had taken several 'good prizes' both Spanish and English.[4] However, about the middle of July the

[1] *APC*, 5, 183–4.

[2] Loades, *Two Tudor Conspiracies*, 161–5. Thomas and Peter were the sons of John Killigrew of Arwenack in Cornwall, and had been in trouble for piracy in the previous reign. *APC*, 4, 245.

[3] *APC*, 5, 99, 24 February 1555.

[4] Wotton to Sir William Petre, 19 June 1556; *Calendar of State Papers, Foreign*, II, 229.

pirates were intercepted by a squadron of the Queen's ships off Plymouth and decisively defeated. No account of this engagement has survived, but the pirates seem to have mustered seven or eight ships, because six were captured and it was noted that one or two had escaped. The royal squadron was probably larger, but we do not know which ships were involved. Among those captured was Peter Killigrew, who was interrogated at length on 21 August, and told an interesting tale of his relations with the Admiral of France. According to him his original ships had been impounded at Brest in the summer or autumn of 1553.

> ... in consyderation whereof after the return of my brother (Henry) ... we were sewtors to thAdmirall to be the meanes to the kinge that we might have the Sacrett for ii yeres with such furnyture to serve her, whiche was graunted us. And after upon service (discharged) demanded the gyfte of the saide shippe with such ordonance which was grantyd us, and which was (conveyed) to us by the Lord Admirall in Newehaven in [i.e. Le Havre] in Lent was twelvemonth (1555) ...[1]

The French authorities denied this, insisting that the ship had been lent to Killigrew for the duration of the Franco-Habsburg war. To complicate matters further, that war had been suspended by the truce of Vaucelles in February 1556, and was not being actively prosecuted at the time when the *Sacrette* was captured. French demands for the return of the ship were rejected, and she appears on subsequent naval lists down to 1562.[2] Peter Killigrew was not eventually prosecuted for either piracy or treason, and after a period of imprisonment was recruited as a captain into the Queen's service.

This victory did not eliminate the problem of piracy, but it significantly reduced it. Among the English exiles only Christopher Ashton remained as a major operator. The exiles continued their somewhat shadowy conspiracies for raids upon the English coast. Wotton's spies unearthed a plot against Portland castle early in 1557, but the only one which came to fruition was Thomas Stafford's raid on Scarborough in April 1557. That episode, which played a major part in bringing England into the renewed Franco-Habsburg war, shows a number of suspicious features. One of these is the fact the English Council knew that Stafford's ships had sailed on 18 April, and had a good idea of their destination, yet made no

[1] PRO SP11/9/25.
[2] Glasgow, 'List of Ships ...'.

attempt to intercept him, in spite of the fact that at least ten royal ships were at sea at the time. The raid was a total failure, but was naturally represented as a piece of gratuitous French provocation, in spite of Henry's earnest, and probably honest, denials.[1]

At the end of 1555 Gonson's account had been over £5 000 in debt, about the same as three years earlier, but by the end of 1556 the deficit had been reduced to £1 154.18s.10d. Receipts for the year totalled £28 385.6s.7d., of which all but £100 had come from the Exchequer, and expenditure amounted to £23 600.9s.11d.[2] This seems to be a clear sign of improving financial management, and was partly a result of the reorganization which had taken place at the Exchequer in 1554. In earlier years when the source of naval income was recorded, it had consisted of warrants drawn on a wide variety of sources, of which the Exchequer had only been one. The pattern of expenditure is also interesting. Sea charges amounted to £5 305, significantly more than in the previous year, and victualling to £12 515, confirming the enhanced level of activity which can be imperfectly reconstructed from other sources. Ordinary expenditure, on the other hand, was down to £5 439, and distribution between dockyards had altered considerably. Deptford was still the largest spender, at £2 966, but this was largely accounted for by the purchase of materials: timber, ropes, pitch and tar and canvas. Most of the work, reflected in wages for labourers, craftsmen and shipkeepers, was carried out at Portsmouth, where £1 916 was expended.[3] Woolwich, Gillingham and Colne spent less than £500 between them. This return to Portsmouth suggests that preparations for war were already commencing before the end of 1556, probably following the breakdown of the truce of Vaucelles in Italy in September. The level of expenditure at the Medway ports also demonstrates that the large new ships which were under construction there were being built on contract and not by direct labour.

The impression which these accounts give of tightening financial and administrative control is confirmed by two sets of Council minutes, one of 11 January 1556 and the other of 8 January 1557. The former consisted of an instruction to the Lord Admiral to take a 'secrete muster' of all the soldiers and mariners then serving in the Queen's ships, without the knowledge of the officers of the Admi-

[1] For a full discussion of this curious episode, see Loades, *Reign of Mary Tudor*, 304–8.
[2] PRO E351/2196.
[3] Ibid.

ralty.[1] Whether fraud or negligence were suspected is not clear, nor what was the outcome of the investigation, but there were obviously several ships on active service in the middle of the winter, as had been customary for a number of years. This instruction was followed by a series of further orders; for a check on the victuals carried on the ships in service; for a monthly muster on all ships appointed for the Narrow Seas; and for a stocktaking of equipment, and of outstanding repair work. The Council was clearly not happy with the effectiveness of the control being exercised by the officials of the Admiralty. There is no record of the immediate outcome of this campaign, and it is hard to see it reflected in Gonson's accounts. However, a year later the whole organization was placed under the direct supervision of the Lord Treasurer, the Marquis of Winchester. The Queen, it was noted '. . . hathe byn sundrie tymes troubled with the often signing of warrants for money to be defraied about the necessarye charges of her Highnes navie' and had decided to make some more convenient arrangement. Ostensibly all that was to happen was that Winchester would undertake this task instead, but in agreeing to perform such routine work, the Lord Treasurer laid down certain conditions which really embodied the whole point of the change.

> First he required to have the somme of xiiii^{m} ^{li} by yere to be advanced halfe yerely to Benjamin Gonson Treasourer of thadmiraltie, to be by him defraied in suche sorte as shalbe prescribed unto him by the saide Lord Treasurer, with th'advice of the Lord Admyrall etc.[2]

In return for this control, Winchester undertook to service and repair all those ships which were in need of such attention, and to build new 'with convenient speede' those that were too far gone for remedial treatment, using timber out of the Queen's 'parkes, forrests, chaces and manours'. He also undertook to ensure that all the ships were properly equipped and victualled. When he was entirely satisfied that the navy was fully ready for action, then he would be willing to remain in charge for an 'ordinary' of only £10 000 a year. Apart from the financial arrangements, the only element in Winchester's programme which represented an innovation was his proposal 'to cause a mass of victuals to be alwaies in a reddiness hable to serve for oone thousande men for a moneth, to be set to the seas

[1] *APC*, 5, 220–21.
[2] *APC*, 6, 39.

upon anye sodayne . . .' The corollary of this, not actually stated, was that there would always be a small number of ships, perhaps five or six, ready to go to sea at a few days warning. Perhaps, in view of the constant activity of the navy over the last few years, that could be taken for granted. Gonson and Baeshe were to account annually and separately, presumably to Winchester himself, although that is not explicit.

The whole of this latter minute is expressive of a lack of confidence in the existing officers on the part of the Council, and this lack of confidence seems to have sprung from the 'secrete searches' ordered a year before. How justified this was, and what improvements resulted from the change, is not easy to determine. The only officer to be dismissed was the Lord Admiral himself, Howard being replaced by the return of Lord Clinton on 10 February 1558. This change is thought to have reflected Philip's influence, but probably had more to do with his conduct of the war than with his role in the administration, and there does not seem to have been any noticeable acceleration of expenditure as a result of the changes. Winchester clearly believed that there was a backlog of repairs and maintenance which needed immediate attention, but beyond that his 'ordinary' of £10 000 a year was not much, if at all, above the level of 1554–5. Probably he wanted to bring Gonson and Baeshe under more effective control, and he may have suspected politically inspired foot-dragging by officers who had all served in the same positions under the previous regime. In the event there was hardly time for Winchester's new system to become established before England was drawn into Philip's war against France in June 1557. From then until the end of the reign the navy was on a war footing, and expenditure inevitably soared. Over the two full years from 30 December 1556 to 30 December 1558 Gonson received £144 941.1s.6d., of which £131 154 came from the Exchequer.[1] According to one set of accounts he spent £157 638, of which victualling accounted for £73 503 and the wages of men at sea £43 492.[2] However his next ordinary statement, commencing on 1 January 1559 starts with a deficit carried over of only £814 – so either he was not responsible for the full expenditure recorded or the statement of his income is incomplete.[3] Whichever total is accepted, it represents something between 20 and 25 per cent of the whole war expenditure for the

[1] PRO E101/64/1, 'A declaration of all such somes of money as have bene payde oute of the receipt unto Benjamin Gonson . . .'.
[2] PRO E351/2195; Oppenheim, *Administration*, 113.
[3] PRO E351/2197.

period. It was also handled by Gonson himself, and not by a specially appointed war Treasurer, as had been normal in the past. Either confidence in the Treasurer of the Navy had been fully restored, or Winchester was satisfied with the effectiveness of his own supervision.

During the first period of the war three new ships were added to the navy, although the exact dates of their commissioning are not known. The *Mary Rose* had almost certainly been launched before January 1557, but the *Lion* of 500 tons and the pinnaces *Sprite* (40 tons) and *Bright Falcon* (60 tons) belong to the last 18 months of Mary's reign;[1] so, probably, does the rebuilding of the 100 ton *Falcon*. Work was also commenced on four other vessels; an 800 ton replacement for the *Great Harry* (provisionally named the *Peter* but eventually the *Elizabeth Jonas*), and three re-builds, the *Jennet* (300 tons), the *Swallow* (300 tons), and the *Hare* (60 tons).[2] This level of construction did not equal that of 1544–5, or even 1512, but it was superior to anything achieved later in the century, with the possible exception of 1587–8 when the Armada was anticipated. In other words Mary's Council did exactly what her father's had done, it stepped up shipbuilding activity in wartime, so there is no particular reason to attribute this to Winchester's new regime at the Admiralty. Only two changes were made to the personnel between the outbreak of war and Mary's death. At the end of July 1557 William Winter, now fully restored to favour, added to his existing office of Surveyor of the Ships that of Master of Naval Ordnance, which had been vacant since Wyndham's death in 1553. He did not, however, get two full salaries, being paid £142 per annum in respect of his second office, instead of the £242.10s. laid down in 1546.[3] The other appointment was that of Peter Pett, who joined the long serving Richard Bull as a second Royal Master Shipwright.

The war of 1557–9 is normally regarded as a failure, and from an English point of view something of a disaster because of the loss of Calais, but the navy acquitted itself as well as the politics of the situation allowed. Philip had no illusions about the nature of his relations with the English, and his determination to bring them into the war was not based upon any high expectations of financial or military support. His honour required that a realm whose title he bore should obey him in a matter of such importance, particularly as

[1] Glasgow, 'List of ships . . .'; Oppenheim, *Administration*, 109.

[2] Glasgow, 'List of ships . . .'. Work on the 'Peter' seems to have commenced in the spring of 1558. Glasgow, 'The navy in Philip and Mary's war', *MM*, 53, 1967, 335.

[3] Glasgow, 'Maturing of naval administration . . .', 9 and n.

he was fully supported by the Queen. He also needed the English fleet, reluctant though it may have been to co-operate with him. Shortly after he had left England in August 1555 it had been expected that his father Charles V would shortly be retiring to Spain, and Philip had requested 12–14 English ships to form a part of the escort. Apparently the English Council had told him that they could not be prepared in time, and the King had reacted angrily, telling them that their fleet should be ready at all times to repel invaders. If this exchange ever took place as reported, it tells us more about Philip's relationship with the English Council than it does about the state of the fleet.[1] There were at least 24 ships in commission at that point, although several of those were probably at sea on other missions and the Council did not feel inclined to recall them for Philip's convenience. It is also possible that they felt that they had been given unreasonably short notice. In the event an order was given on 14 October for 15 ships to be prepared for the Emperor's escort, but they were not needed and Charles remained in the Low Countries for another 11 months.[2] Thereafter the King took more pains to inform himself of the true state of England's maritime preparedness, and had lists, both of the Queen's ships and of available merchantmen, drawn up for his use, which subsequently found their way into his archive at Simancas.[3] When England finally entered the war on 7 June 1557 a fleet of 21 ships was already at sea with 3 192 men on board – not including the new ships, the *Philip and Mary* and the *Mary Rose*, although Sir Thomas Cotton had been especially called home from Calais to take command of the former. The first mission of this fleet was the highly traditional one of sweeping the Channel in preparation for the crossing of the expeditionary force under the Earl of Pembroke, which was to join Philip's main army in the Netherlands. There was virtually no resistance, as Henry had no war fleet in the North at this time. On 12 June Howard reported that he had searched the whole coast from Brittany to Boulogne without encountering any French ships at

[1] Philip's rebuke to the English Council seems to have been contained in a letter written to the select council about a month after his departure from England. It probably reflects his irritation with the uncooperative attitude of that council (of which this is not the only example) rather than a considered encouragement to revitalize the navy. In the first place the navy was in reasonably good condition, and in the second place Philip had had ample opportunity during more than twelve months in England to make his wishes known in this respect. Glasgow, 'The navy in Philip and Mary's war', 322.

[2] PRO SP11/8/61. Loades, *Reign of Mary*, 188.

[3] AGS E811, f. 128.

all.[1] Later in the month there was some action; on the 22nd four French ships were sighted near Dieppe, and at least two were taken; shortly after seven more appeared, but after a brisk chase they escaped into Boulogne.

At the end of June the fleet was recalled to escort the army, which by then was ready to sail, and on 5 July Philip left England for the second and last time, accompanied by about 8 000 English troops. Meanwhile a squadron consisting of the *Pauncey*, the *Mary Fortune* and (somewhat ironically) the *Sacrette* continued to patrol the Channel in case any French warships should put in a belated appearance.[2] In the event the crossing was uneventful, although once ashore the logistical arrangements broke down, and both Philip and the English army missed the decisive battle of St Quentin, fought on 10 August. Honour was to some extent restored by participation in the capture of the town itself on 27 August, an engagement which cost some 200 casualties, but that was virtually the whole extent of England's participation in the land war. By 10 October all but 500 of the English contingent had returned home, presumably in English ships although no details of the arrangements have survived. Having discharged its escort duties the main fleet, by this time numbering 15 and commanded by the Vice-Admiral, Sir William Woodhouse, returned to station in the Channel, where on 26 July it was joined by the *Jesus of Lubeck* commanded by William Winter.[3] At the same time a second fleet, consisting of nine royal ships led by Sir John Clere in the *Minion*, was detailed to bring home the fishing fleet from Iceland and to make a show of strength off the Scottish coast. Unfortunately Clere, who may have lacked experience in naval command, chose to land on Orkney on 12 August. His landing was resisted, and in seeking to escape by boat Clere and three of his captains were drowned.[4] In spite of this mishap the Iceland fleet returned safely; but Woodhouse seems to have achieved nothing of note in the Narrow Seas, and in September he brought his ships back to Portsmouth, where most of them remained rigged and equipped but manned by skeleton crews. About ten ships remained at sea during the autumn, in accordance with what was by then well-established practice, but they did not constitute a war fleet, and could do little to respond to the sudden crisis caused by the Duke of Guise's attack on Calais on 1 January 1558.

[1] PRO SP11/11/12; Glasgow, 'Philip and Mary's war', 329.
[2] BL Stowe MS 571, ff. 77–132; Loades, *Reign of Mary*, 312; PRO SP11/11/26, 27.
[3] PRO SP11/11/26.
[4] Glasgow, 'Philip and Mary's war . . .' 331–2.

It is sometimes said that Calais fell because England had lost command of the seas, but that is true only in the most myopic sense. Had there been a number of fully-armed warships in Calais harbour at the time of the attack the outcome might have been different, but otherwise naval strength could not have helped. The critical factors were surprise and the speed of the French advance. Woodhouse was alerted on 31 December, and instructed to get five ships to sea 'with all possible diligence'. His reaction time could hardly be faulted, and a squadron of English ships tried to enter Calais harbour on 3 January.[1] It was already too late, because Ruysbank fort, which controlled the entrance, had fallen on the 2nd, and the heavy guns which it mounted were in enemy hands. A powerful fleet might have been able to batter its way in, but the ships available were not up to so formidable a task. In moving against Ruysbank the French army had been supported by sea, but the whole operation was completed in less than two days, so unless English ships had actually been within sight of the town at the time, they could have done nothing to intervene. Calais itself surrendered on 7 January, but Guines was still holding out, and the first reaction of the English Council seems to have been to counter attack as quickly as possible with whatever resources were nearest to hand. On 9 January Woodhouse was ordered to put to sea with all available ships.[2] Musters had already been ordered, but circumstances conspired to emphasize the belatedness of the English response. The influenza epidemic which had been raging since the previous summer meant that fit men were few, and much harder to come by than in normal circumstance; and then on 9 and 10 January a violent storm blew up. Whether Woodhouse had managed to get any further ships to sea by then seems very doubtful, but those that had responded to the earlier call caught the full blast of this tempest. As far as we know none were lost, but every one was damaged, one or two seriously. This set-back caused the musters to be cancelled on 12 January, and although the Council continued to toy with the idea of an expeditionary force, after the fall of Guines on 21 January the pretence of an urgent military response was abandoned.[3] Although there are many ways in which the English handling of the Calais crisis can be criticized, a lack of naval preparation or presence is not one of them. There was

[1] PRO SP11/11/66; Henry, Earl of Rutland to the Queen, 3 January 1558, PRO SP69/12/712.

[2] PRO SP11/12/12.

[3] Loades, *Reign of Mary*, 319–20; SP11/12/f. 35; C. S. L. Davies, 'England and the French War', in *The Mid-Tudor Polity*, ed. J. Loach and R. Tittler, 159–85.

an English squadron on normal patrol in the Channel at the time of the attack, and communications between England and Calais by sea were not broken. Woodhouse responded with what was, by the standards of the time, amazing speed to the demands made upon him. But the lack of advance warning and the rapid fall of Ruysbank create an impression of inadequacy which is not justified. The fall of Calais was a political failure, and to some extent a military one, but no cause of shame to the navy, and there is no reason to suppose that it influenced the decision to replace Howard with Clinton as Lord Admiral in the following month.

It took some time to repair the January storm damage, and regular mobilization for the summer seems to have been delayed by about a month, which may account for the timing of Peter Pett's appointment in April. On the 26th of that month instructions were sent to nine West Country gentlemen to join the fleet as captains by 10 May. This group, which included Walter Raleigh the elder, Henry Strangeways and James Kirkham, had mostly been involved in piracy or conspiracy during the earlier part of the reign. Along with Peter Killigrew they provide a good example of the way in which the Government used this war to reconcile some disaffected elements of the gentry.[1] Philip was particularly influential in this connection, and the service of the Dudley brothers in the St Quentin campaign should be seen in the same light. Clinton hoisted his flag in the brand new *Lion*, but was then ordered to Dunkirk for consultations with Philip, leaving the next stage of the preparations in the hands of William Winter. Some part of the fleet was probably at sea by the middle of May, but the French naval presence seems to have been negligible, and there is no evidence of further action until the end of June. The main campaign objective for the season was a combined Anglo-Flemish attack on Brittany, and by late June some 140 ships had emerged from Portsmouth to link up with the 30 which were coming from Flanders. A surviving list of 55 'captains serving at the seas in the King's and Queen's Majesties ships', probably belongs to this campaign, and may well correspond to the number of fighting ships, as opposed to victuallers.[2] It includes Clinton himself, Sir William Woodhouse, Sir Thomas Cotton, William Tyrell and Peter Killigrew, but none of those summoned in April, who must have been allocated to other duties. At about the same time, on 22 June, letters of Marque were issued to a further 23 men to fit out their own

[1] PRO SP11/13/9; Loades, *Reign of Mary*, 312–3.
[2] Bodleian Library, Rawlinson MS 846, f. 95.

vessels for privateering. Clinton also issued a set of fleet orders to be displayed on every ship. Apart from insisting upon the captains' duty of obedience to the Admiral and declaring desertion to be a felony, these were very closely modelled on Lisle's orders of 1545.[1]

However, before anything could be accomplished word was received that the French were moving an army north from Calais towards Dunkirk. Dunkirk had replaced Calais as the staple town for English wool, and its loss would have been a serious blow to trade, as well as a strategic threat. So ten ships under the command of John Malen were detached to assist the Imperial defenders. Before they could get there, however, the French army threatening Dunkirk was cut off by the Count of Egmont, and the two forces collided near Gravelines, within sight of the sea. Malen, on his way north, literally stumbled upon this action. In an inspired moment of improvisation he brought his ships in close to the shore and began to bombard the French lines. Taken completely by surprise, and badly mauled by the heavy guns, they broke and Egmont won a complete victory.[2] Malen earned himself the title of Vice-Admiral of the Narrow Seas and a special commendation from the Queen. Unfortunately the main fleet was to be considerably less successful. Clinton landed 7 000 men near Brest at the end of July without encountering any opposition from the French navy; but the town proved to be too strong to attack and the local military commanders were unusually resolute and effective. After a few days the English re-embarked, having accomplished nothing beyond the burning of the village of Le Conquet. Clinton was then trapped in the roadstead by adverse winds, and his supplies began to run out. As soon as the wind changed, on 3 August, his Flemish allies weighed anchor and departed, leaving him with little option but to return empty-handed to Portsmouth.[3] The campaign was a failure, and the Council was displeased, but it was by no means a disaster, and the losses do not appear to have been significant. Thereafter the bulk of the fleet remained in service, but was split up to discharge a number of different functions. Thomas Malen with one squadron remained on patrol in the Narrow Seas; William Winter with '20 sail of good ships' was sent to intercept a French fleet reported to be about to sail

[1] Bodleian Library, Rawlinson MS 846, ff. 1–16. These are two sets of very similar orders, one issued by William Winter in March 1558, and the other by Clinton in July.
[2] Glasgow, 'Philip and Mary's war . . .' 336; Davies, 'England and the French war', 181.
[3] PRO SP11/13/64; Glasgow, 'Philip and Mary's war . . .' 337.

from Le Havre to Scotland; and Sir Thomas Cotton with nine ships was sent to the aid of the Earl of Sussex, the Lord Deputy of Ireland.[1]

On 17 August Clinton set out again with what must have been little more than a squadron. Having been frustrated by the weather from landing on the Normandy coast, he then made for the Channel Islands, but before anything could be accomplished his ships were struck by a virulent outbreak of sickness. With half his men out of action he retreated again to Portsmouth where, on 24 August, he fell sick himself after what must have been one of the shortest naval expeditions of the century. Winter's errand seems to have been a wild goose chase, and only Cotton saw any significant action. He had been called upon because the MacDonalds of the Isles were interfering in Ulster, and when intercepted had simply taken to their boats. So Sussex planned a punitive expedition against the clansmen, a campaign for which he needed naval support. On 14 September Cotton and the Lord Deputy left Dublin, and five days later, in spite of adverse weather, landed over 1 000 men in Kintyre. Cotton's larger ships, the *New Bark* and the *Mary Willoughby*, were of little use in such confined waters, and the expedition was curtailed by further bad weather, but considerable damage was inflicted upon both Kintyre and Arran.[2] One Irish ship was lost, and sickness again contributed to the decision to retreat. By the time Cotton returned to Dublin it was already 5 October, and too late in the season for anything other than routine patrolling. John Malen, flushed with his success at Gravelines, apparently proposed a sort of commando raid against Le Havre which the Council, desperate for some tangible achievement, approved, but by that time the peace negotiations had already commenced and the plan was abandoned. A month later, on 17 November, Mary died and Philip ceased to be King of England.

When he had received that title, just over four years earlier, pessimists had predicted that England would fall under Spanish control. That had not happened. Optimists had predicted splendid new trade opportunities, particularly access to the rich Spanish colonies across the Atlantic. That had not happened either. Philip had proved consistently unsympathetic to English commercial ambition, not only forbidding direct access to America, but also putting pressure upon Mary to stop the development of trade to West

[1] Glasgow, 'Philip and Mary's war . . .', 337–9.
[2] PRO SP50/1/36, 37; Glasgow, 'Philip and Mary's war . . .', 339.

Africa, which had been going on intermittently for several years. This was not because his own interests were directly involved, but those of the King of Portugal 'which narrowly concern me', as he explained to the disgruntled English Council.[1] In fact Philip had consistently defended the interests, not only of his own Flemish subjects, but also of the Portuguese and of the Hanseatic League against the Merchant Adventurers of London, a circumstance which had contributed significantly to his unpopularity in England. He did not, however, attempt to obstruct the opening of commercial links with Russia. The voyage of Willoughby and Chancellor which had set off in 1553 to find a way to China had failed in its principal objective, and Willoughby had perished. However in 1554 Chancellor returned, not from China but from Moscow. The full story of that venture would not be appropriate here, but he brought greetings from Tsar Ivan IV which were seized upon with enthusiasm by his backers in London. On 6 February 1555 Philip and Mary chartered a new company, soon to be called the Muscovy Company, for the purpose of exploiting this new trade connection, and Sebastian Cabot was named the first governor.[2] In the summer of the same year Chancellor returned to Russia accompanied by a number of factors for the new company, and the Tsar granted them generous trading privileges. Returning in 1556, Chancellor met with disaster. His ships were wrecked and he himself was drowned, but the Russian ambassador who had accompanied him survived, and the newly established trading company was able to consolidate its position. Meanwhile, also in 1556, a second explorer, Stephen Borough, made another unsuccessful attempt (again with Sebastian Cabot's backing) to find the North East passage. He failed, and in the following year Cabot died; but the momentum which had been set up did not falter. In 1558, in complete contrast to his earlier discouragement, Philip invited Borough to visit the *Casa de Contratacion* in Seville – that great repository of Spanish maritime knowledge and expertise. Perhaps he was convinced that English ambitions lay in the North, well off the routes frequented by his own seamen, or perhaps he simply did not believe that any Englishman was capable of benefiting from the experience. Whatever Philip's motive, Borough seized his opportunity with both hands, bringing back not only a unique eyewitness account of the *Casa* and its workings, but charts, note books, and a copy of Martin Cortes's *Arte de Navegar*. This was

[1] Philip to the Count of Feria (his representative in England), 4 February 1558, *Cal. Span*. 13, 351.
[2] Richard Hakluyt, *Principal Voyages and Navigations*, I, 318–20.

rapidly translated into English by his friend Richard Eden, and its appearance in London in 1561 marked the beginning of a new era in English navigational skill and ambition. In the decade between 1550 and 1560 they acquired that appetite for exploration and discovery which was to underpin the whole strategy of seapower over the next two hundred years.

7
POLICY, ADMINISTRATION AND FINANCE, 1558–1588

When Elizabeth came to the throne, negotiations to end the war with France were already in hand. Both Philip and Henry II were bankrupt and in desperate need of peace, a fact which the new Queen of England tried to use to secure the recovery of Calais. She was unsuccessful because Philip, in spite of some twinges of conscience, could not go on fighting for the benefit of his ally, and because the French called her bluff.[1] For several months before the peace treaty was eventually signed at Cateau Cambrésis in March 1559, the fighting had become desultory, and English participation even more so. In anticipation of the end of the war, in February and March 1559, the officers of the Admiralty undertook a stocktaking of the navy, probably on the Queen's orders, and sketched out a policy for the years ahead. Before that, on 12 December 1558, an interim estimate had been made of the current charges, from 1 October to 31 December, which shows that at the moment of Mary's death there were six royal ships and seven hired merchantmen on patrol in the Narrow Seas, carrying 335 masters, mariners and gunners.[2] If the latter figure is accurate, they must all have been very small ships. Together with the charges of shipkeeping at Portsmouth, Gillingham and in the Thames, these patrols were estimated to cost £3 167.4s.9d. over the three-month period. At the same time there were 184 shipwrights and other craftsmen building the *Peter* at Woolwich and a further 120 rebuilding the *Jennet* and the *Hare* at Portsmouth. This work was estimated to cost a further £2 123.14s.

[1] Philip acknowledged that the loss of Calais resulted from a war undertaken on his behalf, but was eventually reduced to suggesting that Elizabeth might wish to continue the war on her own. Loades, *Reign of Mary*, 338.

[2] BL Add. MS 9294, f.1; T. Glasgow, 'Maturing of naval administration', 11.

over the same period.[1] The first ship list of the reign, dated 20 February 1559 was a part of the stocktaking operation, and listed a total of 39 ships. Of these, four were at sea and a further 23 in commission; three at Gillingham, nine in the Thames and the remainder at Portsmouth. Of the 12 ships not in commission but included in the list, seven were in building or under repair, two (the *Minion* and the *Primrose*) had already been disposed of, and three (the *Trinity Henry*, the *Dragon* and the *Lion*) were classed as 'utterly decaied'.[2] The main planning document was then drawn up on 24 March, and entitled 'A boke for Sea causes'.

This document starts with a list of 21 ships 'met to be kept and preserved for the servis of her matie', displacing a total of 5 510 tons and carrying 3 880 men. A further ten are listed as 'very muche worne and of no contynuaunce without greate Reparacyon to be done upon them'. These ships should be 'contynewed during the dowtfull tyme of the pease', but thereafter should be sold or scrapped and the money so saved devoted to the building of new ships. There are estimated to be 45 English merchantmen available to be converted 'in order of war', amounting to 7 040 tons and carrying 4 600 men. If the Queen wishes to mobilize her whole navy she will also need 20 victuallers of 80 tons each, with a further 400 men. The cost of mobilizing such a fleet is estimated at £10 512, and the monthly charge on active service at £11 363, calculating the average wage per man at 8s.6d., with 12s. for victuals, and 12d. a ton for the tonnage of the merchant ships.[3] Demobilization would cost a further £4 000, so the whole cost of a five-month campaign on this scale would amount to £71 377. The authors also note that such a mobilization would require at least two months warning 'and readie money for the doing thereof', as well as a 'staie' of all merchant voyages. As a presentation of the capability of the English navy in 1559, this could hardly be improved upon. Whether the ordinary seaman's pay had been increased from the 6s.8d. a month fixed by Henry VIII in 1545, or whether 8s.6d. was an average, including everyone from boys to officers, is not clear, but the two months' preparation time seems to have been realistic and represents an extremely efficient system by the standards of the time.[4] The second part of the document is a

[1] BL Add. MS 9294, ff. 2–3; T. Glasgow, 'The royal navy at the start of Elizabeth's reign', *MM*, 51, 1965, 73.

[2] PRO SP12/2, 20 February 1558/9.

[3] PRO SP12/3/44, ff. 131r.–134v.

[4] Ibid., f. 133r. There is no other reference to seamen's wages being raised between 1546 and 1582, so the latter is probably the true explanation.

statement of the existing situation, with seven royal ships and eight armed merchantmen at sea 'upon the Queenes chardge extraordinary', an increase of only two ships over the pre-Christmas period, but this time carrying 940 men and estimated to cost £1 597 a month. Of these men 320 appear to have been soldiers under the command of Sir Thomas Cotton, and the *Primrose*, which had only just been sold for £1 800 now heads the list of armed merchantmen upon which tonnage was being paid.[1] For the latter purpose she was 'esteemed' to be of 300 tons, although a few lines previously her displacement was given as 200 tons. This small fleet was commissioned to the end of March, and the authors wished to know the Queen's pleasure 'for the continuance of the charge'.

The third part of the 'Book' is a summary of work in progress at Woolwich, Deptford and Portsmouth, with the charges of keeping the Queen's ships afloat 'within the compass of the ordinary', which is now fixed at £12 000 per annum.[2] At Deptford are the *Hart*, the *Antelope*, the *Swallow*, the *Brigandine* and the *Sun*; upon which are working 170 shipwrights and other artificers at 12d. per man per day for wages, victuals and lodging, and 25 labourers for wages only at 7d. a day. Timber, iron work and other commodities are budgeted at £880, making a total estimate for three months six days of £1 816.13s.4d. At Woolwich are eight ships, 150 artificers and 25 labourers for a total quarterly charge of £1 254.6s.8d.; and at Portsmouth nine ships, 130 artificers and 24 labourers, estimated to cost £1 151. The remaining ships are afloat at Portsmouth and in the Thames, under the care of 372 mariners and gunners, whose wages and victuals are estimated at 20s. a man per month, for a total cost of £1 195.12s.9d. The total Ordinary cost of the first quarter of 1559 is thus estimated at £5 417.6s.9d. – not much less than half the budget for the whole year. There then follow two brief 'position papers', one for peace and the other for war. In peacetime

> . . . yt is thought that Gilligham water is the metest harborowe to kepe the Queenes majesties Shippes in, aswell for that the place will requyre a smaller number of Shipkeepers lesse Spoile of tacle, more suretie for the ships[3]

As we have seen, this had been the thinking of the Admiralty officers for some time, and the familiar point about 'grounding' is

[1] PRO SP12/2/30. According to the record only £1 000 of the agreed purchase price had been paid, so the ship may have been repossessed by the Crown.
[2] By a warrant dated 11 March 1558/9. Bodleian Library MS Rawlinson A.200, f. 165.
[3] PRO SP12/3/44, f. 133v.

made again. It is recommended that ten ships presently at Portsmouth should be brought round to Gillingham at a cost of £435, and that the old blockhouse at Sheerness should be refurbished and kept with six gunners to protect the anchorage. In time of war all the Queen's ships should be rigged and fitted out in the Thames, and then sent to Portsmouth at an estimated cost of £2 000. By remaining at Portsmouth during June, July and August, it is calculated that £1 700 would be added to the cost of their maintenance, so they should return to Gillingham at the end of the campaigning season. Finally, the officers present a 'profile' of the future navy '. . . to be a suffycent nomber for her majestie to have of her owne whiche may be made and brought to ther perfection within v yeres next following, so her majesties pleasure to contynewe the ordynarye . . .' This model navy is to consist of 24 ships of 200 tons and upwards, four Barks of 60–80 tons, and two Pinnaces of 40 tons – a total of 30. Of the ships, four are to be of 600 tons or more, four of 500, four of 400, six of 300 and six of 200 – reflecting the firm professional preference for medium-sized men-of-war. No ship of more than 800 tons is projected.

The importance of these documents for an understanding of the development of the Tudor navy can hardly be overestimated. They come at the end of what used to be thought of as a very depressed period in naval history, but it is now clear that they reflect the very considerable achievements of the previous twenty years. The overall number of ships is lower than it had been in 1547; discounting the rowbarges the figure has declined from 41 to 31, but the number actually in commission is not significantly less. The establishment of the Ordinary two years earlier, although quickly overtaken by the demands of war, had made the whole process of budgeting much easier with the prospect of a return to peace.[1] And we have here unequivocal evidence of a structured policy, as opposed to a series of pragmatic improvisations. There is, however, no sense of innovation. Comparing these estimates with expenditure levels over the previous decade, it is clear that nothing unprecedented was going on. The workforces in the different dockyards fluctuated in response to demand, but that shipkeepers, artificers and labourers should be employed upon a regular basis in each place was clearly normal practice by this time. Such workers were not 'in ordinary wages' in the same sense as the officers, that is on a regular payroll irrespective of whether there was work or not, but the practice of maintaining a

[1] There is no evidence that Winchester's Ordinary of 1557 was applied after Gonson had received £7 000 for the first half year, and the conditions which he had then laid down had been satisfied in the circumstances of war.

number of master craftsmen on a virtually permanent basis, and moving them from place to place can already be detected.[1] Gonson's later accounts show this to have become normal practice by 1570. What role the Lord Treasurer may have played in inspiring these presentations, and how real his oversight may have been at this point, is not very clear. There is no trace of Winchester's emergency victualling provision for 1 000 men, specified in 1557, nor any specific discussion of victualling at all, which suggests that it was not an issue of concern.[2] At the same time there is an underlying anxiety about funding. In February the Ordinary was referred to as £14 000, but by March the Queen had reduced it to £12 000, and it cannot have been accidental that the officers put forward what was, in effect, a case for an Ordinary in the region of £20 000. When the surviving series of quarter books begins in 1562, we are on familiar ground; the distinction between Ordinary expenditure and extraordinary or 'sea charges'; the breakdown by quarters and by dockyards; the steady programme of maintenance and rebuilding. Neither Mary nor Elizabeth made revolutionary changes in naval administration; what we have here is a profile of a gradually evolving organization, firmly rooted in the practices of the past but undergoing constant modification and review.

Over the following 30 years the personnel and structure of the administration changed remarkably little. Sir William Woodhouse died in 1565 and the office of Lieutenant or Vice-Admiral was discontinued.[3] William Brooke, the original Controller, died in 1561 and was replaced by William Holstock, hitherto Keeper of the Storehouses. Richard Howlett, the Clerk of the Ships, was succeeded by George Winter, Sir William's brother, in 1560, and Winter was succeeded in 1580 by William Borough.[4] Benjamin Gonson, the long serving Treasurer, died in 1577 and was succeeded by Sir John Hawkins. Sir William Winter, who combined the offices of Surveyor and Master of the Ordnance from 1557, lived until 1589, after which the second office was discontinued.[5] Edward Baeshe, the Surveyor

[1] Apart from Peter Pett and Mathew Baker, the name of Edward Bright, master shipwright, and a number of other craftsmen appear regularly in the records. Bodleian Library, Rawlinson MSS A.200, A.201 etc.

[2] Victualling was reorganized in 1565 (see below, p. 203). At this point some victualling was still paid through Gonson's account, as is shown by regular ordinary payments to Thomas Wilson at Gillingham, ibid.

[3] T. Glasgow, 'Vice Admiral Woodhouse and shipkeeping in the Tudor navy', *MM*, 63, 1977, 253–63.

[4] Oppenheim, *Administration*, 148–9.

[5] Glasgow, 'Maturing of naval administration', 21. After 1569 his task was considerably lightened by no longer having to account to the Ordnance office in the Tower for the ships' guns. That task was transferred to the Master Gunners of each ship, who became permanent appointments. It was this change which made the Mastership of Naval Ordnance redundant.

of the Victuals, having seen off a number of reversionaries, died at length in 1587 and was succeeded by James Quarles. Apart from the extraordinary longevity of some of these officers, they were closely connected by blood or marriage. Hawkins, for example, was Gonson's son in law, and William Borough was the younger brother of Stephen, the pioneering navigator. This obviously made for stability and continuity, but it also put the navy in the hands of a narrowly defined interest group. In that, it did not differ greatly from other sectors of the Elizabethan administration, such as the Exchequer, but nepotism was eventually to have an insidious effect upon the whole structure. By the end of the century the admirable professionalism of the early Elizabethan navy had become distinctly stale and fossilized, not to say corrupt. Lord Clinton, who had recovered the office of Lord Admiral in 1558, retained it until his death in 1585, becoming Earl of Lincoln in 1572.[1] He was succeeded by Charles, Lord Howard of Effingham, the son of his predecessor. Apart from the discontinuance of the Lieutenantship, the only significant change in administrative procedure before 1588 was the separation of the accounts of the Surveyor of the Victuals from those of the Treasurer after 1564. This had been one of the reforms specified by Winchester in 1557, but Baeshe continued to receive much of his money 'in prest' from Gonson until 31 December 1564.

One year earlier, on 1 January 1564, the Treasurer's Ordinary had been drastically reduced to £6 000 a year, but since this was no longer to cover Ordinary victualling charges, that is shipkeepers and artificers, the effect was probably not great.[2] If there was a funding policy after 1564, it is extremely hard to reconstruct. The Treasurer's income between the end of Elizabeth's adventure in France in 1563 and the outbreak of war with Spain in 1585 varied between 18 000 a year and £5 178.[3] The Ordinary was increased again in 1567 from £6 000 to £7 695 6s.2d. but neither of these figures bears any relationship to the Treasurer's actual receipts.[4] In four years, 1565,

[1] *Dictionary of National Biography*.

[2] Glasgow, 'Maturing of naval administration', 18.

[3] Oppenheim, *Administration*, 161, based on the Audit Office accounts.

[4] It is difficult to be sure what the Ordinary was supposed to be. The figure of £6 000 for January 1564 seems reasonably firm, but whereas the Exchequer Warrant for Issue of 21 February 1567 gives £7 695.6s.2d., the warrant of the same date cited in the Quarter Book for 1570 gives only £5 780.2s.2d. According to John Hawkins the basic figure for the whole period from 1569 to 1587 was £5 714, with a supplement of £2 500 for other dockyard expenses, making a total of £8 214. It would probably be true to say that the Ordinary in the sense originally envisaged by Winchester was abandoned after 1564, although the distinction between ordinary and extraordinary expenditure was assiduously maintained in the Quarter Books at least down to 1600. Oppenheim, *Administration*, 160–1; Rawlinson MS A.201, f.1; PRO SP12/202/35; Glasgow, 'Maturing of naval administration', 18; PRO E351/2213–2221, Hawkins' declared accounts from 1577 to 1585.

1566, 1575 and 1580 his total income was actually less than the Ordinary for those years; but normally it was considerably more, in some cases more than double. In a few years – 1574 for example, or 1577 – income exceeded expenditure, but in most years he was in deficit, sometimes heavily so. Over the same period of 22 years expenditure ranged from £7 486 in 1583 to £21 471 in 1564. There seems to have been no natural tendency to rise in line with inflation, but high spending years can normally be related to periods of political tension, such as 1569 when the total reached £17 800. After 1571 the accounts are clearly divided into Ordinary and extraordinary expenditure, and this distinction makes understanding a little easier. In no year for which the figures survive did the Ordinary expenditure exceed Ordinary income. Normally there was a comfortable surplus; so clearly when the Admiralty was under pressure additional expenditure was classified as extraordinary, no matter what caused it, and was met by *ad hoc* warrants of the same kind which had been used before 1557. The positive way of describing this situation would be pragmatic, but it could equally be called hand to mouth. Either Winchester had changed his mind since Mary's reign, or he was no longer in control. In view of his advanced years, and the fact that the advent of William Cecil as Lord Treasurer in 1572 brought about no very noticeable change, the latter is probably the true explanation. The most telling insight into the Elizabethan funding of the navy is provided by the introduction of contracts or 'bargains' in 1579. These contracts were similar to those entered into with the farmers of the customs, whereby the Crown received a fixed income and enjoyed the performance of a service, in return for the opportunity to make a considerable profit. Hawkins's contract specified that he was to maintain 25 ships to a certain standard, but not to repair them or to provide shipkeepers, in return for £1 200 a year. At the same time Peter Pett and Matthew Baker, the Queen's shipwrights, entered into a similar contract, undertaking to ground and grave the ships at specified intervals (which varied with the size of the ship) and to carry out certain types of repair, in return for £1 000 a year.[1] In neither case was the contractor to account for the money received,

[1] PRO SP12/132/88–91. How these sums were supposed to relate to the Ordinary is not apparent. Perhaps in spite of Hawkins' later testimony, it was suspended during these years. For a recent discussion of these contracts, see S. Adams, 'New light on the "Reformation" of John Hawkins; the Ellesmere naval survey of January 1584', *EHR*, 105, 1991, 97–111.

and the intention clearly was that he should make a profit on the bargain.

By thus sub-contracting part of the Ordinary to the very officers whose duty it was to oversee the whole operation, chaos and mutual recrimination were guaranteed. The intention was probably to motivate efficiency and eliminate waste by giving the officers concerned a personal incentive. The main result was furious quarrels between the officers of the Admiralty as those with contracts tried to shift expensive work onto those without, and between Hawkins on the one side and Pett and Baker on the other. Much of the obloquy to which Hawkins was later subjected arose from this source. The situation had become so bad by January 1584 that a commission of inquiry was instituted, as a result of which all the existing contracts were abrogated. But in a sense Hawkins was exonerated, because he was then offered, and accepted, a further contract for £4 000 a year to carry out virtually all the functions covered by the Ordinary – repairs, moorings, shipkeepers, the maintenance of wharves and storehouses, and the finding of materials, victuals and lodgings.[1] If he could do all that successfully within the contract, and make a profit, then the old system must have been very inefficient. Of course others, and particularly Pett and Baker denied that it could be done and accused Hawkins of default and negligence on a large scale. The charges were never proved, and do not seem to have been justified, but he did cheat, keeping his Ordinary expenditure below £4 000 by making use of extraordinary warrants. In spite of his claims, no overall savings were effected and Hawkins surrendered his contract at Christmas 1587 on account of the rapidly increasing demands upon his office. The system was then abandoned.

By 1562 the dockyards were beginning to develop distinctive functions and identities, foreshadowed earlier but now clearly visible in the detailed breakdown of Gonson's accounts. Deptford was no longer a significant anchorage. In the third quarter of the year only three hoys were afloat there. On the other hand 214 shipwrights had worked a total of 10 135 days between them building the *Triumph*, the *Victory* and the *Aid*.[2] During the following quarter work on these ships continued, while the *Jesus of Lubeck* and the *Great Bark*

[1] Oppenheim, *Administration*, 162–3.
[2] MS Rawlinson A.200, ff. 26–33.

underwent some of the repairs which the survey of 1559 had considered to be scarcely worthwhile. Woolwich at this time was employing only labourers and storekeepers, unloading and storing timber and provisions, while Gillingham had become the main anchorage, in accordance with the policy earlier laid down. In the last quarter of 1562/3 29 ships were afloat there, including all the largest vessels then in commission; the number had hardly fluctuated throughout the year. The new fort at Upnor, built to guard the anchorage and manned by six gunners, was also a charge upon the Gillingham Ordinary.[1] Colne, near Harwich, was still functioning but only as a small-scale timber yard,[2] while Portsmouth housed between four and six ships upon which Peter Pett and 130 shipwrights and caulkers worked for several weeks. Activity was concentrated mainly at Deptford, Gillingham and Portsmouth; the first two specializing and only Portsmouth maintaining a variety of functions, probably as the main basis for the medium-sized ships on short-term standby. It seems also to have been policy to shift as much as possible onto the extraordinary side of the account; not only the wages of seamen on active service, and the hire of small ketches used to deliver special messages to ships at sea, but also the wages and travelling expenses of Peter Pett and other shipwrights when they were sent to repair the *Primrose* at Bristol 'being spoyled at the seas with foul weather'. Thomas Baker took eight days to survey 16 of the ships at Gillingham in late July to ascertain their seaworthiness, and he was also paid on the extraordinary side of the account. By this time the Ordinary simply covers routine work at the main dockyards, while the extraordinary is a mine of information about the day by day operations of the ships and the Admiralty officers. Thomas Baker surveys royal ships at Chatham (so called for the first time); Peter Pett surveys timber in Hertfordshire; a skiff is bought at Deptford for the *Double Rose*; Thomas Jones is paid for letters of intelligence out of France; and 'sea charges' show that 17 of the navy's largest ships were at sea at some point during the year.

According to his quarter book for 1563, Gonson received £9 630 of the £12 000 to which the standing warrant of March 1559 entitled him, and £13 375 in extraordinary receipts, most of the latter by warrants specified for particular purposes in the manner typical of

[1] Oppenheim clearly implies that the fort was not built until after the land had been acquired in 1568 (*Administration*, 150), but the Quarter Book for 1562/3 shows that it was already in use then. Rawlinson MS A.200, f. 75v.

[2] The yard at Colne was sold in 1566. PRO E351/2202.

his father's early days in office.[1] The pattern of expenditure was much the same as in the previous year. At Deptford the 'remaking' of the *Great Bark* and the repairing of the *Jesus* continued. The *Victory* and the *Triumph* were now being fitted out, and a joiner was paid for building 'cabans' in them. Four new 'gallyots', the *Guide*, the *Searcher*, the *Post* and the *Makeshift* were also under construction, and a carver was paid for executing and garnishing figureheads for the new ships. There were rather fewer ships at Gillingham, and rather more at Portsmouth, indicating an increased level of active service. This was the year of the Le Havre expedition, and the extraordinary expenditure details much of that deployment. The next surviving breakdown, of 1570, shows further shifts of emphasis, but generally in the same direction.[2] Gonson's Ordinary receipts totalled no more than £5 780.2s.2d., while extraordinary income amounted to £17 553, of which £11 900 came on a single warrant of 6 March. The number of ships anchored at Gillingham varied from 20 in the first quarter of the year to 11 in the second, while the appearance of Peter Pett and up to 60 shipwrights and caulkers on the Ordinary indicates that routine repairs were being carried out there rather than at Deptford, where the number of craftsmen employed had fallen almost to nothing. The permanent staff at Gillingham remained small, consisting of a clerk, a purveyor and a rat-catcher, in addition to the Upnor gunners, but another indication that it was becoming the chief base can be seen in the addition of a payment of £5 per annum for the 'rent of a house at Tower Hill [Chatham] wherein the officers of her Majesties ships do meet and confer from time to time touching her highness' weighty affairs.'[3] By comparison the Deptford Ordinary for this year is meagre, except at the staff level. Stephen Alexander, the clerk of the cheque, the clerk of the reports, the clerk of the surveys, two purveyors, two storekeepers, Mathew Baker and Augustine Levello,[4] master shipwrights, the keeper of the plug, the porter of the woodyard, a messenger, two carpenters and two mariners, make an impressive headquarters establishment. The only other people to be paid on the Ordinary were six watchmen and a variable number of labourers. The Woolwich Ordinary shows nothing but the keeper of the storehouse, while

[1] MS Rawlinson A.200, ff. 165–6. According to another account his receipts for the two years 1 January 1562 to 31 December 1563 £53 790.12s., PRO E351/2199.

[2] MS Rawlinson A.201.

[3] Ibid., f. 41r.

[4] Augustine Levello was a Venetian, specifically employed to look after the galleys, and paid at the higher rate of 16d. a day.

Portsmouth lists the storekeeper, the keeper of the plug, and the shipkeepers on board the galley *Elinor*.

These changes are partly explained by the fact that much activity which in 1562/3 had been classed as Ordinary was now classed as extraordinary. At Gillingham for example, the wages and victuals of shipwrights and others repairing and mending the *Antelope*, the *Jennet* and the *Primrose*, '. . . and (working) upon the new building and new making of the *Bull* and the *Tiger*, her highness' old ships in the fashion of galleasses . . .' were so described. This employed over 200 men for a total in excess of 20 000 man/days.[1] At Portsmouth 70 men worked a total of 3 598 man/days repairing the *Elinor*, and a painter was paid £5 for '. . . beautifying and garnishing the captains cabin; and for the gilding and limning with gold the letters of her highness' name, and the crown upon the stem and sides of the said galley'. At Deptford a new ship was being built which kept Mathew Baker and 138 craftsmen busy throughout the summer; a total of 9 146 man/days. This new ship, which was probably the *Foresight*, was launched in September with the assistance of 74 mariners who were specially recruited for four days to finish her rigging and trimming. William Lizard of London was paid a princely £49.16s. for 'garnishing' her, and setting up the royal arms.[2] That expenditure which had previously been classed as extraordinary now appears as 'sea-causes extraordinary', and includes not only all missions and the preparation for them, but also the cutting of a new mast pond at Chatham, with four partitions, 'for the better preserving of the said trees' to make masts and spars. Nineteen ships were rigged and provisioned for sea service in the course of the year. By 1574 the shift towards Gillingham has become even more marked.[3] There was little action at sea, and between 26 and 28 ships were in the anchorage in each quarter of the year. There are now three clerks, one of them on the higher rate of £6.13s.4d. On this occasion not only were a number of shipwrights paid on the Ordinary, but also their travelling expenses and the purchase of various items of equipment, such as pump-hoses and stop-leathers. The Deptford, Woolwich and Portsmouth Ordinaries are substantially unchanged, although Deptford now boasts several houses rented by the quarter as accommodation for the dockyard workmen, in place of the former payments for

[1] MS Rawlinson A.201, f. 106r.

[2] Ibid. For a full discussion of the symbolism and techniques of 'garnishing' ships in this period, see S. Rodgers, 'The symbolism of ship launching', (Oxford D.Phil. 1983).

[3] MS. Rawlinson A.202.

lodgings. The Gillingham extraordinary is mainly a list of purchases of raw materials, and no extraordinary payments are recorded at all for Woolwich or Portsmouth. The account is clearly incomplete, as there are no figures for receipt, and no totals for Ordinary expenditure. Other figures suggest that 1574 was a year of above average activity, with expenditure totalling nearly £13 000 exclusive of victualling,[1] so it would be rash to draw any conclusions from the detailed statement, beyond the continued advance of Gillingham.

The first year of John Hawkins' Treasurership, 1578, also has an incomplete account, although slightly more informative than that for 1574.[2] 22 different ships were anchored at Gillingham at different times. The largest, such as the *Triumph*, continued to carry a full set of officers – Master, Boatswain, Purser, Cook and Master Gunner, together with a skeleton crew of 13 seamen – while smaller vessels like the *Achates* of 100 tons carried only the Boatswain, Cook, Gunner and 2 mariners. Payment rates in harbour were about half those at sea, but shipkeeping on this scale was still an expensive business, and absorbed most of the Ordinary budget in every year. Some 130 shipwrights and other craftsmen worked through the summer 'repairing, ransacking, dubbing and caulking her majesties ships against the winter weather . . .'. Two new ships, the *Revenge* and the *Scout* were fitted out, and half a dozen bricklayers were employed to reconstruct the hearths and furnaces in the bowels of the ships under repair. The beakhead of the *Dreadnought* 'decayed and broken with foul weather' was repainted, as was the stern of the *Foresight*. In this year also a number of repairs were carried out to the buildings at Chatham, and a new mast-pond was dug, 140ft. by 44ft., which could also serve as a dock for two or three pinnaces 'yf neded shal requyre'.[3] The *Hope*, the *Philip and Mary* and the *Antelope* spent part of the year docked at Deptford, whither they were moved from Gillingham which seems to have had no drydock facilities until the following century. The *Elizabeth Jonas* was docked at Woolwich, and it took six workmen 14 days to open the dockhead and get her out. Woolwich, indeed, took on a new lease of life with the need for docking. The *White Bear* was docked there for repair, and the old *Jennet* broken down into a lighter. The *Elinor* continued her solitary existence at Portsmouth, and provided most of the work recorded in the Ordinary there. The extraordinary receipts for the year totalled £8 562, but it is even more difficult than

[1] Oppenheim, *Administration*, 161.
[2] MS Rawlinson A.203.
[3] Ibid., f. 108.

usual to understand the line drawn between Ordinary and extraordinary expenditure. Work on the ships docked at Deptford appears under both headings, the expenses of moving them and of opening the dock being classed as extraordinary, whereas the opening of the dock at Woolwich, as we have seen, was ordinary. Shipwrights' wages, and the purchase of timber and ironwork appear in both categories, although for some reason the repair of the *Triumph* at Woolwich appears only upon the extraordinary side. The sea-charges for the year relate mostly to the service of the *Lion*, the *Elizabeth Bonaventure*, the *Dreadnought*, the *Swiftsure* and the *Foresight* upon the coasts of Ireland, and to various comings and goings connected with that service.[1] Extraordinary expenditure for the year totalled £9 221.7s.7d., and total expenditure according to this account was £13 938.11s.9d. There are no figures for Ordinary income, but according to a different record the total which Hawkins received was £14 226.[2]

The timberyard at Colne seems to have been abandoned after 1563, and very little structural work was carried out at Portsmouth. There was a bad fire there in August 1576, and the damage seems not to have been made good until after the outbreak of war nine years later. The fort at Upnor was built sometime between 1559 and 1562, although the site was not finally purchased by the Crown until 1568.[3] The old Edwardian bulwark at Sheerness was at length rebuilt in 1574, but in 1585, with war threatening, these defences were not considered to be adequate and it was decided to lay a chain across the Medway at Upnor. The work was completed by the end of the year, but it had proved a difficult and expensive operation. The chain was fastened to piles at one end, and at the other passed over 'two great wheels' which were used to tension it. Even so it required the support of five lighters.[4] Other precautions were also taken, against sabotage no less than against surprise attack. Two pinnaces were kept at Sheerness on standby, and the largest ships, which were anchored downstream nearest to the chain were required to carry lights at night. In 1585 the Council ordered that the princi-

[1] For example, rigging wages for the *Lion*, the *Elizabeth*, the *Dreadnought* and the *Foresight* amounted to £178. The *Swiftsure* was later diverted to the Narrow Seas 'for the apprehension of pirates'.

[2] Oppenheim, *Administration*, 161. His declared account, on the other hand, shows a total expenditure of £14 956. PRO E351/2214.

[3] Oppenheim, *Administration*, 150.

[4] BL Add. MS 9294, f. 58. In 1574 the way through St Mary's creek at Chatham was blocked with piles in order to prevent a flank attack on the anchorage. PRO E351/2210.

pal officers of the navy should take turns, a month at a time, in sleeping on board one of the larger ships in order to supervise the shipkeepers. How long this regime lasted we do not know. The docks themselves were maintained, but not greatly extended, apart from the creation of the two mast-ponds which we have already noticed. The main dock at Deptford was reconstructed in about 1574, and given a new pair of gates at a cost of £150 four years later.[1] Additional wharves and storehouses were built at Chatham, Deptford and Woolwich, and in 1573 a 'ropehouse' was constructed at Woolwich by an entrepreneur named Thomas Allen. Allen was a 'Queen's merchant', contracted to import cordage from Danzig, but this seems to have been intended to be more than a storehouse. Perhaps Allen planned to import the raw materials and make the ropes himself. If that was the case, he almost certainly failed, because purchases of 'Muscovie rope' continued undiminished and Allen's name does not occur again.

The main infrastructure, both physical and administrative, had been created by Henry VIII. After 1547 the navy did not expand in size, and although there were continual modifications to ship design and structure, to rigging and to armaments, none of these were of a nature to require facilities on a different scale. After the wars ended in 1563, over twenty years of consolidation followed. The administrative structure, slightly diminished at the top, filled out at the lower levels with clerks, storekeepers and purveyors. More master shipwrights were retained on a permanent basis, and by 1588 six master mariners had been added to the regular payroll.[2]

After 1559 the poilicy was to have a navy of modest size but fully maintained and in regular use. John Dee's plea for a 'Petty Navy Royal', set out in *The Perfect Arte of Navigation* in 1577, corresponded to official thinking in strategy, although not in scale. He argued for

> . . . a PETY NAVY ROYAL of Three score Tall Ships, (or more) but in no case fewer; and they to be very well appoynted, thoroughly manned and sufficiently victailled . . . That, henceforward, neither France, Denmark, Scotlande, Spain, nor any other country, can have such liberty, for Invasion, or their mutuall Conspiracies, or Ayds, any way, Transporting; to anny the blessed state of our Tranquillitie . . .[3]

[1] PRO E351/2215.
[2] Ronald Pollitt, 'Bureaucracy and the Armada', *MM*, 60, 1974, 119.
[3] John Dee, *The Perfect Arte of Navigation*, 3.

The purpose of such a fleet did not differ greatly from that set out by Fortescue a century earlier – the defence of the realm, suppression of pirates and protection of merchants – but Dee was presenting a project which was almost feasible. He was quite right to point out that the maritime resources of the kingdom could easily produce 60–80 ships of over 80 tons. The queen had about 30 such ships of her own. An incomplete survey of 1560 lists 79 in private hands, and a much more comprehensive list of 1577 shows 136 ships of over 100 tons, with 656 between 40 and 100.[1] By this time the development of long distance trade was achieving what over a hundred years of royal bounties had failed to do, and large ships for private use were being built in increasing numbers. London alone registered 14 between 1571 and 1576.[2] By 1582 there were 177 registered merchantmen of over 100 tons, with a further 70 between 80 and 100 tons.[3] So the whole country could muster about 250 ships of over 80 tons at the time when Dee was writing, and the number was rising rapidly. Bounty at the traditional rate was paid on some 380 private vessels of 100 tons or more in the course of the reign, the great majority being built in the last ten years, between 1593 and 1603; but it seems clear that the bounty itself was not a factor in this increase. Dee was also right to point out that most of these were '. . . very easily, and [in a manner] contynually, Maynteyn[ed] in Trade at sea.' However, there was a great deal of difference between using ships for profitable commerce and keeping them 'circling the realm' on constant patrol, which is what Dee was advocating. That would have been equivalent to a permanent war footing, and he probably exaggerated only slightly when he predicted that it could cost anything up to £200 000 a year. Even in the Armada year, when naval expenditure touched £91 000, Elizabeth did not have 60 ships regularly at sea. Such a level of spending on an Ordinary basis was out of the question without a fundamental re-structuring of the Crown's revenues.[4] Dee's own solution was that the fleet should pay for itself by enforcing a 10 per cent tax on all foreign fishermen who

[1] PRO SP12/11/27; ibid./96, f. 267.

[2] PRO SP12/107/68, 37 others were recorded for the rest of the country.

[3] PRO SP12/156, ff. 88r–90v. A few years earlier the biggest private ship owner was reported to be 'Hawkyns of Plymouth' who owned 13 ships, one of them being of 500 tons and another of 350. These vessels must have been registered in London as the largest Plymouth registered ship was only 140 tons. Oppenheim, *Administration*, 173. For a survey of the bounty ships, see Dietz, 'The royal bounty . . .', 14–20.

[4] The ordinary annual revenue of the Crown by 1580 was about £300 000, and although Elizabeth raised over £2m. in extraordinary revenue between 1588 and 1600 that was specifically voted by parliament to pay for the war.

ventured into English waters. At that point his plan begins to slide towards fantasy, but neither that nor Dee's extravagant language should blind us to the fact that the principle of a constant naval presence in English waters, paid for by the Crown and backed up by an adequate administrative structure, had been accepted.

In order to achieve this a regular programme of building, repair and disposal was necessary, but such a programme had been in place since long before Elizabeth came to the throne, and needed only to be continued. Elizabeth built steadily, but bought less than her father. Apart from the work which was already in hand in November 1558, she built the *Hope* in 1560; the *Triumph*, the *Victory*, the *Aid* and the *Post* (a brigantine) in 1562; the *Foresight* in 1570; the *Dreadnought*, the *Swiftsure* and the *Achates* in 1573; the *Revenge* and the *Scout* in 1577; the *Merlin* in 1579; the *Brigantine* in 1584; the *Cygnet* (a pinnace) in 1585; the *Rainbow*, the *Vanguard*, the *Tremontana*, the *Charles*, the *Moon*, the *Advice*, the *Makeshift*, the *Spy*, and the *Sun* in 1586; and the *Ark Royal* and the *Popinjay* in 1587.[1] The old *White Bear* was completely rebuilt in 1564; the *Bull* and the *Tiger* in 1570; the *Swallow* and the *Elizabeth Bonaventure* in 1580; the *Antelope* in 1581; the *Lion* in 1582; and the *Nonpareil* and the *Galley Elinor* in 1584.[2] In the early part of the reign this work was mostly done by direct labour, as we have seen, at Deptford or Woolwich, and overseen by one or more of the royal shipwrights, who were also responsible for the design. The *Triumph* was built in this manner for a cost of £3 788, exclusive of rigging and fittings. After Hawkins became Treasurer, however, most of the building and rebuilding was let out on contract. The *Lion* was rebuilt in this manner in 1582 for £1 440, and the *Nonpareil* in 1584 for £1 600.[3] The *Vanguard* and the *Rainbow* cost £2 600 apiece. These contract prices were probably also exclusive of rigging and fittings, since the *Triumph* was the largest of Elizabeth's new ships at 1 000 tons, while the *Vanguard* and the *Rainbow* each displaced 500. Some ships were purchased; the *Christopher* in 1560, and the *Elizabeth Bonaventure* in 1567, while the *Primrose* reappeared without explanation in 1560, having been sold in 1554. There were also a few prizes; the hoy *Mary Grace*, taken at Leith in 1560, and two French galleys taken in the

[1] Glasgow, 'List of ships'.

[2] The *White Bear* may have been the third incarnation of the *Great Galley* of 1515, first rebuilt as the *Great Bark* in about 1540; the *Nonpareil* had started life as the *Philip and Mary*, ibid.

[3] Oppenheim, *Administration*, 128–9.

same campaign and renamed the *Speedwell* and the *Tryright*.[1] A third galley, the *Elinor*, was confiscated from the French Huguenots (theoretically allies) during the Newhaven campaign of 1563. Repair work went on continuously, and features in every surviving set of accounts. Graving, caulking, replacing worn timber and repainting were carried out on a routine basis, and checked by regular surveys. Specific damage inflicted by the weather was often repaired in the nearest port to the ship's station, usually by sending a team of skilled shipwrights from Deptford.

Hawkins' second bargain, of June 1585, seems to have envisaged a more ambitious schedule. A survey taken on 25 January 1584, in connection with the work of the commission of inquiry, not only listed all the major repair work which had been undertaken since 1578, and reported on the condition of 24 named ships, but also set out a programme for the repair of one or two ships a year down to the end of the century, at an estimated total cost of £25 500. Hawkins proposed this scheme, or something very like it, to Burghley in the spring of 1584. It may well have been accepted, but like the bargain itself, it was overtaken by events in 1587, and remains informative principally as a guide to the Treasurer's policy in respect of this important part of his responsibilities.[2]

Disposal is very much harder to identify than acquisition. For the most part ships simply disappear from the records without explanation.[3] However, we do know the fate of some; the *Jesus of Lubeck*, for example, was captured by the Spaniards during Hawkins' ill-fated expedition to the Caribbean in 1568; the *Brigandine* was captured by the French in 1562, and the *Hart* went down off Portsmouth in May 1563. Ships sold included the *Phoenix* in 1573, the *Jerfalcon* in 1562, the *Falcon* in 1575, the *Searcher* and the *Guide* in 1564, and the *Tiger* in 1584.[4] Rather surprisingly, apart from the *Hart*, the only other royal ships to suffer shipwreck during this period were the brigantine *Post*, which sank off the Irish coast in 1566, and the *Greyhound*, which went down in 1563.

Altogether Elizabeth built 25 warships of various sizes between

[1] The two galleys which Elizabeth inherited, the *Red* and the *Black*, disappear from the records in 1560 and 1563 respectively. These two prizes were extensively used in 1562–3, and thereafter maintained, but not much used, until 1579. The *Elinor* was rebuilt in 1584, and remained in service until 1599. T. Glasgow, 'Oared vessels . . .', 371.

[2] Huntington Library, Ellesmere MS 1679, printed and discussed by Simon Adams in 'New light on the "Reformation" of John Hawkins . . .'.

[3] Glasgow, 'List of ships'.

[4] Ibid.

her accession and the coming of the Armada, and 11 of those could be described as capital ships of over 300 tons; but details of their dimensions and design are hard to come by. This is less because of the absence of evidence than because no two testimonies agree. A complete set of specifications for the ships then in service was drawn up in 1602, but its figures are contradicted by other evidence in almost every line.[1] John Hawkins is popularly credited with the most important developments in design, reduction in the height of the castles, and the introduction of a longer and slimmer hull design. It seems from the 'Fragments of Ancient English shipwrightery' drawn up in about 1586, probably by Mathew Baker, that by then the fashionable profile for a warship of 300–500 tons (the favoured size) was low, with a length/beam ratio of 3:1 instead of the 2½:1 of the older carracks or the 2:1 normal for merchantmen.[2] An excellent example of such a ship is the 480 ton *Rainbow*, built by Peter Pett at Deptford in 1586, and for which reasonably firm statistics can be ascertained. She had a keel length of 100ft. and a beam of 32ft; 35 tons of ordnance was disposed upon a single gundeck, and her complement in action was 250 men.[3] Hawkins may well have been responsible for persuading the admiralty to favour such designs, which he had come to appreciate in his privateering days, but he did not invent the galleon. The terminology of the period is confusing, and the distinction between a Portuguese carrack and what was called a 'galleon' seems to have been mainly one of size, but there were certainly ships in Henry VIII's navy which had most of the features favoured by Hawkins. Some of these, such as the *Anne Gallant* and *Grand Mistress*, began life as true galleases with oar propulsion. Others, for example the *Tiger* and the *Bull*, were built as sailing ships, but virtually without castles, and were called galleases because they could be moved by sweeps. The contrast between the *Henry Grace a Dieu*, which was a classic carrack, and the *Grand Mistress* as portrayed in the Anthony Roll is very marked.[4] Opinion among seamen was sharply divided over the relative merits of these two types of ship. The great advantage of the carrack, as Sir William Monson pointed out, was that, being 'high charged' she was difficult to board, and easy to defend from

[1] PRO SP12/286/36; BL Add.MS 9336, f.10; P. Kirsch, *The Galleon*, 116–30.

[2] Magdalene College, Cambridge, Pepys MS 2820, f. 160.

[3] Kirsch, *The Galleon*, 21–3.

[4] Magdalene College, Pepys MS 2992, ff. 51–2 (see also p. 95 above).

'close fights' if she was boarded.[1] She was at her best in formal set-piece engagements of the traditional kind. Her great disadvantage was that she was unweatherly, the high castles making her difficult to steer, and impossible to sail within 8 points of the wind. The galleon was faster, more manoeuverable, at her best in running fights where there was plenty of sea room. That is why she appealed to the privateers, and it was the privateering tradition which prevailed in the navy under Hawkins, although even as late as 1596 the *Warspite* could be built in the style of a carrack, and Monson was still expressing doubts in the 1620s.[2]

The period also saw a number of technical innovations, mostly of a minor nature, which improved the handling quality of the ships. Sprit sails, although known long before, became more common as the desire for precise steering became more pressing; a new method of striking topmasts was introduced; and the use of capstans for weighing anchor. Chain pumps did not improve the sailing quality, but they made dealing with leaks and bilge water a great deal easier. Increased resort to the tropics made the acquaintance of wood boring beetles, unknown in colder waters, and some ships returned almost literally falling to pieces until Hawkins introduced a double skin method of construction, with horsehair between the planking, the best deterrent known until the introduction of copper sheathing.[3] Other innovations, although known and advocated by some seamen, did not find general acceptance. Sir William Winter, for instance, tried very hard in 1578 to persuade his colleagues to replace gravel ballast, which quickly became noisome and sometimes shifted, with stone, but most did not respond. He also advocated the re-location of cooking gallies from the hold to the fo'castle, but the change was not generally accepted until long after his death, although it had many advantages for both hygiene and safety.[4]

Elizabethan warships were faster and handier than their predecessors; they were also much more heavily armed. As we have already seen, the warships of 1540 were more heavily gunned than their predecessors of 1515. Those of 1585 had taken another quantum leap. In 1540 the *Great Bark* of 500 tons (a newly rebuilt ship)

[1] Sir William Monson, 'How to fight at sea, one ship with another', printed in *The Naval Tracts of Sir William Monson*, ed. M. Oppenheim, 91.

[2] Oppenheim describes the *Warspite* as 'one of the few shipbuilding failures of the reign'. In 1598, soon after completion, she needed £712 to be spent on repairs (*Administration*, 130). However, according to Hawkins, several other ships, including the *Revenge*, suffered from similar defects. Adams, 'New light'.

[3] T. Glasgow, 'Sixteenth century English seamen encounter a new enemy', *American Neptune*, 27, 1967, 299–308.

[4] Oppenheim, *Administration*, 127–8.

carried a total of 87 guns, but only 7 of those were heavier than a saker. The *Mary Rose* of 450 tons had no fewer than 96, and of those 6 could be classed as heavy.[1] But in 1585 the 800 ton *Elizabeth* carried 34 guns of demi-culverin size or more, out of a total of 76, and the *Revenge* of 500 tons 22 out of 46.[2] So the overall tonnage of the ordnance had increased considerably, although the total number of guns had not. The technology of gunfounding and of powder making had also improved, and the firepower of the *Revenge* must have been about four times that of the *Great Bark*. A good test of that change is provided by the last stand of the *Jesus* at San Juan d'Ulloa in 1568. She was an old ship, which had been condemned nine years before and was barely seaworthy. She was a carrack with two gun-decks, mounting a total of 61 guns, of which 12 were heavy.[3] The odds against her were too great and she was eventually captured, but Hawkins made devastating use of his heavy guns in keeping a sizeable Spanish squadron at bay and learned, if he still needed to learn, that the future of seafighting lay with firepower. The English tactic of using a ship as a floating gun-platform had probably been developing since the late 1540s, and it came of age in this significant little engagement. By 1585 it was well known and respected by other seafaring powers, but not as yet imitated. In 1584 William Thomas, the master gunner of the *Victory*, complained of the shortage of trained gunners, and other English observers shared his concern, but they were setting themselves a very exacting standard, and the truth seems to have been that there were no warships in the world at that point which could match either the power, or the range, or the rapidity of the English guns. The French navy, so formidable in 1545, and even in 1558, had disintegrated during the civil wars; and the Spaniards, in spite of their victory at Terciera in 1583, were still learning the business of Atlantic fighting.[4] It was in such adverse circumstances that Philip decided to launch the Armada.

The problems which Henry VIII had begun to encounter in recruiting seamen for his warships became noticeably worse in the war of 1557–9. This was no doubt partly the result of the influenza epidemic, but it was also partly caused by the unpopularity of the war. In May 1557 21 royal ships were at sea, and the names of their

[1] From a table dated 13 February 1540, printed in *MM*, 6, 1920, 281.

[2] Oppenheim, *Administration*, 156–7. For a summary of modern research findings on Elizabethan naval ordnance, see Kirsch, *The Galleon*, 48–62.

[3] M. Lewis, 'The guns of the *Jesus of Lubeck*', *MM*, 22, 1936, 324.

[4] I. A. A. Thompson, 'The Invincible Armada', in *Royal Armada*, 160–80.

masters and captains are listed, but 65 private ships had also been hired, and officers for those proved difficult to find.[1] On 26 July royal letters were sent to a number of named gentlemen, summoning them for naval service because '. . . ships presently in the Narrow Seas are not according to our expectation furnished with captains.'[2] How successful this tactic was we do not know, but there were no summonses to attend the Council in consequence of default. The following summer the problem was less with the officers than with the seamen, and seems to have been much worse. On 29 March all masters and mariners retained to serve in the navy were forbidden to depart from their ships without licence upon pain of death.[3] However, that did not solve the problem of the shortfall in recruiting, and on 3 May a further proclamation forbade all other voyages because

> . . . no small number of the best and ablest of the said shipmasters, mariners, gunners, seafaring men and watermen, contrary to the obedience and duty of good subjects, not regarding the premises but in contempt thereof, have withdrawn themselves from her highness' said service, and by colourable means conveyed themselves into divers good ships and other vessels lately set forth towards outward realms and places in voyages for traffic and merchandise, and also in adventuring and warfare . . .

The proclamation then went on somewhat ambitiously to decree that no ship should sail without the Lord Admiral's licence, and that all ships already at sea should instantly return.[4] Finally, at some point during July all watermen and mariners without exception were ordered to be '. . . obedient as well to the said Lord Admiral himself as to his inferior and under officers . . .' upon pain of death.[5] It is difficult to imagine a more eloquent testimony to the unpopularity of naval service at that time. It was not until 1592 that Elizabeth felt constrained to issue any similarly draconian order, but that did not mean that the difficulty disappeared with the new regime. Periodic musters of seamen indicate that the problem did not lie in overstretched resources; an incomplete return (without London) lists 7 014 in 1560, and another, equally incomplete, 6 530 in 1570.[6] The

[1] Magdalene College, Pepys MS 2875, Miscellaneous transcripts; 13, 15, 22.
[2] Ibid., 27.
[3] Hughes and Larkin, *Tudor Royal Proclamations*, 2, 84–5.
[4] Ibid, 89–90.
[5] Ibid, 91–2.
[6] PRO SP12/11/27; SP12/71/74 (i), /73/15 (i), /48; Oppenheim, *Administration*, 176–7.

only complete muster roll, of 1582, gives a total of 16 283, classed as masters, seamen, fishermen and watermen.[1] If all the 28 ships listed as being in commission in 1575 had gone to sea at once 'in fashion of war' they would have required about 7 000 men, of whom about half would have been seamen.[2] A similar sized fleet of armed merchantmen would have needed about 3 000. So, assuming that the 1582 figure is the best guide, and allowing for a steady (but not dramatic) increase in population after 1560, only a major war such as the Armada campaign should have presented the Admiralty with a real problem of man power.

Recruitment difficulties arose for other reasons. One of these was pay, because the 1545 increment of about 30 per cent was quickly overtaken by inflation. Between 1545 and 1560 the price of a standard 'basket of consumables' had risen by over 100 per cent, an unprecedented experience after over a century of static or falling prices prior to 1520 and only a very modest rise thereafter. The 1550s had seen much hardship and social unrest ashore, and although seamen were cushioned to some extent by the fact that their victuals were provided, the real value of their wages had slumped dramatically. By 1560 it certainly compared unfavourably with the kind of profit and loot sharing deal which a seaman could negotiate for himself on board the average merchantman which went in for a little piracy on the side.[3] There is no evidence from the pre-Armada period that the Queen's crews were not promptly paid, and no pay-related mutinies that we know of, but Sir William Monson later confirmed that the seamen's preference for private ships, alleged in the Marian proclamation of May 1558, still applied during his early days of service in the 1580s.[4] The wet, crowded and unhygienic conditions of living on the royal warships had not improved since the days of the first *Mary Rose*, but they were no worse than those on merchant ships – or indeed ashore. Medicine was primitive, and on long voyages the mortality could be as high as 50 per cent, but many private ships carried no physician at all, and losses were even higher. The other main deterrent mentioned by Monson was the code of discipline – the ferocious corporal punishment which was meted out more by custom than by law, and loosely

[1] PRO SP12/156/45.

[2] Bodleian Library, Rawlinson MS A.297, ff. 15r.–16v., giving the manning levels for all the ships in commission.

[3] C. L'Estrange Ewen, 'Organised piracy around England in the sixteenth century', *MM*, 35, 1939, 29–42.

[4] Sir William Monson, *Tracts*.

based upon the ancient Laws of Oleron.[1] Some early Elizabethan captains, notably Hawkins, are known to have been reluctant to resort to such barbarous methods, but we know very little about how order was maintained in the pre-Armada period. Warships had to go where they were sent and remain on station, rather than pursue opportunities for plunder, and that could present the captain with a serious disciplinary problem. The most celebrated mutiny of the period – that of the *Golden Lion* during Drake's expedition to Cadiz in 1587 – arose from such reasons.[2] Gentlemen adventurers could also be a nuisance in this connection, but that is a rather different issue. By 1620 service on the king's ships was generally 'abhorred', and both pressure and force were used to keep crews up to strength. Elizabeth probably survived by making only modest demands upon the seafaring population during the first twenty-five years of her reign, and when the pressure began to increase, in 1582, Hawkins persuaded her to issue a new pay scale.

The basic rate for an ordinary seaman was raised to 10s. a month, and 32 different ranks and grades of officer were recognized.[3] Only a first rate ship, such as the *Elizabeth Jonas* or the *Victory*, carried the full range. The smallest ship (the *Signet*) had only five, and seven different grades or classes of ship were provided for. Broadly speaking, the larger the ship the more the officer was paid; so the master of the *Triumph* was paid £3.2s.6d. a month, the master of the *Revenge* £3, and the master of the *Aid* £2.5s. Similarly the Purser of the *Mary Rose* received 16s.8d. a month, his equivalent on the *Dreadnought* 13s.4d., while the *Signet* made do with a cook/steward. In some cases the grading of posts casts an interesting light on contemporary values. The surgeon was paid more than the coxswain, and the

[1] There were good reasons for strict discipline on board warships. If supplies of food, and more particularly drink, were not tightly controlled, the men rapidly became unfit for duty, as happened at Lisbon in 1589. The unauthorized use of candles, and later tobacco, was also forbidden because of the risk of fire and explosions. The corporal punishments listed by Monson as 'sufficient to subdue the roughest seamen in the world' included various forms of flogging, keel-hauling, and death for striking a superior officer. On a warship the infliction of such punishments was at the discretion of the captain. Similar punishments were sometimes used on private ships, but usually only for endangering the safety of the ship, and then the captain acted with the consent of the remainder of the crew. Julian Corbett, *Fighting Instructions, 1530–1816*, 37, 40; Monson, *Tracts*, 2, 436.

[2] Oppenheim, *Administration*, Appendix B.

[3] PRO SP12/186/43. With the introduction of this graduated scale, deadshares and rewards, which had featured in seamens and officers pay since the fourteenth century were discontinued. In 1568 James Humphrey had listed the wage rates then in use more summarily, from the seaman at 6s.8d. a month to the master of a 'Great Ship' at 40s. Magdalene College, Pepys MS 1266, 190–1.

trumpeter was paid more than the master gunner, while a 'quarter gunner' on 11s.3d. a month was paid little more than an ordinary seaman. The higher-ranking officers were normally kept in pay while the ship was on a care and maintenance basis, and the master's first job when he was instructed to prepare his ship for sea, was to recruit the remainder of the junior officers and craftsmen. Only the master gunner had the separate job of providing his own assistants, and the accounts show a number of instances of these officers or their agents being paid the conduct money for the men they had recruited.[1] Ordinary seamen might be volunteers, who simply turned up at Chatham or Deptford when the word spread that the fleet (or some part of it) was being manned. However, such men supplied only a fraction of the need and the vast majority were pressed. This could be done in a variety of ways. Commissions might be given to selected officers to go into the maritime counties and negotiate quotas with the magistrates there, or commissions might be sent direct to the magistrates themselves; the justices of the peace, or the mayors and aldermen of port towns. The commissioners might then simply round up the designated men, pay them their conduct money, and despatch them to wherever the fleet was assembling. Alternatively they might return the names of those who were to serve to the Admiralty, together with their places of habitation, and one of the clerks would then write letters similar to that penned by James Humphreys to the constables of an unknown hundred on 12 March 1568.[2]

> . . . thes shalbe to charge; as also in the Quenes Maiesties name to commande yow upon the sight hereof; To charge and set forth the viii men here under written . . . and that yow do commande them to be at Chatham in Kent on satterday next; and there to present them selves before the Officers of her highness Shyppes . . .

This letter was accompanied by 4s. conduct money for each of the eight men named in the schedule. Another method, it seems, was to write directly and individually to the men concerned, instructing them as to the time and place of their appearance. A model letter of this kind was also penned by Humphrey on 20 March 1568, summoning seven individuals to Chatham by 1 April.[3] This latter

[1] MS Rawlinson A.203 ff. 327–8.
[2] Pepys MS 2875, 95, the Queen's commission of 16 June 1560; 96, a schedule of 2 000 men to be recruited from 12 different counties. MS Rawlinson 846, f. 114.
[3] Ibid., f. 115.

method can hardly have been in general use for ordinary seamen, unless literacy rates were much higher than anyone has hitherto suspected. Perhaps it was this sort of attention to detail, or administrative efficiency, which kept the ships manned with relatively little fuss and complaint, while the problems both before and afterwards appear to have been so much greater.

As far as can be told from the record of sums of money provided for the paying off of ships and for conduct to and from the ports of embarkation, the seamen of this period were usually paid promptly, but benefits and perquisites were few. In 1587 the crews of three pinnaces were awarded an extra month's pay for their good service in taking Spanish prizes, and in the following year £5 was divided among the hundred men who had manned the Calais fireships.[1] However, such rewards were scarce, and when a royal ship took a prize most of the value went to the Queen, the Lord Admiral and the officers. That was another reason why seamen preferred the more egalitarian system of the privateers, in spite of the extra risks involved. Earlier in the century it had been normal to supply 'coats', and sometimes liveries for seamen in the King's service, but the practice had been discontinued by 1560. Entrepreneurial officers, like Roger Langford in 1586, might provide shoes and clothing, but the price would be deducted from the men's pay.[2] John Hawkins made a habit of ensuring that the men under his command were properly clad, but even he did not provide such a service free of charge. A seaman who was sick or injured might be sent ashore and continue to receive his pay until he had recovered and returned to duty, but a man who was discharged sick could expect little more than a begging licence to see him home.[3] It was to be the experience of war, and particularly of the years 1588 and 1589, which convinced first the Admiralty and then the Queen that some more generous provision would have to be made for the sick and disabled. It was simply not logical to provide for the impotent poor in civilian life and to leave ex-soldiers and seamen to fend for themselves. Apart from any humanitarian consideration, such neglect encouraged others to avoid similar service if they possibly could.

One of the reasons why Elizabeth's Council appears so parsimo-

[1] The accounts show regular payments to the servants of Gonson and Hawkins for collecting large sums in cash from the Receipt of the Exchequer. Oppenheim, *Administration*, 135.

[2] PRO E351/2233. Oppenheim, *Administration*, 138–9.

[3] MS Rawlinson 846, f. 116; signed by William Winter on 10 June 1566, for one William Patch, who had served five weeks in the *Philip and Mary*.

nious in its attitude towards seamen's pay is that wages formed less than half the cost of employing a mariner – considerably less if he was on harbour duty. By the time his sea pay had reached 10s. a month the cost of his victuals for the same period was budgeted at 14s.[1] In 1557 the Lord Treasurer had stipulated that Edward Baeshe, the Surveyor of the Victuals, was to account separately, and after 1564 the victualling totals no longer feature in the Treasurer's books. Baeshe operated through a general commission of purveyance implemented by his agents and assistants in each county. After 1560 he was provided with a headquarters and a number of storehouses. The former Abbey of Grace on Tower Hill, close to the house rented for meetings of the Admiralty officers, was purchased and refurbished in that year at a total cost of £1 900, and other buildings were rented at Ratcliff, St Katherines and Rochester.[2] By 1565 the system was deemed to be unsatisfactory, probably on grounds of cost rather than efficiency, and Baeshe entered into an agreement which was, in effect a contract. Signed on 13 April 1565, this was similar in some respects to that later undertaken by Hawkins, for which it may have served as a model.[3] By its terms Baeshe was to receive annual *pro rata* payments of 4½d. a day for each man in harbour, and 5d. a day for each man at sea. In return he was to provide victuals in accordance with a carefully stipulated schedule which certainly went back to 1545, and probably much further. Each man was to receive every day a gallon of beer, and either a pound of biscuit or a wheaten loaf of 20 oz. The week was then divided into four 'flesh' days and three 'fish' days, not out of deference to the Church but in order to protect the fishing industry. On flesh days (Sunday, Monday, Tuesday and Thursday) every man was to be given either 2lb. of fresh beef, or half a pound of salt beef, or half a pound of bacon. On the fish days (Wednesday, Friday and Saturday) his ration was either a quarter of a stockfish (dried cod) or four herrings, plus quarter of a pound of butter and half a pound of cheese.[4] For a supplementary allowance of 4d. per month for a man at sea and 8d. in harbour, Baeshe was also to provide such necessities as firewood and candles, hitherto the responsibility of individual pursers. He took over the payment of rent for his store-

[1] BL Harleian MS 167, ff. 1–38; Baeshe's quarter books, endorsed by Vice-Admiral Woodhouse. Each entry records the victualling of a single ship, based upon the mustered strength of the crew.
[2] Oppenheim, *Administration*, 140.
[3] PRO E351/2358; Bodleian Library MS Rawlinson 846, ff. 132–3, rates for victualling, *c*. 1570.
[4] Ibid.

houses, and the wages of his clerks and assistants. The 1557 proposal that one month's victuals for 1 000 men should always be kept in hand was revived, and Baeshe agreed not to use purveyance unless he was called upon to provide for 2 000 men or more at short notice. The council had struck a hard bargain with its surveyor, but threw in a couple of sweeteners – a £500 interest free 'float' and a licence to export 1 000 hides a year for his own profit from the oxen slaughtered to provide the beef.[1]

The existence of this contract explains the change in the accounting procedure, although the dates do not exactly coincide. It was terminable by six months' notice on either side, but continued until May 1586, about a year before Baeshe's death. In spite of his willingness to continue, the Surveyor often found it hard going, and was anticipating a debt of £534 when he eventually decided to lay down the burden. He had been in office for 36 years, and must have reached an advanced age. The Council was not altogether unsympathetic to his problems, caused more by a steadily advancing inflation than by either incompetence or mistaken strategy. They advanced him an extra £1 000 without interest in 1569, and put up the rates to 5½d. and 6d. in 1573.[2] Nevertheless he was heavily in debt by 1576, and petitioned for further relief. It does not always do to take such petitions at face value, but Baeshe seems to have been an honest man, and no charge of malfeasance was ever made against him. He claimed that his contract was saving the Exchequer 1 000 marks a year, over and above the great benefit of not having to resort to purveyance, and that he was losing £500 a year while trade with the Low Countries was embargoed and he could not export his hides. The fire at Portsmouth had also cost him £240. All this was no doubt true, but it could equally be pointed out that a man who normally made £500 a year from one privileged licence was not exactly poverty-stricken. There is no record of the response which he received, but it appears that his debts had been substantially reduced by the time that he decided to hand over his office ten years later.

Without resort to purveyance, Baeshe had to bargain for his provisions in the open market, and this was no doubt part of his problem. Prices varied with the circumstances, but his allowances did not, and although this could work both ways, with an underlying inflation it must more often have been to his detriment. He also needed to know where supplies could be located, and to spread his

[1] PRO E351/2362; Oppenheim, *Administration*, 141.
[2] PRO SP12/109/37; Oppenheim, *Administration*, 141–2.

demand as widely as possible to avoid driving up prices. By the end of his career, and probably long before, he had worked out a quota system for most of his requirements '. . . declaringe oute of what Shires the wheate, maulte, Oxen, Butter and Cheese is to be had'.[1] Sussex, for example, was deemed capable of producing 600 quarters of wheat, 600 quarters of malt and 100 oxen. Some were assessed for grain only, others for oxen only; the butter was to come from Norfolk and Suffolk, and the cheese only from Suffolk. Some counties, such as Cornwall and Northumberland, were not expected to contribute at all. How this might work in practice can be seen from a letter written in February 1587 by Lord Hunsdon in his capacity as Lord Lieutenant of Norfolk.[2] The country was already at war, and commissions had been issued to restrict the export of grain and other foodstuffs, so Hunsdon addressed his letter to the Sheriff, the Justices of the Peace, his Deputy Lieutenants, and to 'her majesties commissioners for restrainte of corne and other provisions within the said countie'.

> . . . you shall understand that Edward Bashe Esquier generall surveior of the Queenes majesties victualls for sea causes is especially commanded with all expedition to make ready a greate proportion of victualles for the whole navie; towardes the furnishing wherof ther is alloted to be provided within the countie of norfolk one thousand quarters of wheat, one thousand quarters of maulte, and one hundred barrelles of butter, albeit for this present service I have thought good to reduce the same for the ease of the cuntry, to five hundred quarters of wheat and threescore barrelles of butter; for which provision the sayde Edward Bashe doth now send downe his purveior to lade and send the same away to London with all speede . . .

Baeshe presumably struck bargains of this kind in all counties, reducing his demands in exchange for the collaboration of the authorities. He had some leverage, because a big operation was in prospect, and he was entitled to resort to purveyance if he thought it necessary. Hunsdon's letter continued,

> I doe require you to assemble yourselfes together in your severall divisions and to appointe the sayd provisions to be forthwith had, and delivered at reasonable prices at the waterside, and the same

[1] PRO SP12/107 ff. 39v–40r.
[2] Bodleian Library, MS Tanner 241, ff. 28–9.

> corne to be taken of the great corne masters, Broggers and outbiers of corne without grievance to the people, which speadily may be performed, considering it is for her majesties greate service and that ready money shall be paide upon the delivery thereof . . .

24s. a quarter, he suggested, would be a reasonable price for the corn, and he reminded his readers that Baeshe had promised not to resort to his commission of purveyance 'if the provisions may be otherwise reasonably had . . .'

In spite of both warning and incentive, Norfolk was recalcitrant, and on 16 March Hunsdon wrote again in more peremptory style

> . . . muche marveling that you Mr. Shreife and the residew of the Justices and commissioners are so carelesse of her majesties greate service, being (as I am enformed) so greate store in your shier . . .[1]

This time Baeshe's purveyor arrived armed with the Queen's commission, requiring 500 quarters of wheat and 600 of malt, but willing to obtain the butter from Suffolk instead. What Suffolk said to that, or how quickly the commission was obeyed, we do not know. If every county reacted in the same way, it must have been a wearisome struggle to victual a major operation.

In November 1586 the rates had been increased again, to 6d. and 6½d., but even so when Baeshe's stores were eventually handed over to his successor James Quarles in June 1587, there was only 12 040 lb. of beef and 2 300 stockfish in hand.[2] This would not even have been enough for the 1 000 man reserve. Baeshe's expenditure after 1564 ranged from £1 843 in 1566 to £11 932 in 1580, averaging about £4 000 a year. By contrast, the last year of the war (1563) had required £19 208, and in 1587 Quarles spent £29 563.[3] Baeshe seems to have been a loyal and tenacious servant of the crown, and it is probably significant that the complaints about the quality of victuals, which had been so frequent in each of Henry VIII's wars, were not heard during his long period in charge. They began again with redoubled vigour as soon as he had stepped down, and reached a crescendo in 1588 and 1589. Most of Baeshe's work was done in peacetime, and the wars between 1557 and 1563 were not all-out efforts like that of 1543–6, but he does at least seem to have been

[1] Ibid., 30–31.
[2] Oppenheim, *Administration*, 142.
[3] Ibid., 161.

sufficiently competent and honest to avoid adding another disadvantage to service in the royal navy. He was also spared some of the worst problems of victualling long voyages, which presented special problems, especially if the destination was the tropics. None of the standard provisions would keep at sea for any length of time, and beer had a particularly short life. It also took a ton of stowage space to store the provisions for four men for one month; so to victual a crew of 200 for three months required 150 tons of stowage, which would have been more than half the capacity of a ship of that size, before any allowance had been made for arms, munitions or spare tackle. So it is not surprising that some captains, notably Drake, consistently took the risk of under victualling, preferring the danger of shortages to the dangers of bad food and inadequate space. Such ships had to re-victual as they went, which not infrequently explains their choice of tactical options.

As we have seen, the weight of the ordnance carried had increased significantly by the 1580s, and this had its effect upon ship design, but the range and complexity of other weapons, of ammunition and of auxiliary equipment also increased, and these competed with the victuals, and with the men themselves, for space on board. By 1575 a capital ship like the *Triumph*, which carried 200 soldiers and 50 gunners in her complement of 700 men, also carried a range of personal weapons and armour; 250 arquebuses, 200 pikes, 100 corselets and 200 morions, in addition to older equipment such as 50 bows and 200 bills.[1] Even the little *George*, with 10 gunners and 40 mariners carried 12 arquebuses. These guns were in a sense replacements for the slings and double bases of an earlier generation, but they also needed powder and ammunition. When William Winter accounted as Master of Naval Ordnance, for what he had supplied to the *Lion*, the *Swallow*, the *Antelope* and the *Saker* in the Narrow Seas in 1562, he listed 3 cwt of wrought lead shot for arquebuses and 96 ells of canvas for cartridges among quantities of 38 other items, costing a total of £156.10s.1d.[2] The list of munitions needed by a warship on active service was very considerable; thousands of nails, ladels and swabs for the guns, plates of iron and lead, spare wheels for the gun carriages, bolts of various kinds, and a

[1] Bodleian MS Rawlinson, A.297.
[2] PRO E101/64/31. Winter kept his own accounts, some of which survive in the PRO, of which this, for 1561–3 is one. His whole expenditure for those years totalled £2 437.1s.9d. The account for 1564–5 is in the British Library, Cotton MS Otto E VII, ff.12–18. Others are in Gloucester Record Office (D 421/X 1). Glasgow, 'Maturing of Naval Administration', 19.

huge variety of spare cables. All this needed storage space, and gunpowder, like biscuit, required dry storage. Although the introduction of centralized victualling had made the purser's life much easier in one respect, increasing sophistication of equipment and longer periods at sea gave him new headaches. Not least of these must have been the difficulty of finding space for everything. It is not surprising that sleeping accommodation remained extremely cramped, even for the officers.

The diet provided by Edward Baeshe and his assistants was sufficient in quantity, but desperately monotonous and unbalanced, as had been the case throughout the century. Before 1550 the purser's discretion, as well as the officers' private means, had meant that a variety of other foodstuffs, including fruit and poultry, were often present on board, although it is difficult to say in what quantities. After 1550 this became more difficult, but pursers did still claim and receive sums of money for supplementary victualling, which was probably of this nature.[1] During long voyages, upon which the problems were worst, every landfall provoked a foraging expedition, and the consumption of unfamiliar food and drink sometimes had the most disastrous consequences. With Drake's expedition of 1585 to 1587 naval operations proper extended across the Atlantic for the first time, and the problems of diet-related mortality began to increase alarmingly.

By the time of the Armada, England could get its navy to sea faster, and keep it there longer, than any other power. Its gunnery was advanced and its tactics, based upon a generation of successful privateering, innovative and effective, but against sickness and infectious disease it had as yet no defence. Nevertheless during the generation which separated Elizabeth's accession from the climax of the war with Spain, the English navy had adapted itself to an oceanic role, and had the capability, although on a modest scale, to carry out a blue water strategy.

[1] MS Rawlinson, A.200, A.201.

8
SHIPS AT SEA, 1558–1588

While the peace negotiations continued, from November 1558 to the end of March 1559, naval operations were confined to patrolling. Privateers continued to operate with enthusiasm, as they were entitled to do until the peace was actually signed, but the summer of 1559 saw no major mobilization. However, Cateau Cambrésis was an uneasy peace as far as England was concerned. Not only was Elizabeth very determined to save face over Calais, and consequently made a great show of regarding its loss as a temporary setback, but a strong French military presence continued in Scotland. The Scots were included in the treaty, but the death of Henry II following a tournament accident on 10 July, and the accession of his 15 year old son Francis II intensified the Queen's sense of insecurity. Mary, the titular queen of Scotland was now also Queen of France, and because her husband was technically of age there was no Regency Council. Had there been, it would probably have been under the control of the princes of the blood, but in the event Mary's ambitious Guise kinsmen, the Duke and Cardinal of Lorraine, became all powerful.[1] Henry had recognized Elizabeth's title, but there was no guarantee that Francis would do the same, given the strength of Mary's claim to the English crown, and the fact that a third Guise, the Queen Mother, was Regent of Scotland.[2] Elizabeth was therefore faced with the difficult task of diminishing French influence in the North without breaking the peace. In the

[1] The senior prince of the blood was Anthony of Bourbon, King of Navarre. Bourbon himself was a moderate Catholic, but his wife, Jeanne D'Albret and his nephew, Gaspard de Coligny were strong Protestants, and his younger brother the Duke of Condé became a political leader of the Huguenots.

[2] Mary, the sister of the Duke and the Cardinal, and widow of King James V.

spring of 1559 it seemed that this might be achieved for her without the necessity to take any action, by the Protestant Lords of the Congregation, who were in rebellion against the Regent. However as the summer advanced it became clear that Protestant ardour was no match for professional soldiers. The Lords suffered a number of defeats and their forces began to evaporate. They also had no fleet, and consequently no means of preventing French reinforcements from reaching the Regent. Only Elizabeth could do that, and it was probably the news that such reinforcements had sailed on 13 December which eventually forced her hand.

On 16 December, in a manner which was to be typical of many of her subsequent actions, the Queen ordered Sir William Winter to sea with 34 ships and instructions to act 'as though on his own initiative' in intercepting the French ships.[1] Fortunately Winter was spared the impossible situation into which such orders could easily have led him. He did not actually sail until 26 December, and by that time two things had happened. On 24 December the Council resolved upon open intervention in Scotland, and ordered the Duke of Norfolk to advance cautiously with about 4 000 men who had already been mustered; and secondly the French fleet had been dispersed and driven back by storms.[2] As it turned out, neither of these developments was decisive. A second fleet was soon assembling in the Normandy ports, and there was optimistic talk in France of 10 000 men being in the North by Candlemas. At the same time the Duke of Norfolk's orders were countermanded, and he was told to restrict his intervention to the sending of 'secret succours';[3] on the other hand, Winter's role was now open and acknowledged. On 22 January he reached the Forth, and immediately went into action, cutting the lines of communication between the French garrison in Leith and the army operating in Fife. The latter retreated by way of Dunfermline and Stirling, abandoning their artillery and supplies. There were a few French ships in the Forth, but they were in no position to challenge the English fleet; two galleys and a hoy were captured. Emboldened by this success, and by the frustration of the second French relief expedition through bad weather, on 27 February Norfolk was allowed to conclude a formal treaty of alliance with the Lords of the Congregation. Elizabeth became Protector of the Liberties of Scotland for as long as the marriage between Mary and

[1] PRO SP12/7/169–71. T. Glasgow, 'The navy in the first undeclared Elizabethan war', *MM*, 54, 1968, 23–37.

[2] J. B. Black, *The Reign of Queen Elizabeth*, 43.

[3] S. Haynes, ed., *Burghley Papers*, 217, 220.

Francis should endure. Although the Queen was still reluctant for her army to become involved, circumstances in France conspired to favour her. On 4 February Nicholas Throgmorton, her ambassador in Paris began to write of the 'factions in religion' which were beginning to appear in France, and on 16/17 March a conspiracy against the Guise supremacy erupted in the Tumult of Amboise.[1] Although they were in a sense to his advantage, Philip was not amused by these developments, and was anxious to discourage Elizabeth from re-awakening war with France. He allowed, and probably encouraged, his military men to make threatening noises, but unfortunately for him Elizabeth knew perfectly well that his finances would not permit him to make good such threats – at least for the time being.

Nevertheless, the Queen's chronic indecisiveness almost allowed the opportunity to pass, and it was Cecil, acting with Throgmorton's active encouragement, who took the immense risk of authorizing Lord Grey to advance from Berwick on 28 March.[2] By 5 April Grey had linked up with the Scottish army, and a few days later Leith was invested. Elizabeth accepted the *fait accompli*, but her objectives remained distinct from those of her Scottish allies. She was only concerned to secure the removal of French troops from Scotland, while they wished to overthrow the Regent and secure the control of government for themselves. The Regent, however, totally failed to exploit this difference, perhaps because of her own deteriorating health, or perhaps she was unable to believe that no succour would arrive from France. She refused to negotiate, and the siege of Leith continued with renewed vigour. However it was a bungled operation, and the grand assault on 8 May was a disastrous failure. Had the French been able to hold out, the Anglo-Scottish alliance would probably have fallen apart, but fortune had deserted them. Even if the situation in France had not inhibited any further attempts at relief, it is unlikely that anything short of an armada could have got through Winter's blockade. Negotiations were already taking place when the death of the Regent on 11 June hastened a conclusion. In spite of her strong position, Elizabeth nearly blew the whole settlement by attempting to insist upon the

[1] Black, 46. The 'Tumult' was a Protestant conspiracy to kidnap the King and wrest control from the Guise family.

[2] Exactly how much Elizabeth knew about this decision is uncertain. She did not give any official instruction herself, but it seems very unlikely that she had not given Cecil some intimation of her approval. Haynes, *Burghley Papers*, 267. For a full discussion of these manoeuvres, see Conyers Read, *Mr. Secretary Cecil and Queen Elizabeth*, 164–6.

restoration of Calais, but she allowed herself to be persuaded by wiser counsels, and on 6 July agreement was reached. Both England and France agreed to withdraw their troops, the fortifications at Leith, Eyemouth and Dunbar were to be razed, and Mary and Francis were to stop displaying the insignia of England and Ireland upon their arms.[1] Winter then ensured compliance by evacuating the whole French garrison and their dependents in what was probably the most efficient naval operation of the reign. By the time his fleet was withdrawn it had been on active service for over nine months, and had cost £11 294.11s.9d. a fraction of the cost of the army, which had achieved much less.[2]

1560 was a year of considerable activity. Apart from Winter's fleet in the North, Lord Admiral Clinton was at sea in the South Western approaches, operating out of Portsmouth with up to 42 ships. These probably included the two old galleys, since he had two Venetians among his captains.[3] But it was a summer cruise rather than a sustained operation, since it cost less than £6 000. It was probably at the same time that Sir Thomas Cotton had 20 ships in the Narrow Seas, at a cost of £3 500, which reflected the Queen's nervous anxiety about French intentions rather than any substantial threat. The contrast between a year of normal vigilance and one which included even modest military activity, is startlingly reflected in the Treasurer's accounts. In 1559 Gonson expended £21 868.11s.1d., and in 1560 £84 300 6s.4d.[4] This contrast helps to explain Elizabeth's marked indifference to all suggestions that she should follow up the Treaty of Edinburgh. She ignored Throgmorton's warnings that the French would refuse to ratify the Treaty, and that the Guises were bent on revenge. The Scottish lords who pressed for a closer relationship were scarcely afforded the courtesy of a hearing. It was during these months that the Queen's relationship with Lord Robert Dudley was coming to a steamy climax, and she had scant attention to spare for anything else. Such a major lapse of concentration might have cost her dear, but circumstances conspired to protect her. Francis II died in December 1560, throwing France into deeper confusion, and significantly reducing the risk of any Guise inspired attempt to re-enter Scotland. And although Elizabeth's behaviour

[1] Haynes, *Burghley Papers*, 351–2; Conyers Read, 189–90.
[2] PRO E351/2197, Gonson's accounts, 1 January 1559 to 31 December 1560.
[3] Ibid.
[4] Ibid.; Oppenheim, *Administration*, 161.

provoked scandalized gossip at every court in Europe, it provided neither pretext nor opportunity for hostile diplomatic moves.

By 1562 the Queen had recovered her emotional balance, and had begun to pick up again the threads of her earlier strategy. Broadly speaking this was to use continental Protestants wherever possible to deflect potential Catholic threats against England, preferably without any open agreement or formal obligation. By 1560 the reformed churches everywhere felt threatened, and Germany in particular was thick with rumours of Catholic leagues and conspiracies. The Lutheran princes wanted an evangelical league, but that was not part of Elizabeth's scheme and she used the doctrinal unacceptability of the Confession of Augsburg to escape that particular trap.[1] Her formal obligations to the Scottish lords had come to an end with the death of Francis II, and she could see no need to renew them, particularly after the return of the widowed Queen in August 1561. Mary had embarked with only two galleys and two ships, not waiting for the safeconduct which had been requested on her behalf. Had she wished, Elizabeth could easily have intercepted her at sea, but no such orders were given, and when the galleys encountered the English barks which were patrolling the North Sea, they exchanged salutations and passed on. To Elizabeth, Mary represented legitimacy in the North, and she always preferred to deal with a lawful government. The Scottish lords were quite strong enough to prevent the reappearance of French troops in Scotland, and that was all that interested the Queen of England. Moreover, any such threat could best be countered in France itself, and there the rising tide of religious discord presented the opportunity. In February 1562 the Duke of Guise emerged as the leading Catholic champion, obviously aiming to use the disorder to recover that control of public policy which he had lost to the Queen Mother, Catherine de Medici, on the accession of the infant Charles IX. By the end of March the Huguenot leaders, the Prince of Condé and Gaspard de Coligny were also in arms. They seized Orleans, and appealed to their co-religionists in England and Germany to make common cause against the Counter-Reformation. In spite of Throgmorton's partisan urgings, Elizabeth's first reaction was to offer mediation, seeking thereby to avoid the risk of a Catholic victory without danger or expense to herself. It was only when Catherine had rejected her overture with contempt that the Queen began to listen to those who were urging a more

[1] E. I. Kouri, 'Elizabethan England and Europe; forty unprinted letters from Elizabeth I to Protestant powers'. *BIHR* Supplement 12, 1982.

active intervention. Apart from the ambassador, the foremost among these was Lord Robert Dudley, still in his own eyes, if not in Elizabeth's, a candidate for the Crown matrimonial. Elizabeth's uncharacteristic adventurousness on this occasion is often attributed to his influence, but in fact the temptation lay more in the situation itself than in any siren voice.

By September the Huguenot position was becoming desperate. Both Spain and the Catholic parts of Germany were mobilizing to support the Guise, but there was no sign of equivalent support for them. Elizabeth was therefore able to dictate her own terms. By the secret treaty of Richmond, signed on 20 September, England was to recover Calais in return for 6 000 troops and a loan of 140 000 crowns (about £45 000).[1] Le Havre, called by the English Newhaven, was to be handed over at once as a pledge for Calais, and half the English troops committed were to remain there as a garrison. With exemplary promptness, the Queen despatched her first contingent under Sir Adrian Poynings within a matter of days, carefully explaining both to her own subjects and to the Spanish ambassador that she was not at war with France, and had no desire to see unauthorized hostilities developing, either at sea or anywhere else. Meanwhile naval deployment had more than kept pace with the rapid development of events. Several ships were already at sea during July; the *Saker* and the *Phoenix* transporting provisions to Berwick; the *Willoughby* and two others ferrying artillery to Ireland and chasing pirates in the Irish Sea.[2] By 6 August five others had been sent out under Sir William Woodhouse, to be joined by three more on 10 September, and a further three, including the *Triumph* and the *Victory*, on 1 October.[3] At first it seemed that the gamble was going to pay off. Philip was in no position to intervene, because his moves to assist the Guise had been stopped in their tracks by disorders in the Netherlands. By December he was offering to mediate the return of Calais to England in order to stop Elizabeth's support for Condé. By that time the Earl of Warwick with the main English force had joined Poynings in Le Havre. The larger warships were withdrawn before the onset of winter, but five smaller ships joined the Channel guard on 1 December, and maintained full

[1] Black, 57–8; PRO SP70/42/582–3.

[2] Proclamation of 24 September 1562; 'Wherefore her majesty letteth all her subjects assembled either at Portsmouth or at Rye to understand that this her intent is not to make war or use any hostility against the French king or any of his faithful subjects . . .' Hughes and Larkin, 2, 206–7.

[3] Bodleian Library MS Rawlinson A.200, Quarter Book, 1562–3. PRO E351/2199; Gonson's accounts, 1 January 1562 to 31 December 1564.

communications between England and Normandy throughout the bad weather.[1]

Unfortunately for Elizabeth, however, this was not a war which could be won at sea. On 26 October the Catholic forces took Rouen, cutting Le Havre off from the main Huguenot army, and then in December Condé was defeated and taken prisoner at the battle of Dreux. Catherine had no desire for a more complete Guise victory, and negotiations for a settlement commenced at once. This process was probably aided by the assassination of the Duke of Guise in February 1563, and by the end of March Condé had come to terms, regaining his own liberty and a measure of toleration for his co-religionists in return for laying down his arms and abandoning his ally. Warwick and his garrison had had very little to do while these dramatic events were unfolding, and the main activity of the Huguenot population of Le Havre during the winter seems to have been privateering. In January Philip's ambassador in London complained that French and English ships operating out of Le Havre were causing untold damage to Spanish and Flemish shipping. Some of these held letters of marque from the Protestant governor and some, it was alleged, from the Earl of Warwick. The French Government had declared all English ships to be good prize as soon as Poynings arrived in Normandy, but the Catholics were not strong at sea, and it seems that little serious damage was inflicted. Elizabeth refrained from proclaiming any counter measures because she wished to maintain the position that she had no quarrel with the Crown of France. On 8 February she ordered the arrest of any of her own subjects giving aid or comfort to the Le Havre 'pirates',[2] but the Queen was not above duplicity in such matters. She had no desire to antagonize Philip, but equally no real desire to prevent English seamen from enriching themselves at the expense of the French. A man like Francis Clarke, who is alleged to have fitted out three ships, and to have taken 18 prizes worth £50 000 during this period, would have been officially a pirate, but he may well have been given unofficial countenance, either by Warwick or by Lord Admiral Clinton.[3] Over the next few years Elizabeth's double standards over piracy were to cause her endless, and fully justified, diplomatic problems.

In the short term, however, Le Havre soon ceased to be a problem

[1] T. Glasgow, 'The navy in the Le Havre campaign, 1562–4', *MM*, 54, 1968, 281; MS Rawlinson A.200.

[2] Hughes and Larkin, 2, 208–9.

[3] Laird Clowes, 477. The Earl of Warwick seems to have issued letters of marque during the occupation, although he was not authorized to do so.

in that sense. Warwick had kept his men occupied during the winter with improving the fortifications, but after Condé had signed the peace of Amboise his position soon became politically impossible. The one thing guaranteed to make the French forget their own quarrels was the presence of an English army on French soil, and the spring saw an upsurge of patriotic enthusiasm. By the beginning of June the port was closely invested on the landward side. That in itself was not a disaster because the sea communications remained open and as late as the middle of May a special contingent of mariners was sent across from Sussex 'to fetch diverse French ships' from the haven there.[1] However, by the middle of June a raging epidemic had broken out in the garrison, and although fresh levies were sent out, they died just as quickly as the rest. In early July it was decided to mount a major rescue operation, and 20 royal ships were ordered to sea. There then ensued a race against time. By 15 July Warwick had only 1 200 fit men. On 16 and 17 July 18 ships put out from Chatham and two from Portsmouth, but were held up by contrary winds.[2] On 24 July Warwick lost control of the harbour mouth, which might not have mattered if a large and heavily armed English fleet had arrived quickly, but effectively prevented him from getting any of his own vessels out. Not knowing how long it would take Clinton to arrive, and with his forces still melting away from disease, on 26 July Warwick decided to surrender on honourable terms. By the middle of August the fleet had returned to Portsmouth, having seen no action at all, and on the 25th orders were given for most of the ships to be returned to their anchorages at Gillingham.[3] The Queen was left with an empty diplomatic hand, which not even her subtlety and histrionics could redeem. After resisting the inevitable for more than six months, she eventually signed the treaty of Troyes on 11 April 1564, which virtually annulled all French obligations under the peace of Cateau Cambrésis, and left England without even a shadow of a claim on Calais.

The unfortunate outcome of this adventure strongly reinforced Elizabeth's natural caution, and it was to be over 20 years before she was compelled to intervene again on behalf of beleaguered Protestant rebels. No figure is available for Gonson's expenditure in 1562, but he received about £24 345, and it is unlikely that he spent a

[1] MS Rawlinson A.200, f. 327r. A total of 15 ships were removed, upon what legal pretext is not clear.

[2] T. Glasgow, 'The navy in the Le Havre expedition'; Black, 61–2; MS Rawlinson A.200, f. 327r.

[3] PRO E351/2199.

great deal more. Deficits were normal at this time, and a margin of £5 000 should probably be allowed, but that would still be well short of a wartime level.[1] The equivalent figures for 1563 are £53 790 and £63 290, significantly less than had been expended in Scotland three years earlier.[2] It would, however, be hard to argue that the Queen's parsimony had been in any sense responsible for the debacle. Even if the main fleet had set out earlier in the summer of 1563, and had carried greater reinforcements, that would not have checked the epidemic in Le Havre, or delayed the outcome by more than a short while. Elizabeth's propensity to live now and pay later was at its most marked in this early period of her reign, but it was Warwick rather than Clinton or his officers who complained of inadequate funding in 1563, and his protests were largely of a self-justificatory nature.

The regular deployment of ships was temporarily superseded by these unofficial wars, but continued on a diminished scale, and was resumed as soon as they were concluded. For a short time immediately after Elizabeth's accession the Vice-Admiral of the Narrow Seas was instructed to 'keep', that is close, all passage to the continent, except for those serving the commissioners at the peace negotiations.[3] This embargo was soon relaxed, but similar instructions were regularly sent to the admirals, and sometimes directly to captains actually at sea. For example on 29 August 1562 the Council wrote to Sir William Woodhouse 'presently upon the seas', instructing him to detach the *Swallow*, then under his command to rendezvous with Sir Hugh Paulet, at Hurst Point *en route* to Spain, and to escort him on his mission.[4] In August 1563 Ralph Chamberlain, in command of three ships in the North Sea, was instructed to discharge the *Hope* and to remain on station with the other two until further orders.[5] During the winter of 1563/4 an unusually strong naval presence was maintained in the Channel, perhaps intended to persuade the French that the threats against their shipping and coasts with which Elizabeth was trying to salvage her defeat at Le Havre, were to be taken seriously. The *Elizabeth Jonas*, the *Victory*, the *Philip and Mary*, the *Aid* and the *Black Galley* were all in service between the end of November and the end of January, and the first

[1] MS Rawlinson A.200, ff. 1–7; Oppenheim, *Administration*, 161.
[2] PRO E351/2199.
[3] *APC*, 7, 4, 21 November 1558.
[4] *APC*, 7, 8, 26 November 1558; ibid., 129, 29 August 1562.
[5] Ibid., 138, 10 August 1563.

three were capital ships not normally used for routine patrolling.[1] In the same year James Humphrey, one of the Controller's assistants, was paid expenses for arranging the 'wafting' of the Iceland fishing fleet, and for fitting out the *Mary Willoughby* to protect the herring fishermen.[2] The quarter books, when these survive, show the dates of the manning, victualling and discharge of all ships sent out on the Queen's service. Six ships (unnamed) were victualled for two months on 14 February and 13 March 1563; five more on the 4 April and 16 May; a rowbarge on 19 May, the *Swallow* and the *Falcon* on 25 May; the *Antelope*, the *Jennet* and the *Double Rose* on 1 June; 'certain ships northward' on 27 June; and the main fleet in three batches in the middle of July.[3] In 1570, a year of peace without military expeditions, the *Bonaventure* and the *Philip and Mary* were commissioned at the end of April under the command of John Hawkins, to escort the fleet of the Merchant Adventurers to Hamburg. In July ten ships were ordered to sea 'in warlike order by her majesty's command' under the command of Lord Charles Howard and William Winter, and another ten were sent to Queenborough to be rigged in case of need.[4] This alarm can be traced to two related events; the publication of the papal bull *Regnans in Excelsis* against Elizabeth in May, and the large Spanish fleet assembling at Antwerp during July to escort Anne of Austria, Philip's fourth wife, to Spain. Musters were ordered and the whole coast from Cornwall to Berwick was put on the alert. Howard's ships, headed by the *Philip and Mary* and the *Lion*, were at sea for about six weeks, from late August to early October, before the alarm subsided. In 1578, perhaps a more typical year, the *Lion*, the *Dreadnought* and *Foresight* were sent to Ireland in July, probably accompanied by the pinnace *Handmaid*; the *Swiftsure* was commissioned in June and July 'for the apprehension of pirates in the Narrow Seas'; the *Achates* was used (among other things) to carry Lord Cobham and Sir Francis Walsingham to the Low Countries; and the *Bonaventure* was at sea on service unspecified, which may well have been the escort for the Merchant Adventurers.[5]

By 1578 it seems unlikely that the quarter books were giving anything like the full particulars, but Gonson's general accounts, and those of Baeshe, can be called upon to provide additional

[1] PRO E351/2200, Gonson's accounts from 1 January 1564 to 31 December 1564.
[2] Magdalene College, Pepys MS 1266, James Humphrey's book, 1568, 178.
[3] MS Rawlinson A.200, ff. 342r–344v.
[4] MS Rawlinson A.201, Quarter book, 1569/70, f. 176r.
[5] MS Rawlinson A.203, Quarter book, 1578/9, ff. 335–338.

information. In 1568 the *Swallow*, the *Antelope*, the *Aid* and the *Phoenix* were at sea in October, November and December; the *Saker* made a round trip to Liverpool in June, and provisions were sent to Beaumaris in North Wales for the *Hare*, the *Makeshift* and the *Hoy Elizabeth*, serving in the Irish Sea.[1] In the same year Sir William Winter was also at sea, but neither the size nor the purpose of his fleet is clear. Such uncertainties are innumerable, but the general picture of deployment is not hard to reconstruct. There were routine patrols, varying in size and duration, covering the South and East coasts in most months of every year. Usually these were made up of small ships and pinnaces, but larger warships might be sent out if any particular threat was anticipated. Regular escorts were provided for the cloth fleet, the Iceland fishing fleet, and (probably) the North Sea herring fishers. Royal messengers and ambassadors, both going and coming, were provided with transportation or armed escort. Most years saw ships serving in Irish waters, and there were frequent specific expeditions against pirates, of which more anon. Alarms caused by diplomatic tension were unpredictable, and did not occur in every year, but they kept the Admiralty officers on their toes, and they seem to have had no great difficulty in producing 15–20 ships at a few weeks' notice. The great majority of the ships deployed in response to such emergencies, or on routine service, were the Queen's own vessels, but the traditional practice of hiring private ships did not entirely cease. In 1560 the tonnage of ships hired for the voyage to Scotland amounted to £2 702.12s.2d., which at 12d. per ton per month would account for over 50 small vessels throughout the expedition.[2] In 1563 the *David of Lubeck* was hired at the higher rate of 16d. per ton per month, still paid to foreign 'bottoms', and in 1569 four English merchantmen were taken up for specific duties. The *Trinity Henry* and the *Grace of God*, both of London, were hired for two weeks' guard duty in the Thames estuary; the *Edmund* of London was sent as a victualler to La Rochelle, and the *Primrose* of Harwich served for three weeks in an unrecorded capacity.[3] An unknown number of transports and victuallers were used in connection with the Le Havre campaign, but in normal years of peace there was little need for such supplementation. When hiring did occur, it seems usually to have been a matter of short-term convenience, when a vessel was needed for a particular purpose and the royal ships available were deemed not to be suitable.

[1] PRO E/351/2204, Gonson's accounts from 1 January 1568 to 31 December 1568.
[2] PRO E351/2197.
[3] Pepys MS 1266, 176; a certificate of discharge dated 17 March 1563, E351/2199.

Although it was subjected to relatively few demands for royal service, the merchant marine of England was flourishing and expanding during these years. As we have seen, each census showed a significant increase; 51 ships of over 100 tons were built between 1571 and 1576, and in 1581 the Wardens of Trinity House reported an increase of 114 in the number of fishing boats operating on the East coast.[1] Some contemporaries believed that the Navigation Acts were responsible for this increase, others attributed it to the legislation enforcing fish days, but the basic cause seems to have been a steady and prolonged increase in trade, both local and long distance. The Muscovy company steadily expanded its business with Russia and central Asia, while the Eastland Company, formed in 1579 strove with some success to wrest the Baltic trade from the declining Hanse. The biggest impact on the demand for ships, however, was made by the new Levant Company, founded in 1581. In that year the Company owned no less than 14 ships of between 200 and 350 tons; and between 1583 and 1587 it sent out 27 voyages, using a total of 19 ships.[2] Both the Guinea trade and the new slave trade to the West Indies were illegal and risky, but for precisely that reason required large and well-armed ships, a circumstance which undoubtedly explains John Hawkins heavy investment. The records show about 380 ships receiving the tonnage bounty during the reign, but that may well be less than the true total, and certainly less than the number of eligible ships built.[3] Many owners did not claim the bounty, because it involved entering into a bond not to sell the ship outside the realm, and by 1580 English shipbuilding was well enough thought of to create a demand. The situation of Henry VII's reign was reversed, and Philip II was several times urged to buy English ships for their superior quality. The bounty was not usually paid in cash, but allowed against customs dues, and the same was true of hire tonnage. Whereas in the fifteenth century the demands of royal service pressed constantly upon merchants, and provoked frequent protest and complaint, by the reign of Elizabeth the navy was about 80 per cent self sufficient except in times of major national emergency, when a 'navy royal' in the old-fashioned sense might still be required.

Indeed it could be argued that by 1560 the 'private sector' had more need of the navy than the other way round. Fully-armed warships were not ideal cargo carriers, but if the nature of the cargo

[1] Oppenheim, *Administration*, 167, 172–3.
[2] PRO SP12/149/58; Oppenheim, 169.
[3] PRO SP12/262/126; Oppenheim, 168; Dietz, 'Royal bounty . . .', 14–20.

was low on bulk and high on value – such as spices, gold or slaves – then the degree of protection which they afforded was well worth the inconvenience. This led to one of Elizabeth's most significant innovations, loan investment. Up to the end of Mary's reign royal ships were simply hired out, for a stipulated rent and against a bond of indemnity in the event of loss or damage. However in 1561 the Queen loaned the *Minion*, the *Primrose*, the *Brigantine* and the *Fleur de Lys* to Sir William Chester for a voyage to Africa; the ships and £500 worth of provisions constituting an investment which entitled her to one third of the profit at the end of the trip.[1] Both Edward IV and Henry VII had traded in their own interest, but neither had attempted to use their ships for investment in this fashion. In 1562 Robert Dudley borrowed the *Jesus of Lubeck* upon what looks at first like an old-fashioned hire arrangement, but since he paid only £500 for a two year loan, the Queen probably expected something a little more substantial than gratitude by way of return. The *Jesus* also featured prominently in Elizabeth's next investment project, which was the second of John Hawkins' slaving voyages in 1564. Dudley, the Earl of Pembroke, Lord Admiral Clinton, Gonson, Winter and a syndicate of London merchants formed the rest of the *ad hoc* company backing this project, which had a distinctly naval flavour to it. The great warship turned out to be an invaluable asset because, arriving in Hispaniola with his cargo, Hawkins found the colonists too much in awe of their own government to be willing to trade. It required a demonstration of fire-power to correct the balance of fear, and persuade them to do business. The lesson of this experience, and the angry representations from the Spanish ambassador which followed, at first prompted the Queen to forbid Hawkins' next proposed trip. Captain John Lovell went in his place, and without the weight of a royal warship failed completely.[2] Successful trading in the Caribbean had to be a matter of high politics between England and Spain, and thus of naval strategy.

In spite of Elizabeth's denials, and occasional conciliatory gestures, she had allowed Anglo-Spanish relations to deteriorate steadily since her accession. In this process her seamen had played a prominent part, acting in the spirit of Robert Reneger, if not always with his degree of success. In spite of its total failure the one positive lesson that the Le Havre expedition had taught was that France no longer had a navy to be feared. Consequently England no longer

[1] PRO SP12/17/43 and 26/43.
[2] J. A. Williamson, *Hawkins of Plymouth*, 87–100.

needed the friendship of Spain to protect her interests at sea. Moreover the rising tide of discontent in the Netherlands, and Philip's reaction to it, had already deposited some 18 000 Flemish fugitives in southern England by 1563, a total which had risen to about 30 000 by 1566. Most of them were Protestants, and their stories of oppression and maltreatment met with a sympathetic response. There had been considerable anti-Spanish feeling in England during Mary's reign, which had helped to sour relations between the royal couple, and everything that had happened since 1558 had served to aggravate that hostility. Consequently when a squadron of Spanish warships arrived uninvited at Plymouth in August 1567, the reaction was predictable. Hawkins was already in the anchorage with several armed ships, and when the intruders refused to salute his flag, he opened fire and drove them out.[1] It seems unlikely that this encounter was a coincidence, because Hawkins had taken advantage of the deteriorating situation to persuade the Queen into another, and more elaborate collaboration. The objective was basically the same as in 1564; by using force and the threat of force to acquire slaves in West Africa, and to sell them at a large profit in the Spanish colonies. But there were some significant differences. On this occasion Hawkins had two royal ships, the *Jesus* and the *Minion*, and he also held the Queen's commission, in spite of the fact that it was theoretically a private trading voyage.[2] The Spaniards undoubtedly suspected his intentions, and possibly hoped to use a 'friendly' visit to gather further information. The response can have left them in no doubt about the expedition's hostile intentions.

The outcome is well known. In spite of the warnings which must have been sent, no attempt was made to intercept Hawkins, and only the usual displays of reluctance when he arrived in the Caribbean – reluctance which he overcame in the customary way. However, more by bad luck than by miscalculation, he encountered the *flota* under the personal command of the Viceroy, Don Martin Enriquez. Trapped in the harbour at San Juan d'Ulloa, he found the royal banner of England no defence against being regarded as a pirate. After a brisk and highly significant engagement he managed to extricate himself and three of his ships, but the *Jesus* and her armament had to be abandoned.[3] As a result the voyage was a financial disaster, but more important, Elizabeth had compromised herself up

[1] Williamson, 107. For a full list of the original accounts of the voyage, see ibid., 105.
[2] Williamson, 102, which fully explores the complicated arrangements surrounding the voyage.
[3] Ibid., 132–46; Michael Lewis, 'The guns of the Jesus of Lubeck', 324.

to the hilt. Illicit English voyages to the Caribbean continued – there were 13 between 1570 and 1577 – but they did not enjoy a high level of success and became increasingly piratical in their nature. The first two independent voyages of Francis Drake, in 1570 and 1571, were typical. Drake had been with Hawkins at San Juan d'Ulloa, and was motivated partly by a desire for revenge, partly by anti-Catholic zeal, and partly by a simple greed for plunder. Drake made no pretence of an intention to trade, and kept away from the main harbours, but by preying upon the virtually unarmed barks which plied along the coasts of Panama and Mexico, and among the islands, he collected booty to the value of over 40 000 ducats (about £13 000).[1] The Queen was not in any way involved in this venture, but she was kept informed because Drake had, through Hawkins, strong court connections. He was on a winning run, and his third voyage in 1572/3 was the best yet. Operating in loose collaboration with French Huguenot corsairs, who were thirsting for revenge after the destruction of their Florida colony by the Spaniards in 1562, and with bands of escaped slaves known as *cimarrones*, he ambushed a mule train near Nombre de Dios and returned with a small fortune in silver bullion. The Spaniards suspected that these raids also served a long-term political purpose, which explained the Queen's interest, namely the establishment of English colonies at suitably located spots to challenge the Spanish hegemony in the New World. Richard Grenville did indeed produce such a scheme in 1574, which the Queen refused to license, and the existence of that scheme became known when John Oxenham and two other Englishmen were captured in Panama in 1577.[2]

In a sense Grenville was unlucky, because he found Elizabeth in a cold mood, when her relations with Philip were fairly amicable and she was keenly aware of the risks. Such a mood was bound to pass, and when a further group of projectors approached her in 1577 with a plan to go through the strait of Magellan and explore the western seaboard of South America, they found her responsive, in spite of the implications. They asked for the *Swallow* as her investment and symbol of recognition, but that was refused, and Elizabeth confined herself to being a private shareholder. Nevertheless, with Francis Drake in command and strong court backing, the Spaniards had

[1] K. R. Andrews, *Trade, Plunder and Settlement*, 129–31; I. A. Wright, *Documents concerning English voyages to the Spanish Main*, 1569–80, xix.

[2] PRO SP12/95/63, Grenville's petition to the Queen; SP12/235/1, draft letters patent to Grenville and his associates; R. Pearce Chope, 'New light on Sir Richard Grenville', *Trans. Devonshire Assoc.*, 49, 1917, 210–282.

every reason to regard this as another undercover state operation.[1] For a variety of reasons, what had been intended as a voyage of exploration, with a little piracy on the side, turned into an heroic circumnavigation which lasted almost three years. Drake returned, having established direct connections with the spice islands and collected about £150 000 worth of loot, on 26 September 1580. He became a popular hero, and the Queen knighted him on the deck of his own ship,[2] thereby confirming the worst Spanish suspicions. Elizabeth's relations with Drake, Hawkins, and the numerous other captains who traded, fought and robbed in Spanish waters, are very hard to interpret logically. She was certainly not consistent, and her reaction to individual proposals varied greatly with the immediate circumstances and the identity of the promoters. The level of recognition accorded to Hawkins in 1567/8 was unusual but not unique, and even when the Queen had no active involvement at all she still had to license the voyage, and vetoed a fair number of proposals as she did Grenville's. What is clear is the very strong connection which existed between this kind of enterprise and the royal navy. The men, the guns, the equipment, and sometimes the ships, were interchangeable; so it is quite legitimate to regard the development of these voyages, and the form which they took, as an aspect of public policy. Unfortunately for Elizabeth it was a policy which she could not entirely control, but it dramatically affected both strategy and tactics at sea. The navy could now reach any part of the world that English ships could reach, and would soon have the need to do so; at the same time the qualities of gunnery and seamanship necessary for survival in perilous and hostile waters were equally at the disposal of Her Majesty's ships for the waging of more formal war.

The ambiguous adventures of Hawkins and Drake, and the countenance given to them, created an acceptable face for piracy in the Caribbean. Eventually the onset of war would turn pirates into privateers, and ruthless adventurers into heroes of the Reformation. But in European waters the unpalatable truth of constant robbery and occasional murder on the high seas was harder to evade or disguise. There was nothing new in that situation, but the noticeable growth of commerce after 1560 aggravated the problem by making the rewards greater and somewhat easier to come by. Piracy had not traditionally been an offence in common law, and until 1536 it had

[1] BL Cotton MS Otho E VIII, f. 9, is the original plan. For a full discussion see K. R. Andrews, 'The aims of Drake's expedition of 1577–80', *AHR*, 73, 1968, 724–41.

[2] Z. Nutall, ed., *New Light on Drake*, passim; Andrews, *Trade, Plunder and Settlement*, 141–58.

been tried under maritime law in the Lord Admiral's court. In that year it was removed from the Admiralty jurisdiction by statute, on the grounds that the procedures of civil law, which the maritime law followed, required either a free confession or the testimony of two witnesses to secure a conviction.[1] The difficulty of producing such witnesses in court, even if they had survived to tell their tale, was so great that convictions were hardly ever secured. So piracy was made triable by commission of Oyer and Terminer under the common law, where the only rule of evidence was that it had to convince the jury. Executions under this procedure commenced almost at once and continued sporadically thereafter. However, it was one thing to have a law and another to enforce it effectively. Some known pirates evaded capture for years on end, often through the collusion of the magistrates and Vice-Admirals of the regions in which they operated. Substantial gentry families, such as the Bulkelys, the Killigrews and the Perrotts had one foot on the pirates deck and the other in the service of the Crown. Moreover the great majority of victims were more concerned to secure redress than they were to see the guilty parties punished, and for that they still had to resort to the High Court of Admiralty. If the pirate and his victim were both English, and the identity of both parties was known this court, although slow, could be reasonably effective; but if the victim was English and the pirate French, or vice versa, then the chances of success were small. For example, in 1576 two notorious English pirates named Callis and Court plundered five ships out of Rouen, and sold their cargoes in Cardiff. The aggrieved merchants swore before their own Admiralty court that their losses amounted to 20 000 livres Tournois (about £2 000). One of their number, Pierre Chambellan, then came to London and petitioned the French ambassador to help them secure justice.[2] Partly because this was the culmination of a long series of complaints, and partly because the Rouen merchants had a privileged status, the English Council acted. One of Chambellan's ships was found at Bristol, and although the citizens were at first completely uncooperative, a peremptory letter from the Council restored the vessel to its owner. Meanwhile Chambellan had taken his case to the English Admiralty court, and the Government was sufficiently aroused to send a special commission into the West Country which resulted in the arrest of the two pirates, who appeared before the court in November 1577. In May

[1] 'An Acte for the punyshment of Pyrotes and Robbers of the See', 28 Henry VIII, cap. 15.
[2] F. E. Dyer, 'Reprisals in the Sixteenth Century', *MM*, 21, 1935, 187–97.

1578 they were released on bonds of £4 000 each, Court on the grounds that he was needed for the Queen's service at sea. Chambellan protested vigorously, but gained no further satisfaction before he had to return to France. The two men bonds were eventually declared forfeit in December 1580, but the sureties defaulted and the pirates were not re-arrested. Numerous petitions were addressed to Lord Admiral Lincoln without result over the next two years, and in 1582 the French appealed to their own Admiral. At length in 1585, all else having failed, the surviving Rouen merchants were granted letters of reprisal in 40 000 francs by their own Admiralty court.[1]

Letters of reprisal were simply a recognized method whereby the victim took the law into his own hands, and nearly always resulted in an escalation of the original dispute. They did, however, have the great advantage of not involving the government concerned in any effort or expense. A case like that of Callis and Court raises the whole question of how serious Elizabeth's Council was in tackling the issue of piracy. Having taken what at first appeared to be prompt and effective action, the Council simply failed to follow up its own initiative; the culprits escaped with a few weeks of imprisonment, and innocent English merchants were belatedly and quite unnecessarily exposed to reprisals. These in turn caused a fresh round of protest and complaint. The English were not always the original offenders. In 1574 the merchants of Bristol complained that the town of St Malo had sent out a semi-official fleet of seven vessels to prey on their commerce. By 1586 the dispute had escalated, and a correspondent wrote to Lord Burghley,

> being at St Malo last month (I) heard that sixteen of their ships had been rifled or taken by Englishmen . . . and that their hatred of the English was such that our merchants dared not walk about in public . . .[2]

The French did at least have the excuse that the authority of the Crown was virtually in abeyance during these years, and no effective action could be expected from central government. The English Council was effective enough in other ways, and it is therefore the will which is in question. Between December 1558 and November 1580, no fewer than 16 proclamations were issued relating to piracy.

[1] F. E. Dyer, 'Reprisals in the Sixteenth Century', 193. The franc was money of account, approximately the same value as the livre Tournois, so presumably their legal costs, and the delay, were also taken into account.

[2] PRO SP15/29/126. The state papers are full of claims for compensation.

Of these five, all dated between 1561 and 1564 were aimed at preventing attacks on Spanish and Flemish ships.[1] Their repetition, and the steady crescendo of complaint from the Spanish ambassador suggests that they were totally ineffective, and the fact that the Queen and her leading courtiers were already investing in what were virtually piratical attacks against Spain's colonial empire, points to the reason why. The Court was sending out contradictory messages, and the seamen rightly believed that although the Queen might be angry today, and vow the punishment of those who embarrassed her in public, by next week she would be privately rejoicing over their exploits. Corrupt officials who turned a blind eye when Spanish cargoes were brought ashore had found a means of making their offices profitable, and were undemanding servants when it came to seeking rewards of a legitimate nature. Moreover, as Anglo-Spanish relations became more strained, Elizabeth progressively gave up the pretence of friendliness. After Cecil's *coup* in seizing Genoese bullion bound for the Duke of Alva's armies, Alva had retaliated at the beginning of January 1569 by arresting all English ships and merchants in Low Countries ports.[2] On 6 January Elizabeth reciprocated by ordering the detention of all Spanish ships in English ports, and within a few days 43 had been secured. The dispute continued until 1573, and during that period, although no letters of Marque or reprisal were issued, English seamen had every reason to suppose that attacks on Spanish shipping would be even less risky than usual.

However, although the Queen might have political reasons for allowing her seamen to harrass the Spaniards, such attacks were only one aspect of their activities. Between 1564 and 1586 Englishmen were alleged to have spoiled the Scots of goods to the value of £20 717 – a healthy 'balance of trade' since the Scots had only managed to steal £9 268.[3] Scotland was not even potentially hostile during these years, and there was not a shadow of a justification for such aggression. The great majority of victims were probably other Englishmen from neighbouring or rival towns, and one of the great problems about this kind of piracy was its casual nature. For every pinnace or bark which set out with nefarious intent, there must have been a dozen legitimate traders who could not resist the temptation to pick up an easy prize on the way. Merchant ships were supposed to be licensed to carry arms, but guns were increasingly available, and self-defence provided a constant and reasonable pretext.

[1] Hughes and Larkin, *Tudor Royal Proclamations*, 2, nos. 482, 499, 513, 519, 523.
[2] *Cal. Span., Elizabeth*, 2, 91–3; R. B. Wernham, *Before the Armada*, 296–7.
[3] BL Additional MS 11405, ff. 91, 103. Oppenheim, *Administration*, 179.

Moreover it seems that letters of reprisal were issued somewhat casually. In June 1563 William Strachey was licensed by the Lord Admiral to 'go upon' the French with 'one, two or three shippes to be well furnyshed for their defence', 'beinge lately spoyled of his shypes and goodes at the seas by the Frenche as he alleageth . . .'[1] The only control was the depositing of bonds. Strachey was required to enter into a recognizance not to harm any of the Queen's subjects, or those of the King of Spain. Similarly when Martin Frobisher set forth his ship *John Appleyard* towards Le Havre in March 1562, he was required to enter a bond for £50 not to harm English, Spaniards or 'Portingals'.[2] However, as we have seen, it was one thing to forfeit such a bond in theory, and quite another to be required actually to pay. But it would not do to conclude from all this that the Admiralty court or the Council were simply supine in their attitude to piracy. It was much more complicated than that, and often depended upon the priorities of the moment. In almost every year for which there are records royal ships were sent out 'to apprehend divers pirates and rovers': the *Mary Willoughby* for 73 days in 1562; the *Aid* for 90 days in 1563; the *Aid,* the *Bull* and the *Tiger* for 43 days in 1570; the *Achates* for four months in 1574. These patrols were specific, and were distinguished from other routine duties such as escorting the Merchant Adventurers, or transporting ambassadors. They were, however, only the sharp end of an operation which was pursued in several other ways.

In November 1564 the Mayor and Aldermen of Bristol were granted a commission out of the Admiralty 'to furnishe and set to the seas certaine Shippes for the repressing and aprehending of pirattes haunting the Seas betwene Silley and the porte of Bristowe'. This they were to do at their own expense, and all other magistrates in the area were called upon to help them.[3] Shortly afterwards, on 24 December, the Council sent a series of letters to the Vice-Admirals of the coasts and the mayors of the port towns, ordering them to arrest certain named pirates, and to proceed by law against those already captured.

> . . . sundry and divers piracies and spoils have been committed upon the seas by the Quenes Maiesties subjectes of the West Parts since the conclusion of the last peace with the French, and divers

[1] PRO HCA/25/1, bond dated 13 June 1563.
[2] Ibid., dated 6 March 1562.
[3] *APC*, 7, 164; 14 November 1564.

> of them apprehended and not one executed or punished according to their deserts . . .[1]

Sessions of Oyer and Terminer, by virtue of the commissions already issued, were to be convened at once. However, one of the problems with common law procedure was that it could be obstructed by an uncooperative jury, and on 16 March the commissioners in Cornwall were instructed to send up to Star Chamber the jury which had acquitted a pirate called Abers, together with the relevant evidence.[2] Clearly in 1565 circumstances were propitious for a drive against piracy, and the Council spared no effort. On 1 March Sir John Chichester and Sir Peter Carew were paid £40 to conduct a survey of likely haunts and landing places along the coasts of Devon and Cornwall – information which they could probably have supplied from personal experience.[3] On 16 August the Vice-Admirals of Norfolk, Suffolk and Essex were instructed to search all the coastal villages for stolen goods, and the Vice-Admiral of Essex was ordered to send out two barks to apprehend offenders 'without burdening the Queenes Maiestie with extraordinary charges'.[4] Finally, on 8 November, commissions were issued in every coastal county 'for the repressing of pirates and other disorders executed upon the sea coasts . . .', with a rigorous schedule of instructions, including a census of all ships and barks, a ban on all unlicensed sailings, and strict supervision of all cargoes landed.[5] These instructions were clearly intended to stifle robbery at sea by making it impossible to get ships or victuals out, or plunder in. They probably went as far as administrative action could, but the incident of the Cornish jury, and the Queen's notorious reluctance to accept 'extraordinary charges' indicate a large gap between intention and achievement.

There were similar bursts of activity in later years. In May 1577 some of the poachers of the Cinq Ports decided to turn gamekeeper, and offered to send out ships at their own expense 'so as they might have reasonable recompense of such pirattes goodes as shold be taken . . .', and Lord Cobham was asked to assess the volunteers. In

1 *APC*, 7, 180–82.
2 Ibid., 206–7.
3 Ibid., 202.
4 Ibid., 244, and 253–5, 29 August 1565.
5 Ibid., 278–9, 'Form of commission for the suppressing and apprehending of pirates'; 280–90, 'Articles for the repressing of pirates and other disorders executed upon the sea coastes'. The model is for Norfolk, but commissioners are listed for all maritime counties and for 189 port towns. The normal number of commissioners per county is four, but Sussex has four for each rape (12).

July 1578 another general commission was sent down to the counties 'for the arming forthe of Shippes' against pirates and other criminals.[1] Such efforts were not always futile. In 1580 two marauders called Bayte and Atkinson who had taken an Italian ship, were caught and hanged. The same fate befell the notorious John Peers after a long life of crime, and in the same year the navy staged a successful ambush along the lines of the one which had caught Peter Killigrew in 1556. When a situation became particularly bad, effective action was possible. Between 1581 and 1583 Studland Bay in Dorset became infamous as a pirate refuge; it was reported that over 40 stolen vessels had been unloaded and stripped there. Finally, in the summer of 1583 William Aldburgh and Benjamin Gonson junior were commissioned as pirate hunters, and as a result of their efforts some three dozen prisoners were interrogated between 6 and 8 August. Several were sent to the Tower, and on 20 August, 9 were hanged at Wapping.[2] After 1585 the onset of open war with Spain changed the situation considerably. Many pirates became privateers, and gained in both respectability and freedom of action; others were pressed into service in a navy whose level of formal activity naturally increased. Piracy was not so much defeated as sublimated, and before peace returned in 1604 the Admiralty court itself had begun to find a more effective strategy. The years between 1560 and 1585 probably saw the climax of piracy, both in scale and profitability. Every maritime country participated in the vicious circle, but it was a matter of somewhat equivocal pride to the Elizabethans that they outdid even the French in barefaced robbery, and the Queen's own attitude reflected the popular mood in this, as in so many other things. No wonder her diligent ministers and councillors sometimes wondered whose side she was on.

The relationship between piracy and international politics was close, but not consistent. It was not always the Spaniards who were offended. In spite of the improvement in Anglo-French relations signalled by the Treaty of Blois in 1572, English seamen showed an inveterate tendency to collaborate with the Huguenots, particularly the Rochellais, and in 1569, for example, Charles IX ordered the arrest of English goods at Rouen.[3] It was, however, Elizabeth's relationship with the rebellious Netherlanders which caused the main problems. Her willingness to receive Protestant refugees, and

[1] *APC*, 9, 348, 14 May 1577; ibid., 10, 279, 7 July 1578.
[2] PRO SP12/161/20; C. L'Estrange Ewen, 'Organised piracy around England in the sixteenth century', *MM*, 25, 1949, 29–42.
[3] Black, *Reign of Elizabeth*, 131.

to allow the Dutch privateers known as 'Sea Beggars' to operate out of English ports provoked Philip's ambassador Guerau de Spes to conspire her overthrow, and to urge the Duke of Alva to come to the assistance of the northern rebels in 1569. After the failure of the Ridolfi plot in 1571, the Queen was anxious to reduce international tension, and the Sea Beggars were expelled from England on 1 March 1572. La Marck, the Dutch captain, held letters of marque from the Prince of Orange which Elizabeth recognized, but neither he nor his followers had conducted themselves discreetly, and had even indulged in attacks on English shipping.[1] Elizabeth's move was therefore both justified in her own interests and intended as a conciliatory gesture towards Philip. At first it was accepted in that sense, and the commercial dispute with Spain which had run since 1568 was brought to an end, but in the long run the situation was greatly aggravated. Not only did the resumption of direct trade with Spain once again bring English merchants and seamen within reach of the Inquisition, but within a month of their expulsion from England, La Marck and his men had seized the port of Brill on the coast of Holland. There is no reason to suppose that Elizabeth either wanted or expected such a development, but it marked a crucial turning point in the revolt of the Netherlands. Partly because of the terrain, and partly because of his distractions in the south, Alva was unable to retake Brill, and within a few months several other towns had fallen to the insurgents, giving them a territorial base from which they continued to operate for the remainder of the war. The Queen had no desire to become involved, and no great sympathy with rebels, but it was not in her interests for the revolt to be completely suppressed. Moreover many of her subjects strongly sympathized with their co-religionists, and in spite of her prohibition English volunteers began to appear, fighting alongside the Dutch. By 1575 William of Orange, the rebel leader, had a small but effective navy, and wished to cut off the trade of Antwerp by blockading the Scheldt. Elizabeth would not hear of any such strategy, having made a major effort to reopen the trade, and threatened to use her own navy to keep the port open. William was understandably angry, and even more so when she threatened hostilities if he should call upon French support. However, at the same time the Queen was threatening war against Philip if he would not make concessions to the just grievances of his Netherlandish subjects.

[1] Hughes and Larkin, 2, 585 and notes. The Queen had written to the Lieutenant of Dover castle on 21 February, instructing him to tell La Marck to remove himself.

Elizabeth was wholly bent on ending the war by a negotiated settlement, but neither of the protagonists was willing to compromise, or make any kind of concession. All that happened was that both sides became convinced of her duplicity and bad faith, a conviction which was greatly strengthened in the case of the Spaniards by the maritime activities which we have already examined. Briefly it seemed that she might be let off the hook by the *Paix des Prêtres* of 1577,[1] but William was soon angling for an English alliance, pointing out the advantages which would accrue to England if their two navies joined forces, and Elizabeth was toying with the idea of marrying the Duke of Anjou as a means of injecting a controlled French presence into the Netherlands. The Anjou marriage failed to materialize, and French intervention was a disaster, so by 1583 the Queen was back with the same dilemma, now made more acute by Spanish successes. Philip's acquisition of the Crown of Portugal by lawful inheritance in 1580 was a major blow both to England and to the Dutch rebels. Not only did it give him a second colonial Empire, it also gave him an oceanic war fleet of a kind which Spain had never hitherto possessed. The effectiveness of that fleet was demonstrated in July 1583 when, under the command of the Marquis of Santa Cruz, it destroyed a Franco–Portuguese fleet operating in support of the Portuguese pretender Dom Antonio. This victory at Terciera, in which the experienced French commander Philip Strozzi was killed, was an unmistakable warning to both England and Holland, and encouraged Philip to think in terms of settling with the northern heretics once and for all. After his victory Santa Cruz hanged his surviving opponents out of hand as pirates, on the grounds that they were not fighting under any recognized flag. Two years earlier Lord Grey had done the same thing to a small Spanish force which had landed at Smerwick in support of an Irish insurrection, and had displayed a papal banner. Both sides were becoming increasingly ruthless, and as the Spanish armies began to advance in the Netherlands in 1582 and 1583, Elizabeth's diplomatic wrigglings began to look increasingly desperate. The crisis came in June 1584 with the assassination of William of Orange, and a real possibility that the revolt would collapse. In November 1584 she commenced serious negotiations, and as the situation continued to deteriorate, on 10 August 1585 was driven to make a general undertaking for the defence of the United Provinces by the

[1] So called because it was organized by the Catholic party. Otherwise known as the 'Perpetual Edict'.

treaty of Nonsuch. In September the Earl of Leicester received a commission as Lieutenant General, and by December was in the Low Countries with 7 000 men.[1]

Although this move was not accompanied by any formal declaration of war, both England and Spain accepted that such a state existed by the end of 1585. Without the treaty of Nonsuch war might have been avoided, but that is by no means certain, given the commitment to hostile preparations on both sides. On 23 December 1584 the English Council had authorized the fitting out of a fleet of 35 sail, including 11 warships, in expectation of an attack by the forces of the French Catholic league.[2] Civil war had recommenced there when the death of the Duke of Anjou left the Huguenot leader Henry of Navarre next in line to the throne, and Elizabeth's subjects, as usual, had made no secret of where their sympathies lay. The attack did not materialize and the Council order was countermanded, but not before a lot of work had been done, leaving more ships ready for the sea than would have been normal at that time of the year. In the spring, Spain was afflicted by a shortage of wheat, and Philip authorized large-scale importations, guaranteeing the safety of all ships engaged in the trade, most of which came from England and the Baltic. On 29 May he then changed his mind, and ordered all such ships to be seized, their guns confiscated and their crews imprisoned. Some provocation may have been given, or he may have responded to pressure from his own council, but in England the reaction was one of self-righteous outrage. The Admiralty court was besieged with claims for heavy losses; £39 100 from London, £29 000 from Ipswich, £29 300 from Bristol, and £22 300 from other ports.[3] Such claims cannot have arisen from a short-term trade in grain; they may have been accumulated over many years, or they may have been deliberately inflated, but there was no way in which they would be recovered by judicial process. Inevitably, on 9 July the issue of letters of reprisal was authorized. Letters were only to be issued to those who could produce proof of loss, and the recipients were to give bond not to injure other than Spanish shipping. But against Spain they were authorized to act 'as if it were in the time of open war', and reprisals upon such a huge scale would have been difficult to distinguish from hostilities. At the same time, on 1 July Sir Francis Drake was commissioned to undertake a specific campaign of retaliation.

[1] Wernham, *Before the Armada*, 377–8.
[2] *Sir William Monson's Naval Tracts*, ed. M. Oppenheim, I, 125 and n.
[3] Ibid., 125–6.

This expedition was set up in the same manner as that of John Hawkins in 1567. It was a joint stock venture with a capital of £60 400 and a fleet of 22 sail, towards which the Queen contributed £10 000 cash, and the ships *Bonaventure* (600 tons) and *Aid* (250 tons). Six of the private ships were over 200 tons, including the *Primrose* and the *Galleon Leicester* (each 400 tons), but the majority were small. The full complement of soldiers and seamen was 2 300.[1] Drake himself bore the Queen's commission as Admiral, and Martin Frobisher of Vice-Admiral, so there was no doubt as to their official status, although there may well have been a discrepancy between official and unofficial instructions. Publicly, Drake was to demand the lifting of the embargo, and the release of all ships, goods and men. Privately he seems to have been authorized to take whatever he could lay his hands on by way of recompense, and probably had his eyes on one of the fleets due to arrive from the New World in the autumn. He sailed from Plymouth on 14 September, and arrived off Vigo on the 27th. There he followed his public instructions, and was informed that the embargo was already lifted. Philip seems to have known every detail of the composition of Drake's fleet, but nothing of his real intentions, perhaps because he had been given very wide discretion. Getting no satisfaction and very little plunder either at Vigo or at the next place he tried, Palma, he learned while still off the Spanish coast that both the incoming fleets had eluded him and were safe in harbour. Faced with the prospect of a fruitless trip, and running low on victuals, Drake headed for Santiago in the Cape Verde Islands, where he arrived on 16 November. Landing in force, he found both Santiago and San Domingo deserted. Much needed victuals were obtained, but no plunder, and after firing the towns, Drake pressed on in search of a dividend for his shareholders.[2] During the crossing of the Atlantic his forces were seriously depleted by disease, but when he reached San Domingo in Hispaniola on 1 January 1586, he had his first stroke of good fortune. Warning had been sent of his coming, but it had not arrived in time, and he was able to take the City almost totally by surprise. After destroying part of it he accepted a ransom of 25 000 ducats (*c.* £8 000), and left after a month.

By February the threat of Drake's presence in New Spain was widely known. Individual pirates, mostly French, had appeared in

[1] BL Harleian MS 366, f. 146; Monson's *Tracts*, I, 124.

[2] Ibid., 127–8. It is necessary to remember that as a result of the adoption of the Gregorian calendar, Spanish dates in this period are ten days ahead of English. I am following the English chronology.

the area before, and the towns were by no means undefended, but a hostile warfleet (which this was in substance if not in form) was something altogether new. The Spanish officials panicked, obstructing each other, and in spite of the warning no effective defensive preparations were made. On 11 February Drake appeared before Cartagena, one of the wealthiest cities in the colonies, and ostensibly well fortified. The fortifications, however, were improvised and the defence less than resolute. God, as one English participant significantly commented, put it into their heads to attack before dawn, and Christopher Carleill, commanding the soldiers, found a weak spot in the breastwork, where it did not quite reach to the water's edge.[1] In spite of being supported by 500 local tribesmen armed with poisoned arrows, the 400 or so Spanish defenders broke and fled under a fierce attack. Once in possession of the town, Drake demanded a ransom of £100 000, and began to destroy the buildings to enforce his demand. The governor offered 100 000 ducats (*c.* £32 000), and time was on his side. Not only could he expect support from the neighbouring colonies, but the English were seriously weakened by disease. After prolonged bargaining, and a consultation with his own officers, Drake decided to accept the governor's offer and set out for home before the Viceroy's fleet could be mobilized against him. He eventually left on 18 April, his force now reduced to about 700 fit men.[2] In spite of this, he seems to have been in no hurry, and stayed off Cape Antonio at the westward end of Cuba for about three weeks, from 26 April to 19 May. His objective may have been to intercept passing ships, but if so knowledge of his presence seems to have frustrated the enterprise, for little or nothing was taken. On 27 May he reached the small settlement of St Augustine on the Florida mainland, and took it without difficulty, coming away with some £2 000 in cash. Finally, Drake sailed north to the newly established English settlement at Roanoake, where the discouraged colonists begged for a return passage in his ships. He was already carrying some 300 galley slaves liberated at Cartagena, but the depletion of his own crews was so great that the extra numbers were welcome rather than the reverse. Leaving Roanoake on 18 June, he made a smooth passage, and arrived back at Plymouth on 28 July.[3]

The impression created by this voyage was far greater than its actual achievement. On 19 February 1586, before any knowledge of

[1] Monson's *Tracts*, I, 131. J. S. Corbett, *Papers relating to . . . the Spanish War, 1585–7*, 18–20.

[2] J. S. Corbett, ed., *Papers relating to . . . the Spanish War, 1585–7*, 69–70.

[3] Monson's *Tracts*, I, 132.

the fall of Cartagena could have reached Europe, the Venetian ambassador to Spain wrote that 'Lisbon is in an uproar on account of the mischief he (Drake) has done, so too Castile, yet there are no signs of preparations'.[1] When the truth became known the King was mortified and enraged as he had not been by two decades of ordinary piracy. Spanish prestige was damaged far more severely than the colonial economy, and both the Dutch and the dissident Portuguese were encouraged. Elizabeth was pleased, and Drake's fellow countrymen welcomed him again as a hero, more impressed by the audacity of his exploit than by its military significance, which in fact was slight. Nor did he make a vast profit. The declared plunder amounted to £67 000, which once the Queen's share had been deducted, paid only about 15s. in the £ to the ordinary investors.[2] There may well have been more which passed without record into the pockets of the surviving officers and men, but it seems safe to assume that no one made a fortune out of the seizure of Cartagena and St Augustine. A few years later with the benefit of hindsight Sir William Monson declared that the whole voyage had been a wasted opportunity. Had Drake held Cartagena and garrisoned it, he argued, the whole focus of the war would have been shifted from Europe to the New World, because the Spanish silver supplies would have been strangled at source.[3] In the event all that had happened was that the Spaniards had learned their lesson from a mild setback. Within a few years the Indies were adequately fortified and properly patrolled, so that later English attacks could be successfully beaten off. On the second point Monson was undoubtedly right, although it is difficult to see how such an outcome could have been avoided; but on the first he was writing without knowledge of the actual circumstances. It seems clear that Drake's Council did debate the feasibility of holding Cartagena, and decided against because of the ravages of disease among their men and the length of time which it would have taken for any reinforcements to have reached them. As an act of war, the expedition was not a heavy blow, but it was a telling one in a period when honour was so highly prized, and when

[1] Ibid., 133. It was not only rumours of Drake's depredations that were causing alarm. It was known in Lisbon that Elizabeth was in communication with the Sharif of Fez-Morocco to formulate a common strategy against Spain, reawakening ancient Spanish fears of attack from the south. These negotiations had been fronted by the formation of the Barbary Company in 1584. The development of these various threats had placed Philip's financial credit under severe strain. M. Rodriguez Salgado, *Armada; an international exhibition to commemorate the Spanish Armada*, 16–17.

[2] Monson's *Tracts*, I, 133.

[3] Ibid.,123.

messages of Divine favour were so quickly distilled from the fragmentary results of military action. The English undoubtedly felt their sense of special providence enhanced by this foray, and the story lost nothing in the telling.

Drake was not, of course, the only English captain at sea in 1586. The naval charges for the year amounted to £29 391, of which £8 905 was classed as 'sea charges'.[1] This was very light for wartime – less than half of what had been spent in 1563 – but it did not include the £10 000 invested in Drake's voyage, or any other similar investment.[2] Normal patrols were maintained. Henry Palmer, on board the *Foresight*, is described as Admiral of the Narrow Seas in that year. Also, on 6 August, instructions were issued to John Hawkins as Admiral of what can only be described as an Atlantic patrol. His exact orders do not survive, but he led a fleet of 18–20 sail of which five were the Queen's ships.[3] Four of these, the *Nonpareil*, the *Lion*, the *Hope* and the *Revenge*, were of 500 tons or more, so he had greater fire-power than Drake. The private ships do not appear to have been on a joint stock basis, but rather to have been taken up and paid for in the traditional manner. According to the Venetian ambassador in France, the original purpose of this patrol was to shadow suspect French shipping movements and to protect English commerce, and it was only when the alarm turned out to be a false one that Hawkins was given leave to go 'buccaneering' against Spain. He was at sea for about two and a half months, and caused considerable disruption to Spanish commerce, although the value of his prizes appears to have been small. He is known to have taken at least three ships between 27 August and 20 September, one of them a medium-sized trader from the Indies, but the whole operation was low key, and may well have had more to do with supporting the Huguenots of La Rochelle than disrupting Spanish commerce.[4] Meanwhile, Philip had taken the momentous decision to launch his full power against England, not with the object of conquest but for the purpose of knocking her out of the war, and hopefully replacing Elizabeth with some amenable Catholic, such as Mary Stuart. He had toyed with such a project as early as 1574, but it was the treaty

[1] Oppenheim, *Administration*, 161. There was also an unheralded but destructive raid on Spanish fishing interests on the Iceland banks; Rodriguez-Salgado, 16.

[2] These investments, and the equipping and provisioning of ships which were used as investments, were paid direct out of the Exchequer by occasional warrant, and no trace of them can be found in the accounts of the Treasurer of the Navy.

[3] Bodleian Library MS Rawlinson 192, f. 210; Drake, Hawkins and Palmer were all commissioned as Admirals in that year; *APC*, 14, 206; Monson's *Tracts*, I, 134.

[4] *Cal. Ven.*, 8, 214, 24 October 1586.

of Nonsuch which made up his mind, as he had become convinced that England was the key to victory in the Low Countries. In January 1586 he turned back to a plan originally proposed by the Marquis of Santa Cruz in August 1583, when he was fresh from his victory at Terciera. This had envisaged an enormous fleet of over 500 sail bearing an invading army of 55 000 men direct from Spain. Philip had ignored the proposal at the time for the perfectly good reason that it was beyond his resources.[1] However, with the additional incentives which he had acquired by 1586, some of its features began to have a renewed appeal, and the successful experience of Santa Cruz in mounting a similar operation on a smaller scale in the Azores encouraged him to decide upon the attempt. The Admiral had meticulously costed his original plan at 4 million ducats (about £1 300 000), but in April 1586 another very experienced commander came up with a much cheaper alternative which looked more practicable. On the 20th of the month, when he had already decided in principle to launch an attack, Philip received a long letter from the Duke of Parma, commanding the army in the Netherlands. Parma suggested that he should himself invade England with 30 000 men, thus saving the enormous cost of transporting an army from Spain. Secrecy would be essential, he argued; the situation in the Netherlands would have to be sufficiently under control, and the French neutralized; above all, the papacy must not be made privy to the attempt until everything was prepared.[2] Despite all these problems, and conflicting advice from his council, the King at length decided to accept Parma's plan. A large warfleet would still be needed to wrest control of the channel from the formidable English navy for a few crucial days, but 150 ships was a very different proposition from 500. Philip was under no illusions; even this scaled-down enterprise would be a severe strain upon his resources, not so much of money as of ships, guns and organization. But it was feasible, and both his strategic sense and his religious duty urged him to strike a crippling blow with the least possible delay.

No sooner was the decision taken, however, than it began to be

[1] In November 1583 Philip informed the Pope that the operation would be too difficult. National Maritime Museum MS PHB 1A, f. 435. Santa Cruz's original proposal had been contained in a series of position papers, and was not worked out in detail. C. Martin and G. Parker, *The Spanish Armada*, 109.

[2] Parma had commented favourably upon Santa Cruz's original plan in January 1584, but Santa Cruz had upped the stakes in a revised version of March 1586, which required 800 ships and 94 000 men. Parma was not, however, commenting directly on the revised plan. He seems to have changed his mind about the original strategy. Archivo General de Simancas, E. 590, f. 125. Martin and Parker, 115.

modified. This was partly because the obvious man to lead the navy was the Marquis of Santa Cruz, and he remained wedded to some features of his original proposal. Moreover, one of Philip's most senior and respected advisers, Don Juan de Zuñiga, although enthusiastically endorsing Parma's scheme, continued to believe that there was a case for sending a force direct from Spain. The combined influence of these two elder statesmen therefore re-introduced the idea of a long distance seaborne invasion, and the King was persuaded that some 16 000 soldiers should be sent with the armada, thus bringing the total invasion force much closer to Santa Cruz's original 55 000.[1] August 1587 was fixed as the target date for the armada to depart. By the autumn of 1586 Elizabeth knew perfectly well that a formidable navy was being prepared against her, although she did not know exactly how it was to be used. Her first reaction was to make repeated attempts to keep peace negotiations alive, and the Duke of Parma humoured her, believing that if she could be deceived into thinking that a settlement was imminent, her defensive preparations would be less resolute. If Elizabeth had been entirely responsible for policy he would probably have been correct, but neither Cecil nor the sea-captains were so unreasonably optimistic. Naval preparations were stepped up; 11 new ships were completed in 1586 and two more in 1587, including the *Vanguard*, the *Rainbow* and the *Ark Royal*, each over 400 tons. Expenditure went up to £44 000, most of it in the dockyards and warehouses rather than at sea.[2] Drake's return in the summer had also alerted others to the possibilities of private warfare, in which patriotism and profit could be most satisfactorily combined. In December 1586 Robert Flicke of London petitioned for, and was granted, licence to equip ten ships at his own expense to intercept the inward bound East India fleet off Lisbon.[3] By the time Flicke's preparations were well in hand, however, the Queen had been persuaded that she must do something about the preparations being made against her. Characteristically she decided to combine public and private enterprise, and instructed Drake to mount an operation along the same lines as his voyage to Cartagena. His orders were to intercept supplies arriving at Lisbon, and to prevent the fleet from assembling, if necessary 'by

[1] Philip in fact changed his mind several times during 1586. At one point he was proposing to abandon the large-scale attack on England and launch a smaller Armada against Ireland. It was not until after Zuñiga's death in November that he finally decided upon the plan eventually carried out. Martin and Parker, 117–18.

[2] Oppenheim, *Administration*, 161; Monson's *Tracts*, I, 138–9.

[3] Ibid., 141.

distressing the ships within the havens themselves'. Robert Flicke was persuaded to combine his enterprise with that of Drake, and a fleet of 23 ships was assembled. Of these six, including the *Bonaventure* (600 tons), the *Golden Lion* (500), the *Rainbow* (500) and the *Dreadnought* (400) were contributed by the Queen; eleven by the city of London (Flicke's squadron); four by Drake himself; and two by the Lord Admiral Charles Howard, who had taken over from the Earl of Lincoln after the latter's death in 1585.[1]

Drake knew his mistress, and no sooner had he received his commission at the end of March than he hastened to set sail, leading his own ships out of Plymouth on 2 April and rendezvousing with the remainder of the fleet at sea.

> The wind commands me away . . . our ship is under sail. God grant we may so live in His fear as the enemy may have cause to say that God doth fight for her Majesty as well abroad as at home.[2]

God was keener on Elizabeth's cause than she was herself. On 12 April she revoked Drake's commission, but it was already too late. According to Monson's later account he did not decide to make for Cadiz rather than Lisbon until he was informed at sea by two ships out of Middleburg that the real focus of operations was in the south. However, it seems clear that Drake knew perfectly well where his target was to be, but had refrained from advertising the fact for obvious reasons. By using his own fast pinnaces to intercept any possible advance warning, he achieved total surprise, sailing into Cadiz harbour on 19 April bearing no insignia and quite unrecognized. Within 24 hours he had destroyed or captured 24 Spanish ships lying in the haven, some of them large and powerful, together with large quantities of stores and equipment.[3] At first the only resistance was offered by fourteen royal galleys, which were quickly repulsed and severely damaged by the weight of the English broadsides. Even in the confined waters of the harbour, which should have favoured them, they were no match for warships. No assault was made upon the town, partly because there was no need and partly because the Duke of Medina Sidonia was quickly on the scene with reinforcements which would have made the operation unjustifiably hazardous. On 21 April the English left Cadiz as suddenly as they

[1] Monson's *Tracts*, I, 136–51, which also gives a full account of the operation.
[2] Corbett, *Spanish War*, 104.
[3] Ibid., 113–6; Monson's *Tracts*, 143–5; Rodriguez Salgado, 22.

had arrived, and there was urgent speculation as to their next destination. Medina Sidonia sent out warnings in all directions, but Drake's intention seems to have been to catch the 12 galleons of the Biscay squadron, one of the core ingredients of the Armada, at sea between Lisbon and Cadiz. In that he failed, but on 30 April descended instead upon the castle and harbour of Sagres, on the extreme south western tip of Portugal, which he captured almost without resistance. There he remained until the end of May, dominating the sea lanes in all directions and taking or sinking every ship that tried to pass out into the Atlantic. The Venetian ambassador reported '. . . the English are masters of the sea, and hold it at their discretion; Lisbon and the whole coast is, as it were, blockaded . . .'.[1] Philip fired off instructions in all directions, but none could be implemented in time to be effective.

Drake, however, had his shareholders to think of, and the great military success at Cadiz did not offer very much by way of dividend. On 31 May he left Sagres for the Azores, with the express intention of intercepting both the Portuguese Indies fleet and the *flota* from the New World. Panic ensued, and exaggerated rumours of the depradations of 'el Draque' spread throughout Spain and Portugal.[2] In fact the English fleet was scattered by a storm and never completely reassembled, while a mutiny took place on board the *Golden Lion*, and she returned to England without authorization.[3] More by chance than good planning, about the middle of June Drake came upon and captured the large Indies carrack *Sao Phelipe*, with a cargo later valued at £140 000, and therefore probably worth a good deal more. Deciding that he now had enough to satisfy his patrons, as well as having discharged his military duty, the English Admiral abandoned his station and brought his prize triumphantly into Plymouth on 7 July. Meanwhile Philip, determined to prevent further losses, and if possible to exact revenge, ordered Santa Cruz to sea with all the ships and men who could be mustered. On 12 July, when Drake was already safe at home, the Marquis left Lisbon with 37 ships, and scoured the ocean for three months in search of his elusive prey. By the time he returned, with his vessels weather-beaten, his supplies exhausted, and his crews depleted by disease,

[1] *Cal. Ven.*, 8, 227, 21 May 1587.

[2] Council to Philip, 4 May 1587, AGS GA 208, ff. 267–8; Rodriguez-Salgado, 22.

[3] This seem to have arisen out of a quarrel between Drake and his Vice-Admiral William Borough, who was in command of the *Golden Lion*. The ship returned to England without authorization on 5 June, and the officers and crew were imprisoned, but Drake's attempt to insist on a court martial was unsuccessful. See Corbett, *Spanish War*, and Oppenheim, *Administration*, Appendix B.

there was no chance of launching the Armada in 1587.[1] In every respect, Drake's voyage had been a total success. He had enhanced his already formidable reputation, spread alarm and despondency, and tempted the Spanish Admiral into a massive waste of time and resources. By comparison the actual destruction wrought at Cadiz had been minor; both the supplies and the ships could be, and were, soon replaced. The raid itself was a minor inconvenience, but to an operation which was already running into major logistical difficulties, it was a severe discouragement. The capture of the *Sao Phelipe* was a more mixed blessing. By guaranteeing a handsome profit on the venture, it encouraged the citizens of London to undertake subsequent voyages of a similar nature, but it also encouraged the Queen to believe that it was possible to make a sea war pay for itself, and that the allocation of public funding need not be increased. The pernicious consequences of this were to become apparent in the next decade.

The loss of momentum caused by Drake's success also caused the strategy of the Armada itself to be revised. Zuñiga had died in November 1586, and the Duke of Parma had become increasingly critical of the way in which his original plan had been tampered with.[2] Since the Armada had become public knowledge, his original insistence upon secrecy and surprise had become pointless. By the end of the year Philip had resolved upon the strategy which he was then to stick to in the face of all criticism until its inadequacy was convincingly demonstrated in the following August. The Armada, with a small force on board, was to sail up the Channel, not offering battle to the English navy and not deviating from its path, until it reached 'Margate roads', that is, the Downs. There it was to provide cover to enable Parma's army, already embarked in landing barges, to sail across to Kent. The plan was littered with tactical loose ends. How was the rendezvous to be accurately synchronized, given the uncertainties of the weather? How were Parma's barges to get out to sea, given that the Dutch had shallow-draft

[1] Philip at first refused to accept this, and issued orders that the expedition should set out forthwith, in the middle of winter if necessary. For a few weeks the King's state of mind seems to have bordered on the unstable. Both Santa Cruz and Parma were ordered to proceed in spite of the impossibility of the situation, but in December Philip's health collapsed, and by the time he recovered in January he had been forced to accept the inevitable. Martin and Parker, 136–42; Rodriguez-Salgado, 24–6.

[2] The situation was also complicated by competition between Parma and Santa Cruz for the overall command of the operation, and by Parma's incessant demands for money, e.g. Parma to Philip 18 September 1587, AGS E.592 ff. 117–8; Rodriguez-Salgado, 26.

warships which would obstruct their passage? How was the lack of a convenient deep-water harbour to be overcome? Parma became so querulous that the King eventually imposed silence upon him, but his doubts were fully justified, and the question remains as to why Philip, normally so cautious should on this occasion have been willing to leave so many crucial details to the good providence of God who had not, so far, shown much sign of being on the Spanish side.[1] On 16 January 1588 Santa Cruz assured the King that the fleet would be ready to set out by the end of the month, but the truth was that the old seaman was mortally ill, and the preparations were in total confusion. The men were deserting and dying of disease faster than they could be mustered, and consuming the victuals faster than they could be collected. In the middle of February Santa Cruz died, and Philip's special commissioner, the Count of Fuentes, sent him a candid and accurate report of the situation. Only an administrative genius could salvage the wreck, because if the Armada was not launched in 1588 it would not sail at all, since costs running at over £100 000 a month could not be sustained much longer even by Philip's enormous wealth. At last the King made the right decision, and entrusted the rescue of his cherished enterprise to Alonso Perez de Guzman, the Duke of Medina Sidonia.

[1] The King was well aware of the shortcomings of his strategy, but could clearly see no way round them and was too deeply committed to withdraw. Rodriguez-Salgado, 27–8.

9
THE ARMADA AND AFTER

Without the energy and efficiency of the Duke of Medina Sidonia, the Armada would never have sailed at all. Having failed in a desperate bid to avoid the honour, he managed to convert the chaos which he had taken over in mid-February 1588 into the impressive looking fleet which he was able to lead out of the Tagus on 30 May. However, nobody knew better than he how deceptive the impression was. Of his 130 ships only about 30, mainly from the squadrons of Portugal and Biscay, were properly armed warships. Guns had been a constant problem; neither Spanish gunfounding nor powder manufacture being equal to the demands being placed upon them.[1] In 1586 Santa Cruz had envisaged his ships carrying no more than an average of four of five guns each, but the experience of Drake's raid on Cadiz had convinced the King of the inadequacy of such a scale of armament, and he ordered a dramatic increase. When they eventually set out, the Armada ships carried an average of 19 guns each, but only six in the entire fleet carried more than 40, which was the normal level by then for any English ship of more than about 250 tons.[2] Moreover, many of these guns were old, or unsuitable in other ways, designed for siege work on land rather than sea-fighting. Nor were they properly mounted, most of them being on the large two-wheeled carriages used ashore, so that their long trains inhibited re-loading. There may have been a shortage of trained sea-gunners in England, but the Spanish plight was much worse. The Armada guns were handled by soldiers with no experience of sea fighting, and a deeply rooted reluctance to pay any attention to seamen. There

[1] I. A. A. Thompson, 'The Invincible Armada', 165–6.
[2] Martin and Parker, *The Spanish Armada*, 196–7.

was no general shortage of powder or shot, but much of the powder was of inferior quality, and because of the haste which had been necessary the shot was not always matched to the guns.[1] Also the guns, having been scraped together from all over the place, were very miscellaneous in size and design, so that a gunnery expert was needed on every ship to make sure that each piece was correctly primed and fired. It is hardly surprising that, when it came to combat, the Spanish gunfire was desperately slow and inefficient.

Manning and provisioning had, in a sense, been Medina Sidonia's great triumph. He actually got over 29 000 men, soldiers and seamen, onto his ships with enough food for about two months. But again it was a fragile triumph. Not only were most of his seamen inexperienced – many of them pressed from the inland provinces – but the majority of his soldiers were also raw recruits. The battle hardened *tercios* whom the English feared were with Parma in the Netherlands, not on board the Armada. The food was adequate, both in quantity and quality, but there were some awkward shortages, such as barrel staves, which meant that much of the water was kept in green barrels and rapidly became undrinkable. Finally, there were the ships themselves. Santa Cruz had originally proposed a large number of oared warships, galleys and galleases, as a part of the fleet, but when it actually set sail there were only four of each.[2] This may have been partly because of the poor performance of the galleys against Drake's ships at Cadiz, but more probably it was felt that they could not be spared from the Mediterranean, where the threat from North Africa was still acute, even though the Turks for the moment were not menacing.[3] Whatever the reason, the decision to take so few oared ships was fully justified by the outcome, since none of the galleys even got as far as the Channel, and the galleasses played almost no part in the fighting. The sailing ships varied greatly in quality. A few were modern galleons, which the Portuguese already had and the Spaniards were just learning to build, but most were much older in design; towering, high sided carracks, or small pinnaces – pataches and zabras. The main strategic problem for the fleet was created by the urcas, or hulks, large, cumbersome and slow moving transports carrying the horses, the

[1] *Armada*, ed. M. Rodriguez Salgado, pp. 173–5.

[2] Galleases; *San Lorenzo, Napolitana, Zuniga* and *La Girona*; galleys; *La Capitana, Princesa, Diana* and *Bazana*. Of these the *San Lorenzo, La Girona* and *Diana* were lost; the *Capitana, Princesa* and *Bazana* left the fleet before it reached the Channel; the *Napolitana* and the *Zuniga* returned safely. Martin and Parker, *Armada*, 155.

[3] Thompson, 'The Invincible Armada', 165–6.

siege trains, and large numbers of soldiers. The need to protect these hulks necessitated the highly disciplined formation which Medina Sidonia adopted, and also dictated the extremely sedate pace at which the whole Armada was compelled to advance. In spite of the long period spent in preparation, not all these ships were in good condition when they set out. There were no royal dockyards in Spain, and the organization of repair and overhaul left too much to chance or private initiative. Both Santa Cruz and Recalde had suffered damage to their ships in the autumn of 1587, and some had been hastily patched up rather than properly repaired.

The King's instructions to his Admiral, issued on 1 April, were a strange mixture of the practical and the visionary.[1] Insistence upon the divine mission of the Armada was strong. There was to be no swearing on board, and the brothel ship which often accompanied an army royal was left behind as inappropriate to a crusade. More important, the exact manner of the conjunction between Parma and Medina Sidonia was left in the hands of God. On the other hand Philip was totally explicit that the whole purpose of the Armada was to make that rendezvous. The Admiral was not to attack the English fleet, nor was he to seek to make any landfall on his own initiative. His task was to get his fleet intact to the Downs, and to fight off any attempt by the English navy to impede him. The King was under no illusions as to the difficulty of the task, nor as to the tactics which his enemy would adopt.

> . . . it must be borne in mind that the enemy's object will be to fight at long distance, in consequence of his advantage in artillery . . . The aim of our men, on the contrary, must be to bring him to close quarters and to grapple with him . . .[2]

It was one thing, however, to identify a problem, and quite another to find a solution to it. Having confined himself to stating what any Spanish captain would have known, Philip had no helpful suggestions to offer. These were not the kind of orders to go out of date, and the fact that almost two months elapsed between their issue and the actual departure of the fleet mattered very little. What was much more serious was the fact that the Armada spent two weeks bottled

[1] The document commenced 'Victory is a gift from God: He gives it or takes it away as He wills. Since you are in charge of executing His work, we can expect Him to favour and assist us, unless we become unworthy of this through our sins'. AGS E. 165, f. 29; Rodriguez Salgado, *Armada*, 32.

[2] AGS E. 165, f. 29; 'Spanish documents relating to the Armada', *Naval Miscellany*, ed. C. Lloyd, 4, 16.

up in Lisbon by adverse winds before it could get to sea, and another two weeks painfully inching up the coast to Coruna. This not only meant that victuals were being consumed at an alarming rate, it also meant that some of the more perishable commodities were already going putrid before the campaign proper had begun. Medina Sidonia sent urgent messages ahead to Coruna for fresh provisions, but as he tried to get his large fleet into the haven, it was struck by a south-westerly gale on 21 June. About a third of the ships reached safety, and the other two thirds were scattered all over Biscay and the western approaches.[1] The Admiral, in despair at one more misfortune, tried to persuade the King that God must have turned against the whole idea of the enterprise. But to make such a suggestion to Philip in his current frame of mind was to invite rebuke, and on 1 July he ordered the expedition to proceed, with many theological exhortations about the justice of the cause.[2] Medina Sidonia redoubled his efforts; the straggling ships returned; fresh provisions were obtained; and on 21 July the Armada was at sea again. But the storms had not been without their effect; there was no time for substantial repairs, and some of the ships were not as seaworthy as they had been when they left Lisbon.

Nevertheless, the bad weather had not been an unmitigated misfortune. In spite of Elizabeth's determination to continue with the desultory peace negotiations which she was keeping alive at Bourbourg, England had been mobilizing since the beginning of the year. By March it was realized that Drake's spectacular raid of the previous year had merely postponed the attack, not frustrated it. The Armada was still coming. Consequently this was no ordinary mobilization of the Queen's ships to patrol the Channel, or despatch a few adventurers to the New World. For the first time since 1545 the full maritime resources of the country were called upon. The whole fleet was never actually together in one place, but between March and August a total of 197 ships were in service. Of these 34 were the Queen's own ships; a further 53, mostly small, were 'taken up' in the traditional manner for service under the Lord Admiral, and paid for by the Queen; and another 23, described as 'coasters' under the command of Lord Henry Seymour, were mostly financed in the same way. However, almost half the fleet was provided by various forms of private contribution, which partly reflected the keen sense of national emergency, and partly the 'contract warfare' which had

[1] Martin and Parker, 159.
[2] Ibid.

become such a feature of Elizabeth's reign. Thirty vessels, 13 of them over 200 tons, were provided and paid for by the City of London; and a further 34, under the command of Drake, seem to have been provided by a variety of nobles and individual merchants.[1] They bore such revealing names as *Galleon Leicester, Galleon Dudley, Bark Hawkins* and *Bark Talbot*, and four of them were over 300 tons. Measured simply in terms of large fighting ships, the two fleets were not ill-matched. Medina Sidonia had far more large ships, but most of them were not fighting ships in the proper sense, while many of the smaller English ships were heavily armed and able to give a good account of themselves. The English had many advantages. They were operating close to their own coasts, where fresh supplies and munitions could be obtained; they carried more and better guns, and knew how to use them; and many of their large ships were newer and more seaworthy than anything in the Spanish fleet. On the other hand Medina Sidonia had a unity and firmness of control which the English could not match. Lord Howard was a competent admiral, but he was far exceeded in experience (and daring) by subordinates such as Drake, Hawkins and Frobisher, and Drake in particular was always sure he knew better than his commander. This problem was exacerbated by the manner in which the fleet was made up, and there were a number of captains who saw themselves virtually as freelance operators.[2]

It was Drake who persuaded Howard to make his forward base at Plymouth, rather than at Portsmouth as had been the case in previous wars. He moved many of the ships under his own command there in February, but it was the beginning of June before Howard joined him, which would have been barely in time if Medina Sidonia had not been delayed. At that point there were 105 ships at Plymouth; 19 Royal warships, 46 large auxiliaries, and 40 smaller ships and victuallers. Fifteen galleons, under the command of Lord Henry Seymour, remained in the Narrow Seas with a number of support vessels.[3] Howard's intention was not to await the arrival of the Armada, but to repeat the successful tactic of 1587, and carry out a pre-emptive strike. However, he did not know exactly where the Spanish fleet was, whether at sea or in harbour, and the weather

[1] Martin and Parker, 65. See also BL Royal MS 14 B XIII, printed in J. Charnock, *History of Marine Architecture*, 59–72.

[2] For Drake's conduct in the case of the Rosario, see PRO E133/47/3, 'Drake v. Drake'. Martin and Parker, 286.

[3] Martin and Parker, 164; Charnock, 63.

which had scattered the Armada frustrated all his attempts to leave harbour until 4 July. Had the winds been favourable, he could easily have caught Medina Sidonia in Coruna as Drake had caught Santa Cruz's supplies at Cadiz. However, the winds were not favourable. First there were storms off the Scillies, and then a flat calm, which left the English fleet 60 miles off the Spanish coast, and finally a south-westerly which drove them back to Plymouth. They arrived there, with their victuals completely exhausted and some of the ships in need of repair, on 22 July, the day after the Armada finally left Coruna. Just a week later, on 29 July, a scouting pinnace spotted the Spanish fleet off the Lizard, advancing in tight formation and with a following wind. The next two days could have been extremely dangerous for the English, as they rushed to complete their revictualling, and struggled to get their fleet to sea against the adverse wind. Fortunately Medina Sidonia knew nothing of their difficulties, and even if he had strict adherence to his orders would have prevented him from seizing the advantage. As the Armada advanced looking, so to speak, neither to right nor left, by skilful seamanship Howard and Drake managed to warp their ships out into Plymouth sound against the wind, and even to seize the weather gauge as the Spanish fleet disdained to engage in competitive manoeuvring. Instead the Armada fanned out slightly into a defensive battle formation, and continued to advance. Although the Spanish crews may have been inexperienced, the captains were not, because only expert seamen could have controlled their vessels so tightly, and continued to do so over many days.[1]

What then followed was a running battle over six or seven days, which went through several distinct phases, but produced no conclusive result. The most striking and original tactic was the initial use by the English of what the Spaniards called an attack *en ala*, that is, in line ahead.[2] Howard and Drake, leading their respective squadrons, swept around the wings of the Spanish formation, raking them with continuous gunfire. It was a dramatic innovation in a major sea battle, and clearly disconcerted the Spanish captains, but it did not do a great deal of damage. The Armada lost two large ships during this opening phase, but neither as a direct result of English action. There was a massive explosion aboard the *San Salvador*, and she had to be abandoned; and soon after the *Nuestra Senora del Rosario* was involved in a collision. Seeing this mishap, which left the *Rosario*

[1] C. Fernandez Duro, *La Armada Invencible*, 2, 101–5.
[2] Martin and Parker, 165–6.

struggling at some distance from the fleet, Sir Francis Drake abandoned his own station, contrary to Howard's orders, and secured the prize. It turned out to be a rich one, and the English commanders could not afford to fall out, but Drake's action showed that the risk of serious indiscipline was never very far below the surface. Henry White, captain of the *Bark Talbot*, commented somewhat sourly that

> The majesty of the enemy's fleet, the good order they held, and the private consideration of our own wants did cause, in mine opinion, our first onset to be more coldly done than became the valour of our nation and the credit of the English navy . . .[1]

English gunfire may not have done much physical damage, but its rapid and continuous discharge, together with the elusive nature of their enemies, began to undermine Spanish morale after the first two days. Medina Sidonia was forced to pull in the wings of his formation, and to seek for means to counter-attack his tormenters. On 2 August off Portland a sudden change of wind gave him the weather gauge, and it seemed that his opportunity had come. However, skilful seamanship and superior knowledge of the local water enabled Howard and Frobisher to extricate their endangered ships and renew the attack.

No one on either side had experience of this type of sea fighting on such a scale, and if the Spaniards were somewhat unnerved, the English soon found themselves running out of powder and shot. By the evening of 2 August Howard was forced to disengage, and for a few hours it looked as though Medina Sidonia was going to take advantage of the situation by occupying Portsmouth harbour until his rendezvous with Parma was assured.[2] He may even have intended to do so, but on 3 August Howard re-organized his fleet into four squadrons, and having replenished his munitions, resumed the attack with the specific purpose of forcing the Spanish past the eastern end of the Solent, and on up the Channel. A series of engagements then followed over the next two days, each English squadron acting independently but in conformity to an agreed plan. Although they retained the initiative throughout this period, and frustrated any intention which Medina Sidonia may have had to

[1] Martin and Parker, 167.

[2] Medina Sidonia and his council did actually decide to enter the Solent to await word from Parma, and notified the king of their decision. But they did not, apparently, tell the other captains of the fleet, because the decision is not mentioned in any of the standard accounts. AGS E.455/492, Medina Sidonia to the King, 30 July.

enter the Solent, the English again failed to inflict any significant damage on the Spanish ships, or to disrupt their formation. Having caused a fair number of casualties and a lot of exertion to their enemies, by the evening of 4 August the English squadrons were again running out of ammunition. Howard disengaged, and on the evening of 6 August the Armada anchored, more or less intact, in Calais roads. So far, in spite of some virtuoso displays of seamanship and gunnery by individual English ships, and the periodic use of line-ahead attacks, the strategic advantage lay with the Spaniards. The army of Flanders was only 25 miles away, and the critical stage of the whole operation had arrived. However, in spite of the fact that Medina Sidonia had been firing off messengers at regular intervals since early June, and three within the previous week, no word of his progress had reached Parma before the fleet itself reached Calais.[1] There were a number of reasons for that, and Parma was certainly not to blame. The weather conditions were bad; English, Dutch and Huguenot barks were scouring the Channel for small Spanish or Flemish vessels; and the messengers did not necessarily know exactly where they were going. So on Wednesday, 3 August, Parma sat down and wrote to his opposite number, informing him that his barges would be ready to move on Friday, 11 August, and not before.[2] That message reached Medina Sidonia, through a number of hazards, on the evening of his arrival off Calais, and the appalling difficulty of their whole undertaking became suddenly apparent.

The Armada had arrived, but it had not secured command of the seas, and it had no secure refuge. Although Calais was in more or less friendly hands, and the governor was willing to provide supplies, the open roadstead provided safety neither against the weather nor against English attack. Moreover another difficulty had made itself extremely obvious, which Medina Sidonia should have understood before. His own deep-draught ships could not approach the Flemish coast, which was skirted with shallows and sandbanks. Therefore Parma had to devise some means of evading or deceiving the Dutch warships, some of them of shallow draught specifically designed for the coastal waters, which would be on the lookout to frustrate his emergence.[3] Consequently Parma had to keep his embarkation

[1] Martin and Parker, 179–80.

[2] AGS E.594/122; Martin and Parker, 287.

[3] These ships, commanded by Justin of Nassau, were not well-informed about Parma's intentions, but they were fully capable of destroying the lightly armed barges, which was the main reason for their deployment. They played only a minor part in the subsequent battle.

plans secret, and his barges scattered about in many places. He would be in no position to set sail at a few hours notice, however urgent the Armada's situation. In fact the Duke had laid his plans with skill, and his enemies were in complete ignorance of his tactics, many of them believing that the great fleet was directed against themselves. But the price of this success, which gave him at least a fighting chance of getting to sea, was inevitably further delay. Parma's barges were the weak link in the chain, and everybody knew this except, apparently, Medina Sidonia. If the Dutch could be deceived, and if the weather was calm, they might get out; if the Armada commanded the channel, they might get across . . . if. At this point, on the morning of 7 August, Lord Henry Seymour's squadron joined Howard in mid-Channel, giving him a total of about 140 ships, and it was decided to launch a fireship attack upon the Armada that night.[1] This was not an original tactic, and Medina Sidonia was expecting it. He put out a screen of pinnaces to intercept the unmanned vessels, and gave strict orders that, in the event of an attack, his ships were to slip their anchors, and as soon as the danger was past, return and pick up the same moorings. Eight fireships were prepared at a cost of £5 111.10s.0d., and sent in with the wind and tide behind them at midnight.[2] Two were successfully intercepted and towed aside, but the remaining six got through, and it was at that point that the hitherto excellent discipline of the Spanish fleet cracked. Only the flagship and four of its immediate neighbours successfully executed the planned manoeuvre and remained on station. The remainder cut their cables and scattered in panic, to the Admiral's rage and chagrin.

Once the formation was broken, much of the defensive strength of the armada disappeared, and if Howard had not allowed himself to be distracted for two hours by the capture of the galleass *San Lorenzo*, the outcome might have been a total rout.[3] In the event a proportion of the fleet was given time to rally round its flagship, and that may well have saved it from annihilation in the battle which rapidly developed. The English were both upwind and to seaward of the Armada, much of which was now scattered along the Flemish coast. Seeing their advantage, Howard's ships now began to do what they had hitherto avoided, and moved in to close range to get the maximum effect from their heavy guns. For nine hours, until they

[1] *Armada*, 240. Pages 233–242 contain an illustrated, day by day account of the campaign.
[2] Martin and Parker, 186.
[3] *Armada*, 241.

once again ran out of ammunition, the English galleons pounded their enemies, and for the first time inflicted serious structural damage. Only one ship, the *Maria Juan*, was sunk outright, but several others were so battered that they had to be run ashore, or were left as helpless hulks, to be picked off by Julian of Nassau's Dutch cromsters.[1] Others again survived the battle only to be wrecked subsequently because their weakened timbers could no longer stand up to the weather and the sea. Human casualties were also high, at least 1 000 killed and 800 injured. On the English side no ships were lost, and casualties in action were light. The victory was completely decisive, in that there was no longer any chance of conducting the army of Flanders to England, but two factors enabled a significant part of the Armada to extricate itself; the English guns fell silent, and the wind changed, driving the whole melée off the Flanders banks and out into the North Sea. Medina Sidonia rallied his ships so effectively that he still seemed to present the threat of a raid on the English coast as he sailed away north, and the English fleet shadowed him until he was north of the Tyne before turning back. By then their own victuals were exhausted as well as their ammunition, and plague had broken out on many of the ships. There was at first little sense of euphoria. There were still at least 100 Spanish ships in the North Sea, and some, including Drake, thought they were heading for Norway to refit and return.[2] It was only later that the truth was learned, as stories began to come back of wrecks upon the Scottish and Irish coasts.

The aftermath was a sad story in terms of naval history. So widespread and virulent was the disease that discharged seamen were dying in the streets as they left their ships. They had been eight months at sea, and had neither clothing, money, nor proper medical care. 'It would grieve any man's heart to see them that have served so valiantly die so miserably', commented Lord Howard in early September,[3] adding that this was hardly the way to encourage such service in the future. Perhaps as many as half of the 16 000 who served against the Armada perished in this way, against a few dozen who died in battle. At this point the normally efficient Admiralty administration, which had coped so well with the gigantic task of mobilization, finally broke down. The scale of the human tragedy, coming on top of the enormous efforts required to victual and arm a fleet for a campaign of such unprecedented severity and length, was

[1] *Armada*, 241.
[2] Martin and Parker, 251.
[3] Ibid., 253–4.

simply too much. As Hawkins wrote to Burghley on 4 September 'our ships (are) utterly unmeet and unfitted to follow any enterprise from hence without a thorough new trimming, refreshing and new furnishing with provisions, grounding and new men . . .'.[1] Nevertheless, it is not entirely fair to ascribe the attitude of Burghley or the Queen to a simple callous indifference to human suffering. Elizabeth knew better than anyone that the Spanish threat had not gone away; that the navy would have to be repaired, refitted and prepared again for sea by February or March, and that all such operations were very expensive. So much of the relief work was left to the initiative of the officers, and the charity of urban and other local authorities, while the Council strained every nerve and resource to prepare for another tough campaigning season.[2] The Armada campaign had been both more and less than a victory at sea. Less, in that the Spaniards were defeated at least as much by the weather and by the flaws in their own strategy and logistics as by the English fleet. More, in that it also offered conclusive proof that the new style of sea fighting could be as effective in large pitched battles as it was in raids and minor skirmishes. The age of the artillery duel, the synchronized broadside and the line ahead formation had finally arrived. No longer were such tactics the expedient of the weaker party, and it at last became possible to cripple, or even destroy an enemy fleet at sea without boarding any of its vessels. Moreover, the contrast between the effort and expense involved upon the two sides was staggering. The Armada had taken two years of hard work on the part of an army of officials, and had cost about £100 000 a month to assemble.[3] Even then it set out in certain respects ill-prepared. The English fleet was assembled in less than three months, victualled, armed and equipped to at least as high a standard as its enemy, and in the case of armament much higher, at a total cost to the Queen of less than £100 000.[4] There was much unquantified private investment, but even so the true cost was probably no more than £200 000, as against £2½m. for the Armada. The reason for this was not the Queen's notorious meanness, penny-pinching on the wages and relief payments of sick and disabled seamen. It lay partly in the tradition of private enterprise which Elizabeth had revived and strongly fostered, and partly in the efficient infrastructure which had

[1] PRO SP12/216/3. R. B. Wernham, ed., *The Expedition of Sir John Norris and Sir Francis Drake to Spain and Portugal*, 1589, 5–6.
[2] Ibid., Introduction, xii–xv.
[3] Thompson, 'The Invincible Armada', 172.
[4] Oppenheim, *Administration*, 161.

been developed from the early days of the century. The Armada campaign provided the supreme test for the Council of Marine Causes, and what it stood for. Only over the discharge and demobilization arrangements did it fail conspicuously; in every other way the policy which it represented was thoroughly vindicated.

After 1588 a degree of anti-climax was inevitable, and it was not long in coming. The Queen and Burghley were very anxious to strike another blow against Spain, before either her crippled navy or her morale could recover. Plans were being discussed before the end of September, but it was obvious that only a limited number of royal ships could be properly docked and repaired for service early in the following year. So it was decided to launch another joint-stock enterprise, similar to Drake's raid on Cadiz.[1] There was no shortage of willing entrepreneurs, and within a few weeks a scheme had been prepared whereby the Queen would authorize and commission the expedition, contributing six of her own ships and £20 000, while a consortium of adventurers would put up another £40 000. At this stage the aims were unclear. Drake and some of his friends, such as Sir John Norris, believed that the time had come to place Dom Antonio on the throne of Portugal, and he encouraged that notion with ample promises, both concerning the strength of his following there and the rewards which would be forthcoming for his backers. Others believed that the most telling blow (and the largest profit) would derive from the interception of the Indies silver fleet, believed to be weakly defended after the recent debacle. By December it had been decided to attack Lisbon; musters of soldiers were ordered, and negotiations opened with the States General to withdraw some contingents from the Netherlands. Estimates of the cost began to escalate past the £60 000 which was assured.[2] Attempts to attract a positive Dutch contribution to the expedition failed, and the States General proved less than co-operative about the need for troops. Nevertheless, in spite of delays, the preparations continued and the Queen significantly increased her financial stake. In so doing, she also made it clear that she was not happy with the objectives which had hitherto been decided upon, and on 23 February she issued explicit instructions that

> Before you attempt anything either in Portugal or in the said islands [Azores] our express pleasure and commandment is that you first distress the ships of war in Guipuzcoa, Biscay, Galicia,

[1] Wernham, *Expedition*, xviii, xxi, 24, 25.
[2] Ibid., xxiv.

> and any other places that appertain either to the King of Spain or his subjects, to the end that they may not impeach you . . . [nor] take encouragement in the time of your absence to attempt some what against this our realm or our realm of Ireland.[1]

In other words the prime objective of the expedition was to be the military task of destroying the survivors of the Armada. After that the leaders would be at liberty to assist Dom Antonio in the securing of his inheritance, and if his own estimate of that task was correct, they would still have time and resources to ambush the silver fleet in the Azores.

The Queen realized that in shifting the priority of the voyage in this fashion she was making it less attractive to the other investors, and also probably to the commanders. Sir Francis Drake and Sir John Norris were called before the Council and bound in solemn oaths to obey the Queen's orders, but she trusted them so little that she sent a clerk of the Council, one Anthony Ashley, along with them to keep their sense of duty fresh and green. By 19 March 97 ships, of which eight belonged to the Queen, and over 17 000 men had been assembled at Plymouth.[2] There they remained, imprisoned by adverse winds, for a month while the victualling difficulties escalated, and the costs got close to £100 000 – 30 per cent above budget. For a second time the Queen rescued the adventurers by producing another £12 459, increasing her stake to over half, and reinforcing the public and military nature of the expedition. Nevertheless, by the time that the fleet actually set sail on 18 April her suspicions had returned in full measure, and rightly so. Drake and Norris made not the slightest attempt to go to Santander. More as a gesture than anything else, they went first to Coruna (which is on the direct route to Lisbon) professing to have heard that a valuable merchant fleet had arrived there. Arriving at Coruna on 23 April they found no merchant fleet, but two or three Armada survivors, which were duly destroyed. The town was taken completely by surprise, and almost undefended, but offered little plunder beyond additional victuals. An unsuccessful attempt having been made to take the citadel, Norris and Drake re-embarked their men on 8 May, having suffered very few casualties, but also achieved little beyond the satisfaction of having violated Spain with impunity.[3] In spite of having learned that a Spanish fleet was indeed refitting at Santander,

[1] Wernham, *Expedition*, xxix.
[2] Ibid., 332–34.
[3] Laird Clowes, *The Royal Navy*, 491. Wernham, *Expedition*, 149–54.

the commanders then made straight for Lisbon, pursued by the Queen's angry letters of remonstrance as word reached her of what was happening. Acting in accordance with a pre-arranged plan, Norris disembarked the bulk of his force some 45 miles north of the city on 16 May. The idea was that he would march south, rallying Dom Antonio's supposedly great popular support, and enter Lisbon in an overwhelming display of force. Drake, meanwhile would bring the fleet and the remainder of the troops up the Tagus to join them. The plan failed, not because of Spanish resistance, which hardly appeared, but because Dom Antonio had in reality no popular support. On 23 May Norris reached the suburbs of Lisbon to find the city held against him and no sign of a Portuguese rising. There was no sign of Drake, either, who, it was discovered, was still at the mouth of the Tagus having got wind of the situation and fearing to sail into a trap. After a few days skirmishing, and finding sickness growing among his men, Norris decided to cut his losses and retreat while he could. He marched down the Tagus and rejoined Drake at Cascais on 26 May.[1] By 3 June, with their effective strength down to 4 000 men, the commanders decided that there was no longer any hope of success in Portugal and re-embarked. In an attempt to salvage some hope of profit, they decided to make for the Azores, but were becalmed off the Portuguese coast and compelled to fight off an attack by a dozen Spanish galleys – the only resistance they encountered at sea. Thereafter a southerly wind arose, and carried the fleet northward, frustrating the last of its declared purposes, and breaking it up. By 19 June several ships had already set course for home, and the remainder, after making a successful but entirely fruitless raid on Vigo, followed. By 3 July they were back at Plymouth, having lost only two small ships, but many thousands of men by disease, and having neither profit nor military success to show for their efforts.

Drake and Norris understandably expected a rough reception from the Queen, but at first she was surprisingly gracious. This may partly have been because Ashley had put a favourable gloss upon his reports, but also because from her point of view the voyage had not been a complete waste of money. In the first place the defenceless condition of the Spanish coast had again been demonstrated, to the great dishonour of its King; and secondly it had revealed conclusively that Dom Antonio was a broken reed, a lesson which could

[1] Norris and Drake to the Privy Council, 2 June 1589, PRO SP12/224/78; Wernham, *Expedition*, 179–81.

have been very much more expensive. On this occasion, however, the Council was not so easily satisfied. John Thomas and Christopher Baker, two officials of the Admiralty, were sent down to Plymouth post haste to receive custody of the Queen's ships, and of the guns and munitions which had been captured in Spain.[1] Immediate steps were taken to discharge the other ships, soldiers and mariners, and on 27 July Drake and Norris were summoned to attend upon the Council, bringing their accounts with them.[2] As with the Armada campaign, and partly for the same reason, demobilization proved difficult. As early as 22 July it was felt necessary to ban the plague-stricken survivors of the expedition from approaching the Court, for fear of infection; and a month later that ban was repeated and reinforced. The reason for these 'disordered assemblies' was that the men had not been paid, or at least not fully paid, and the Council acknowledged that there could be some justice in their complaints;

> . . . to the end the said parties employed in the said voyage might receive reasonable contentment after the examining what sums of money are due to so many of them as have been impressed either by virtue of her majesty's commission or by letters from the lords and others of her highness Privy Council it hath been ordered . . .

that Norris and Drake were to enquire into the grievances and make reasonable redress.[3] On 14 November a Provost Marshall was appointed, and any who continued their protests beyond that point were liable to the penalties of martial law. These demonstrations were the work of desperate men who felt that they had nothing to lose, and coming on top of the heavy casualties provide an ominous comment on the deficiencies which were beginning to reappear in the organization of manpower. The soldiers and seamen had, after all, done all that had been asked of them in the course of the voyage, and the same could not be said of the commanders. In October the Council conducted an enquiry into their conduct, and they were charged with ignoring orders, and with failing to establish proper intelligences in Portugal before venturing to land there.[4] Their replies have not survived, but the vital ingredient of royal indig-

[1] Wernham, *Expedition*, lvii; *APC*, 17, 396, 398–400.
[2] Ibid., 450–51.
[3] Hughes and Larkin, *Tudor Royal Proclamations*, Vol. 3, 39, 44–5.
[4] PRO SP12/227/35; Wernham, *Expedition*, 291–4.

nation was not present to give substance to the Council's very justifiable annoyance, and neither was penalized except by a temporary loss of favour.

The Portugal voyage was not a disaster, but it was a failure, and in human terms an expensive one. Most of all it was a wasted opportunity. Before the end of 1589 no fewer than 60 Armada ships from Santander and San Sebastian were again at sea, not ready for action but substantially repaired; and a dozen new galleons of the latest design were on the slipways of Santander and Bilbao. Spain's naval strength was recovering fast, and it was being allowed to do so unmolested. Just as the Cadiz expedition of 1587, or the response to the Armada, had been examples of how successful Elizabeth's curious hybrid technique of making war at sea could be, so the Lisbon expedition was the classic demonstration of its hazards. Private investment meant private motives, divided loyalties, and inadequate control. If Medina Sidonia had shown more enterprise, and less respect for his orders, he might have done better, but the English method was to go too far in the other direction, and it did not always work. The lesson seems to have been learned, because although Elizabeth did not cease to invest both ships and money in privateering ventures upon the high seas, the major voyages undertaken during the remainder of the war showed a significantly higher degree of royal participation and control. The Lisbon voyage only occupied a handful of the Queen's ships, and many others were at sea during the year, some like the *Victory*, in service with privateers, others on regular patrol and escort duty. Some spent most of the year in dock recovering from the exertions of 1588. Altogether £47 836 was expended by the Treasurer of the navy, and that did not include the Queen's investment with Drake and Norris.[1] Up to this point the English had shown very little strategic imagination, having been mainly concerned with 'annoying' the King of Spain in a piecemeal fashion, and defending themselves against his counter attacks. But in 1590 a new approach can be glimpsed, which was to have a long and distinguished future in naval strategy. John Hawkins and Martin Frobisher were commissioned to cruise off the coast of Spain in order to intercept all ships passing to or from the Indies.[2] How large these squadrons were is not clear, but they were powerful enough for Philip to command the *flota* to delay its departure. More important, they remained on station for seven months, being

[1] Oppenheim, *Administration*, 161.
[2] Laird Clowes, 494.

victualled at sea. They took virtually no prizes, but paralysed that aspect of Spanish commerce, an unsung exploit which testifies to the high level of discipline which could be maintained, and points to the whole fleet consisting of royal ships. An overall naval expenditure for the year of £60 370, and the absence of other recorded exploits, points in the same direction.[1]

A few years later Sir Robert Cecil was presented with 'A project how to make war upon Spain', which worked out this experimental strategy much more fully.

> First, and principally, we must keep employed two main fleets upon the coast of Spain eight months in the year, that is from March to November. Every fleet to consist of forty-five ships, to be divided into three squadrons; one to lie off the Rock [Cape Roca] to intercept all traders of Lisbon; the second at the South Cape [St. Vincent], to stop all intercourse to San Lucar and Cadiz, and to and from the Indies; the third to the Islands [Canaries], lest they should there stop and put their goods ashore, having intelligence of our being upon the coast of Spain . . .[2]

'Perhaps', the author added sensibly, 'the number of these ships will exceed the proportion her majesty is willing to employ. But if Holland will be drawn from the trade of Spain, and join with us the number may be easily raised by them and our maritime towns in England, so that her majesty need but employ six ships of her own in each fleet, to serve for the Admiral and Vice-Admiral of every squadron.'[3] Long-term deployment upon such a scale was never to be feasible during the Tudor period, but the strategy of blockade which it represented was still the dominant element in naval policy at the time of the Napoleonic wars. It represented at least as important a breakthrough as the tactics which had been employed for the first time on a large scale against the Armada. Undeterred by the meagre results of the voyage of 1590, another squadron was put on station in the Azores in the summer of 1591, commanded by Lord Thomas Howard and consisting of seven ships of the royal navy with a similar number of support vessels. This time their six-month vigil was worse than fruitless, for it ended in the quixotic self sacrifice of

[1] Oppenheim, *Administration*, 161.

[2] 'A project how to make war upon Spain, written in the Queen's time and presented to Sir Robert Cecil, by her Majesty's appointment', in *The Naval Tracts of Sir William Monson*, 5, 53–6.

[3] Ibid. The Regents of Holland had successfully insisted upon trading with the enemy, on the grounds that it was the only way they could pay for the war effort.

the *Revenge*, surely one of the most heroic and pointless actions ever fought at sea.[1] Howard took some small prizes, but was dislodged from his station before the silver fleet arrived, and it was obvious that a much more powerful presence would be needed to bring off that major coup. Since it was impossible to keep a large enough fleet in place long enough to be sure of an interception, success would depend almost entirely upon chance, and the experimental strategy was abandoned. Over the next three years naval expenditure averaged no more than £27 000, and no significant military operations were mounted.[2] Patrols, escort work and privateering continued.

By 1594 rumours of a second Armada were in the air, and a number of scouting squadrons were sent out, which produced no reliable information. The only substance behind the reports seems to have been provided by a small-scale galley raid on Cornwall, which resulted in the burning of Newlyn and Penzance. This was an incident of no particular significance, but it provided a warning against complacency, since the small Spanish force managed to evade the English patrols which were at sea to prevent just such an occurrence. The main naval operation of 1594 was conducted in support of Henry of Navarre in Brittany. Henry, who had become King Henry IV of France on the assassination of Henry III in 1589, had deemed it prudent to secure his throne by converting to Catholicism in 1593, at which point his hitherto cordial relationship with Elizabeth became somewhat strained. Since, however, the Spaniards continued to exploit an unsettled situation in Brittany to their advantage, the Queen soon came to the conclusion that it would still be expedient to support her former ally. Consequently a force of soldiers under Sir Henry Norris was despatched to assist the French in dislodging a Spanish garrison which had occupied the peninsular of Camaret, close to Brest.[3] At the same time Sir Martin Frobisher with four large warships and about half a dozen other vessels, proceeded to the Bay of Crozon to link up with Norris and cooperate in the reduction of the fort there, which was threatening Brest harbour. The operation lasted only a few days, and was completely successful, but in the course of the assault Frobisher received a wound from which he died a few weeks after bringing his ships back to Plymouth. Death had already claimed a number of the Queen's loyal and most effective servants; Sir Nicholas Bacon in

1 Laird Clowes, 495–6.
2 Oppenheim, *Administration*, 161.
3 J. B. Black, *The Reign of Elizabeth*, 416.

1579, the Earl of Leicester in 1588, Sir Francis Walsingham in 1590; and 1595 was to claim the lives of both Sir John Hawkins and Sir Francis Drake. The cause was an expedition which they proposed between them in the latter part of 1594. Like the famous raid of ten years previously (but unlike recent operations in European waters) this was to be a joint investment between the Queen and the two leaders, for the purpose of attacking and plundering Spain's colonies in the New World, particularly Panama. The Queen provided six ships, £30 000, and the commission authorizing the enterprise.[1] Hawkins and Drake with their city backers provided 21 ships and about £60 000. Inevitably there were disagreements over the instructions. Elizabeth, in spite of the lesson of Lisbon, attempted to treat the expedition as though it were at her sole disposal, ordering a raid on the Spanish coast, followed by the interception of the *flota*. The captains pointed out that they had prepared for an amphibious operation in the Caribbean, and suggested delicately that if the Queen liked to foot the whole bill they would, of course, be entirely at her disposal.[2] The result was a compromise; Elizabeth modified her instructions, and the captains ignored them. The expedition sailed from Plymouth on 29 August 1595. It was well found and victualled, but the Spaniards knew more about its true objectives than the Queen did. Drake and Hawkins were temperamentally ill suited to co-operation, and there were endless disagreements about tactics, first in the Canaries, then in Dominica and finally in Guadeloupe. By the time the expedition reached its main objective at San Juan de Puerto Rico the town had been heavily fortified and prepared to receive them. The English attack was launched with the customary courage and panache, and considerable damage was done to the ships in the harbour, but it was repulsed after heavy fighting. Sir Nicholas Clifford, second in command of the troops was killed in the action, and Sir John Hawkins died at sea the same day. Frustrated at Puerto Rico, Drake then took his forces across to *Tierra firma*, taking and sacking a number of towns, from La Hacha on 1 December to Nombre de Dios on the 28th. A certain amount of plunder was secured, but an attempt to attack the town of Panama by a march across the isthmus failed, and the expedition was already returning, having been frustrated of most of its purposes, when

[1] J. S. Corbett, *Drake and the Tudor Navy*, 2, 402–37; J. A. Williamson, *Hawkins of Plymouth*, 332–43.
[2] G. M. Thompson, *Sir Francis Drake*, 290–91.
[3] Ibid., 302.

Drake died off Puerto Bello on 28 January 1596.[3] On its way back the fleet was intercepted off Cuba by a Spanish squadron, but fought off the challenge, sinking one of the enemy ships.

By the time that Sir Thomas Baskerville brought this fleet back to Plymouth in May 1596, an altogether more serious operation was in hand. Fears of a new Spanish Armada were mounting, with some justification. The defeat of 1588 still rankled, but the damage had long since been repaired and Spain was now far stronger at sea than she had been ten years before. Ireland always provided a tempting target, and the Spanish presence in Brittany had still not been eliminated. Moreover, in early April troops from the Netherlands under the command of the Cardinal Archduke Albert made a sudden descent on Calais and captured the town. Elizabeth immediately ordered a relief force to be raised to assist the French in recovering their possession, but then tried to revive the ancient question of England's own right, and while the two sides wrangled the citadel also fell, and the expedition was called off.[1] But a riposte was urgently needed, and the preparations for a fresh attack on mainland Spain, which had been gathering momentum for some nine months were hastily brought to completion. This was planned as an Anglo-Dutch operation, with Lord Howard, the English Lord Admiral, in overall command of the fleet. Under him were to serve 18 royal ships, 68 merchantmen of various sizes, 18 hoys and flyboats, and a squadron of 24 Dutch warships commanded by Jan van Duijvenvoorde, the Admiral of Holland.[2] The soldiers, some 7 000 in number were under the command of the Earl of Essex, the Queen's favourite, a young man who already had a reputation as a brave but headstrong captain. Most of the English side of the expedition was paid for by the Queen, but both Howard and Essex seem to have made substantial personal contributions. The merchant ships were 'taken up', and there was no commercial investment of the kind which had supported Hawkins and Drake. This was to be a military operation under Elizabeth's full control, whose purpose was to be the 'annoyance' of the King of Spain

> . . . by burning of [his] ships of war in his havens before they should come forth to the seas, and therewith also destroying his magazines of victuals and his munitions for the arming of his

[1] Black, *Elizabeth*, 418.
[2] S. and E. Usherwood, *The Counter Armada, 1596*, 39–42.

> navy, to provide that neither the rebels in Ireland should be aided and strengthened, nor yet the king be able, of long time, to and have any great navy in readiness to offend us.[1]

A council of five senior officers was appointed, ostensibly to assist the two generals, but in reality to ensure that their disagreements, and particularly the volatility of Essex, did not frustrate the enterprise. They were Lord Thomas Howard, Sir Walter Raleigh, Sir Francis Vere, Sir Conyers Clifford and Sir George Carew.

During April the ships began to assemble at Dover and the army at Plymouth. On the 30th Howard took his fleet down to Plymouth Sound, and the last phase of the preparations began. Meanwhile the Queen had changed her mind at least twice. On 28 April she summoned the Admiral back to court, apparently with the intention of revoking his commission. He did not respond, and within two days his friends at court had persuaded Elizabeth to adhere to her original plan.[2] Nevertheless both he and Essex were anxious to be away, and chafed constantly at the expensive delays caused by the non-arrival of expected ships and supplies. By contemporary standards these delays were certainly not excessive, and the real reason for their jumpiness was fear of the Queen's changeability, so it was with great relief as well as a keen sense of anticipation that Howard finally led his fleet out to sea on 1 June. No mention had yet been made of the expedition's target, but it seems certain that, as in 1587, Cadiz had already been privately determined upon. Howard had no desire to repeat the mistake which Hawkins and Drake had made in the previous year. A few days later, off Cape Ortegal, the fleet was organized into its five battle squadrons, and sealed instructions were distributed to the captains, for use in the event of the ships becoming scattered or detached from the main fleet.[3] Howard then sailed south, out of the sight of land, and used his fast scouting boats to ensure that no word of his coming should reach the city. When he arrived on 20 June, the surprise was complete. Howard lost some of his advantage by not attacking until the morning of the 21st, but there was little that the Spaniards could do in that time to improve their defences. Fort San Felipe, at the entrance to the harbour, and the galleys that were moored inside, opened up a brisk fire on the English ships as they entered, but did little to impede their advance.

[1] BL Cotton MS Otho E IX f. 313; Usherwood, 18.
[2] Ibid., 30–2.
[3] Laird Clowes, 512.

As they were driven steadily further into the narrowing harbour, the Spanish ships began to get entangled and to impede each other. A few managed to escape by way of a narrow channel to the south of the Isle of Leon, but Sir John Wingfield in the *Vanguard* later blocked that off.[1] The action continued throughout the morning and into the afternoon, by which time the cornered Spanish ships had been almost totally destroyed. The flagship *San Felipe* blew up; two large galleons, the *San Mateo* and the *San Andres*, were captured; and the remainder sunk, burnt or driven ashore.

While this action was in progress, the Dutch attacked and captured the island of Puntal, and a force of English soldiers under Sir Conyers Clifford destroyed the bridges leading from the city to the mainland, in order to prevent reinforcements arriving from that direction. The Earl of Essex, with the main force then attacked the city itself, and in spite of the fact that it was walled, carried it in a few hours of brisk fighting, with remarkably little loss of life. The garrison surrendered for a ransome of 520 000 ducats (about £180 000), giving 40 hostages, and the bulk of the civilian population was then evacuated.[2] Before these negotiations were completed, Howard detached Raleigh with a squadron of warships, to proceed to the secondary harbour of Puerto Reale and to carry out the remainder of their instructions by destroying the merchant shipping that was gathered there. Thinking that they knew their enemy, the officials of the port offered a ransom of 2 million ducats, but on this occasion they misjudged. Howard responded that his instructions were to destroy, and he proceeded to do just that. By the time that he had finished, apart from the two galleons taken earlier, 13 men-of-war, 11 Indiamen, and a large number of other miscellaneous merchantmen had been destroyed, and 1 200 pieces of ordnance captured; a total loss to Spain calculated at 20 million ducats.[3] The victory had been complete, and executed with remarkable efficiency, given the notorious proneness of English fighting men to drunkenesss and disease. But having discharged their commission, the commanders then had to decide what to do next, and unity of purpose deserted them. Essex and Duijvenvoorde wanted to retain the city and garrison it as a base for continued harrassment of the Spanish coast. Howard and the other members of the Council demurred, and decided to return to England, much to the Earl's chagrin. The fortifications of Cadiz were razed, many of its principal buildings destroyed, and the rest

[1] Laird Clowes, 514. Lambeth Palace, Codex 250; Usherwood, 68–9.
[2] Laird Clowes, 516; Usherwood, 84–6.
[3] Ibid.

systematically pillaged. 'It is plainly', wrote the Duke of Medina Sidonia, 'a chastisement from our Lord, and His will alone. Blessed be His name, although the loss has been very heavy.'[1] The English departed on 5 July, and Essex, not satislfied with having been the scourge of the Lord, made several attempts to persuade his colleagues to some further enterprise on the way back. They called at Faro, and found it deserted; they called at Coruna, and found not a single ship. The Council would not agree either to an ambush in the Azores, nor to an attack on Santander or San Sebastian. And so the fleet returned in triumph with a great deal of booty, but one very disgruntled commander who felt that his warlike energies and skills had been very largely wasted.

The taking of Cadiz was in many ways the most striking achievement of the English navy during this Spanish war, and indeed of the whole Tudor period. Neither storm, nor disease, nor indiscipline disrupted it; it was positively conceived and boldly executed, and the presence of a useful Dutch squadron should not detract from the credit due to the English Admiralty. It was a victory which crowned, even more than the defeat of the Armada, a century of naval development. It was also a hard act to follow. In the following year, 1597, Philip tried a quick counter-stroke against England, not making the mistakes which he had made in 1587–8, but endeavouring to use speed and secrecy instead of overwhelming force. The English certainly knew nothing of his plans, and he might easily have salvaged some honour with a telling blow if storms and adverse winds had not frustrated his endeavours.[2] And if English defensive vigilance was not all that it might have been in 1597, her offensive capabilities also seem to have run out of luck. Probably on his own insistence, the Earl of Essex was given sole command of a force of 19 warships, a few support vessels, and a Dutch squadron of 10, for the purpose of seizing one of the islands of the Azores group (probably Terciera) and converting it into a base for long-term operations against the

[1] Usherwood, 94.

[2] This expedition had been planned in the previous year, as an immediate response to the raid on Cadiz, and the Governor of Castile had gathered over 100 ships and 16 000 men at Ferrol. This fleet was driven back by adverse weather off Finisterre, and the attempt was postponed to the following year. The English knew that a fleet was at Ferrol, and in July 1597, Essex's first instructions were to attack it. But by the time he eventually left it was believed that the Spanish fleet had dispersed, and that part of his instructions was cancelled. In fact the Governor set out at the same time with a smaller force, intending to attack Falmouth, and the two fleets passed on the high seas without encountering, but the gales ensured that the Spaniards never reached their destination.

Spanish Atlantic trade.[1] This expedition attempted to sail on 9 July, but was driven back by storms, and eventually left Plymouth on 17 August. What followed was a tale of confusion and ineptitude, of orders disobeyed, of personal rivalries and of missed opportunities. Some minor towns were taken, some ships, and a fair amount of booty, but no serious attempt was made to challenge any of the larger islands, possibly because the expedition was short of soldiers, and the main Indies fleet was missed by a whisker. On October 9 the fleet set sail for home, having achieved nothing.[2] Like the Portugal voyage, it was not so much a disaster as a non-event; and like Drake and Hawkins in 1589, Essex had to take most of the blame. Angry at having been, as he saw it, frustrated at Cadiz, he was left even more upset by the Islands voyage. In desperation to restore his credit, he sought further adventures in Ireland, eventually with fatal consequences. Ironically, the Islands voyage seems to have cost much more than the Cadiz expedition. Ocean service in 1597 cost £27 263, and there seems to have been no other expedition of note, while the accounts for 1596 show no more than £14 415 for Howard's great exploit.[3] Perhaps the Queen allowed her share of the profits to be set against the costs, but that does not seem very likely, and if so the accounts do not show it. In neither case were there shareholders to pay off, although presumably both Essex and Howard were entitled to claim their substantial expenses.

The next two years saw much privateering, but only routine naval operations, apart from one remarkable episode in 1599. In the early summer there was something of a panic, occasioned by reports of large-scale Spanish naval preparations. It eventually transpired that these were directed against the Netherlands, but the Council was right to take no chances, and ordered the emergency mobilization of 18 warships. According to contemporary accounts the whole process of rigging, victualling and fitting out was accomplished in 12 days, and as Sir William Monson declared 'the Queen was never more dreaded abroad for anything she ever did'.[4] In its own small way, this story is also a remarkable testimony to the efficiency of the Council for Marine Causes. The Queen's ships were kept at a high level of maintenance, repaired and ready to be fitted out at very

[1] Laird Clowes, 519–24; Samuel Purchas, ed. *Hakluytus Posthumus or Purchas his Pilgrimes*, 4, 1035.

[2] Laird Clowes, 523.

[3] This latter figure is probably exclusive of victualling; Oppenheim *Administration*, 161.

[4] Laird Clowes, 528.

short notice. The fleet so impressively prepared was not actually needed on that occasion, but the moral was not lost, either at home or abroad. In 1598 Elizabeth's long time enemy Philip II died, having made his peace with France at the treaty of Vervins some two months previously; and between these two events Lord Burghley also died, leaving the Queen an isolated and aging figure. Perhaps in consequence, there were some motions towards ending the war, but they came to nothing, and late in the season Sir Richard Leveson was sent to the Azores with some half dozen warships, for the usual purpose of intercepting the *flota*.[1] Aware of his expedition, the Spaniards fitted out 18 ships against him, but the two squadrons missed each other, and Leveson missed the silver fleet. Meanwhile the deteriorating situation in Ireland, and the victories of Hugh O'Neill, Earl of Tyrone, continued to offer tempting possibilities to England's enemies. By midsummer 1601 35 ships had been assembled at Lisbon under the command of Don Diego Brochero to transport 4 500 troops to Ireland, and Sir Richard Leveson had been given six warships, with instructions to intercept them.[2] He was fractionally too late to prevent the landing at Kinsale, but in time to destroy several of the Spanish ships in the harbour, and to blockade the invaders from the sea. Kinsale was in the wrong place to support O'Neill's rebellion, and by the end of October it was closely invested by Lord Mountjoy, the English Deputy. Leveson's ships remained on station through the two months' siege, bombarding the garrison, and destroying any Spanish ships which came within reach. On 23 December the Irish relieving force was defeated, and on 2 January Aguila, the Spanish commander, surrendered on terms. A few days later the English fleet returned to the Thames.[3]

The last two naval expeditions of the reign were fitted out in 1602, under the command of Sir Richard Leveson and William Monson. Leveson sailed with five warships on 19 March, with instructions to patrol the Spanish coast and to do as much damage as possible to enemy shipping – a strategy not very different from that being pursued by the many privateers which were operating at the same time. Monson followed on 26 March with four further vessels, but Leveson unfortunately encountered the Plate fleet before either Monson, or a Dutch squadron which was in the offing, could join him, and he

[1] Bodleian Library, Rawlinson MS 192, f. 210.

[2] J. J. Silke, *Kinsale; the Spanish intervention in Ireland at the end of the Elizabethan Wars.*

[3] Ibid. Laird Clowes, 530.

was lucky to escape.[1] Shortly after the two English squadrons joined forces, but of the Dutch there continued to be no sign. At the beginning of June they received word that a rich Indiaman had reached the small Portuguese port of Cezimbra, and the two commanders decided to attack, which they did on June 3rd. After a scrappy action, in which the English warships again demonstrated their immense superiority to the galleys which were endeavouring to defend the harbour, the carrack was taken and proved to be worth a million ducats.[2] Well satisfied with this small exploit, Leveson and Monson set sail for home the following day. During September the survivors of the galleys which had endeavoured to defend Cezimbra entered the Channel on their way to the Netherlands, but they were intercepted by a squadron of English warships under Sir Robert Mansell, and eight out of the nine were destroyed.[3] No sooner had Monson returned to Plymouth than he was given fresh instructions for another mission of a similar nature, and set sail again on 31 August with nine fresh ships, carrying his flag in the *Swiftsure*. On 26 September he unexpectedly encountered a large Spanish fleet off Lisbon, and was forced to extricate himself with some difficulty.[4] After laying off the coast for almost another month he made a further unsuccessful attempt to take a substantial prize. On this occasion the *Swiftsure* got the worst of a hard hitting artillery dual, and was forced to return in a damaged state, reaching Plymouth sound on 24 November, a few days ahead of her consorts. The war at sea had been an affair of fluctuating fortunes, but the English had certainly scored more direct hits on Spain than vice versa. Philip had made repeated attempts to attack England and Ireland, and only the Armada itself was actually frustrated by the royal navy. In 1596 and 1597 serious attempts were dispersed by storms, in one case without the English even being aware of its existence. Nevertheless, the same wind blew for Englishman and Spaniard, and the English attacks repeatedly got through, even after Spanish sea-power had fully recovered. One of the reasons for this was the quality of the English commanders, but another was the efficiency of the support services, which could turn a vessel round in half the time taken by the private dockyards of Spain. The English navy was professional in the same sense that the Spanish army was professional, and as a result it was

[1] Laird Clowes, 532–5.
[2] Ibid., 533.
[3] Ibid., 534, 537.
[4] Ibid.

able to operate on resources which were less than a quarter of those which were available to its opponents.

In the midst of so many high profile operations, it is difficult to glimpse the navy going about its routine work, and we often do not know how many ships were at sea in a given year, or for how long. Only one quarter book survives from the war years – that for the relatively quiet year 1600 – but if that was in any sense typical it presents a picture of ceaseless small-scale activity.[1] The *Lion* and the *Victory* were sent out to guard the Thames estuary, the former going on station on 3 March, and the latter on 17 April; on 11 August the purser of the *Lion* was paid for maintaining Admiralty lights, presumably to mark the channels.[2] Sir Henry Palmer, captain of the *Golden Lion*, was also paid for guarding the entry to the Thames from 24 April to 5 July, and for transporting the Earls of Northumberland and Rutland to the Netherlands. Several other ships were involved in this round-the-year watch; a few, like the *Daisy Drombler*, were hired merchant ships, but most were the Queen's own. Altogether £2 126.18s.5d. was spent upon this guard. The *Antelope* and the *Charles* were moved from Portsmouth to Chatham; the *Vanguard*, the *Adventure* and the *Answer* were sent out in February on some unspecified mission, possibly to Berwick, since the *Answer* is later referred to as being on the north east coast. The *Crane* and the *Advantage* were upon the same station later in the year, and the *Vanguard* went twice to the Isles of Scilly. The *Vanguard* was also stationed in the 'Narrow Seas' during the summer, along with the *Adventure* and the *Rainbow*, while the *Repulse* and the *Warspite* went southward under the command of Sir Richard Leveson from 4 June to 13 October. A constant naval presence was maintained upon the coast of Ireland, consisting of the *Sun* and the *Moon*, along with about a dozen dromblers and pinnaces, hired mostly from the Suffolk and Essex ports. Long experience had shown that these small craft were the most suitable for policing that very difficult region. A detailed reconstruction of the navy's work for a routine wartime year can be pieced together from these accounts, and it makes an impressive record. Here is the conclusive proof that the Admiralty has outgrown its occasional nature, geared mainly to the launching of infrequent major enterprises. Ships are constantly at sea; returning, refitting, and changing stations;

[1] Bodleian Library, Rawlinson MS 206. There is also some supporting information in Rawlinson MS 192, f. 210 et seq.

[2] Ibid., f. 37. The Statute 8 Elizabeth c.13 had given this responsibility to Trinity House, but it is difficult to see what other kinds of light could have been meant.

demands, both routine and exceptional, have to be met; dockyards and buildings have to be maintained; men have to be recruited, paid and discharged; victuals have to be provided and accounted for. All this is unglamorous work by comparison with Drake's voyages to Cadiz or Cartagena, but it is the work which makes such exploits possible. By 1600 the Admiralty is a fully-fledged department of state.

Nevertheless, it was a department which exercised only partial control over operations within its own theatre of war. Not only did the Queen occasionally enter into partnership with groups of her subjects, she also allowed, and later encouraged, warfare which was entirely private in its funding and direction. Whether this was privateering or piracy depended upon your point of view. In 1582 at least eleven English ships were sailing under the flag of Dom Antonio, the Portuguese pretender.[1] At other times English ships operated under letters of marque issued by William of Orange, or the Protestant Governor of La Rochelle. Elizabeth's official policy was entirely defensive, even after 1585, so she relied heavily upon these entrepreneurs to carry the war to the enemy and to debilitate his capacity for attack. It was not until 1597 that letters of marque were officially proclaimed, because the mercantile community needed no encouragement to expand and develop what it was already doing. Control over these privateers was officially exercised by the Lord Admiral through the Admiralty court, but in practice such control was lax and easily evaded. As we have seen, the Queen had suffered constant diplomatic embarrassment earlier in her reign, and the onset of open war did not entirely remove that problem. Dr Julius Ceasar, the judge of the Admiralty Court, was besieged by complaints from Italian, French and Hanseatic merchants that their ships had been looted on the more or less flimsy pretext that they were doing business with Spain, or with a Spanish dependency.[2] Even if a political will for total honesty had existed, it would have been virtually impossible to deal out even-handed justice on such claims, and that will did not exist – or at least only intermittently. The English were accused, with much justice of making up the laws of contraband as they went along, and a powerful reason for this disingenuous attitude is suggested in a comment made by Dr Ceasar in 1590; '. . . her majesty hath gotten and saved by these reprisals

[1] K R. Andrews, *Elizabethan Privateering*, 202, gives the names of several of these ships. The English merchants trading to Iberia were strongly opposed to this involvement.

[2] BL Lansdowne MS 157, f. 208; Andrews, 26.

since they began above two hundred thousand pounds'.[1] It was only when political embarrassment outweighed the profit that action had to be taken, or at least seem to be taken. In 1592 privateers were ordered to declare their prizes to the Lord Admiral (which was a condition of their authorization), on pain of being treated as pirates; in 1591 and again in 1599 the plundering of friendly ships was prohibited; and in 1602 the laws against piracy were ordered to be strictly enforced.[2] Much of this was parade indignation – a bit of political theatre – but as Ceasar himself recognized, it needed to be taken seriously. Once the war was over the problem of domestic piracy, which was a minor matter when so many acquisitive instincts were directed outward, would recur with redoubled force unless the Admiralty court could strengthen its hand. Part of the trouble arose from the fact that the court was at the same time an aspect of the Queen's government and a private franchise of the Lord Admiral. It was an anachronism, as the Admiralty itself had been in the earlier years of the century. Ceasar knew what was needed; a regular judicial circuit to bring to book 'such great personages who dare do and speak whatsoever them listeth'.[3] But these great personages were also the pillars of the Elizabethan regime, and a judicial circuit would cost a great deal of money. So the Admiralty court remained unreformed, in spite of a clear perception of what needed to be done. A document of instruction for the Lord Admiral's solicitor, drawn up in 1601, listed the essential elements; the indictment of all who had taken ships to sea after 1585 without letters of reprisal, or who had disposed of prizes before adjudication; the arrest of all private and unauthorized men-of-war; the enforcement of the statutes concerning the duties of vice-admirals; and the signing and sealing by the Lord Admiral of all compoundings or pardons for faults, fines and forfeitures.[4] The will and resources necessary to carry out such a reforming programme were not available. In the last years of her reign Elizabeth and her Council were increasingly turning a blind eye to the reappearance of what were virtually medieval franchises in

[1] Ceasar to Howard, 18 December 1590; Lansdowne MS 157, f. 434; Andrews, 22.

[2] Hughes and Larkin, 3, 29 December 1591, 8 January 1592, 3 February 1591, 8 February 1599, 99, 100, 71, 197.

[3] BL Lansdowne MS 157, f. 210. For a full discussion of Ceasar and his role in this situation, see Andrews, 22–31. Although he was a place hunter, Ceasar was a reasonably honest man, but like all other Elizabethan officers, he was expected to make the majority of his income from fees. For the effect of this on the Vice Admirals, see R. G. Marsden, 'The Vice-Admirals of the coasts', *EHR*, 22 (1907), 468–77; and 23 (1908), 736–57.

[4] Lansdowne MS 145, f. 15.

many parts of the administration. The Queen either could not, or did not choose to, reorganize her finances in such a manner as to be able to pay and reward her servants at an acceptable level. Consequently she felt obliged to permit them to reward themselves, through monopolies, unofficial fees, bribery and all manner of extortion.[1] It is against this background that the failure of the Admiralty court to control privateering or provide remedies for piracy must be seen.

Strictly speaking, privateering is not naval history, but it would give a very distorted picture of the sea war against Spain to omit all reference to it. As we have seen the Queen herself was a privateer, having authorized and participated in a number of expeditions which, without her sanction, would have been simply piratical. After 1585 her ships frequently collaborated with the privateers, even when the latter were not part of an official naval operation. A classic example of such a collaboration was the taking of the great carrack *Madre de Dios* in 1592, an event which has been recorded in full and graphic detail.[2] A squadron of royal ships under Sir John Burgh, a squadron of the Earl of Cumberland's privateers, and a few freelance operators, all lurking around the Azores in the hope of intercepting incoming shipping, combined to take a vessel which would have been too big and powerful for them individually. She was a fabulous prize. Even the declared wealth amounted to nearly £150 000, and that was after an orgy of plunder by all the privateering crews. The total value probably exceeded £250 000, and we know so much about the incident because the wrangling went on for years, and Elizabeth, characteristically, insisted on retaining far more than Sir John Burgh's part in the operation would have justified.[3] In the same year Christopher Newport successfully raided the Bay of Honduras, and William Parker of Plymouth took Puerto de Caballos in both 1594 and 1595, demonstrating that skill and daring could still find its rewards, even in the newly fortified Indies.[4] Sir Henry Palmer, William Winter junior, Robert Crosse and Thomas Fenner all belonged to that class which K. R. Andrews has called 'the professionals'; men who operated as privateers on a substantial scale over a number of years, attacking both Spanish shipping and the

[1] There are a number of discussions of the declining integrity of late Elizabethan administration, well summarized in A. G. R. Smith, *The Government of Elizabethan England.*

[2] There are a number of contemporary accounts of this exploit, extracts from which were printed and discussed by C. L. Kingsford in the *Naval Miscellany*, 2, 87–121.

[3] Ibid., 93–4.

[4] Andrews, 172–3.

Spanish colonies.[1] By far the greatest entrepreneur, however, was George Clifford, Earl of Cumberland. Cumberland waged what was virtually his own private war against Philip, sending out or leading over a dozen squadrons in as many years, culminating in the great voyage of 1598. On 6 March he led out from Plymouth a fleet of 18 ships, headed by his own 900 ton *Scourge of Malice*.[2] Warned of his coming, the Indies fleet stayed in port, and Cumberland sailed for the Canaries, where he took and plundered the island of Lanzarote. From there he proceeded to Dominica, remaining from 23 May to 1 June, and arrived off San Juan de Puerto Rico on 6 June. After a determined resistance the town was taken and occupied, being used as a base for extensive raiding in the area, until the unhealthy climate and the spread of disease forced the English out on 14 August. Although he succeeded in obtaining a ransom for San Juan, the rest of the voyage was an anti-climax. In the Azores he missed a large Spanish convoy by a matter of days, and arrived home on 16 September, having made a substantial loss on the enterprise.[3] In spite of taking many rich prizes during his privateering career, Cumberland mortgaged a substantial part of his estate, and ended up in serious financial difficulties. The beneficiary was the Queen, on whose behalf Cumberland had struck several blows against Spain as substantial as all but the most important naval operations, without costing either the Admiralty or the Exchequer a penny. Perhaps his sense of patriotic achievement was a compensation, but it may be doubted.

Looking back on this period a few years later, John Hagthorpe wrote in *England's Exchequer* that, in the Queen's time there were 'never less than 200 sail of voluntaries and others' upon the Spanish coast, and modern research has tended to vindicate his claim.[4] 236 English vessels are known to have been privateering in the three year period 1589–91, and there is no reason to suppose that this list is either complete or untypical. 86 voyages can be confirmed for 1598. They came overwhelmingly from London and the West coast ports, and belonged to individual adventurers, merchant consortia, and the 'professionals' already noticed. At first there were good pickings, even for the small ship, provided that she was well armed and

[1] Andrews, 81–99.

[2] Laird Clowes, 526–7.

[3] Andrews, 78. For a full biography, see G. C. Williamson, *George, third Earl of Cumberland*.

[4] John Hagthorpe, *England's Exchequer, or a discourse of the sea and navigation*, 25; Andrews, 32–50.

manned; but the myth of profit outlived the reality. As the prey became both scarcer and more wary the small men, the 'amateurs' were increasingly driven out of business, or taken over. Most of the professionals overreached themselves, as Cumberland did, and the men who made the business work consistently to their advantage were the London merchants. Sir Thomas Mydleton and his partners invested in Weymouth privateers; Henry Cletherow, John Davies and others managed the Southampton ships.[1] The marriage of London capital with local expertise provided the most successful formula, and kept up the attacks until the end of the war. It would not be true, therefore, to claim that privateering was not profitable, but the fate of the most pretentious operators provided a warning that a sea war could not be expected to pay for itself, a message which the Queen learned but many of her aristocratic subjects did not. Nevertheless as a form of auxiliary warfare it was extremely effective, and the damage done to Spanish commerce was immense. In a sense it never recovered. The privateers contributed a good 50 per cent of the war effort between 1585 and 1604, and their destructive impact far outweighed the profits which they made. They also constituted a superb training ground for seamen and gunners, who had much to teach the naval officers who strove to recruit them. Although their motives were certainly not altruistic, and only partly patriotic, it is hard to see how the Admiralty could have fought the war without them.

The Admiralty itself was partly protected from the malaise of late Elizabethan administration by the substantial legitimate remuneration of its officers. The fees themselves had not been increased since the positions were established, but the Treasurer could still expect to receive £194 a year, in addition to 1s.4d. a day for two clerks; the Master of the Ordnance the same; the Controller £138; the Surveyor £128; the Victualler £140, and the Clerk of the Ships £100.[2] Such rewards did not make the officers immune from corruption, and the charges flew thick and fast, even during Hawkins' early days in office. However, there seems to have been a great deal more smoke than fire, at least down to the time of his death in 1595. Howard, although he was an effective Lord Admiral at sea, does not seem to have taken much trouble to oversee the administration. He remained in office until 1618, and long before then the Admiralty had fallen into deep discredit, as was made clear by the results of the

[1] Andrews, 120.

[2] Bodleian Library, MS Rawlinson 297 ff. 24–54, a complete list of fees etc. of every officer of the Crown.

Commission of Enquiry in 1608.[1] One of the reasons adduced for this sad state of affairs was neglect of the regular meetings of the chief officers; '. . . they should at the House at Chatton Hill (instituted for the same purpose) meete, there to resolve all such busines as shall tend to the best benefit and good of his majesty's affairs in the same Navy Royal'.[2] There had been no Lieutenant of the Admiralty since the death of Sir William Woodhouse, and it is not clear who had convened such meetings since 1565. Sir William Winter was the Senior Admiralty Officer after Woodhouse, and the trouble may have begun with his death in 1589. But Hawkins was also an effective leader, and it is more likely that his departure created confusion and led to a lack of administrative control. His replacement was Roger Longford, a mere accounts clerk, and it was not until 1598 that Fulke Greville was given the full powers of Treasurer. Greville is reputed to have been an honest man, but somewhat unworldly and lacking in energy, and it seems likely that his subordinates took advantage of him in a way which they would not have been able to do with Hawkins.[3] Winter's death, as we have seen, resulted in the discontinuance of the separate office of Marine Ordnance, but this made little practical difference as most of the work had been done by the main Ordnance office for some years. Sir Henry Palmer took over his position as Surveyor of the Ships and was succeeded in his turn by John Trevor in December 1598. At the same time Palmer succeeded William Borough as Controller. Bemjamin Gonson jnr became Clerk of the Ships on Borough's promotion in November 1588, and was succeeded in 1600 by Peter Buck.[4] James Quarles, who had taken over the office of Surveyor of the Victuals from Edward Baeshe, died in 1595 and his place was taken by Marmaduke Darrell. As with previous Admiralty appointments, nearly all these men were experienced sea-captains before their appointment to the Admiralty, so the problems did not arise from the intrusion of unqualified place hunters.[5]

The trouble arose originally from Elizabeth's unwillingness to be

[1] Bodleian Library, MS Rawlinson 192, ff. 12 et seq. Several texts have been collated and edited by A. P. McGowan, *The Jacobean Commissions of Enquiry, 1608 and 1618*.
[2] BL Cotton MS Otho E.VII, f. 63. Chatham Hill is referred to.
[3] Oppenheim, *Administration*, 149.
[4] Ibid.
[5] While this was true of the Admiralty officers, it was not always true of the sea commanders. Patronage and family connections had always played a part in appointments, but Sir Richard Leveson seems to have owed his promotion less to ability than to his marriage connection with the Howards. The successors of Hawkins and Drake – Leveson, Sir William Monson, Sir Robert Mansell, were not their equals in either ability or honesty. J. S. Corbett, *The successors of Drake*, 301.

honest with her parliaments about the amount of money which she needed to prosecute the war, and with the irresponsible optimism of certain members concerning the profits of privateering. Between 1590 and 1602 the navy absorbed some £656 000, an average of £54 700 a year.[1] This was a great deal of money, but it was far from exorbitant, and just as the Queen's enthusiasm for private enterprise warfare undermined her Council's control of military operations, so her pathological suspiciousness over expenditure undermined the morale of her officers. This was clearly reflected in a lament which Hawkins addressed to Lord Burghley in April 1590.

> . . . the matters in thoffice growe infenyte and chargeable beyond all measure and soche as hardly any man can gyve a reason of the innumerable busynesses that dayly growe; yet the mistrust ys more troblesome and grievous than all the rest for with the answerynge of thone and towle of thother there ys hardly any tyme left to serve God or to sattysfie man. The greater sort that serve in this office be growen so proud obstinate and insolent nothynge can sattysfie them and the commen sort very disobedyent so as a man that must answere the immoderate desyres of all theise were better to chuse to dye than so lyve . . .[2]

Although Hawkins could not say so openly, this suspicion originated from a Queen who was always calling her servants to account, and who encouraged them to check on each other. As long as he lived, Burghley was able to mitigate the effects of this, but when he died in 1598, there was no one to disguise the fact that Elizabeth was trying to make control of expenditure supply the place of adequate income. Nowhere was this more clear than in the case of victualling. During his first year in office James Quarles was accused of serious malpractices, but the charges originated from a subordinate who was hoping to secure his office by undertaking to discharge it more cheaply, a problem which we have already encountered a decade earlier in respect of Hawkins.[3] In 1589 the victualling rate was reduced to 5½d. in harbour and 6d. at sea, which was clearly not adequate, since Quarles had to be given special supplements in both 1590 and 1591, and still petitioned that he had lost £3 172 between April 1590 and April 1591 on account of the dearth.[4] His

[1] Oppenheim, *Administration*, 161.
[2] PRO SP12/231/83.
[3] Oppenheim, *Administration*, 142.
[4] Ibid., 143.

successor, Marmaduke Darrell struggled along with the same rates with annual special allowances until 1600, when they were put up to 6d. and 7d. respectively. The system of victualling was efficient. Commissions of purveyance were issued county by county, and were used where composition agreements failed, or were not honoured.[1] Like his predecessors, Darrell was responsible for the contracts which turned malt and barley into beer, wheat into bread or biscuit, and oxen into salt beef. He was instructed to victual all ships in accordance with their manning certificates, drawing on the nearest storehouse to the port of commissioning; Tower Hill for ships in the Thames, Rochester for those in the Medway, and Portsmouth for the vessels there.[2] In spite of the frequency with which it was used, and the difficulties which had arisen while Howard's fleet awaited the Armada there, no storehouse was built at Plymouth, and no ordinary establishment was created there. Another storehouse existed at Dover, as we have seen, for the ships victualled in the Downs. In most respects Darrell's instructions were the same as those of Quarles or Baeshe, including the emergency rations for 1 000 men, but he was required to present monthly or quarterly accounts within the Admiralty, as well as annually to the Exchequer. On 24 March 1601 he gave a bond in £5 000 to repay the prest of £2 500 which he had received for the discharge of his duties in the previous year. If Darrell was guilty of any malfeasance, it was not for lack of vigilant oversight.[3]

In most respects the structure of administration and accounting remained the same. The tendency to diminish Ordinary expenditure in favour of sea charges can be seen very clearly in the quarter book for 1600, where the former totalled £8 170, and the latter £28 200.[4] The dominance of Chatham, visible 30 years before, is now very pronounced. 39 of the 42 ships then in commission were anchored there at some time during the year, and the Ordinary accounted for £7 033; far more than Deptford, Woolwich, Portsmouth and the Steelyard altogether. The Steelyard was the old London base of the Hanseatic League, recently converted into a naval store. Apart from

[1] Bodleian Library, MS Rawlinson C.340, ff. 44 et seq. contains drafts of commissions, letters to commissioners, price lists, quantity schedules, and numerous other documents relating to victualling in this period. See also MS Tanner 241, ff. 28 et seq.
[2] MS Rawlinson 340, f. 71. For orders respecting victualling commissioners, see also MS Rawlinson 168, ff. 108–9.
[3] MS Rawlinson C.340, ff. 84–88.
[4] MS Rawlinson A.206 f. 41 gives a total figure of £36 370; f. 15 gives an ordinary figure of £8 170.6s.10d. The ordinary figure corresponds to that given by Oppenheim, but he gives a total of £35,200.

the shipkeepers at Chatham and 30 watchmen at Deptford, most of the Ordinary is accounted for by the wages of clerks and under-officers, and by small labouring jobs, such as the repair of a wharf at Deptford and the Storehouse at Portsmouth. All the major repair work is classed as extraordinary, including £2 281.18s. spent upon the *White Bear* in dry dock, and upon the docks themselves at Woolwich and Deptford. The repair and repainting of the royal ships, nevertheless, is still being carried out by direct labour and featuring in the main accounts; whereas the building programme is now mostly contracted to the royal shipwrights. The *Merhonour*, the *Garland* and the *Defiance*, all built in 1590, were contracted at a fixed price per ton.[1] The last decade of the reign saw a considerable amount of building. Altogether nine ships were constructed in 1590, most of them by Mathew Baker, the Petts and Richard Chapman; the *Flight* and the *Mercury* were built in 1592; the *Adventure* in 1594; the *Minikin* in 1595; and the *Warspite* and *Due Repulse* in 1596. Of these the *Merhonour, Garland, Defiance, Warspite* and *Repulse* were all capital ships of 450 tons or more. There was then a pause; two galleys and a hoy were built in 1601, and two more galleys in 1602, completing the list for the reign. The galleys seem to have been intended for work in the Thames estuary, perhaps to relieve some of the smaller warships for other duties. They were medium sized, with 60 oars apiece, but were never used, and were eventually sold in 1629.[2] The *Mercury* was also built as a galley, but was converted into a pinnace in 1605. Oared warships had died a very lingering death in the Tudor navy, and in theory there were still five in service in 1603; but they saw no further action. Only the royal barge continued to be propelled by oars, and that was not under the control of the Admiralty.[3] Two ships were bought after 1584; the *Eagle of Lubeck* in 1592, for use as a transport hulk, getting the guns on and off the warships; and the *Lion's Whelp*, purchased from the Lord Admiral in 1601. The latter had already seen quite a lot of service with the navy, and had proved her value. By contrast with her father, Elizabeth bought very few ships at any time, always preferring to build her own. Nor did she take many prizes into service. The vast majority of the ships taken after 1585 were sold. Only five ended up in the navy; *Nuestra Senora del Rosario*, taken

[1] Oppenheim, *Administration*, 129.
[2] J. E. G. Bennell, 'English oared vessels of the sixteenth century', *MM*, 60, 1974, 9.
[3] The Master of the Royal Barge was an officer of the Court, and he contracted with the boatbuilders who constructed the barges, and with the watermen who rowed them.

during the Armada, which lasted until 1594; *San Mateo* and *San Andres*, taken at Cadiz in 1596; and two of uncertain provenance, the *Black Dog* and the *French Frigott*, which appear in 1591 and 1592 respectively. At the time of her death, Elizabeth owned between 40 and 45 ships, all but a handful of them seaworthy and in good repair. There were also, according to a survey of 1588, 183 merchant ships of over 100 tons available as auxiliaries.[1] The country was at war, and the war was being fought largely at sea, so a high level of preparedness was to be expected; moreoever a considerable proportion of the merchantmen were probably doubling as privateers. Nevertheless, the so-called decline of the Elizabethan navy after the Armada can be easily exaggerated. In major exploits it probably failed more often than it succeeded, and it certainly failed to destroy Spain's power at sea, but the overall achievement after 1590 was still considerable. After 18 years of war, the navy was stronger in ships and firepower than it had been at the beginning, had a far larger merchant pool to call on and had inflicted enormous damage on its powerful adversary at remarkably little cost to itself. Apart from the *Revenge*, only a handful of small ships had been lost in action, and the English coast had been kept virtually intact from an enemy whose harbours had been raided at will.

The main weakness was in funding policy, where control was sacrificed to economy, and unnecessary temptations placed in the way of men who were not particularly dishonest, but who were expected to take their own profit from every public transaction. Inflation played havoc with careful budgeting, as it always does, and in 1602 extreme difficulties in recruiting forced another wage increase, again by about 30 per cent. Whether this effectively counteracted the rival attractions of the privateers may be doubted, but it pushed up the sea charges for the year by about £8 000.[2] After the tragedy of 1588 and the fracas of 1589, it was also recognized that some provision had to be made for soldiers and seamen discharged from service, particularly the sick and disabled, and three statutes were enacted in 1594, 1598 and 1601 for that purpose. Like the contemporary Poor Law, this provision was made less for humanitarian reasons than for the preservation of public order, and encouragement to respond to the call of duty.[3] The final Act, 44 Elizabeth c.3, created a very limited entitlement to pensions for the disabled, graded according to rank, from £10 a year for ordinary

[1] BL Cotton MS Otho E.IX, 152.
[2] Oppenheim, *Administration*, 153.
[3] *Statutes of the Realm*, 4, pt. 2, 966–8.

soldiers and seamen up to £20 a year for a lieutenant (or equivalent). This money was not, of course, to come from the Exchequer, but from special funds established in each county and under the control of a County Treasurer. Every parish was to be rated by the Justices of the Peace – not less than 2d. nor more than 10d. per week – and the money paid into the county chest. It was in many ways similar to the Poor Law, and it was hardly an act of generosity upon the Queen's part, but it was more than a gesture, and when it worked must have provided a substantial measure of relief. The Government had at least recognized some obligation to those who made sacrifices in its service. Like Rudyard Kipling's soldiers, Elizabethan seamen were not much loved when they had finished standing between their fellow countrymen and the foreign foe, and before these statutes it had been largely up to their own officers to provide, as the nobles of an earlier generation had provided for their superannuated retainers. In 1594 Sir John Hawkins and Sir Francis Drake had acted in the spirit of that tradition by establishing a small hospital for disabled seamen, known as the 'Chatham Chest',[1] which reflects admirably upon their sense of responsibility, but was a mere drop in the ocean. A long war was bound to create social as well as economic problems, and the 'Acte for the necessarie releefe of souldiers and Maryners' was a symptom of that situation. It was also a recognition that the mariner, no less than the soldier, was essential to the defence of the kingdom. By 1603 the navy had come of age as a fighting service, and the Admiralty as an institution. There were serious problems and setbacks ahead over the next half century, but this was the period to which Samuel Pepys and the other architects of the late seventeenth century navy looked back for inspiration. Like the Battle of Britain, the defeat of the Armada and the capture of Cadiz were made of the stuff of legend. In reminding ourselves how fragile and imperfect those victories were, we must also remember the years of creative work and thinking which created the infrastructure. In many respects that was the real triumph, because without it no Drake or Hawkins or Howard would have been able to challenge the power of Spain upon the seas.

[1] Oppenheim, *Administration*, 145.

NOTE ON SHIPS' NAMES AND IDENTIFICATION

In spite of much research, and the publication of several carefully composed lists of the Tudor navy, the identification of particular ships can be hazardous. When a ship was rebuilt, sometimes it retained its original name, as the *Mary Rose* did in 1536; sometimes it acquired a new one, as the *Philip and Mary* did in 1584 when it became the *Nonpareil*. Often the same name was reused, as was done when a new *Mary Rose* was launched in 1556. It is difficult to be sure whether a designation like *Great Bark* or *Less Bark* was really a name, or simply a description. There was a *Great Bark* in service before the *Great Galley* was rebuilt and given that designation about 1540, and the two may have been in existence together for a time. Similarly a *Great Bark* was rebuilt as the *White Bear*, but it seems unlikely that this could have been the *Great Bark* which had originally been the *Great Galley*. If it was, it went through three incarnations and remained in service for nearly the whole century! There were also privately owned ships with the same names as royal ships, such as *Anne Gallant*, and it is not always clear whether the vessel referred to belongs to the navy or is 'taken up'. Later in the century, as the accounts become fuller, it is possible to track many ships with reasonable certainty from their building, through years of service, to sale or breaking up; but earlier on it is much more difficult, and gaps in the evidence have to be jumped. Consequently we cannot always be sure that ships which appear a few years apart with the same names are actually the same vessels. Names were not usually changed, except on rebuilding, but some ships were known by more than one – as the *Great Galley* was also the *Mary Imperial*. Prizes were also renamed, although often in rather obvious ways, as the *San Andres*, captured at Cadiz, became the *St Andrew*. I have endeavoured as far as possible to make common sense assumptions about identity when the evidence is not conclusive, but many specific points may need to be corrected when, and if, the gaps can be filled.

GLOSSARY

Affinity the retainers and supporters of a nobleman or other prominent person, including servants and family. An affinity was held together by a mixture of loyalty and self-interest, and could decline sharply if the position of its head was weakened.

Almoner an officer whose responsibility it was to distribute money (alms), food, or other charitable gifts to the poor. The king's almoner was an important member of the court.

Arquebus an early form of handgun, fired with a piece of burning tow or 'match'. Normally used with a rest.

Assignment the allocation of a payment to be made out of a designated source of revenue or income. Often used to pass money directly from a debtor to a creditor without passing through the Exchequer.

Backstaff a navigational instrument for measuring the altitude of the sun; so called because the user had the sun behind him when making his calculations.

Balinger a small sea-going sailing vessel, usually single masted and flush decked. Noted for their speed and manoeuvrability.

Bill a simple short-hafted spear.

Bonnet a strip of canvas laced to the lower edge of a sail in order to increase its area, and hence its drawing power.

Cannon a large gun, cast in either bronze or iron, firing an iron shot of 40–60lb. weight. Not often used at sea.

Cannon – perrier a similar gun, but firing a stone shot, and used more in the manner of a mortar.

Carrack a large three or four masted ship, originally developed as a merchantman in southern Europe. Characterized by deep draught, relatively broad beam, and very high fore and aft castles.

Carvel built a type of hull construction in which the planks are placed edge to edge, and the strength of the structure depends entirely upon the frame.

Casa de Contratacion the Spanish Academy of Nautical Sciences in Seville. Modelled on the earlier Portuguese academy at Sagres.

Clinker built a type of hull construction in which the planks overlap and consequently have an inherent strength of their own.

Confession of Augsburg a statement of Lutheran doctrine, drawn up by Philip Melanchthon for presentation to the Imperial Diet at Augsburg in 1530. Later used as the standard test of Lutheran orthodoxy.

Culverin a long-barrelled medium-calibre gun, cast in iron, and firing an iron shot of 15–18lb. weight. The favoured English naval gun of the late sixteenth century.

Customer an official employed to collect the customs dues at a port.

Crayer a small single masted vessel, normally used for trade. Designed for maximum carrying capacity.

Deadshares the wages of soldiers or seamen who were on the captain's payroll, but did not actually exist. A recognized perquisite which was allocated among the officers (and sometimes the crew) of a ship. Introduced in the reign of Henry VIII in imitation of an established military custom, and discontinued in 1695.

Declination the angular distance of a celestial body north or south of the equator, measured from the centre of the earth; corresponding to the geographical latitude of the body.

Demi-culverin a smaller version of the culverin, throwing an iron shot of 9–10lbs.

Denizen a person born outside the dominions of the King of England, who had taken out letters of naturalization, as distinct from an alien, who had not.

Dromond a large ship of Mediterranean origin, propelled by both oar and sail; obsolete by the mid-fifteenth century.

Falcon a light cast gun, either of bronze or iron, firing an iron shot of 2½–3lb.

Falconet a similar gun, but firing a shot of 1½–2lb.

Flanders Galleys an annual trading fleet despatched from Florence to northern Europe. So called because its original destination was Bruges, and later Antwerp, but Southampton, and later London, were included in the itinerary.

Franchise a jurisdictional area in which the king's writ did not run, and where a private lord was responsible for the enforcement of the law. Also known as a liberty. The Earldom of Chester and the Bishopric of Durham were franchises in the early sixteenth century. Franchises were ended in all but name by a statute of 1536.

Galleass a large oared warship, also propelled by sail, usually three masted, with a gun deck over the rowers benches. A cross between a carrack and a galley, it tended to suffer from the disadvantages of both.

Galleon a term with many meanings, but usually used to describe a medium or large sailing ship, built flush-decked and without castles. Galleons were normally somewhat longer and narrower than carracks, and had superior handling qualities.

Galley a lightly-built fighting ship, chiefly propelled by oars. Galleys were fast, and could move independently of the wind, but they could not carry heavy armament, and were at risk in rough weather.

Hanseatic League (Hanse) a trading confederation of north German towns, established in the thirteenth century. At the height of its power, in the early fifteenth century it held a virtual monopoly of maritime trade in and out of the Baltic. In the sixteenth century it was heavily challenged by national trading interests, including the Merchant Adventurers of London.

Mare clausum (literally 'closed sea') the principle that the sea may be exclusively controlled by a sovereign authority, in the same manner as the land. A work of that title was written by John Selden in 1631, in response to the *Mare Liberum* of the Dutch jurist Hugo Grotius, who had argued (1609) that all ships should have unrestricted rights of access to all waters.

Morris pike a shafted weapon, mounting a blade as well as a spear head. Originally 'Moorish pike'.

Orlop the lowest deck of a ship, laid on the timbers immediately above the ballast.

Oyer et Terminer a commission directed to justices and others empowering them to 'hear and determine' indictments on a specified crime or crimes committed within a certain area. Used for the trial of piracy under a statute of 1536.

Patent of Privilege a document issued under the Privy Seal, granting the recipient certain rights, such as manufacturing or trading monopolies.

Pinnace a small vessel of 20–40 tons, usually fitted with two masts. Every large warship had a pinnace as tender, which was usually towed behind when not in use.

Portolan a form of sailing directions, giving details and particulars of the coasts, ports, anchorages, rocks and shoals. A portolan chart was a very detailed coastal chart, covered with a fine mesh of compass bearings.

Port piece an early heavy gun, firing a stone shot.

Prest (or imprest) money given in advance of anticipated expenditure.

Purveyance the right of the monarch to take up provisions for his/her own use at fixed rates. Originally used to supply the royal household, it also extended to victualling the navy (and army).

Pilgrimage of Grace a major rebellion which broke out in Yorkshire in October 1536, and spread to many other parts of the north of England. It had many causes, including resentment at the dissolution of the smaller monasteries. The name was adopted by the rebels themselves, who displayed the banner of the five wounds of Christ, and claimed to be defending the traditional faith.

Readeption the term used to describe the brief recovery of the throne of England by King Henry VI. Henry had been deposed in favour of Edward IV in 1461, but recovered his crown with French help in 1470. He was defeated, and killed in prison in 1471.

Reversionary a person who is given the right to a preferment or a possession after the right of the present incumbent has expired.

Robinet a very light gun, firing a shot of less than 1lb. in weight.

Saker a medium-sized cast gun, of iron or bronze, firing an iron shot of 5–6lb. weight. Much used at sea in the later part of the sixteenth century.

Sergeant at Arms originally a soldier in attendance upon a court to enforce its decisions. By this time a court officer.

Serpentine an early form of heavy gun, with a built up iron barrel and a separate iron breech block. Serpentines could be of almost any size.

Steelyard the London headquarters of the Hanseatic League. After the final withdrawal of the League's privileges in England in 1563, it became a store for naval equipment.

Subsidy a type of direct taxation, developed originally by Cardinal Wolsey, it was based upon the direct assessment of individuals by commission. After 1530 it became the standard form of parliamentary taxation.

Tellers of the Exchequer the officials whose responsibility it was to receive money coming into the Exchequer, to store it, and to issue it upon warrant. There were normally four Tellers, who divided the work between them upon a traditional basis.

Tierra firma the mainland of Spanish America, as distinct from the Caribbean islands.

Trade the approaches to the Breton harbour of Brest.

Vail to lower sails in token of submission or salute.

Wolding welding; softening metal by heat and joining together.

BIBLIOGRAPHY

Primary Sources

Manuscripts

Public Record Office

State Papers – Domestic, Henry VIII (SP 1)
Domestic, Edward VI (SP 10)
Domestic, Mary and Philip and Mary (SP 11)
Domestic, Elizabeth (SP 12)
Domestic, Addenda, Edward VI to James I (SP 15)
Scotland, Edward VI (SP 50)
Foreign, Elizabeth (SP 70)

Chancery – Miscellanea (C 47)
Patent Rolls (C 66)

High Court of Admiralty – Instance and Prize court, Acts (HCA 3)
Assignation Books, examinations (HCA 13)
Letters of Marque, bonds etc. (HCA 25)

Exchequer – Treasury of Receipt, Council and Privy Seal (E 28)
Miscellaneous Books (E 36)
Pipe Office, Declared accounts (E 351)
Miscellaneous Books (E315)
King's Remembrancer, Accounts various (E 101)
King's Remembrancer, Depositions before the Barons (E 133)

Lord Treasurer's Remembrancer, Foreign accounts (E 364)
Lord Treasurer's Remembrancer, Issue rolls (E 403)
Lord Treasurer's Remembrancer, Warrants for Issue (E 404)

British Library

Cotton MSS – Titus E
Julius E
Caligula D
Caligula B
Caligula E
Galba B
Otho E

Additional MSS
Additional Charters
Harleian MSS
Lansdowne MSS
Royal MSS
Sloane MSS
Stowe MSS

Bodleian Library, Oxford

Ashmole MSS
Rawlinson MSS
Tanner MSS

Magdalen College, Cambridge
Pepys MSS

Gloucester Record Office

MSS D421

Archivo General de Simancas

Secretaria de Estado – Estado Inglaterra
Estado Flandes

Diversos de Castilia

Guerra Antigua

Printed (London unless otherwise stated)

Acts of the Privy Council, ed. J. R. Dasent (1890–1907)

Armstrong, C. A. J., *The Usurpation of Richard III by Dominic Mancini* (1936)

Bain, J., ed. *The Hamilton Papers* (Edinburgh, 1892)

Borough, Sir John, *The Sovereignty of the British Seas . . . written in the year 1633* (1651)

Botfield, B., ed. *Manners and Household expenses of England in the Thirteenth and Fourteenth centuries* (Roxburgh Club, 1841)

Burnet, Gilbert, *The History of the Reformation of the Church of England*, ed. N. Pocock (Oxford, 1865)

Bytharne, Jehan, 'Book of War by land and sea (1543)', *Naval Miscellany*, Vol. 1, (1902)

Calendar of the Patent Rolls, 1416–1422 (1911)

Calendar of the Patent Rolls, 1429–1436 (1907)

Calendar of the Patent Rolls, 1452–1461 (1910)

Calendar of the Patent Rolls, 1461–1467 (1897)

Calendar of the Patent Rolls, 1467–1477 (1900)

Calendar of the Patent Rolls, 1476–1485 (1901)

Calendar of the Patent Rolls, Edward VI (1924–1929)

Calendar of the Patent Rolls, Mary and Philip and Mary (1936–9)

Calendar of the Patent Rolls, Elizabeth (1939 – ongoing)

Calendar of State Papers, Foreign, ed. W. Turnbull et al. (1861–3)

Calendar of State Papers relating to Scotland, ed. J. Bain et al. (Edinburgh, 1898–1952)

Calendar of State Papers, Spanish, ed. Royall Tyler et al., (1862–1964)

Calendar of State Papers, Venetian, ed. Rawdon Brown et al., (1864–1898)

Chambers, R. W., and Batho, E. C., *The Chronicles of Scotland by Hector Boethius* (Scottish Text Society, 1938–41)

Clifford, A., ed. *The State Papers and Letters of Sir Ralph Sadler* (Edinburgh, 1809)

Corbett, J. S., ed. *Papers relating to the navy during the Spanish War, 1585–7* (Navy Record Society, Vol. 11, 1898)

__________'The voyage to Calis in Andalusia', *Naval Miscellany*, Vol. 1, (1902)

__________ *Fighting Instructions*, 1530–1816 (Navy Record Society, Vol. 29, 1905)

Debate between the Heralds of England and France, Henry Pyne (1870)

Dee, John, *The Perfect Arte of Navigation* (1577)

Dictionary of National Biography (1885–1900)

Elton, G. R., *The Tudor Constitution* (Cambridge, 1982)

Firth, C. H., ed. *Naval songs and ballads* (Navy Record Society, Vol. 33, 1908)

Gairdner, J., ed. *Letters and Papers Illustrative of the Reigns of Richard III and Henry VII* (Rolls Series, 1861)

__________*The Paston Letters* (1900)

Gairdner, J. et al., eds. *The Letters and Papers, Foreign and Domestic, of the Reign of Henry VIII* (1862–1910)

Guns from the Sea, reprinted from the *International Journal of Nautical Archaeology*, Vol 17, no. 1, 1988

Hagthorpe, John, *England's Exchequer; or a discourse of the sea and navigation* (1625)

Hakluyt, Richard, *The Principall Navigations, Voiages, Traffiques and Discoveries of the English Nation* (1589) (ed. 1907)

Hall, Edward, *The union of the two noble and illustre famelies of York and Lancaster* (1543) (ed. H. Ellis, 1809)

Haynes, S., ed., *Burghley Papers* (1740)

Hearne, T., ed., *Vita Henrici Quinti* (Oxford, 1716)

Hingeston, F. C., ed., *Liber de Illustribus Henricis* (Rolls Series, 1858)

Hughes, P. F. and Larkin, J. L., *Tudor Royal Proclamations* (Cambridge, Mass., 1964–1968)

Jordan, W. K., *The Chronicle and Political Papers of Edward VI* (1966)

Kingsford, C. L., ed., 'The taking of the *Madre de Dios*, 1592', *Naval Miscellany*, Vol. 2 (1912)

Kouri, E. I., 'Elizabethan England and Europe; forty unprinted letters from Elizabeth I to protestant powers', *Bulletin of the Institute of Historical Research*, Special Supplement 12 (1982)

McGowan, A. P., *The Jacobean Commissions of Enquiry, 1608 and 1618* (Navy Record Society, Vol. 116, 1971)

Marsden, R. G., *Select Please in the Court of Admiralty* (Seldon Society, Vols. 6, 9, 1892–7)

Moore, A., 'Accounts and Inventories of John Starlyng, Clerk of the King's Ships to Henry IV', *Mariners' Mirror*, 4, 1914, 20–26, 167–73.

Naish, G. P., ed., 'Spanish documents relating to the Armada', *Naval Miscellany*, Vol. 4 (1952)

Nasmith, J., ed., *Itineraria Symonis Simeonis et Willelmi de Worcestre* (Cambridge, 1778)

Nichols, J. G., ed., *The Diary of Henry Machyn* (Camden Society, Vol. 42, 1848)

__________*The Literary Remains of Edward VI* (Roxburgh Club, 1875)

Nicolas, N. H., ed., *Proceedings and Ordinances of the Privy Council of England* (1834–7)

Oppenheim, M., ed., *The Naval Tracts of Sir William Monson* (Navy Records Society, Vols. 22, 23, 43, 45, 47; 1902–1914).

__________*Naval Accounts and Inventories of the Reign of Henry VII* (Navy Records Society, Vol. 8, 1896)

Patten, William, *The Expedition into Scotland, 1547* (1548) in A. F. Pollard, ed., *Tudor Tracts* (1903)

Plummer, C., ed., *The Governance of England by Sir John Fortescue* (Oxford, 1885)

Purchas, Samuel, *Hakluytus Posthumus or Purchas his Pilgrims* (Hakluyt Society, Extra Series, Vols 14–33, 1905–7)

Rose, S., ed., *The Navy of the Lancastrian Kings* (Navy Records Society, Vol. 123, 1982)

Rymer, T., *Foedera, conventiones, literae . . . et Acta Publica* (1704)

Spont, A., ed., *Letters and Papers relating to the war with France, 1512–13* (Navy Records Society, Vol. 10, 1897)

Spufford, P. *Handbook of Medieval Exchange* (Royal Historical Society, 1986)

Stevenson, J., ed., *Wars of the English in France during the reign of Henry VI* (Rolls Series, 1861–4)

State Papers of Henry VIII (1830–1852)

Statutes of the Realm, ed. J. Luders et al. (1810–28)

Strachey, J., et al., *Rotuli Parliamentorum* (1767–77)

Studer, P., ed., *The Oak Book of Southampton* (Southampton Record Society, 1910–11)

Surtz, E., and Murphy, V., eds., *The Divorce Tracts of Henry VIII* (Angers, 1988)

Taylor, E. G. R., ed., *The Troublesome Voyage of Captain Edward Fenton, 1582–3* (Hakluyt Society, Vol. 113, 1957)

Twiss, Sir Travers, ed., *The Black Book of the Admiralty* (Rolls Series, 1871–6)

Warner, Sir George, ed., *The Libel of English Policy* (Oxford, 1926)

Wernham, R. B., ed., *The Expedition of Sir John Norris and Sir Francis Drake to Spain and Portugal, 1589* (Navy Records Society, Vol. 127, 1988)

Williams, B., *Gesta Henrici Quinti* (English Historical Society, 1850)

Williamson, J. A., *The Cabot Voyages and Bristol Discovery under Henry VII* (Hakluyt Society, Vol. 120, 1962)
Wright, I. A., *Documents concerning English voyages to the Spanish Main, 1569–80* (1932)

Secondary sources

Books (London unless otherwise stated)

Anderson, R. C., *A list of English men of war, 1509–1649* (Society for Nautical Research, occasional publications, 7, 1959)
_________*Oared Fighting Ships* (1962)
Andrews, K. R., *Elizabethan Privateering* (1964)
_________*Trade, Plunder and Settlement* (1984)
_________*The Westward Enterprise* (1978)
Bell, D., *Elizabethan Seamen* (1936)
Black, J. B., *The Reign of Queen Elizabeth* (2 ed. Oxford, 1959)
Bonfils, Lepeyrouse, de, *Histoire de la Marine Francaise* (Paris, 1845)
Bovill, E. W., Canny, N., and Hair, P. E. H., *The Westward Enterprise; English activities in Ireland, the Atlantic and America, 1480–1650* (Liverpool, 1978)
Burwash, D., *English Merchant Shipping, 1460–1540* (1969)
Charnock, J., *History of Marine Architecture* (1802)
Chrimes, S. B., *Henry VII* (1972)
Clowes, W. Laird, *The Royal Navy; a history from the earliest times to the present*, Vol. I (1897)
Colvin, H. M., *The History of the King's Works* (1963–76)
Connell-Smith, G., *Forerunners of Drake* (1954)
Corbett, J. S., *Drake and the Tudor Navy*, 2 vols (1898–9)
_________*The Successors of Drake* (1900)
Duro, C. Fernandez, *La Armada Invencible* (Madrid, 1884–5)
Elton, G. R., *Reform and Reformation* (1977)
_________*The Parliament of England, 1559–1581* (Cambridge, 1986)
Fernandez Armesto, Felipe, *The Spanish Armada; the experience of war in 1588* (1988)
Foster, Sir William, *England's Quest of Eastern Trade* (1933)
Fowler, E. W., *English Sea Power in the early Tudor Period, 1485–1558* (1965)
Gardner, J. *Warships of the Royal Navy* (1968)
Guilmartin, J., *Gunpowder and Galleys* (1974)

Gunn, S. J., *Charles Brandon, Duke of Suffolk* (Oxford, 1986)
Guy, J. A., *Tudor England* (Oxford, 1988)
Ives, E. W., *Anne Boleyn* (Oxford, 1986)
Jordan, W. K., *Edward VI; the young king* (1968)
_________ *Edward VI; the threshold of power* (1970)
Keevil, J. J., *Medicine and the Navy, 1200–1900* (1957)
Kemp, P., *The Oxford Companion to Ships and the Sea* (Oxford, 1976)
Kenny, R. W., *Elizabeth's Admiral; the political career of Charles Howard, Earl of Nottingham, 1536–1624* (1970)
Kirsch, P., *The Galleon* (1990)
Knecht, R. J., *Francis I* (Cambridge, 1982)
Lewis, M., *The Spanish Armada* (1960)
_________ *Armada Guns* (1961)
Lloyd, C., *The British Seaman; 1200–1860, a social survey* (1969)
Loades, D. M., *Two Tudor Conspiracies* (Cambridge, 1965)
_________ *The Tudor Court* (1986)
_________ *The Reign of Mary Tudor* (1991)
Marcus, G. J., *A Naval History of England*, Vol. 1 (1961)
MacDougall, P., *The Royal Dockyards* (Newton Abbot, 1982)
Mackie, J. D., *The Earlier Tudors* (Oxford, 1951)
McKee, A., *The Queen's Corsair; Drake's journey of circumnavigation, 1577–80* (1978)
Mallett, M. E., *The Florentine Galleys in the Fifteenth century* (1967)
Martin, C., and Parker, G., *The Spanish Armada* (1988)
Mattingly, G., *The Defeat of the Spanish Armada* (new ed., 1983)
Miller, H., *Henry VIII and the English Nobility* (Oxford, 1986)
Morley, B. M., *Henry VIII and the development of coastal defence* (1977)
Nutall, Z., ed., *New Light on Drake* (1914)
Oppenheim, M., *The History of the Administration of the Royal Navy 1509–1660* (1896 repr. 1988)
Padfield, P., *Guns at Sea* (1973)
Quinn, D. B., *Sebastian Cabot and Bristol Exploration* (Historical Association (1969))
_________ *England and the Discovery of America, 1481–1620* (1974)
Read, Conyers, *Mr. Secretary Cecil and Queen Elizabeth* (1955)
_________ *Lord Burghley and Queen Elizabeth* (1960)
Redknap, M., *The Cattewater wreck; the investigation of an armed vessel of the early sixteenth century* (1984)
Redworth, G. R., *In Defence of the Church Catholic; a Life of Stephen Gardiner* (Oxford, 1990)

Richardson, W. C., *Stephen Vaughn* (Baton Rouge, 1953)

Rodriguez Salgado, M., ed., *Armada; an international exhibition to commemorate the Spanish Armada* (catalogue, 1988)

Ross, C., *Edward IV* (1974)

Rowse, A. L., *Sir Richard Grenville of the Revenge* (1937)

Rule, M., *The Mary Rose* (1982)

Scarisbrick, J. J., *Henry VIII* (1968)

Sellman, R. R., *The Elizabethan Seaman* (1963)

Silke, J. J., *Kinsale; the Spanish intervention in Ireland at the end of the Elizabethan Wars* (1970)

Smith, A. G. R., *The Government of Elizabethan England* (1967)

Taylor, E. G. R., *Tudor Geography, 1485–1583* (1930)

_________*The Haven finding Art: a history of navigation* (1967)

_________*Later Tudor and Early Stuart Geography, 1583–1650* (1934)

Thomson, G. M., *Sir Francis Drake* (1973)

Tytler, P. F., *The History of Scotland* (1828–43)

Uden, G., *Drake at Cadiz* (1969)

Usherwood, S. and E., *Armada of Spain* (National Maritime Museum, 1975)

_________*The Counter Armada, 1596* (1983)

Waters, D. W., *The Art of Navigation in England in Elizabethan and Early Stuart times* (1958)

Waters, D. W., and Naish, G. P. B., *The Elizabethan Navy and the Armada of Spain* (1975)

Wernham, R. B., *Before the Armada* (New York, 1966)

_________*After the Armada* (Oxford, 1984)

Williams, N. J., *The Sea Dogs: privateers, piracy and plunder in the Elizabethan Age* (1975)

Williamson, G. C., *George, third Earl of Cumberland* (1920)

Williamson, J. A., *Hawkins of Plymouth* (1949)

_________*Maritime Enterprise, 1485–1558* (Oxford, 1913)

Wright, L. B., *Religion and Empire; the alliance between piety and commerce in English Expansion, 1558–1625* (1943)

Youings, J., *Raleigh in Exeter; privateering and colonisation in the reign of Elizabeth I* (Exeter, 1985)

Zeller, Gaston, *Les Institutions de la France au XVIe siecle* (Paris, 1948)

Articles and theses

Adams, S., 'New light on the "Reformation" of John Hawkins; the Ellesmere naval survey of 1584', *EHR*, 105, 1991

'An inventory of guns, 13 February 1540', *MM*, 6, 1920

Anderson, R. C., 'The *Grace de Dieu* of 1446–1486', *EHR*, 34, 1919.

_________'Armaments in 1545', *MM*, 6, 1920

_________'Henry VIII's *Great Galley*', *MM*, 6, 1920

_________'A list of Royal Ships in 1590–91', *MM*, 43, 1951

_________'The *Mary Gonson*', *MM*, 46, 1960

Andrews, K. R., 'Appraisements of Elizabethan privateersmen', *MM*, 37, 1951

_________'The aims of Drake's expedition of 1577–80', *American Historical Review*, 73, 1968

_________'The Elizabethan seamen', *MM* 68, 1982

Baldwin, R. C. D., 'The Development and interchange of navigational information and technology between the maritime communities . . . 1500–1620' (Durham University, M. Litt., 1980)

Bennell, J. E. G., 'English oared vessels in the sixteenth century', *MM*, 60, 1974

Bovill, E. W., 'The *Madre de Dios*, 1592', *MM*, 54, 1968

Boxer, C. R., 'The taking of the *Madre de Dios*', *MM*, 67, 1981

Brooks, F. W., 'The Cinq Ports', *MM*, 15, 1929

Callender, C. S., 'The evolution of sea power under the first two Tudors', *History*, 5, 1920–21

_________'The naval campaign of 1587', *History*, 3, 1918

Carpenter Turner, W. J., 'The building of the *Holy Ghost of the Tower* and her subsequent history', *MM*, 40, 1954.

Carr-Loughton, L. G., 'Early Tudor Ship Guns', *MM*, 46, 1960

_________'The square tuck stern and gun deck', *MM*, 47, 1961.

Carus Wilson, E., 'The overseas trade of Bristol', in *Studies in English Trade in the fifteenth century*, ed. E. Power and M. M. Postan, (New York, 1933)

Croft, Pauline, 'English mariners trading to Spain and Portugal, 1558–1625', *MM*, 68, 1983.

Davies, C. S. L., 'The administration of the Royal Navy under Henry VIII; the origins of the Navy Board', *EHR*, 80, 1965

_________'England and the French war, 1557–9' in *The Mid-Tudor Polity c. 1540–1560* ed. J. Loach and R. Tittler (1980)

de Beer, E. S., 'The Lord High Admiral and the administration of the navy', *MM*, 13, 1927

Dietz, B., 'The royal bounty and English shipping in the sixteenth and seventeenth centuries', *MM*, 77, 1991.

Dowling, M., 'The gospel and the court; reformation under Henry VIII', in *Protestantism and the National Church in the sixteenth century* ed. P. Lake and M. Dowling (1987)

Dyer, F. E., 'Reprisals in the sixteenth century', *MM*, 21, 1935

Ewan, C. H. L'Estrange, 'Organised piracy around England in the sixteenth century', *MM*, 35, 1949

Glasgow, T., jnr., 'The shape of ships which defeated the Armada', *MM*, 50, 1964

_________ 'The royal navy at the start of Elizabeth's reign', *MM*, 51, 1965

_________ 'Oared vessels in the Elizabethan navy', *MM*, 52, 1966

_________ The Elizabethan navy in Ireland', *Irish Sword*, 29, 1966

_________ 'The wreck of the *Greyhound*, 1563', *MM*, 52, 1966

_________ 'The navy in Philip and Mary's war', *MM*, 53, 1967

_________ 'Sixteenth century English seamen encounter a new enemy', *American Neptune*, 27, 1967

_________ 'The navy in the first undeclared Elizabethan war', *MM*, 54, 1968

_________ 'The navy in the Le Havre campaign, 1562–4', *MM*, 54, 1968.

_________ 'List of ships in the royal navy from 1539 to 1588', *MM*, 56, 1970

_________ 'The maturing of naval administration, 1556–1564', *MM*, 56, 1970

_________ 'Comments on "the list of ships in the royal navy from 1539 to 1588" ', *MM*, 61, 1975

_________ 'Vice Admiral Woodhouse and shipkeeping in the Tudor navy', *MM*, 63, 1977

Glasgow, T., jnr., and Salisbury, W., 'Elizabethan ships pictured in the Smerwick map', *MM*, 52, 1966

Goldingham, C. S., 'The navy under Henry VII', *EHR*, 33, 1918

_________ 'The personnel of the Tudor navy and the internal economy of the ships', *United Services Magazine*, 177, 1918

_________ 'Warships of Henry VIII', *United Services Magazine*, 179, 1919

Gunn, S. J., 'The Duke of Suffolk's march on Paris in 1523', *EHR*, 101, 1986

Holmes, G. A., 'The Libel of English Policy', *EHR*, 76, 1961

Holmes, P. J., 'A sea fight in the 1480s', *MM*, 64, 1978

Howard, G. F., 'Gun port lids', *MM*, 67, 1981.

_________ 'Early Tudor rigging', *MM*, 68, 1982.

_________ 'Early ships' guns, I: Built up breech loaders', *MM*, 72, 1986

_________ 'Early ship's guns, II: The swivels', *MM*, 73, 1987

Johns, A. W., 'The Principal Officers of the navy', *MM*, 14, 1928

Lander, R. J., 'An assessment of the numbers, sizes, and types of English and Spanish ships mobilised for the Armada campaign', *MM*, 63, 1977

Lewis, Michael, 'The guns of the *Jesus of Lubeck*', *MM*, 22, 1936

Loades, D. M., 'The king's ships and the keeping of the seas, 1413–1480', *Medieval History*, 1, 1991

McGurk, J. M. M., 'A levy of seamen in the Cinq Ports in 1602', *MM*, 38, 1952

McKee, A., 'The complement of the *Mary Rose*', *MM*, 72, 1986

Marsden, R. G., 'The vice-admirals of the coasts', *EHR*, 22, 1907

Mathew, David, 'Cornish and Welsh pirates in the reign of Elizabeth', *EHR*, 39, 1924

May, W. E., 'The history of the magnetic compass', *MM*, 38, 1952

Moore, A., 'Rig in northern Europe', *MM*, 41–2, 1955–6

Nance, Morton, 'Ships of the renaissance', *MM*, 41, 1955

Oppenheim, M., 'The royal and merchant navy under Elizabeth', *EHR*, 6, 1891

_________'Maritime history' and 'The royal dockyards', in *The Victoria History of the County of Kent*, Vol. 2 (1926)

Pearce Chope, R., 'New light on Sir Richard Grenville', *Transactions of the Devonshire Association*, 49, 1917

Perrin, W. G., 'Early naval ordnance', *MM*, 6, 1920

_________'The Lord High Admiral and the Board of Admiralty', *MM*, 12, 1926

Pistono, S. P., 'Henry IV and the English privateers', *EHR*, 90, 1975

Pollitt, R., 'Bureaucracy and the Armada; the administrators' battle', *MM*, 60, 1974

Potter, D. L., 'The Duc de Guise and the fall of Calais', *EHR*, 98, 1983

Prynne, M. W., 'Henry V's *Grace Dieu*', *MM*, 54, 1968

Quinn, D. B., 'Spanish Armada prisoners in Ireland', *MM*, 70, 1984

Richmond, C. F., 'The keeping of the seas during the Hundred Years War', *History*, 49, 1964

_________'English naval power in the fifteenth century', *History*, 52, 1967

Robinson, Gregory, 'The development of the capital ship, 2', *MM*, 6, 1920

Rodger, N. A. M., 'The English fleet' in *Royal Armada* (Manorial Research, 1988)

Rodgers, S., 'The symbolism of ship launching' (Oxford University, D. Phil, 1983)

Rose, S., 'Henry V's *Grace Dieu* and mutiny at sea; some new evidence', *MM*, 63, 1977

Round, J. H., and Oppenheim, M., 'The royal navy under Queen Elizabeth', *EHR*, 9, 1894

Ruddock, A. H., 'The earliest original English seaman's rutter' (1539), *Journal of the Institute of Navigation*, 14, 1961

Rule, M., 'The sinking of the *Mary Rose*', *History Today*, 32, 1982

Runyon, T. J., 'Ships and mariners in later medieval England', *Journal of British Studies*, 16, 1977

Salisbury, W., 'Early tonnage measurements in England', *MM*, 52, 1966

Scammell, G. V., 'War at sea under the Early Tudors', *Archaeologia Aeliana*, 4 series, 38 (1960) and 39 (1961)

———'Shipowning in England *c.* 1450–1550', *TRHS*, 5 series, 12 (1962)

———'Manning the English merchant service in the sixteenth century', *MM*, 56, 1970

———'European seamanship in the great age of discovery', *MM*, 68, 1982

———'The English in the Atlantic Islands, *c.* 1450–1650', *MM*, 72, 1986

Schubert, H., 'The first cast iron cannon made in England', *Journal of the Iron and Steel Institute*, 146, 1942

Smith, L. B., 'The last will and testament of Henry VIII; a question of perspective', *Journal of British Studies*, 2, 1962

Smith, T. C., 'The artillery defences at Gravesend', *Archaeologia Cantiana*, 89, 1974

Sparling, H. H., 'Mariners of England before the Armada', *English Illustrated Magazine*, 8, 1891

Stanford, M. G., 'The Raleighs take to the sea', *MM*, 48, 1962

Standing, P. C., 'Henry VIII's Lord Admiral (Sir Edward Howard)', *United Services Magazine*, 144, 1901

Taylor, A. H., 'Carrack into Galleon', *MM*, 36, 1950

Thompson, E. K., 'English and Spanish tonnage in 1588', *MM*, 46, 1959

Thompson, I. A. A., 'Spanish Armada guns', *MM*, 61, 1975

———'The Invincible Armada' in *Royal Armada* (Manorial Research, 1988)

Tomlin, K. M., 'The influence of the introduction of heavy ordnance on the development of the navy during the early Tudor period' (University of West Michigan, MA, 1980)

Tomlinson, H. C., 'The ordnance office and the navy', *EHR*, 90, 1975

Waters, D. W., 'The Elizabethan navy and the Armada campaign', *MM*, 35, 1949

__________'Limes, lemons and scurvy in Elizabethan and early Stuart times', *MM*, 41, 1955

Watt, James, 'The surgeons of the *Mary Rose*; the practice of surgery in Tudor England', *MM*, 69, 1983

Webb, John, 'William Sabyn of Ipswich', *MM*, 41, 1955

__________'Elizabethan piracy; the evidence of the Ipswich deposition books', *Suffolk Review*, 2, 1960

Whitlock, P., 'King Henry VIII',s *Mary Rose*, 1511–1545; an outline of the project', *MM*, 66, 1980

Wood, A. B., 'The Laws of Oleron', *MM*, 4, 1914.

INDEX